Up, Down, and Sideways

Studies in Public and Applied Anthropology

General Editor: **Sarah Pink,** University of Loughborough, and **Simone Abram,** Town and Regional Planning, University of Sheffield

The value of anthropology to public policy, business and third sector initiatives is increasingly recognized, not least due to significant innovations in the discipline. The books published in this series offer important insight into these developments by examining the expanding role of anthropologists practicing their discipline outside academia as well as exploring the ethnographic, methodological, and theoretical contribution of anthropology, within and outside academia, to issues of public concern.

Volume 1
Anthropology and Consultancy:
Issues and Debates
Edited by Pamela Stewart and Andrew Strathern

Volume 2
Applications of Anthropology:
Professional Anthropology in the Twenty-First Century
Edited by Sarah Pink

Volume 3
Fire in the Dark:
Telling Gypsiness in North East England
Edited by Sarah Buckler

Volume 4
Visual Interventions:
Applied Visual Anthropology
Edited by Sarah Pink

Volume 5
Ethnography and the Corporate Encounter:
Reflections on Research in and of Corporations
Edited by Melissa Cefkin

Volume 6
Adventures in Aidland:
The Anthropology of Professionals in International Development
Edited by David Mosse

Volume 7
Up, Down, and Sideways:
Anthropologists Trace the Pathways of Power
Edited by Rachael Stryker and Roberto J. González

Up, Down, and Sideways

Anthropologists Trace the Pathways of Power

Edited By

Rachael Stryker and Roberto J. González

berghahn
NEW YORK · OXFORD
www.berghahnbooks.com

Published by
Berghahn Books

www.berghahnbooks.com

© 2014 Rachael Stryker and Roberto J. González

All rights reserved. Except for the quotation of short passages
for the purposes of criticism and review, no part of this book
may be reproduced in any form or by any means, electronic or
mechanical, including photocopying, recording, or any information
storage and retrieval system now known or to be invented,
without written permission of the publisher.

Library of Congress Cataloging-in-Publication Data

Up, down, and sideways : anthropologists trace the pathways of power / edited by Rachael Stryker and Roberto J. González.
　　pages cm. — (Studies in public and applied anthropology ; volume 7)
　　Includes bibliographical references.
　　ISBN 978-1-78238-401-4 (hardback : alk. paper) — ISBN 978-1-78238-402-1 (ebook)
　1. Political anthropology--Case studies. 2.　Power (Social sciences)—Case studies.　I. Stryker, Rachael, 1972– , author, editor of compilation.　II. González, Roberto J. (Roberto Jesús), 1969– , author, editor of compilation.
　GN492.U7 2014
　306.2—dc23

2014000995

British Library Cataloguing in Publication Data

A catalogue record for this book is available from the British Library

Printed on acid-free paper

ISBN: 978-1-78238-401-4 hardback
ISBN: 978-1-78238-402-1 ebook

Contents

Foreword   vii
    Laura Nader

Acknowledgments   xi

Introduction   On Studying Up, Down, and Sideways:
    What's at Stake?   1
    Roberto J. González and Rachael Stryker

PART I. STUDYING WEALTH AND POWER

Chapter 1   On Debt: Tracking the Shifting Role of
the Debtor in U.S. Bankruptcy Legal Practice   27
    Linda Coco

Chapter 2   On Commerce: Analyzing the
Asian Financial Crisis of 1997–1998   44
    Jay Ou

Chapter 3   On Bureaucracy: Excessively Up at
the International Labour Organization   63
    Ellen Hertz

PART II. STUDYING ENVIRONMENT AND SUBSISTENCE

Chapter 4   On Dispossession: The Work of Studying
Up, Down, and Sideways in Guatemala's
Indigenous Land Rights Movements   85
    Liza Grandia

Chapter 5   On Food: Manufacturing Food
Insecurity in Oaxaca, Mexico   107
    Roberto J. González

| Chapter 6 | On Environment: The "Broker State," Peruvian Hydrocarbons Policy, and the Camisea Gas Project
Patricia Urteaga-Crovetto | 127 |

PART III. STUDYING RELATIONSHIPS AND BUREAUCRACIES

Chapter 7	On Family: Adoptive Parenting Up, Down, and Sideways *Rachael Stryker*	149
Chapter 8	On Truth: The Repressed Memory Wars from Top to Bottom *Robyn Kliger*	170
Chapter 9	On Common Sense: Lessons on Starting Over from Post-Soviet Ukraine *Monica Eppinger*	192
Chapter 10	On Caring: Solidarity Anthropology (or, How to Keep Health Care from Becoming Science Fiction) *Adrienne Pine*	211
Conclusion	On Power *Barbara Rose Johnston, Roberto J. González, and Rachael Stryker*	233

Notes on Contributors	243
References	247
Index	263

Foreword

Laura Nader

The plan for this volume arose from discussions addressing the theme "Studying Up, Down, and Sideways," a theme derived from an article I wrote for Dell Hymes's collection *Reinventing Anthropology* (1969) entitled "Up the Anthropologist: Perspectives Gained from Studying Up." The essays in this volume are both exciting and novel, indicating how far the writings of ethnographers have come since *Reinventing Anthropology*, and how much can be accomplished by expanding the ethnographic paradigm to include both daily life issues in the contemporary world and connections that enhance understandings of the workings of power and control. The essays here reflect a growing movement that has received little attention but is nevertheless a dynamic force in American anthropology.

Ethnography, as a theory of description, has to move beyond earlier ethnographies of island societies modeled after the laboratory sciences to take fuller account of the complexities of social life today, using more of a natural history approach. The authors in this book have spent years, not months, in fieldwork that covers many sites to connect the local with the global or the powerless with the powerful—what I have elsewhere referred to as the "vertical slice" approach.

The impact of this new work is not yet fully felt in a world that is closing down to democratic practice, becoming increasingly militarized, and taking on the controlling processes so characteristic of both *Brave New World* and *1984*. The crudity of earlier, valiant interpretations of fieldwork is already evident, indicating that much good work in the human sciences falls short of meeting the world's challenges today. At times the very connectedness and disconnectedness of modern society almost paralyzes the will to understand it. Understanding power has eluded us. However, understanding society as if it were bereft of power is not an option. It bears repeating that "Never before have so few, by their actions and inactions, had the power of life and death over so many members of the species."

The topics included here—family, land dispossession, post–cold war parliaments, bureaucracy, health care, memory, natural resources, debt, food, and commerce everywhere, not just in the so-called underdeveloped world—are of interest to young and old readers alike. As the chapters indicate, the central question of how power and control structure upheavals and their context—colonial expansion, world wars, endless wars, revolutions, conflicts over religion, unemployment—also reaches into all of our daily lives, here as well as there.

What is at stake becomes clearer with each passing day. It is the *longue durée*, that is, *Homo sapiens* and the survival of human life on the planet. It is not only protection of the environment, but the search for natural resources to feed our constricted, solely technological ideas of progress, as well as the pursuit of alternative technologies to overtake the destruction wrought by the world's use of coal, nuclear, and oil. Land dispossession to further special interests, the ongoing contamination of our food supply to favor the prospects of a dominant agribusiness, health care and higher education costs that lead families and individuals into debt and bankruptcy, the stress on families that contextualizes our materialism, the changes in the third world or postcolonial world as related to empire, the place of bureaucracy in regulating world finance—our daily lives. Making daily life analyses of this sort is at once serious, exciting, and transformative.

A final word concerns scope. The audience for this book was discussed during a meeting in the summer of 2010 at Mills College in Oakland, California. At the time I said that in the 1950s, a series of writers in and out of the academy expressed concern about the direction of life in the United States—specifically about materialism, loneliness, and what constitutes freedom—and that these authors had *scope*. I meant that they had an understanding of who they were talking to and what they were talking about in relation to the big picture, the dynamics that link macro to micro and vice versa. These authors wrote with scope to create a dynamic between the reader and what is written. The audience or reader was not (and is not) a static entity. Scope, as one participant said, can place readers within a wider context that helps them understand the impact and consequences of power in their own lives, thus demonstrating individuals' power to create their own alternatives.

My own work stimulating studying up, down, and sideways appeared at critical periods in American history. I published "Up the Anthropologist" in 1969, at the height of the Vietnam War, civil rights, and environmental rights movements of the 1960s. "The Vertical Slice" appeared in

1980 as I witnessed professionals' inability to connect how children's lives are impacted by hierarchies both governmental and corporate, in addition to parenting influences. "Controlling Processes" came out first in relation to how hierarchies work in law firms (1993), and then as the Mintz Lecture in 1997 as a consequence of the political turn and media reactions to the 1960s movements, once again rendering the "best and the brightest" unaware of the dynamics of power. Fears of the kinds of reactions that would follow 9/11 were already in our and others' national consciousnesses. But the purpose of education in democratic societies is to enable the mind, is it not?

Notes

1. Laura Nader, "Up the Anthropologist—Perspectives Gained from Studying Up," in *Reinventing Anthropology*, ed. Dell Hymes (New York: Pantheon Books, 1972), 285–311.

Acknowledgments

The editors thank Laura Nader and Barbara Rose Johnston for their encouragement and support as this project developed. We are also grateful for the comments and suggestions of three anonymous reviewers. We greatly appreciate the efforts of all those at Berghahn Books who helped us realize this project, especially Marion Berghahn, Ann Pryzyzcki DeVita, and Adam Capitanio, as well as the Studies in Public Applied Anthropology series editors, Sarah Pink and Simone Abram.

Introduction

ON STUDYING UP, DOWN, AND SIDEWAYS
What's at Stake?

Roberto J. González and Rachael Stryker

This book is a collection of essays that explore problems of power in the United States and beyond. It is also a series of hopeful models for transcending them. Its authors are anthropologists who are concerned about the undemocratic, sometimes authoritarian uses and abuses of power today, yet believe independent, creative thinking has the power to actualize alternatives to living with these abuses. The contributors to this volume take the firm stance that anthropologists are well positioned to speak with knowledge and insight about the workings of power. This is because the anthropological lens focuses on humans holistically and cross-culturally, while never losing sight of long-term historical processes. Anthropology integrates culture, language, biology, and history to address questions about *Homo sapiens*, the societies that we have created for ourselves, the challenges of survival facing our species, and the human talents available to meet these challenges.

Connecting the Dots

In some ways, life has become easier for millions of people in our society and around the world. Technological developments in medicine, engineering, and other fields have increased human longevity, facilitated transportation, and improved communication. In addition, more people

---

Notes for this chapter begin on page 20.

everywhere are contributing and connected to the global economy, potentially opening the way for cross-cultural contact and a deeper understanding of different lifeways.

But in other ways, life has become more difficult, more complicated, and more frustrating than ever before. A wide range of social problems and personal troubles weigh heavily on the lives of many. Despite the wondrous inventions and scientific breakthroughs of recent years, powerful institutions have often failed to provide citizens with security, safety, or satisfaction and indeed have stood in the way of people solving these problems at the grass roots.

Events from the last few years illustrate the scope of the problem. For example, in August 2005, Hurricane Katrina struck New Orleans and other parts of the Gulf Coast, killing nearly 2,000 people in the United States. U.S. District Judge Stanwood Duval ruled that the flooding caused by the hurricane was largely a man-made disaster created by the "lassitude and failure" of the U.S. Army Corps of Engineers.[1]

Another example comes from the field of public education. Faced with budget cuts, public-school teachers across much of the United States are resorting to unusual measures to cover classroom expenses. In one San Diego–area high school, calculus teacher Tom Farber raised $350 to cover photocopy costs by selling advertising space on his test papers.[2] In the meantime, public university systems throughout the country are undergoing a series of crises related to the corporatization of higher education.

Apart from environmental and educational dilemmas, many Americans are contending with problems associated with housing. Between 2007 and 2012, banks issued foreclosure filings on more than 16 million U.S. properties. According to the *Wall Street Journal*, approximately 5 million Americans lost their homes through foreclosure between 2007 and 2012.[3]

On a global scale, human suffering is also an outcome of ongoing wars and military occupations. Civilian and military fatalities have steadily increased in the U.S.-led war in Afghanistan since it began in 2001. The United Nations reports that more than 3,000 Afghan civilians were killed and more than 4,500 injured in 2011, making it the war's deadliest year on record.[4]

Meanwhile, the global energy system is dominated by inherently risky methods and technologies prone to periodic catastrophes. For example, in April 2010 an offshore well belonging to British Petroleum exploded and sank in the Gulf of Mexico, killing eleven workers and spewing more than 4 million barrels of oil into the ecosystem with disastrous ecological, economic, and health consequences. It was the largest offshore spill in U.S. history.[5] And in March 2011, an earthquake rattled Japan's east coast, creating a massive tsunami that severely damaged several nuclear reactors at

Fukushima in the second-largest nuclear reactor disaster in history, whose long-term effects may prove harmful to many species' environment and biological integrity.

As if this were not enough, the U.S. food supply has been compromised. In 2010, the FDA ordered the Las Vegas–based company Basic Foods to recall ten thousand products containing "hydrolyzed vegetable protein" (a flavor enhancer used in products ranging from potato chips to tofu) because of salmonella contamination. This was only the latest in a series of high-profile recalls revealing persistent problems in the American food system.[6]

At first glance, these human tragedies look unrelated. But closer consideration reveals that they share a disturbing commonality: each occurred largely as the result of the misdeeds (either intentional or unintentional) of decision makers in powerful organizations—banks and financial firms, governmental bodies, military institutions, and corporations. Compounding these actions is the apathy of the many people who feel powerless to effect meaningful change in the world around them. The pattern of "organized irresponsibility" of men and women in the higher circles—and the organized irresponsibility underlying these outrageous situations and many others—are phenomena in need of serious analysis and action.[7] The words of the anthropologist Laura Nader appear as a warning call: "Never before have a few, by their actions and inactions, had the power of life and death over so many members of the species."[8]

There are other symptoms. Economic, natural, political, and social capital are more highly concentrated than at any other time in human history. Approximately 1 percent of the world's population owns 40 percent of the world's wealth; average CEO pay has grown 442 percent in the last twenty-five years while average worker pay has increased just 1.6 percent; and five corporations control most of America's daily newspapers, magazines, radio and television stations, book publishers, and movie companies.[9] Ours is a time of endemic crises affecting billions of people: a man-made environmental crisis of potentially catastrophic proportions that threatens to inundate coastal regions and radically disrupt weather patterns; a housing crisis created by predatory lenders, a corrupt financial sector, and ineffective regulatory bodies; a food crisis sparked by shortsighted multinational agribusiness firms; and an energy crisis connected to shortsighted politicians, obscene revolving-door relationships between government and industry officials, and a refusal to search for alternatives.

Those confronting the problems of power—its concentration, its abuse, and its anti-democratic manifestations—must realize that at its core, these are not *technological* so much as *social* problems. If millions of people today are chronically exhausted, afraid, depressed, ill, angry, nervous, paranoid, nauseous, addicted, overworked, desperate, or just unmotivated, no pill or machine or computer algorithm stands much chance of alleviating their maladies. As C. Wright Mills asserted, when these feelings are experienced en masse they are not only individual ailments but social problems.[10]

Power and Freedom

American intellectuals have a long tradition of critically examining issues of power, reason, and freedom. Revisiting some of this work is worthwhile, for much can be learned about the present state of affairs by looking to a past when thinkers wrote for a broad audience of open-minded citizens. This legacy may be partly rooted in the notion, shared by many of our country's founders, that democracy is not possible without well-informed citizens who have access to a wide range of ideas.

Thomas Jefferson's writings provide a clear example of a set of liberating and democratic ideas in American culture. Jefferson adamantly believed democracy is much more likely to survive in an egalitarian agrarian society based upon independent-minded small farmers rather than a powerful commercial class: "Dependence begets subservience and venality, suffocates the germ of virtue, and prepares fit tools for the designs of ambition," he noted in 1787.[11] His words express a sophisticated understanding of the connection between an egalitarian society and democracy—or in other words, power and freedom. Some of the founders of the United States likely were deeply influenced by the democratic practices of Native Americans, particularly the Iroquois Confederation.[12]

Another distinguished American thinker, Henry David Thoreau, further exemplifies the intellectual tradition, though from a somewhat different perspective. Perhaps Thoreau's most valuable contributions to thinking about public life are his creative ideas for confronting and challenging institutions that impede individual freedom. His powerful work and actions amount to a blueprint for defending democratic social life from the predations of totalitarian government. In his 1849 book *Civil Disobedience*, Thoreau suggested nonviolent resistance as a means by which citizens might challenge oppressive government. Vehemently opposed to slavery and the Mexican-American war, he famously wrote: "Law never made men a whit more just; and, by means of their respect for it, even the well-disposed are daily made the agents of injustice. . . . I cannot for an instant recognize as my government [one] which is the slave's government also."[13] Several years later, he based his book *Walden* on two years of living along the shores of Walden Pond in Massachusetts. It reads like an economic declaration of independence, advocating, among other things, the ideas of self-reliance and autonomy.[14]

In a similar vein, the novels, essays, and characters of other nineteenth-century American writers and thinkers such as Mark Twain and Herman Melville contain critical analysis of the relationship between power, reason, and freedom. For example, Twain's protagonists—Tom Sawyer, Huckleberry Finn, and Pudd'nhead Wilson, to name but a few—are typically iconoclasts who defy authority, sometimes with wide-eyed innocence. Later, Twain played a prominent role in the American Anti-Imperialist League and staunchly opposed the U.S. colonization of the Philippines. In the early twentieth century, other intellectuals from Randolph Bourne to Upton Sinclair to Thorstein Veblen continued this tradition, though in different ways.

By the mid twentieth century, social scientists had entered this American dialogue on freedom, reason, and power. Reflecting on the first and second World Wars, psychologist Erich Fromm wrote in 1964: "Freedom is not a constant attribute which we either 'have' or 'have not.' In fact, there is no such thing as 'freedom' except as a word and an abstract concept. There is only one reality: the *act* of freeing ourselves in the process of making choices. In this process the degree of our capacity to make choices varies with each act, with our practice of life."[15] In the early twentieth century, new systems—Nazism, Fascism, and an emerging Stalinism—essentially took command of humans' entire social and personal lives, effecting, as Fromm put it, "the submission of all but a handful of men to an authority over which they had no control."[16] Soon after, in 1950, sociologist David Riesman, reflecting on the increasing power of government and corporate hegemonies in the United States, asked a similar question in his classic work, *The Lonely Crowd*: Why did a postwar, increasingly suburban and middle-class America seem to be so much more open, tolerant, and empathic towards others, yet also so politically and personally passive?[17]

Fromm and Riesman shared another important similarity: each recognized and attempted to explain a not-always-obvious "crisis of democracy" within his own culture. Fromm in particular knew that such a crisis was not a peculiarly Italian or German or "totalitarian" problem, but one that confronted every modern state. His work aimed more broadly to better understand freedom by analyzing the character structure of modern man and the problems of interaction between sociological and psychological factors. He wondered why human beings yearned for freedom even as they sought to escape opportunities for freedom when they arose. He argued that although freedom brought people independence and rationality, it also isolated them, making them anxious and powerless. This isolation, he claimed, was unbearable, and the only alternatives confronting people were to escape the burden of this freedom by entering into new dependencies and submission, or "to advance to the full realization of positive freedom which is based upon the uniqueness and individuality of man."[18]

Sociologist Robert Lynd also contributed fruitfully to this discussion, suggesting, for example, that in the "go-as-you-please culture" of the United States, institutions such as finance capitalism, organized labor, big business, and institutionalized religion, much like totalitarian states, actually enacted "coercive power of deliberate organization" that efficiently hid the very contradictions social scientists were charged to illuminate.[19] Reisman was similarly concerned with Americans' adherence to society's prescriptions, but instead of focusing on the contradictory nature of U.S. culture, he traced a linear shift in American consciousness from what he called a nineteenth-century "inner direction" to a mid-twentieth-century "other-direction":

> Ironically, for all its moralistic rigidities, the inner-directed type looked more individualistic, hence more attractive to many Americans, although Riesman insisted that in other-direction he did not depict more conformity but rather a change in "modes of conformity"—the way people were induced to conform.... Ultimately, Reisman argued, other-directed people were "at home everywhere and nowhere." They forged bonds quickly but not deeply. That is why the lonely crowd was lonely.[20]

Clearly, this line of American scholars, writers, and thinkers stretching back to the earliest years of our country—Jefferson, Thoreau, Twain, Melville, Bourne, Veblen, Sinclair, Fromm, Riesman, Lynd, and many others—introduced a range of ideas with broad scope. They established connections between seemingly disparate phenomena to shed light on the more obscure workings of power in their own times. They were also citizen-scholars united by their concern about the directions their country and world were taking. Armed with an understanding of whom they wanted to speak to and what they were talking about, they sought to explain their concerns in terms that rang true to others who, like them, were troubled about the state of global affairs.

Anthropology with Scope

Anthropologists have also undertaken new projects, some of which relate directly to the search for a clearer understanding of the dilemmas of contemporary social life. During the global turmoil of the late 1960s, one group of scholars set out a vision for *Reinventing Anthropology*.[21] Among the most incisive contributions to that collection of essays was Laura Nader's groundbreaking article "Up the Anthropologist," which offered some observations on how to reinvent anthropology by studying up, down, and sideways: "What if, in reinventing anthropology, anthropologists were to study the colonizers rather than the colonized, the culture of power rather than the culture of the powerless, the culture of affluence rather than the culture of poverty?"[22] These words ring even more clearly and urgently today than they did forty years ago, though we might add that the "few" now have the power of life and death over *all* species and the ecosystems upon which they depend.

A central theme in "Up the Anthropologist" is anthropology's need for a dramatically innovative approach to the study of social life, one much more inclusive of all of humankind. Nader argued that the scope of previous anthropology had been too narrow in terms of both method and theory. She suggested that *indignation*—particularly the indignation of anthropology students—could be a powerful energizing factor, something not to be snuffed out or repressed but rather harnessed as an engine. Indignation as a motive for doing anthropology was a new idea whose relevance stemmed from several factors, including debates about (and student opposition to) the Vietnam War; the rise of the military-industrial complex and the nuclear arms race; the rapid rise of corporations and increased concentration of power worldwide; the "de-skilling" of the workplace and the alienation of professionals from their work; the bureaucratization of society, including many faceless government agencies; and the Cold War and the lasting impact of McCarthyism, especially in universities. It is worth noting that the University of California, Berkeley (where Nader was a professor) was a flash point for these debates, and that students were more active at this institution than at most others. Rather than condemn, chastise, or ignore students' energy and indignation regarding these issues, she eschewed the possibility of "objectivity" and used the opportunity to encourage students to critically examine important aspects of the bureaucracies that wielded so much power over their lives, keeping in mind the potential for making these institutions more accountable. Just as importantly, she had students participate rather than stand by passively.

Indignation continues to motivate scholars, though the issues may have changed. The campus teach-ins developed by anthropologist Marshall Sahlins are now a frequently used method for educating people on urgent contemporary problems and spurring action. The nationwide struggle to save higher education, which has prompted massive student walkouts in

California and protests at the state capitol, tops the list of concerns, alongside the permanent war economy.[23]

Intellectually, the theme of indignation might be seen as a significant contribution to the debates raging in the late 1960s and early 1970s over whether a "value-free" social science was possible, and what the nature of anthropologists' social responsibility was:

> Anthropologists have favored studying non-Western cultures as a way of fulfilling their mission to study the diverse ways of mankind; they have not had an intense commitment to social reform because of their relativistic stance and a belief that such a stance was necessary to a truly "objective, detached, scientific perspective...." While scientific findings may be ideally viewed as "value-free," certainly the choice of subject for scientific inquiry is not.[24]

This observation is striking because it implies that anthropology itself has been shackled by the dubious notion of scientific "objectivity." (On this point, Thomas Kuhn's 1962 book, *The Structure of Scientific Revolutions*, had exposed the shaky philosophical foundations underlying such claims.) The very process of selecting "a subject for scientific inquiry"—a band of hunter-gatherers rather than an investment banking firm, for example—reveals a subjective bias. In some ways, a kind of "bureaucratic ethos" was shrouding the work of many anthropologists.[25] Yet ethnographic analysis of the process of bureaucratization (and the bureaucratic organizations that enable them) is precisely what Nader proposes in "Up the Anthropologist."

At this time a number of criticisms of applied anthropology emerged in Latin America regarding the approach of top-down development programs.[26] Such initiatives, often sponsored by nationalist governments, economic development agencies, and international financial institutions like the World Bank, tended to serve the interests of elite groups rather than the "target populations" (often indigenous people or peasant farmers). Nader, who conducted research in rural Oaxaca, Mexico, in the late 1950s and 1960s, understood how such top-down programs were likely to create more problems than they solved:

> How has it come to be, we might ask, that anthropologists are more interested in why peasants don't change than why the auto industry doesn't innovate, or why the Pentagon or universities cannot be more organizationally creative? The conservatism of such major institutions and bureaucratic organizations probably has wider implications for the species and for theories of change than does the conservatism of the peasantry.[27]

Such proposals showed anthropologists a way out of imperialist applied anthropology to a more democratic anthropology that would meet the needs of ordinary people.[28]

Nader also posed the innovative theme of *democratic relevance*. For much of the twentieth century, some interpreted the Boasian legacy among American anthropologists as a strong tendency toward cultural relativism—to the point that many steered clear of taking what might be considered "political" stands on their own society. This reluctance appears to have led to a double bias within the discipline: some derided research based in the United States as opposed to the more typical setting of a small-scale non-industrialized society; and some, still reeling from the red-baiting McCarthy period in the U.S. Congress, were reluctant to involve themselves in any political questions at all. The tendency toward apolitical anthropology was ironic in more ways than one. Although Boas formulated the perspective of cultural relativism, he did not equate it to *moral* relativism. Indeed, Boas famously took political stands and radical positions in very public venues. In speeches, essays, op-ed pieces and other popular media, he harshly criticized U.S. imperialism, discriminatory immigration policies, domestic racism, and war.

The idea of a more democratically relevant social science represented something that was straightforward, yet radical for a discipline in which so many practitioners had implied that cultural relativism precluded such a possibility. From this perspective, one could argue that anthropologists and others, as scientists who are also citizens, should strive to make their work relevant to the continuation (or recuperation) of a democratic society where democracy itself was under siege. For many readers, however, the most interesting part of Nader's argument in "Up the Anthropologist" had to do with the importance of "studying up" for the purpose of *scientific adequacy*. Since anthropology purported to represent all humankind, clearly the ethnographic record of powerful contemporary societies, institutions, and individuals was impoverished. By this point in the history of anthropology, researchers had conducted hundreds of studies of foraging societies, countless ethnographies describing the minutest details of village life among agriculturalists, untold numbers of monographs analyzing the cultures of pastoral nomads. Yet precious little anthropological work had focused on contemporary U.S. society and the institutions that dominate it: multinational corporations, governmental agencies, the Supreme Court, the New York Stock Exchange, the families making up the "power elite."

From a scientific point of view, this argument revealed a huge hole in the scholarly literature both here and elsewhere in the world. Apart from the clear logic behind her observation, Nader's insistence on making this a key theme forestalled any criticisms from those who might charge her with taking a gratuitous ideological stand against the political and economic establishment. Had it not been for a strong position reaffirming the scientific nature of the anthropological enterprise, critics might very well have charged her thusly, or viewed "Up the Anthropologist" as little more than an anti-corporate text, suggesting as it did a class analysis that would examine the interrelationships between different groups within U.S. society in particular.[29]

Nader was by no means the only anthropologist calling for a more sophisticated analysis of the workings of power. In fact, during the 1960s and 1970s a range of scholars produced work that pushed the limits of conventional anthropology. Eric Wolf's book *Peasants* (1966) suggested that colonialism (and resistance to it) created new kinds of cultures. In short, peasant societies resulted from political processes linked intimately to capitalist development. Wolf's work, which relied on a model that in many ways resembled what was eventually called "world systems" analysis, led to conclusions about the nature of peasant societies that differed markedly from the findings of Robert Redfield, George Foster, and others.[30] In a similar vein, June Nash's ethnographic work (e.g., *We Eat the Mines and the Mines Eat Us* [1979]) exposed the complex ways in which capitalist development had upended and remade indigenous Bolivians. Like Wolf, Nash chronicled the creation of an industrial proletariat.[31] Marshall Sahlins's research on "stone age" economic systems (1974) forced readers to question basic assumptions underpinning consumer society. By analyzing the affluent lives of hunter-gatherers (who tend to have much more leisure time than their counterparts in agricultural or industrial societies), Sahlins was able to cast a spotlight on a salient aspect of our society: "Infinite Needs."[32] And Sidney Mintz, who had earlier written a deeply contextualized life history of a Puerto Rican *Worker in the Cane* (1963), used sugar as a vehicle for analyzing the political and economic connections linking sugarcane plantation owners in the Americas, slaves of African descent, and the European working classes.[33] Taken together, the work of Nader, Wolf, Nash, Sahlins, Mintz, and others signaled that anthropology's reinvention had begun.

Power and Controlling Processes

Laura Nader, having clearly delineated the terms of studying up in her original 1969 article and mentioned the idea of "studying up, down, and sideways" (implying that a reinvented anthropology should study not only power elites but also their relationships and interconnections with people and institutions of subordinate socioeconomic strata), later explicated the relationships between these three dimensions, which eventually became known as "the vertical slice." Over the 1970s and early 1980s, she published a series of works that used a spatial metaphor to illustrate the idea of analyzing the dynamics of power by examining the links between various strata of society. Nader called on anthropologists to more thoroughly connect the problems facing ordinary citizens, children, parents, and consumers to decisions and policies created by powerful people and institutions—policy makers, corporate executives, and government officials. Only by analyzing a "vertical slice" that exposes the different layers of power can the anthropologist construct a complete picture of cause and effect. In a 1976 article, "Professional Standards and What We Study," she clarified the reasons for the lack of attention to vertical linkage in the field, arguing that anthropological research of the time was less motivated by academic interest in social relationships than by the needs and desires of individual researchers. And Nader later came to more clearly define the concept of vertical linkages in her 1980 article "The Vertical Slice: Hierarchies and Children," where she challenged the notion that family life could be treated in isolation, and investigated the complex linkages between children and institutions. There is a connection, for example, between the production of a highly flammable shirt for children, Washington lobbyists, and governmental regulations. She also defined vertical linkages as the objects of study that one may anticipate upon applying the network model "vertically rather than horizontally."[34] By extension, "the vertical slice" refers to the act of applying the network model in this way.[35]

By the 1980s, studying up, down, and sideways had taken Nader's research in unexpected directions. Following an invitation to participate in the National Academy of Science's Committee on Nuclear and Alternative Energy Systems, she published "Barriers to Thinking New about Energy," a short piece in the popular magazine *Physics Today* that not only described the experience of studying up, down, and sideways, but also analyzed the controlling processes that prevented physicists and engineers from assessing the full range of alternatives for future energy scenarios.[36] Studying up (by interacting with and analyzing the work organization and language of scientists) while studying down and sideways (by taking into account the energy consumption patterns and habits of ordinary people) allowed Nader to make striking observations: this professional group was characterized by "a good deal of standardized thinking, a lack of respect for diversity, and an absolute taboo on the word solar."[37] She noted that the physicists "seem to relish something complicated, hazardous, difficult, and risky, something that requires high technology and big money," even though simpler solutions (such as solar power or improvements in efficiency to existing technologies) were available.[38] They also tended to favor top-down rather than bottom-up solutions and to view human beings as objects; for example, one "risk specialist" suggested that if safety improvements were made to automobiles, household appliances, and the like, "then we could afford to have a nuclear disaster."[39] Another proposition—that if sufficient energy efficiency improvements were made to automobiles, household appliances, and the like, then there would be no need to go nuclear—was apparently not obvious enough:

> We have gotten to the point in our society at which we can no longer entertain obvious solutions. This is where anthropologists come in. The coming era will require practical, general, earthy types of thinkers who understand problems and conflicting value systems. We need people who can look at mundane and straightforward problems, people who will not choose complicated solutions when simple ones are available.[40]

The professional mind-sets of the physicists, engineers, "risk specialists" and others were a prime example of what Nader would later call controlling processes, "the mechanisms by which ideas take hold and become institutional in relation to power"—for example, "the creation of new consumption needs . . . the internalization of codes of behavior by means of which institutional structures transform social relations and consumption patterns" for a wide range of products and services ranging from sugar and breast implants to casinos and pharmaceuticals.[41] This innovative approach to ethnographic studies of systems of ideological and hegemonic controls was possible because the methodological and theoretical groundwork had already been laid and adopted by numerous anthropologists in the United States and elsewhere.[42]

Revisiting "Up the Anthropologist"

Reinventing Anthropology, the volume in which "Up the Anthropologist" originally appeared, received mixed (and sometimes hostile) reviews in the United States.[43] Some accused the contributors of focusing too narrowly on anthropology's role in constructing and maintaining hegemonic structures, some claimed that the authors too harshly judged the impact of institutionalization and bureaucratization on society, and others bristled against what they called "muckraking anthropology."[44] However, Nader's piece fared better than most of the contributions to the volume and was generally recognized as proposing much more than a simple redirection of anthropological research. For example, one reviewer noted that "Nader implicitly recognizes that problem, method, and theory are locked together in a dialectic where they create each other. For this reason, Nader's essay will be of far greater use than any of the others to an anthropologist wanting to do some reinvented anthropology rather than merely talk about it."[45] Other reviewers might have misread Nader's words by assuming that she was simply proposing studies of powerful people, something others had already attempted. For example, George Marcus noted that "In studying elites in the 1970s and 1980s, I was never happy with the idea of an ethnography of elites expressed as 'studying up' (Nader 1969), which carried the connotation of compensating for the preponderant interest of anthropology in studying the dominated, but also of 'getting the goods'—the ethnographic 'goods'—on elites."[46]

Comments such as these demonstrate that some anthropologists failed to understand that studying up, in its original conception, actually meant studying up, down, and sideways by seeking to locate and analyze the connections between powerful institutions (particularly bureaucracies and corporations) and relatively powerless individuals—that is, the "interlocked institutions" mentioned by Clyde Mitchell. As Hugh Gusterson has noted, studying up is more than a simple call to study powerful groups and individuals—it entails "hybrid research and writing strategies that blur the boundaries between anthropology and other disciplines" and "offer[s] the chance to incite new conversations about power in the U.S." as part of a "democratizing project" examining the interconnections between the rich and powerful and the rest of us.[47]

That said, it would be difficult to underestimate the impact of "Up the Anthropologist" across the field of anthropology, for few articles have made as deep an impression. For many, "studying up" has become synonymous with analyzing powerful institutions; for others, it represents research focusing upon elites; for others it is simply shorthand for "radical" anthropology. Some have misinterpreted studying up as an opportunity to study powerful groups so as to make them more powerful, or at least more efficient in their work. Examples of this genre include the "organizational culture" literature of some anthropologists of work.[48] Such uses of "studying up" do not address democratic relevance, scientific adequacy, and indignation as motive. In such work, Nader's proposals ironically become mere instruments used by entrepreneurial anthropologists serving the very institutions that have helped to erode American democracy—General Motors and the Department of Defense among them.

If we use the goals outlined in Laura Nader's original article "Up the Anthropologist" as a barometer for determining whether studying up has hit home for anthropologists, these interpretations of "studying up" prove problematic for several reasons. First, Nader originally attempted to outline a paradigm for studying power that was *both* methodological and theoretical. By contrast, current formulations of studying up sometimes reduce it to a purely methodological convention—a series of bulleted items for action about the wealthy to produce field notes and a full written representation of a culture. Second, such ethnographies isolate the concept of "studying up" from the larger epistemological project of vertical integration. Third, "Up the Anthropologist" provided a process by which anthropologists could historically and culturally contextualize power. However, in some current formulations of studying up, power is so decontextualized that such important phenomena as neoliberal projects, the "war on terror," the erosion of democratic norms in the United States and abroad, and other contemporary global transformations are divorced from their historical context or left out of the discussion altogether. Such work may claim to target power as its object of inquiry, but it actually demonstrates nothing about the source, content, and consequences of the flows of economic and cultural capital. "Up the Anthropologist," on the other hand, outlined a clear paradigm for making anthropology scientifically adequate and at the same time politically relevant.

Many anthropologists have incorporated the methodological and theoretical paradigm of studying up, down, and sideways in their work, both implicitly and explicitly. Reviewing just a few examples will reveal a wide range of the topics, settings, and situations illuminated by "vertical" analysis. The work of anthropologists studying the world of high finance describes fascinating applications of studying up, down, and sideways. Gillian Tett's book *Fool's Gold* (2009), an account of how bankers at J.P. Morgan created risky new financial products that would eventually throw the world into economic crisis, is a good example. So too is Karen Ho's *Liquidated: An Ethnography of Wall Street* (2009), which provides a fine-grained analysis of how ideologies of "shareholder value" serve as controlling processes that lock bankers into closed mind-sets.[49]

Others have examined questions of war, peace, and militarism by employing a version of the "vertical slice" approach. Catherine Lutz's ethnography *Homefront: A Military City and the American Century* (2001) broke new ground by examining the political, economic, and cultural roots of

U.S. militarism. Although the ethnography is set in a single location, Fayetteville, North Carolina (near Fort Bragg, one of the biggest military bases in the United States), it explores the historical connection between this region and the broader "military-industrial complex" of defense contractors and Pentagon officials. Similarly, Carolyn Nordstrom's *Shadows of War* (2004), for example, traces the networks linking weapons manufacturers, arms traders, smugglers, and other profiteers to people and families living in war zones. Hugh Gusterson takes a somewhat different approach in *Nuclear Rites* (1998), which delves into the complex, often contradictory worldviews of U.S. nuclear weapons scientists. Like Lutz and Nordstrom, Gusterson is not satisfied with a one-dimensional description of culture but instead places his research participants within deeper structural contexts that reveal the intersections between their lives and those of others. David Vine's *Island of Shame* (2009) recounts the ways that military elites' decisions have affected the lives of the Chagossians, indigenous peoples native to Diego Garcia, an island in the Indian Ocean. Over the course of the twentieth century, the United States converted the island into a massive military base, forcing the Chagossians to abandon their lands and be relocated to Mauritius and the Seychelles.[50]

Others have cast a critical eye toward the most powerful institution of our time: the multinational corporation. Dimitra Doukas's ethnography *Worked Over* (2003) details the process by which a locally based family enterprise in upstate New York was gradually taken over by corporate "trusts" in the late 1800s and early 1900s, leading to what she calls the "sabotage" of the region's towns. Janine Wedel's *The Shadow Elite* (2009) documents the emergence of a new network of transnational elites, men and women who are able to leverage themselves as global power brokers by virtue of their revolving positions as corporate executives, academics, and government agents.[51]

A vast range of other studies too numerous to mention illustrates the kind of connecting work anthropologists have undertaken in recent years. These include Paul Farmer's *Pathologies of Power* (2004), which exposes the ways in which "structural adjustment" policies and other neoliberal arrangements undermine public health; Steve Striffler's *Chicken: The Dangerous Transformation of America's Favorite Food* (2005), which reveals how global agribusiness firms have evaded regulatory oversight and subjected consumers, workers, and others to grave danger; and Alisse Waterston's *Street Addicts in the Political Economy* (1997), a book that paints a sensitive picture of people denigrated and demonized by the corporate media and demonstrates that the plight of addicts is intimately linked to gentrification and urban "redevelopment" schemes.

Taken together, these ethnographic works indicate just how thoroughly Laura Nader's call to "study up, down, and sideways" has been absorbed by anthropologists today.[52]

This Collection

This volume contains several essays that, taken together, serve to reintroduce Laura Nader's concept of the vertical slice and demonstrate its value for historically and culturally contextualizing power in ways that make anthropology politically relevant. At the same time, the book reminds us of what is at stake when anthropologists do not study up, down, and sideways—for both anthropologists and those we study.

Coco's chapter examines institutions that contribute to global financial crisis, tracing the messaging through which *consumers* both contribute to and internalize financial failure. Specifically, she explores the institutional construction of the consumer debtor in the United States, focusing on the normative discourses that enable U.S. Federal Bankruptcy structures to practice a particular rationalized exercise of power that denies the *necessity* of debt in the wealth creation process. In particular, she asks—and answers—a pointed question: By what processes has the consumer debtor come to be considered a social failure, while the corporate debtor has not?

Ou's chapter examines one of the most pressing issues of the twenty-first century: global financial crisis. Ou's essay, an example of vertically integrated research, examines social organizations such as Korean-owned factories in Indonesia and Korea, and civil society, government, and corporations in the United States to provide a more comprehensive understanding of global corporate capitalism and its relation to society and culture. By analyzing the complex linkages connecting these social groups, he contextualizes the policies and practices that contributed to the onset of the terrible Asian financial crisis of 1997–1998. He also demonstrates the central role of institutions like corporate banks and international financial organizations in the larger global economic crises ten years later.

Ou's and Coco's chapters illuminate some fairly obvious and "lofty" centers of financial power in the United States and abroad. Hertz's chapter, however, examines the practices of power as it travels within state organizations that emulate the bureaucracies of financial institutions. She ethnographically details the seemingly benign and ordinary proceedings of minor bureaucrats at a meeting at the International Labour Organisation in Geneva, exploring attributes of "upness": high levels of generality that allow for certain forms of compromise and, more importantly, loftiness of principle that can then be siphoned back into national and local settings. She argues that the price of this "height" is a feeling of enormous distance between the grandeur of the mission of international organizations such as the ILO and the reality of their impact "on the ground." "Studying up" in the twenty-first century, she argues, will thus involve repeatedly taking the measure of this distance and asking whose interests it advances, when, and where.

Grandia's chapter is the first of three that specifically address multinational corporate expansion and traces the global connections and interlocking directorates that fuel corporate globalization. These chapters also ethnographically deconstruct neoliberal abuses, or the deleterious consequences of neoliberal ideology put into practice on a large scale. For example, Grandia reviews the work of five leading voices on worldwide corporate expansion and dispossession trends: Michael Hardt and Antonio Negri on "empire," David Harvey on "the new imperialism," and Ugo Mattei and Laura Nader on "plunder." Studying cattle ranchers, evangelical missionaries, petroleum companies, World Bank bureaucrats, foreign trade representatives, and transnational conservationists, she also connects the Q'eqchi' case of land dispossession in Belize and Guatemala with global trends. The conclusion compares Q'eqchi' dispossession with the impact of British Petroleum's 2010 oil spill on Gulf Coast residents. In both cases, she argues, the loss or spoliation of territory threatens people's immediate livelihoods and the cultures upon which those are based.

Roberto González's chapter explores the important topic of food, power, and control. It first describes Zapotec foodways—which have been local, sustainable, and organic for more than fifty centuries—and then analyzes the processes that are leading to their erosion. Global migration, international trade laws, the expansion of agribusiness, and the diffusion of genetically modified organisms have all played a part in the degradation of food security among the Zapotec of Talea, a mountain village in Oaxaca, Mexico. Gonzalez examines how the loss of control over food in both Zapotec and our own society presents serious health, environmental, and economic dilemmas, some of which are being challenged by the informed actions of concerned farmers, consumers, and citizens. By tracing the linkages between different strata of global society—studying up, down, and sideways—the chapter gives some sense of the processes by which control over food can be regained.

Urteaga Crovetto's chapter details the emergence of the Camisea Gas Project in Peru, in which the Peruvian state, Multinational Corporations, and the International Development Bank worked in tandem to pursue gas exploitation of Peru's indigenous communities. She regards the development of the Camisea Gas Project as a case study in which discourses of "inevitability" (of the assumedly intrinsic benefit of economic development) work to threaten communities and dispossess them of their resources. She examines the interlocking institutions that, she argues, steadily undermine indigenous peoples' material and symbolic world, cause their gradual loss of identity, and decimate their population in the name of progress. Her essay concludes with thoughts on how identifying discourses of inevitability provides new directions for indigenous activism.

Stryker's chapter is the first of two that use the vertical slice to deconstruct notions of public/private separations between family and commerce or governmental institutions. It looks at the tendency and consequences of American families' over-reliance on institutional messaging (corporate or state surrogacy) to raise children in the United States, particularly within the realm of international adoption. Her chapter offers a fresh analysis of some old concerns about "neontocracy" (the child-centered culture), particularly whether institutional narratives and practice should replace parental intuition in family building. Examining the controlling processes associated with the making—and breaking—of adoptive families illuminates certain practices within a professional field where families must interact with institutions more often than is typical, prompting consideration of how institutions usurp the autonomy of the American family more broadly. The chapter discusses many ideas for rethinking the family as a site for creating present and future forms of freedom and citizenship for its members.

Kliger's chapter explores the value of studying up, down, and sideways for understanding the proliferation in North America of sexual abuse complaints based on delayed discovery of traumatic memories. A vertical research orientation demonstrates that the law, as both discourse and site (the courtroom), has been drawn into the process of scientific fact making about traumatic memory, giving scientists incentive to conceptually shift the way they understand human memory and consequently to alter their research foci. Kliger argues that this process has resulted in a revision of legal and scientific standards, accelerating the rate at which particular types of scientific knowledge are produced and concomitantly increasing dependence upon notions of "good science" as defined by legal discourse.

Eppinger's chapter is the first of two closing essays that draw direct parallels between studying up, down, and sideways and projecting into a future based on citizenship and collective democracy. Based on vertically integrated research in post-Soviet Ukraine, the essay outlines certain contexts of discursive rupture that studying up, down, and sideways, as a mere methodology, may not immediately address. However, Eppinger argues, investigation and deconstruction of the spatial metaphors behind the notion of studying up, down, and sideways point us to certain quite interesting, perplexing questions of how humans discern or create which way is up, particularly at times of great political upheaval. Using theories of language, performance, and performativity, her chapter looks at these problems and makes some methodological proposals, including use of the vertical slice to address them. Ultimately, she argues for rethinking studying up, down, and sideways to understand how people construct and restore common sense in scenarios where the concept of "the commons" is in flux.

Finally, Pine's chapter draws parallels between the act of caring about society and the act of conducting militant anthropology influenced by the vertical slice methodology. As an anthropologist who formerly served as an educator/researcher for the California Nurses Association, Pine studied the politics of the health care industry and of the small, fractious U.S. labor movement. Here, she draws from these experiences to examine how studying up, down, and sideways can inform health care providers', health care patients', and labor organizers' efforts to develop effective direct-action political strategies to subvert—at various levels—an increasingly bureaucratized U.S. health care system. Ultimately, she argues that studying up, down, and sideways is integral to understanding the world in which nurses and their patients work and live, and to fighting to make it a better one.

Conclusion

Eduardo Galeano has written, "One hundred and thirty years ago, after visiting Wonderland, Alice stepped into the mirror and discovered the world of the looking glass. If Alice were born today, she'd only have to look out the window."[53] Today we face daunting "upside-down" challenges to freedom, democracy, and well-being. Confronted with literal and metaphorical seismic world events, we are easily confused as to the patterns that govern them. But just as scholars like Fromm, Lynd, and Riesman found their way through the maze by illuminating contradictions, and just as Nader did so by making connections between institutions and individuals—indeed, just as Alice retooled her thinking to understand that the looking-glass world was actually a chessboard—one needs to think up, down, and sideways to figure out an upside-down world. The contributions to this volume confront some of our day's biggest challenges—corporate hegemony, development thinking, environmental oversight, and the standardization of thought and action, to mention just some of the most pressing. To address these challenges is to rethink not just the scope of what is visible, but of what is ultimately possible.

Notes

1. Giles Whittell, "Flooding from Hurricane Katrina Was Man-Made Disaster, Judge Rules," *The Sunday Times* (U.K.), 20 November 2009, http://www.timesonline.co.uk/tol/news/world/us_and_americas/article6924125.ece.
2. Greg Toppo and Janet Kornblum, "Ads on Tests Add Up for Teacher," *USA Today*, 2 December 2008, http://www.usatoday.com/news/education/2008-12-01-test-ads_N.htm.
3. See Forbes.com, "US Foreclosures Rise in December, Reach 2.2 Mln in 2007," 29 January 2008, http://www.forbes.com/feeds/afx/2008/01/29/afx4584956.html; RealtyTrac, "Record 2.9 Million U.S. Properties Receive Foreclosure Filings in 2010 Despite 30-Month Low in December," 12 January 2011), http://www.realtytrac.com/content/foreclosure-market-report/record-29-million-us-properties-receive-foreclosure-filings-in-2010-despite-30-month-low-in-december-6309; RealtyTrac, "2011 Year-End Foreclosure Report: Foreclosures on the Retreat," 9 January 2012, http://www.realtytrac.com/content/foreclosure-market-report/2011-year-end-foreclosure-market-report-6984; RealtyTrac, "1.8 Million U.S. Properties With Foreclosure Filings in 2012," 14 January 2013, http://www.realtytrac.com/content/foreclosure-market-report/2012-year-end-foreclosure-market-report-7547; Robbie Whelan, "Foreclosure Machines Still Running on 'Low,'" 31 July 2012, http://blogs.wsj.com/developments/2012/07/31/foreclosure-machines-still-running-on-low/.
4. Damien Pearse, "Afghan Civilian Death Toll Reaches Record High," *The Guardian*, 4 February 2012. Although civilian casualties decreased slightly in 2012, the number of attacks (including fatal attacks) on women and children increased significantly. See United Nations News Centre, "Afghan Civilian Deaths Drop but Attacks on Women, Children, and Political Targets Rise," 19 February 2013, http://www.un.org/apps/news/story.asp?NewsID=44170#.UdITdpyfb2Z.
5. For a ground-level view of the economic devastation wrought by the BP oil spill, see Ken Wells et al., "From the Gulf, a Portrait of Business Owners on the Brink," *Bloomberg Businessweek*, 10 June 2010, http://images.businessweek.com/ss/10/07/0708_lost_summer/2.htm.
6. Lyndsey Layton, "FDA Says Basic Food Flavors Knew Plant Was Contaminated with Salmonella," *Washington Post*, 10 March 2010.
7. Sociologist C. Wright Mills developed the term "organized irresponsibility": "Organized irresponsibility, in this impersonal sense, is a leading characteristic of modern industrial societies everywhere. On every hand the individual is confronted with seemingly remote organizations; he feels dwarfed and helpless before the managerial cadres and their manipulated and manipulative minions." C. Wright Mills, *White Collar: The American Middle Classes* (New York: Oxford University Press, 1951), 111.
8. Laura Nader, "Up the Anthropologist—Perspectives Gained from Studying Up," in *Reinventing Anthropology*, ed. Dell Hymes (New York: Pantheon Books, 1972), 285–311.

9. See James Randerson, "World's Richest 1 percent Own 40 percent of All Wealth, UN Report Discovers," *The Guardian* (U.K.), 6 December 2006, http://www.guardian.co.uk/money/2006/dec/06/business.internationalnews; Holly Sklar, "CEO Pay Still Outrageous," *Dissident Voice*, 1 May 2003, http://dissidentvoice.org/Articles4/Sklar_CEO-Pay.htm; Ben Bagdikian, *The New Media Monopoly* (Boston: Beacon Press, 2004).
10. C. Wright Mills, "The Promise," in *The Sociological Imagination* (New York: Oxford University Press, 1959), 3–24.
11. Thomas Jefferson, *Notes on the State of Virginia* (New York: Penguin Books, 1999 [1785]), 171.
12. Jack Weatherford, *Indian Givers: How Native Americans Transformed the World* (New York: Three Rivers Press, 1988), 171–193.
13. Henry David Thoreau, *Civil Disobedience* (New York: Empire Books, 2011 [1849]), 3.
14. Henry David Thoreau, *Walden* (New York: Empire Books, 2013 [1854]).
15. Erich Fromm, *The Heart of Man: Its Genius for Good or Evil* (Religious perspectives; v. 12) (New York: Harper and Row, 1964), 132. For Fromm, the need to define individual freedom was strong: many in his lifetime had anticipated World War I as the final struggle for global democracy and seen its conclusion as the ultimate victory for freedom. Indeed, immediately after that war, existing democracies appeared strengthened and new ones replaced old monarchies. But only a few years after the war's end, emerging new authoritarian systems denied everything individuals believed they had won in centuries of struggle.
16. *Escape from Freedom* (New York: Farrar & Rinehart, Inc., 1941), 4. Around the same time that Fromm published *Escape from Freedom*, American sociologist Robert Lynd published a book called *Knowledge for What?* Like Fromm, Lynd was concerned about the rise of totalitarian regimes. He wondered why, in the face of the broadscale dismantling of intellectual freedom in Germany and the militarizing of the academy in Italy, the U.S. social sciences had failed to analyze these social phenomena to help understand and build a more democratic culture in the United States. See Robert S. Lynd, *Knowledge for What?: The Place of Social Science in American Culture* (Princeton: Princeton University Press, 1939).
17. David Riesman (in collaboration with Reuel Denney and Nathan Glazer), *The Lonely Crowd: A Study of the Changing American Character* (New Haven and London: Yale University Press, 1950).
18. Fromm, *Escape from Freedom*, viii.
19. Lynd, *Knowledge for What?* 65.
20. Rupert Wilkinson, "'The Lonely Crowd,' at 60, Is Still Timely", 12 September 2010, *Chronicle of Higher Education*, http://chronicle.com/article/The-Lonely-Crowd-at-60-Is/124334/.
21. Hymes, *Reinventing Anthropology*.
22. Nader, "Up the Anthropologist," 289.
23. In September 2009, tens of thousands of students and faculty from various University of California campuses walked out in what one newspaper called "the biggest student protest for more than a generation." UC President Mark Yudof responded by telling the *New York Times Magazine* that "being president of the University of California is like being manager of a cemetery." See Deborah Solomon, "Big Man on Campus," *New York Times Magazine*, 24 September 2009.
24. Nader, "Up the Anthropologist," 303.
25. The term "bureaucratic ethos" was developed by C. Wright Mills in *The Sociological Imagination*, 100–118.

26. See Guillermo Bonfil Batalla, *Diagnóstico Sobre el Hambre en Sudzal, Yucatán* (Mexico City: INAH, 1962) and "Conservative Thought in Applied Anthropology: A Critique," *Human Organization* 25, no. 2 (1966): 89–92; Rodolfo Stavenhagen, "Decolonizing Applied Social Science," *Human Organization* 30, no. 4 (1971): 333–344; Arturo Warman et al. (eds.), *De Eso Que Llaman Antropología Mexicana* (Mexico City: Nuestro Tiempo, 1970).
27. Nader's article may have been impacted in part by breakthroughs in the 1950s in British social anthropology—a kind of maverick anthropology developed by scholars dissatisfied with aspects of structural functionalism. In particular, Max Gluckman and others who collectively became known as the "Manchester School" may have influenced the idea of studying up, down, and sideways. These scholars focused on problems of change and conflict rather than stability and "social solidarity." Politically, some members of the group were controversial because they spent a great deal of time doing participant observation among blacks and "coloreds" in Africa and many insisted on including colonial administrators, mine owners, and other elites within the frame of analysis. What they found was that blacks, whites, and "coloreds," mine managers and workers, rural people and city dwellers, colonial administrators and their subjects were connected in interlocking institutions that made notions of "tribe," "city," or "community" obsolete. Their work exposed the power relations inherent in the rapidly urbanizing African societies in which they conducted much of their research. Sometimes this work critically examined British colonialism's role in destabilizing African societies. The work of Clyde Mitchell succinctly explains the approach: "The classical anthropological study takes a unit—a 'tribe' or 'society' or 'community'—and presents the behavior of its members in terms of a series of interlocking institutions, structures, norms, and values. It is not only anthropologists working in urban areas who have found this sort of assumption difficult to maintain, but also those who have been conducting 'tribal' studies in modern Africa (and presumably also elsewhere). They have found that the effect of groups and institutions not physically present in the tribal area influences the behavior of people in it" (Clyde Mitchell, quoted in Laura Nader, "Up the Anthropologist," 291).
28. Laura Nader, "Up the Anthropologist," 289.
29. Nader's call to harness indignation was also part of a more general response to currents in anthropology that for much of the 1960s favored an overly scientific cognitive model based on "componential analysis." Critics of this model approached the methodological obsessions of the linguistically based approach as one way of escaping power analyses. Inherent in much of this sort of criticism was the idea that componential analysis was "anemic" and led to the study of trivial subject matter—hardly the kind of thing that students might be indignant about. For an example of componential analysis, see Ward Goodenough, "Componential Analysis and the Study of Meaning," *Language* 32 (1958): 195–216. For a critique, see Gerald Berreman, "Anemic and Emetic Analyses in Social Anthropology." *American Anthropologist* 68, no. 2 (1966): 346–354.
30. Eric Wolf, *Peasants* (Englewood Cliffs, NJ: Prentice-Hall, 1966).
31. June Nash, *We Eat the Mines and the Mines Eat Us* (New York: Columbia University Press, 1979).
32. Marshall Sahlins, *Stone Age Economics* (Chicago: Aldine-Atherton, 1972).
33. Sidney Mintz, *Sweetness and Power: The Place of Sugar in Modern History* (New York: Viking, 1985). This is only a partial list of anthropological work highlighting the analysis of powerful institutions or anthropology's potential to contribute to solving social problems. See, e.g., Thomas Weaver, *To See Ourselves: Anthropology and Modern Social Issues* (New York: Random House, 1973); James Bodley, *Anthropology and Contemporary*

Human Problems (Menlo Park, CA: Cummings Publishing, 1976); Maria Patricia Fernandez-Kelly, *For We are Sold, I and My People: Women and Industry in Mexico's Frontier* (Albany, NY: SUNY Press, 1983); and Eric Wolf, *Europe and the People without History* (Berkeley: University of California Press, 1982).

34. Laura Nader, "The Vertical Slice: Hierarchies and Children," in *Hierarchy and Society: Anthropological Perspectives on Society*, ed. Gerald M. Britan and Ronald Cohen (Piladelphia: Institute for the Sutdy of Human Issues, 1980), 38.

35. Nader's call to study up originated in part from the work of network theorists such as anthropologist Jeremy Boissevain, which illuminated the value and method of studying networks (temporary, egocentric social forms such as cliques, interest groups, and factions) rather than groups (enduring social groups such as tribes, villages, bands, etc.) in the social sciences. See Jeremy Bossevain, *Friends of Friends: Networks, Manipulators, and Coalitions* (Oxford: Basil Blackwell, 1974).

36. Laura Nader, "Barriers to Thinking New about Energy," *Physics Today* 34 (1981): 99–102.

37. Ibid.

38. Ibid.

39. Ibid.

40. Ibid.

41. Laura Nader, "Controlling Processes: Tracing the Dynamic Components of Power," *Current Anthropology* 38, no. 5 (1997): 711–737.

42. By the 1990s, when Nader developed the idea of controlling processes more fully, the strategy of studying up, down, and sideways had been deeply absorbed in such work as *Harmony Ideology: Justice and Control in a Mountain Zapotec Village* (Stanford: Stanford University Press, 1990 and the edited book *Naked Science: Anthropological Inquiry into Boundaries, Power, and Knowledge* (New York: Routledge, 1996).

43. Walter Goldschmidt, "*Reinventing Anthropology* (Review)," *Science* 180, no. 4086 (1973): 612–613; J. L. Fischer, "*Reinventing Anthropology* (Review)," *Journal of American Folklore* 87, no. 346 (1974): 376–377; David Kaplan, "The Anthropology of Authenticity: Everyman His Own Anthropologist," *American Anthropologist* 76, no. 4 (1974): 824–839.

44. Walter Goldschmidt, "*Reinventing Anthropology*," 613.

45. Leland Donald, "Review: Reinventing Anthropology by Dell Hymes," *American Anthropologist* 76, no. 4 (1974): 8.

46. George Marcus, *Ethnography through Thick and Thin* (Princeton: Princeton University Press, 1998), 27.

47. Hugh Gusterson, "Studying Up Revisited," PoLAR 20, no. 1 (May 1997): 119.

48. Marietta L. Baba, "Beyond Dilbert: The Cultural Construction of Work Organizations in America," in *Ethnographic Essays in Cultural Anthropology: A Problem-Based Approach*, ed. R. Bruce Morrison and C. Roderick Wilson (Itasca, IL: F.E. Peacock Publishers, 2001), 183–210. See also Marietta L. Baba, "Organizational Culture: Revisiting the Small-Society Metaphor," *Anthropology of Work Review* 10, no. 3 (September 1989), 7–10.

49. Gillian Tett, *Fool's Gold: The Inside Story of J.P. Morgan and How Wall St. Greed Corrupted Its Bold Dream and Created a Financial Catastrophe* (New York: Free Press, 2009); Karen Ho, *Liquidated: An Ethnography of Wall Street* (Durham, NC: Duke University Press, 2009).

50. Catherine Lutz, *Homefront: A Military City and the American Twentieth Century* (Boston: Beacon Press, 2011); Carolyn Nordstrom, *Shadows of War: Violence, Power, and International Profiteering in the Twenty-First Century* (Berkeley: University of California Press, 2004); Hugh Gusterson, *Nuclear Rites: A Weapons Laboratory at the End of the Cold War* (Berkeley: University of California Press, 1998); David Vine, *Island of Shame: The Secret*

History of the US Military Base on Diego Garcia (Princeton: Princeton University Press, 2009).
51. Dmitra Doukas, *Worked Over: The Corporate Sabotage of an American Community* (Ithaca, NY: Cornell University Press, 2003); Janine Wedel, *Shadow Elite: How the World's New Power Brokers Undermine Democracy, Government, and the Free Market* (New York: Basic Books, 2009).
52. Paul Farmer, *Pathologies of Power: Health, Human Rights, and the New War on the Poor* (Berkeley: University of California Press, 2004); Steve Striffler, *Chicken: The Dangerous Transformation of America's Favorite Food* (New Haven: Yale University Press, 2007); Alisse Waterston, *Street Addicts in the Political Economy* (Philadelphia: Temple University Press, 1997).
53. Eduardo Galeano, *Upside Down: A Primer for the Looking-Glass World* (New York: Metropolitan Books, 2001), 2.

Part I

Studying Wealth and Power

Chapter 1

ON DEBT

Tracking the Shifting Role of the Debtor
in U.S. Bankruptcy Legal Practice

Linda Coco

In autumn 2008, the United States experienced an unprecedented financial crisis defined by Wall Street's securitization schemes and the unethical practices of financial institutions deemed "too big to fail." Reckless securitization of real estate mortgages led to unsustainable lending practices, creating the conditions for the collapse of the U.S. housing market. Thousands of Americans lost their homes, and several major financial institutions failed, including AIG, Lehman Brothers, and Bear Stearns. The federal government directed taxpayer funds into bailing out a few select financial institutions. Stock markets plummeted in turn, and several large corporations such as Chrysler and General Motors became insolvent.

During the first few months of the 2008 economic crisis, individual bankruptcy filings rose by 8 percent.[1] As consumers turned to bankruptcy to deal with the economic downturn, so did large corporations. On 15 September 2008, Lehman Brothers filed a bankruptcy petition in the Southern District of New York's Bankruptcy Court. In May 2009, Chrysler filed a bankruptcy petition in the same district. By turning to bankruptcy courts for relief from burdensome debt, consumers and institutions both assumed the identity of "debtor"—but their status and conduct were perceived differently.

In the United States, financial institutions and corporations are viewed as economic actors in a marketplace, rather than as moral actors connected

---

Notes for this chapter begin on page 41.

to communities. A higher bar is set for individuals, however, as their behavior is not only measured against the rational-actor standards of the marketplace but must also meet the moral standards of social relations and obligations. For example, since the 2008 financial crisis, individual homeowners with underwater mortgages have been treated more strictly than similarly situated corporations. The investment firms Morgan Stanley and Tishman Speyer Properties walked away from properties in San Francisco and New York City that were billions of dollars underwater rather than continue to pay untenable mortgages.[2] Yet as former Secretary of the Treasury (and former Goldman Sachs Chairman) Hank Paulson admonished, "any homeowner who can afford his mortgage payment but chooses to walk away from an underwater property is simply a speculator—and one who is not honoring his obligations."[3] In other words, the individual debtor who walked away from an unprofitable deal was reprimanded for failing to honor his obligations, but the corporate investor was not. Likewise, corporations were lauded for increasing shareholders' profits, yet individual debtors were demonized for what might be interpreted as wholly rational economic decisions to increase their own profits and lessen their own expenses. In fact, the individual was told to continue paying on a bad investment.

The difference between these cultural attitudes is born of the construction of the individual debtor at various sites in the legal world of bankruptcy. This chapter is an anthropological examination of the construction of the consumer debtor.[4] I explore the normative discourses that enable a particular rationalized exercise of power in U.S. Federal Bankruptcy structures that denies the *necessity* of debt in the wealth creation process.[5] Enlightenment notions of rational conduct and the Protestant ethic combine to shape normative discourses about the debtor. This invites a question: By what processes has the consumer debtor come to be considered a social failure while the corporate debtor has not?

Ethnography on Home Ground

This chapter discusses results of vertically integrated ethnographic research[6] on the place of the debtor in the experience of bankruptcy. This research is partially informed by methods of traditional ethnographic fieldwork, a process defined by key characteristics: graduate-school theoretical training, native language training, a distant (untouched) population or "the other" as object, an exotic landscape, long-term immersion, little contact with native Westerners, illness and suffering or culture shock, assumption of the role of pupil or child to learn the culture, and the use of one or more central interlocutors.[7] Here, however, I apply these methods to home ground. Nader's concept of "studying up, down and sideways" is central to this insider ethnographic research.[8]

In September 2002 I was working as a civil enforcement attorney at the Department of Justice, Office of the United States Trustee in Oakland, California, located in Oakland's federal government buildings. I then moved my field site to a Chapter 13 Trustees office in Hayward, California, where I worked as a staff attorney contacting mortgage lenders. I worked for four months with the Chapter 13 Trustee and after that in the office of an individual consumer debtor attorney in Oakland, California, where I assisted with debtor cases. I then worked in several East Coast field sites. In 2004, I spent five months in Baltimore, Maryland, at a large law firm specializing in bankruptcy practice among larger corporate debtors using Chapter 11 of the Bankruptcy Code, and then again moved my field site to the U.S. Bankruptcy Courts. From 2005 to 2007, I worked in two separate federal districts as a federal law clerk for three different federal bankruptcy judges.

At each of these sites, individuals and institutions constructed the identity of the "debtor" through their spoken words, behavior, texts, official documents, and conduct. A debtor is any individual or corporation who has violated the delicate debt-asset balance that characterizes the experience of individuals and institutions in modern corporate capitalism. As anthropologists and sociologists have noted, debt relations are not unique to the present-day social, political, and economic space, but the particular current form of these debt relations has emerged from specific socio-historical processes rooted in normative discourses.

The debtor is a salient identity in the legal bankruptcy field. Theoretical use of the term "field"[9] is useful in this discussion because the notion helps conceptualize a particular social space where the debtor, as a manifestation of law and legal processes, is located. The emergence of the debtor is situated and relates to all the legal actors' positions and position taking in each location.

Debt and the Debtor in Social Space

Gift giving and obligation are a foundational aspect of all human relationships.[10] The notion of "debt" or "obligation" also features in many social configurations, including traditional indigenous social groups and nation-states, and is important to social organization. The idea of the "gift" and the role of gift giving between social agents create and stabilize social networks of exchange and thus works to strengthen social ordering. In highly specialized societies with distinct professional fields, such as the United States, capitalism, as an economic structure, defines, creates, and manifests a particular form of exchange relations and economic social order. Flows of economic capital (currency) shape exchange networks. And debt and debt relations in these networks impel the circulation of economic capital that is central to the vitality of the economy.

The sociologist Max Weber once wrote that "debt bondage is the normal result of the differentiation of wealth in commercial cities."[11] In other words, the circulation of economic capital is essential to modern experiences of wealth, and so are debt relations. It might even be said that the relationship between the seemingly opposed social positions of wealth and debt is similar to that between the healthy and pathological states of the body.[12] The experience of debt (and bankruptcy) is a fundamental part of social networking in the United States. Debt does not subvert the social order; rather, it "reorganizes relations through the multiplication of possibilities."[13] Most individuals and corporations participating in the U.S. economy are involved in some form of debt relation, and most individuals are debtors.

More often than not, however, debt is not recognized as a normal part of social and economic relations in the United States. Debt or bankruptcy is understood as social failure or lack of economic progress. In most instances, debt and bankruptcy are regarded as marginal to the stable social, economic, and political order; meanwhile, individual debtors are often pathologized, especially when they fail to pay debts on time. A person who fails to pay is seen as a problem. And individual debtors who are no longer able to pay their debts must atone for the failure—more precisely, they must be punished for affecting the collective. In the bankruptcy process, which can be understood as somehow "civilizing" the debtor, the individual develops a particular *habitus* (psychology, behavior, bodily knowledge) with its own history of rationalization and self-control, which links one person's conduct to the collective *doxa* of the group.[14] The circumstance of debt or bankruptcy shows the individual to have failed as a fiscally responsible member of society. Such a person is considered unable to regulate his or her conduct so as to create a stable social order.[15] Having failed to control or constrain conduct appropriately, agents are seen as violating the tempo of the chain of interdependence and thus threatening to destabilize the trend toward civilization.[16]

In the United States, individuals learn about self-restraint and rational behavior through myriad social experiences. Historically, the dominant ethos in capitalist society took its shape from the Puritan ethic of "economic virtue,"[17] in which Calvinist values of self-sufficiency, frugality, and hard work regulate individual behaviors for the benefit of the collective. Individuals who work hard and save money are lauded as having long-term vision, restraint, and strength of character for resisting temptations to their pocketbooks. Self-denial is associated with salvation, whereas the inability to save money or have money is historically associated with lack of self-restraint and construed as a result of self-indulgence. Because free will and choice are attributed to social agents, individuals are held responsible for the debts they have incurred. Their "unrestrained hedonism in the sea of fiscal responsibility" got them into their mess, so they will have to overcome their fiscal sins by learning self-control.[18] Therefore, debt and the debtor are constructed through the combined, interconnected normative discourses of personal responsibility (Enlightenment) and personal failure (Calvinist).

The debtor in the bankruptcy experience is also embedded in Anglo-American legal doctrine, which is rooted in Kantian notions of rational thought and action.[19] The "reasonable man" standard—the idea that a free man will act reasonably and within the norms of the social good—organizes much of the common law. As sociologist Nikolas Rose put it: "As the twenty-first century begins, the ethics of freedom have come to underpin our conception of how we should be ruled, how our practices of everyday life should be organized, how we should understand ourselves and our predicament."[20] Through these notions, individuals are ruled and rule themselves. Rose adds that " . . . there is agreement over the belief that human beings are, in their nature, actually, potentially, ideally subjects of freedom and hence that they must be governed, and must govern themselves, as such."[21]

Constructing the Individual Debtor in Bankruptcy

Various documents and interactions construct the debtor's position, experience, and identity. The 1978 Bankruptcy Code defines debtor identity, and case law delimits it. As the locus of bankruptcy practice, the U.S. Bankruptcy Courts are the most salient area of social construction of the debtor identity. The transformative process of legal authority, found most powerfully in the courts, produces the individual debtor identity at various sites in the bankruptcy field. Legal practice in the Offices of the United States Trustee (UST) further disciplines the debtor identity. The trustee, creditors, and attorneys from the UST office also shape debtor identity at a public hearing known as the meeting of creditors, held at the Offices of the United States Trustee. Finally, attorney offices are also an arena of debtor identity construction.

Textual Constructions

The Bankruptcy Code states who and what constitutes a debtor in both its eligibility and definitions sections. In the code's eligibility section, a "person" can file under Chapter 7 and Chapter 11. A "person" is defined as a "[human] individual, partnership, and corporation." The code further states that the "debtor means a person or municipality concerning which a case under this title has been commenced." Therefore, a person becomes a debtor by invoking the protections found in the Bankruptcy Code. The code is clear that "debtor" means a "person" or "municipality." The term "debtor" may be substituted for "person" wherever "person" appears in the text. An individual who files a bankruptcy petition in the bankruptcy court becomes "the debtor" in the bankruptcy experience. Only a human individual with regular income can file a Chapter 13 bankruptcy. These seemingly benign code sections are further interpreted by federal bankruptcy case law.

The Supreme Court interprets the Bankruptcy Code's definition of the individual "debtor" to mean that only the moral individual debtor is eligible for the bankruptcy discharge. Thus, the court manifests the dominant discourses of rational/free behavior and punishment/forgiveness. The Supreme Court has also discussed the "social policy" that underwrites notions of acceptable and unacceptable individual consumer debtors. Crucially, the articulated standard does not relate to the corporate or institutional debtor. In the 1934 Supreme Court opinion *Local Loan v. Hunt*, the court articulated the standard for the eligible individual debtor in bankruptcy:[22] only the "honest, but unfortunate debtor" is eligible for the bankruptcy discharge of burdensome debts. In a recent Supreme Court case, *Marrama v. Citizens Bank of Massachusetts*, a Chapter 7 debtor who had transferred his real property on the eve of bankruptcy to prevent his creditors from acquiring it was found to be a dishonest debtor, and the court denied him the protections of the bankruptcy code.

The Supreme Court further shapes the debtor's identity by stating that "one of the primary purposes of the Bankruptcy Act is to 'relieve the honest debtor from the weight of oppressive indebtedness, and permit him to start afresh free from the obligations and responsibilities consequent upon . . . misfortunes.'" According to the court, the debtor must have acted honestly—with good intentions and reason—and experienced misfortune, and must not have acted in a fraudulent or purposeful manner. In other words, the debtor must be unlucky, not morally blameworthy. A debtor who has acted appropriately and complied with the actors and mandates of the bankruptcy process is entitled to forgiveness. The court states, "The honest but unfortunate debtor who surrenders for distribution the property which she owns at the time of bankruptcy to the trustee is entitled to a new opportunity in life and a clear field for future effort, unhampered by the pressure and discouragement of pre-existing debt."[23]

Thus, individual debtors must establish that they deserve to have their financial burdens forgiven. Particularly, they must show that they have experienced unexpected misfortune not of their own making. The prevailing discourse of morality requires an honest failure, and only on this condition does the court grant forgiveness. However, no similar standard exists for the corporate debtor, who is simply seen as part of the natural ebb and flow of the capitalist market, where the morality of the actor is irrelevant. The business judgment of the bankruptcy courts applies only to corporate officers—not to individuals.

Bankruptcy Courts

The Bankruptcy Courts are physical and symbolic arenas of debtor identity construction. As spaces of legal processes and pronouncements, they are typically perceived as spheres of impartiality, reason, and results. As one judge in the Northern District of California explained: "Judges have to be fair and impartial deciders of fact. We cannot indulge in vicarious generosity. Judges have to do what the law requires them to do." A debtor who files a bankruptcy petition with the clerk of the court is no longer a person, but a list of assets, liabilities, and calculated fiscal risk. His or her identity is constructed on the pages of the petition. The petition is assigned a case number, a judge, and a trustee, and all the information contained in its pages is listed on the court docket as public record. The docket becomes the official representation of the debtor to the judge, the trustee, the creditors, and the world.

The Bankruptcy Court staff must limit the content of their contact with the debtor to the information provided in the public record. The petition systematizes the debtor's financial information in particular court-created patterns, and the court actors view the debtor through this lens. Debtors are no longer living, breathing, feeling entities. For example, in a discussion with a fellow law clerk, I asked her to define the individual debtor.

She coolly responded, "Debtors are our inventory. The court needs the debtors as the debtors need the court." Upon filing the petition, the individual becomes a debtor—an object of the court process, stripped of individual identity. Thus a complex "historical" person is transformed into a "debtor" whose importance, potential, and fate are defined by a near history of fiscal responsibilities and responses alone.

Furthermore, rules and codes strictly manage the debtor's conduct. The debtor must act in accordance with the rational steps assigned by the court to achieve desired results. In the court, the debtor must know to act docile and apologetic. The debtor must also know when to speak and when to remain silent. The debtor learns to provide the court with the requested information. As a judge explained, "The debtor wants something from our court, and in exchange, the debtor has to do things. The debtor has to follow our rules and behave appropriately. The court counts on debtors to understand the rules." Debtors who do not understand and follow the rules face severe consequences: the court can deny them the requested discharge and force them to pay all their debts.

United States Trustee Office, Department of Justice

The role of the UST is to "prevent fraud and abuse in the bankruptcy process"[24] through "civil enforcement" of bankruptcy laws and processes. A UST attorney reviews the petition filed by a debtor, researches the debtor on government databases, checks public records, and attempts to locate inconsistencies between the research data and the papers the debtor has filed. Upon finding inconsistent information indicating hidden assets, the attorney publicly questions the debtor at the meeting of creditors.

UST attorneys in the bankruptcy process are primarily concerned with enforcement and punishment. A UST attorney described his role as follows:

> I think of myself as a cop. It is interesting that you mention the role we play, because there is case law in the 9th Circuit that states that the UST is the policeman of the bankruptcy system. I think the case law cites legislative history, which says that the US Trustee is the watchdog of the bankruptcy system charged with preventing fraud and abuse.

In the bankruptcy process, the role of the "cop" is to regulate and ultimately change the behavior of the participants (the debtor and the debtor's attorney). As another employee at the UST said, "I change behavior. Particularly, I change debtor and attorney behavior. I want to make their conduct conform to the laws and rules. My role is to teach the debtors and their attorneys the appropriate conduct in the bankruptcy process." The bankruptcy process constructs and shapes the conduct of the debtor. Upon failure to adapt, the debtor's case is dismissed and the protections of the federal court are no longer available.

Although a very small share (less than 1 percent) of debtors actually engage in any kind of fraud or misconduct,[25] debtors are sometimes viewed and constructed as consummate liars. In an interchange with a fellow UST employee, I discussed my investigation into an Oakland couple who had filed a Chapter 7 petition. The husband worked for a tire shop, and the wife was a state police employee. They had two children, a combined income of approximately $65,000, and credit card debt totaling around $70,000. The wife had not listed her overtime pay:

Me: Good morning, Lee.
Lee: Good morning, Linda. What are you doing today?
Me: I am filing a motion to dismiss a case because the debtors did not state their income accurately. I requested their paycheck stubs and the debtors really make about $2000 more a month than they stated on their schedules.
Lee: So they lied to the court?
Me: Yes.
Lee: Debtors are all liars. You go get them. Make them pay those credit cards.

The perception of debtors as liars often characterizes UST staff's relation to and interaction with the debtor, who is viewed with suspicion and sometimes even jealousy. For example, UST trustees often expressed disgust when reviewing debtors' schedules, remarking to one another about debtors' spending and saving habits and debtors' need to pay for their mistakes. As one trustee summarized it: "Why should they not pay their debts when the rest of us have to?" As is common in all areas of the bankruptcy experience, the regulating participants applied the discourse of reason: the speaker would suggest that the debtor should have behaved more rationally under the same life circumstances. They also used standardized punitive discourse to frame debtors' situations, no matter how different those situations might be.

The Meeting of Creditors

The meeting of creditors is another social space that creates, constructs, and reproduces the identity of the debtor.[26] The meeting of creditors originates from Section 341 of the 1978 Bankruptcy Code, which orders the specific practice and space for the workings of the bankruptcy legal process. The actual meeting is held forty-five days after the filing of the bankruptcy petition in the Office of the Department of Justice rather than in bankruptcy court. During the meeting of creditors, creditors (i.e., those to whom the debtor owes money) can, in front of the trustee overseeing the case, question the debtor in public. The debtor and the debtor's attorney appear at the meeting, and the trustee facilitates the meeting. The meeting of creditors is the only direct contact many individual debtors will ever have with U.S. bankruptcy institutions. Debtors often experience intense dread and fear during the meeting of creditors.

Many of the debtors I interviewed recounted feeling guilty and like criminals at the meeting of creditors for being unable to pay their debts. In one case, a debtor who was ill had lost his job and gone through a painful divorce. He described his response to the public meeting of creditors: "I waited for the cops to come in and take me away . . . I was so scared I felt I was sitting on peach nuts." This debtor had worked his entire life, experienced several financial stresses in a short period of time, and been unable to pay his medical and credit card bills. When the judge called his name, he appeared so fearful that he could barely walk to the table at the front of the room. When questioned, he had a difficult time speaking and answering.

At the meeting of creditors, a debtor must manifest contrition. The debtor must feel sorry for his or her status as a social failure, and must also seek forgiveness to obtain a "discharge" of debts. The debtor must not appear arrogant, entitled, reticent, withholding of information, or dismissive toward the trustee (and even less so toward the creditor). Should the debtor act in such a manner, the trustee will often respond by investigating the debtor further, asking for more documents or requesting a debtor oral examination (testimony taken under oath). The trustee may also attempt to delay or withhold the debtor's discharge of debts.

Creditors' questioning of the debtor also shapes debtor identity. At the meeting of creditors, creditors often want to see that the debtor is sorry for being unable to repay the debts. For example, consider the following exchange I had with a creditor immediately after a meeting of creditors concerning an individual who had received several deposits from a company for work that he did not ultimately complete:

Me: Why did you ask the debtor, "Are you sorry for what you did to all these people?"
Anna: Because I want to know that he is sorry. What kind of person is that, that does what he does? I want to know if he was sorry.

Me: How did you feel about the question you asked and the response you got from it?

Anna: I want him to say he was sorry, and I want him to return our money. I want the whole story about the relationship between [him and my company]. I want to know, so that I can make sense of the situation. I did want to make him feel bad.

The Attorney's Office

A final site of debtor identity construction is the attorney's office. The attorney is responsible for correctly organizing the debtor's information to present to the UST, the trustee, and the court so as to attract the least negative attention from the trustee and the creditors. The goal is to methodically present (through the bankruptcy petition) the debtor's fiscal body to the court, the trustee, and the creditors.

A consumer debtor typically first appears at the bankruptcy attorney's office with a bag of unopened bills and stacks of personal financial documents such as car loan papers, mortgage loan documents, and tax returns. The attorney examines and organizes this information to create the bankruptcy petition, which is subsequently compared with the official standards for consumer debtor conduct and behavior found in the Bankruptcy Code and case law. Therefore, the debtor attorney's creation and representation of the debtor's fiscal identity determines the manner in which the various legal actors engage the debtor in the bankruptcy process. The debtor's attorney acts as a navigator and translator for the debtor in the bankruptcy process by explaining to the debtor the content and meaning of the bankruptcy petitions and filing process, and by representing the debtor in various hearing procedures.

The close interaction between the debtor and the attorney can give the bankruptcy attorney a deep understanding of how an individual came to be a debtor and why he or she had to file for bankruptcy—one that usually differs from that of UST employees, trustees, and creditors. These other types of bankruptcy professionals might lament the disappearance of the shame associated with bankruptcy, but debtors' attorneys, in contrast, are much more likely to view the debtor as being in need of the "great fiscal hug" that bankruptcy can provide. In other words, they understand that sometimes even the most well-intentioned, responsible people are not immune to fiscal crisis. They may also attribute debt to the fact of the debtor simply never having been taught fiscal responsibility. As one California debtor's attorney explained:

> We are all debtors for the most part. The people who come into my office have often experienced a life of hardship. These people are not dishonest, and the debtors are not trying to play the system to get things for free. Debtors are people who have lost jobs, have excessive medical bills, children to feed, and hard money loans. There is a phenomenon of depression and denial that sets in once a person cannot pay his bills. At that point, the debtor is unable to face reality. The debtor does not open his or her mail. When the debtor reaches my office, the debtor often appears disorganized, stressed, and a mess for us to clear up.

This attorney also believed that her role was to alleviate the debtor's suffering in the face of social stigmatization: "The stigma has not disappeared from filing bankruptcy for my clients. The debtors come into my office with serious guilt and pain about not being able to pay their bills."

Indeed, the debtors I researched exhibited a range of feelings about filing for bankruptcy, the most common being great personal responsibility for their situation. They often believed they had failed their children, community, and society because of their financial problems. As noted earlier, they approached the meeting of creditors with many feelings of shame and self-hatred. A particularly interesting tendency among the debtors I interviewed was that they discussed their financial failure in relation to how their parents would feel and what they would think. One debtor who had lost her job stated that she would never tell her mother or father about filing for bankruptcy: "Not in a million years. They would suffer to think that I could not pay my bills. I was raised to pay my bills."

The shame and personal responsibility felt by a debtor who cannot pay his or her debts reflects back on the debtor in daily activities in the community and society. For example, one debtor described her interactions with her bank: "My mortgage lender treated me horribly when I missed two payments. I was treated with disrespect at the bank branch office. I had paid on time for 10 years, and I am still treated as dirt. When I left the bank, I thought everyone could see that I was a debtor."

Moreover, debtors can experience identity crisis, questioning their personal history and family upbringing. One woman shared the following story about her family and her father's approach to money:

> I was raised in Sacramento, California. I was born in 1941, and I had a war-years childhood experience. There was a lot of poverty when I was growing up. I remember that the depression years were still hanging around our region. It was not over. My family came from poor people. My father was a truck driver. . . . He would never take help. His attitude toward money was that if you did not have it, you did not spend it.

This debtor learned from her father that people were not supposed to spend money they did not have, but somehow she had failed to live as he prescribed. After her bankruptcy, she saw her decisions to borrow money for an education and her first home as wrong. In her eyes, she had failed herself, her community, and her father. She had come to believe that she was personally responsible for her economic and financial situation.

Conclusions: Individualism and Personal Responsibility

The individual in American culture often follows the axiom "himself rules him."[27] Starting early in life, individuals internalize the notion of personal freedom, believing themselves to be in control of their own daily economic lives. The bankruptcy process shapes, and is shaped by, this deeply encultured notion of individual responsibility. It is implicit in bankruptcy actors' conduct and speech about debtors and debt. The underlying assumption is that the individual debtor is free, and the results and circumstances of the debtor's life, particularly financial failure, are simply a result of failed self-rule.

The concept of failed self-rule within bankruptcy processes occurs within a broader U.S. culture where Americans attribute both their successes and their failures to their individual attributes, qualities, power, and acumen rather than to their location within the social and economic structure. To understand the pervasiveness of the narrative that links individualism to personal responsibility, one can look to other U.S. field sites, even ones as seemingly disparate as drug-dealing cultures, the American middle class, and particle physics. For example, anthropologist Phillipe Bourgois has noted that "the blame-the-victim theories of individualism are common place" among crack dealers in New York City.[28] Similar to debtors in the bankruptcy process, Puerto Ricans receive blame in popular and institutional discourse for their economic dislocation within the U.S. economic and social structure. One such narrative is that the individual Puerto Rican who fails to find a legitimate job is responsible for his failure. Americans fail to recognize the relationship between socially structured restraints (such as race, class, citizenship status) and individual failure. Bourgois critiques this attribution error, observing that whereas individual agency is an important consideration in analyzing actions of human behavior, one must also consider those actions in the context of a social structure analysis, particularly where there might be structural and/or symbolic forms of violence.

America's "frontier mentality" is another helpful framework for thinking about the U.S. preoccupation with individualism. As anthropologist and lawyer Katherine Newman has written: "In the world of corporate downsizing, our culture—as evidenced in popular opinion—continues to believe that worthy individuals rise to the top and the undeserving fall by the way side. The Frontier mentality is one within which no one likes to hear of failure. It is one where individuals are makers of their own fate and people get what they deserve."[29]

Finally, while comparing the worlds of high-energy particle physics in the United States and Japan, anthropologist Sharon Traweek discovered a clash of "ideal types" in sharing innovation. America's cultural value of individualism was at loggerheads with Japan's value of *amae* or interdependence. The individualistic laissez-faire economic approach to innovation and decision-making in the American lab often contrasted starkly to the collective approach of Japanese physicists. In the United States, the head of the lab makes decisions, tells others what to do, and receives the credit for a discovery. In Japan, however, innovation results from a collective decision-making process involving all lab members, and credit is assigned to the research group.[30]

In this chapter, I have traced some pathways through which actors in the field of United States bankruptcy law normalize consumer debt as a direct result of personal irresponsibility. Particularly, I demonstrated the complex ways in which legal actors present debt as a personal issue rather than a political and social construct, thus characterizing debtors as morally suspect. The interconnected normative discourses of personal responsibility and personal failure shape the identity of the individual debtor at various locations in the bankruptcy field. In the bankruptcy experience, the debtor is embedded in Anglo-American legal doctrine rooted in Kantian notions of rational thought and action. Debtors are viewed as isolated individuals and attributed with free will and choice. Debtors are held, and hold themselves, responsible for their debts, believing that their own individual decision-making processes have led to financial failure. Just as individuals are solely responsible for their success, they are also solely responsible for their failure, and debtors must overcome their behavioral sins by learning self-control.

In addition, the individual debtor—unlike the corporate debtor—experiences bankruptcy from a highly personalized position. This shows no signs of stopping. Under recent 2005 bankruptcy code amendments, new means tests scrutinize individuals and hold them accountable more than did previous bankruptcy laws. The corporate debtor, on the other hand, is not required to undergo such a review.[31] Moreover, special protections for the corporation continue to dominate American legal culture.[32]

Throughout various bailouts, the U.S. government has continued to view corporations and financial institutions as purely economic actors in the marketplace.[33] When AIG, Chrysler, and General Motors became insolvent, U.S. Secretary of the Treasury Timothy Geithner left the morality of officers and managers unquestioned.[34] Under U.S. capitalism, therefore, individuals must continue to bear the moral burden of the larger marketplace forces. They also bear the burden of structural failure. In other words, there but for the grace of God—or bankruptcy court—go we.

The disciplining of debtors is not merely an individual issue. Overemphasizing the "degenerate" qualities of human debtors is a powerful controlling process[35] that obscures far more degenerate neoliberal economic and social policies that strive for accumulation by imposing debt structures on actors at the local, national, and international levels. For example, "debtor countries" inextricably bound to a turbulent world banking system primarily shaped by the Great Depression and Cold War politics are consistently subject to moral profiling, yet very few people consider the inherent conflicts of interest facing lending institutions in a Western global power projection of which world banking systems are a part. For instance, the United States (ironically, itself plagued by domestic and global debt) exerts a "dollar hegemony"[36] to control the terms of currency production on which that very debt system operates. Meanwhile, despite its massive debt load, the United States continues to spend more on its military than do all other countries combined—expenditures that, if abated, would likely erase the U.S. deficit.[37]

Examining this expanded field of debt raises questions. Who exactly owes what to whom? And who are the real morally suspect actors in a global economy? This chapter begins to answer by examining the construction of the debtor up, down, and sideways specifically within bankruptcy circuits in the United States, while also providing a model for thinking about how the construction of debtors operates as a controlling process on a global stage.

Notes

1. Tara Siegel Bernard and Jenny Anderson, "Downturn Drags More Consumers into Bankruptcy," *New York Times*, 16 November 2008, 1.
2. Shahein Nasiripour, "Don't Look Back: Major Players Continue to 'Walk Away' From Poor Mortgages," *Huffington Post*, 26 January 2010. http://www.huffingtonpost.com/2010/01/25/dont-look-back-major-play_n_435965.html

3. Ibid.
4. When I use the term debtor, I mean consumer debtor. Otherwise "institutional" or "corporate" will be placed in front of the term debtor. For a broad anthropological analysis of debt, see David Graeber, *Debt: The First 5,000 Years* (London: Melville House, 2011).
5. Nikolas Rose, *Powers of Freedom* (New York: Cambridge University Press, 1999).
6. Laura Nader, "The Vertical Slice: Hierarchies and Children", in *Hierarchy and Society: Anthropological Perspectives on Society*, ed. Gerald M. Britan and Ronald Cohen (Philadelphia: Institute for the Study of Human Issues, 1980).
7. George Stocking, *The Ethnographer's Magic and Other Essays in the History of Anthropology* (Madison: University of Wisconsin Press, 1992).
8. Laura Nader, "Up the Anthropologist: Perspectives Gained from Studying Up," in *Reinventing Anthropology*, ed. Dell Hymes (New York: Vintage Books, 1972).
9. Fields are social spaces or arenas for the production, distribution, and circulation of capital. Fields are magnetic in that they draw people together; they are spaces of struggle between such actors and spaces of positions and position taking. Fields have rules of the game, and actors have a sense for the game. Most significantly, the field is a space for the researcher to think relationally. Pierre Bourdieu, *Invitation to Reflexive Sociology*, (Chicago: University of Chicago Press, 1992), 96–97.
10. Marcel Mauss, *The Gift: The Form and Reason for Exchange in Archaic Societies*, trans. H. W. Halls (New York: W.W. Norton, 1950).
11. H. H. Gerth and C. W. Mills, eds., *From Max Weber: Essays in Sociology* (New York: Oxford University Press, 1946), 185.
12. Francois Delaporte (ed.), *A Vital Rationalist: Selected Writings from Georges Canguilhem*, (New York: Zones Books, 2000).
13. Janet Roitman, "Unsanctioned Wealth, or, The Productivity of Debt in Northern Cameroon," *Public Culture* 15, no. 2 (2003): 213.
14. *Doxa* is a set of ineffable cognitive and evaluative presuppositions whose acceptance is implied in membership itself. Included in this definition are intra-field debates or polemical positions that share a common backdrop of meanings that are often defined in relation to each other. Pierre Bourdieu, *Practical Reason: On the Theory of Action* (Palo Alto: Stanford University Press, 1998), 23.
15. Norbert Elias, *The Civilizing Process: Sociogenetic and Pyschogenetic Investigations*, trans. E. Jephcott (Oxford: Blackwell, 1994), 379.
16. Ibid., 379.
17. Max Weber, *The Protestant Ethic and the Spirit of Capitalism* (New York: Routledge, 1930).
18. Robert Manning, *The Consequences of America's Addiction to Credit* (New York: Basic Books, 2000), 23.
19. It is important to note that the identity of "debtor" originated in text in the Bible as it related to crop failure. The failure of a crop was considered a result of fate, not related to the acts or omissions or misdeeds of the individual.
20. Rose, *Powers of Freedom*, 61.
21. Ibid., 62.
22. Honest. n. (1) Of persons: Held in honor; holding an honorable position; respectable. v. (1) to confer honor upon; to honor; (2) To cause to appear honest or honorable; to justify, defend, or excuse. *The Compact Edition of the Oxford English Dictionary* (Oxford University Press, 1971).
23. *Local Loan Co. v. Hunt*, 292 US 234, 243 (1934) (citing *Williams v. US Fidelity &Guaranty* 236 US 549, 554 [1915]).
24. 11 U.S.C. § 28 U.S.C. Section 586. Duties; supervision by Attorney General.

25. Less than 1 percent of the 400 cases I reviewed each month during 2002–2003 involved fraud by the debtor. Field notes from the United States Trustees Office, Oakland, California.
26. Section 341 of the 1978 Bankruptcy Code mandates that creditors be able to question the debtor about the debt in a public arena. The meeting of creditors is run by a trustee, whom debtors often believe to be a judge; however, very few individual debtors actually appear in bankruptcy court.
27. Rose, *Powers of Freedom*, 61.
28. Phillipe I. Bourgois, *In Search of Respect: Selling Crack in El Barrio*, (New York: Cambridge University Press, 1995), 15.
29. Katherine S. Newman, *Falling From Grace: Downward Mobility in the Age of Affluence*, (Berkeley: University of California Press, 1999), 35.
30. Sharon Traweek, *Beamtimes and Lifetimes: The World of High Energy Physicists*, (Cambridge: Harvard University Press, 1988).
31. Bankruptcy Abuse Prevention and Consumer Protection Act of 2005. 11 U.S.C. § 707. Dismissal of a case or conversion to a case under chapter 11 or 13.
32. Jeffery D. Clements, *Corporations Are Not People: Why They Have More Rights Than You Do and What You Can Do About It* (San Francisco: Barrett-Koehler, 2012). The best example of the legal protections afforded a corporation is found in U.S. Supreme Court opinions that describe the corporation as a fictitious person. See Felix Cohen, "Transcendental Nonsense and the Functional Approach," *Columbia Law Review* 35, no. 6 (June 1935): 809–849.
33. House of Representative Hearings in the Committee on Oversight and Government Reform: The Federal Bailout of AIG, Wednesday, 27 January 2010, p. 18, Statement of Timothy F. Geithner, Secretary of U.S. Department of Treasury: "Deciding to support AIG was one of the most difficult choices I have ever been involved in in over 20 years of public service. The steps that were taken were motivated solely by what we believe to be in the public interest. We did not act because AIG asked for help. . . . We acted because the consequences of AIG failing would have been catastrophic for our economy and for American families and business." Throughout the testimony, Geithner characterized government action as saving the economy for American by giving public money to a private institution. His comments held no consideration of the immoral actions of banks and of AIG management.
34. Ibid. See also Paul Ingrassia, *Crash Course: The American Automobile Industry's Road to Bankruptcy and Bailout* (New York: Random House, 2010); Mike J. Roe and David Skeel, "Assessing the Chrysler Bankruptcy," *Michigan Law Review* 108 (2010): 728–772.
35. Laura Nader, "Controlling Processes: Tracing the Dynamic Components of Power," *Current Anthropology* 38, no. 5 (1997): 711–737.
36. Henry C. K. Liu, "U.S. Dollar Hegemony Has Got to Go," *Asia Times Online*, 11 April 2002. Retrieved on 11 July 2013 from http://www.atimes.com/global-econ/DD11Dj01.html.
37. Graeber, *Debt*, 365–367.

Chapter 2

ON COMMERCE
Analyzing the Asian Financial Crisis of 1997–1998

Jay Ou

During the 1980s in Seoul, South Korea, foreign, brand-name consumer products became wildly popular with teenagers—including me. By watching Hollywood blockbusters and American television, my friends and I learned what was cool. Suddenly, we were inundated with jackets by Members Only, jeans by Jordache, and Reebok and Nike Air Jordan sneakers. Brand names were symbols of social distinction in Korea's nascent consumer society, and these manufactured consumer goods signaled status. My friends even sneered at anyone wearing "fake" versions of the brands, unaware of the irony: the "fake" and the "real" goods were both produced in the same Korean factories.

But as Korean youth became captivated by the marketing messages of Michael Jordan and Tom Cruise, many major U.S. companies began to relocate their subcontracting manufacturing from Korea to other countries such as Indonesia and China. Increased labor costs in a newly politically democratic Korea led these companies to seek subcontractors in countries that offered what Korea no longer did: a cheap, docile labor force, economic incentives and subsidies, and a strong military-backed dictatorial government.

Years later, as a graduate student, I became interested in studying corporate capitalism and was drawn to the particular case of Korean industrial investments in Indonesia. My academic interest was twofold. Korea's economic success was considered a model for developing countries like

---

Notes for this chapter begin on page 61.

Indonesia, where Korea had become a major industrial investor in the 1980s and 1990s. However, as critics pointed out, Korean-owned factories in Indonesia often participated in widespread labor suppression. These critics considered "Korean management" extraordinarily inhumane.[1]

To adequately understand these ideologies of Korean management and development, I embarked on ethnographic fieldwork in Korea, Indonesia, and the United States in 1997. I began in Seoul. Within weeks of my arrival, with its currency devalued by nearly 50 percent, Korea was close to defaulting on its debt until it capitulated to the demands of the International Monetary Fund (IMF). This marked the beginning of the "IMF era" in Korea, so called in reference to the neoliberal program that the IMF and Western financial institutions imposed in exchange for a massive $57 billion loan bailout of the Korean economy. The IMF-imposed austerity conditions included massive cuts in social spending and extensive loosening of corporate and financial regulations and practices. Thousands of companies large and small went bankrupt overnight, leading to a horrifying, dramatically sharp increase in suicide mortality.[2]

Indonesia fared even worse. Its currency plummeted to a fraction of its initial value within weeks. In one seven-day period, the government devalued the Indonesian rupiah by more than 700 percent, rapidly driving up the cost of basic necessities like food and fuel.[3] Violence and rioting erupted across the country as people struggled to make ends meet. Industrial areas became sites of massive demonstrations and strikes. Unable to prop up the economy with proper emergency measures, the Suharto government instead used violence to quell social dissent. In February 1998, as I waited in Korea for the violence to subside in Indonesia, media reports of attacks on Chinese Indonesians appeared. Journalist contacts in Java warned me not to go to Indonesia, fearing that my Korean ethnicity would make me a target of the violence. Koreans I knew in West Java confirmed these warnings by recounting mass mob attacks on their compatriots in the streets. A U.S.-based academic colleague who had just returned from Java warned me that a national uprising was imminent, and that when it did occur, it would be targeted at Chinese and people who looked Chinese. Media reports confirmed that Chinese Indonesians and East Asian businessmen were fleeing the country for fear of violent reprisals. Korea, Indonesia, and the entire region were in a state of shock. The social and cultural effects of the economic crisis continued for several years.

With these tumultuous events forming the backdrop to my research, I decided to focus on a wide range of social groups and organizations comprising laborers and managers in Korean-owned factories in Indonesia and Korea, and employees of civil society, government, and corporate organizations based in Indonesia, Korea, and the United States. This vertically integrated research examined social organizations in all three countries to contribute to a comprehensive understanding of global corporate capitalism and its relation to society and culture. By conducting research among socially stratified groups such as workers, corporate elites, and government officials, I sought to elucidate the machinations of power in contemporary commerce.

In this chapter, I argue that to fully understand Indonesian and Korean workers' lives, one must apprehend the influence of the corporate-capitalist model of development, which encompasses finance capitalists, corporations, individually owned businesses, educational institutions, government bureaucrats, and the military-industrial complex. The picture is incomplete without understanding the history and struggles of labor movements and civil society movements in each country. By analyzing some of the complex linkages connecting these social groups, I hope to contextualize the policies and practices that contributed to the onset of the Asian financial crisis of 1997–1998. The global reach of this economic crisis demonstrated the vulnerability of the global financial marketplace. Indeed, the Asian financial crisis in many ways foreshadowed the global financial crisis of 2007. Corporate banks and international financial organizations were central to creating and resolving these crises, reaping economic benefits from them in many cases. This should stand as a warning to anyone concerned about the consequences of global economic integration.

Taking a "Vertical Slice" to Analyze the Global Economy

In her influential article "Up the Anthropologist: Perspectives Gained from Studying Up," Laura Nader called for ethnographic research on critical contemporary issues, noting that "If one looks at the great social theorists—Karl Marx, Max Weber, Emile Durkheim—their works were inspired by the problems of their day, and we are still working on the problems of their day."[4] Nader also suggested that more ethnographic research should take a "vertical slice" approach to critical analysis of contemporary social issues. A vertical slice requires using "the network model vertically rather than horizontally" to understand the interconnections between groups of unequal power.[5] A vertical slice approach is particularly well suited to understanding global financial crises, as well as the lives of those affected.

When I began research in 1997, I planned to conduct vertically integrated ethnographic fieldwork and participant observation—first in a Korean-owned factory in Indonesia, and then in industrial training centers for Indonesian workers in Korea. I also wanted to do research among those in positions of power—corporate executives and government officials.

Given the complexity of the project, I planned to conduct multi-sited ethnographic research in three Indonesian cities (Tangerang, Jakarta, and Karawaci) and four Korean cities (Seoul, Busan, Ansan, and Changwon).

The project began smoothly. I conducted interviews and shorter periods of participant observation with approximately 30 executives from Korean multinational corporations and approximately 20 executives from U.S. multinational corporations with investments in Indonesia and Korea. The executives ranged from CEOs and chairmen of the board to middle-management employees such as factory managers. Their Korean and U.S. corporate employers had industrial investments in Indonesia and Korea. I also interviewed approximately 20 political party leaders and national and state government officials in Korea and approximately 10 in Indonesia, including party chairmen, ambassadors, and mayors among others.

My original research proposal also included a plan to interview workers in Korean "industrial training centers." However, research plans were changed to reflect the fact that in reality there were no "industrial training centers" in Korea. Industrial trainees (often foreign workers) were sent straight to their respective factories in Korea after an initial briefing that lasted no longer than a day. There were no follow-up training programs or formal organizational structures. The industrial trainee program was effectively a rubber stamp for cheap industrial labor. Due to the fragmented nature of worker distribution, I conducted research for this part of my project primarily in the Ansan Industrial Complex just south of Seoul, which boasted a high concentration of factories and Indonesian industrial trainees. During my two years of fieldwork, I had the opportunity to interview approximately 110 Indonesian workers and Indonesian "industrial trainees" working in Korea.

My primary concern was to understand what motivated both Indonesian and Korean workers to join the ranks of corporate labor in both Korea and Indonesia, as well as how members of each of these groups defined, rationalized, and negotiated their experiences once they joined the global assembly line. I also wanted to examine the role of NGOs and labor unions in workers' lives at this time.

Working on the Global Assembly Line

Indonesian "Industrial Trainees" in Korea

Ethnographic fieldwork with Indonesian industrial trainees yielded information about their overall experiences in the industrial trainee program, as well as their experiences after they left the program to find work as illegal laborers. My research revealed that Indonesian workers often suffered difficult experiences—for example, the majority of workers were negatively impacted by the economic crisis and had to deal with such problems as sudden unemployment, nonpayment of wages, unilateral wage reductions, and fear of deportation.

Workers also regularly experienced cultural conflicts stemming from abusive workplace behavior, managers' failure to accommodate workers' religious and dietary needs (most of the Indonesian workers were, of course, Muslim), and the challenges of living in Korea's culturally homogenous society. They also suffered the more mundane difficulties of homesickness and challenging weather conditions.

Interestingly, the cultural conflicts increased as Indonesians stayed longer and learned the language. Time and language competency allowed the workers to better understand the behavior and conversations of their Korean colleagues. Although it undoubtedly aided communication, it also allowed them to understand demeaning language or tones they otherwise might have missed. The non-use of the polite form was the most demeaning linguistic act in this category of interaction. (Like other East Asian languages, Korean uses honorifics to denote the speaker's relationship to the person he or she is addressing.)

Indonesian workers disliked being pressured in the workplace with overtime and extra work without transparency. Retaining practices that emerged in the development years, Korean industrial workplaces are exemplary theaters of the *bballi, bballi* (fast, fast) culture that many foreigners and Koreans themselves see as synonymous with Korean business and management culture. Many economists and policy makers have upheld the remarkable speed of economic and industrial development in Korea as a shining example for other developing nations, including Indonesia.

Most of my Javanese worker interviewees pointed out that working at such a fast pace was not necessarily productive. They thought that many times, the quality of their work had suffered precisely because of this constant time pressure. In addition, workers frequently raised the issue of nonpayment of overtime work, a major labor rights violation. Once they learned their rights through local labor networks, workers often challenged their employers.

Many Indonesian workers complained about the difficulties of living in a culturally and linguistically homogenous society without speaking the local language. Most Indonesians learned a rudimentary level of Korean inadequate to form strong bonds and networks. It thus was difficult for them to do such basic things as banking, shopping, and traveling. The Seoul and Ansan city governments have made concerted efforts to translate and transliterate key signs and infrastructure for foreign workers, but at the time of my research most private establishments did not. Most of the laborers lacked a command of English as well, which posed further difficulties.

The most positive aspect of being an Indonesian laborer in Korea was the relatively higher pay. Their main reason for participating in the program was to accumulate greater monetary earnings than they could in their home country. Therefore, their spending was very minimal. The companies provided most of their meals, and the workers rarely ate out. Minimal expenditures went toward calling cards, cigarettes, and increasingly, computer rooms for Internet communication. Every Indonesian worker I met reported sending remittances back to Indonesia at least once every three months. They all shared an implicit ethic of sacrifice for long-term economic betterment. This view was most pronounced when they discussed their homesickness and difficulties with food and religion.

Because their daily practices consisted mostly of work and rest in their accommodations, which were usually in or around their workplace, their lives were very circumscribed geographically. The boring routine was broken periodically by visits to the mosque, shopping areas, and rare cultural events. Almost all Indonesian workers became involved in intra-ethnic communities through the mosque or personal connections and thereby learned of other job possibilities and also about labor rights in Korea.

This network was complemented by Korean migrant labor support centers. Some Indonesians worked with these centers to help other migrant laborers and seek their own labor rights advice. Very few of them socialized with people from other ethnicities outside of the workplace. Language was a major barrier, as were many Korean social practices that were not conducive to spontaneous, informal relationships between different ethnic groups.

The Indonesian industrial trainees came from many different regions in Java, so it was difficult to make anything but a generalized demographic analysis. Unlike other anthropological factory studies,[6] my research was conducted among factories in different industrial sectors. The commonality was that all factories involved low-skilled, intensive labor. Also, as participants in the same bilateral government-corporate migrant labor program between Korea and Indonesia, they all were subject to the same policies and regulations.

All the Indonesian industrial trainees I met were working to better the long-term economic well-being of their families in Indonesia. A third of the workers I surveyed had families with one or two children. They very often felt lonely and stuck closely to their community while in

Korea. Indonesians were concerned about losing their jobs but seemed to be pragmatic about finding solutions if something happened. After some time in Korea, many of them navigated the illegal labor market well, and most of them wound up saving much more than they would have, had they worked similar jobs in Java.

Korean Factory Managers in West Java

The global assembly line has created odd, seemingly contradictory arrangements. At the same time that Korea was importing Indonesian migrant workers to work in its factories, it was exporting Korean managers to offshore factories in Indonesia. Like the Indonesian industrial trainees in Korea, all the Korean factory managers I met had lived in their host country five years or less. They hailed from different parts of Korea, although all had lived in Seoul in recent years. Although their structural positions differed greatly from those of the Indonesian industrial trainees or workers, they had several things in common. Most were married with children. Like the trainees, they worked for their company for the economic betterment of their families. And during the economic crisis, workers and managers alike in both countries worried about losing their jobs.

Korean managers tended to have a nationalistic outlook on their work. Based on past experiences with Western countries, they understood that Korea had to compete on a global economic scale. Korea had just been accepted into the Organization of Economic Co-operation and Development (OECD) in 1997. Japan, a country that once colonized Korea and had long been an economic rival, joined the OECD in the 1960s. Japan was a constant competitor; in fact, many managers commented that Korea was at economic war with Japan. Due to the nature of their work, most were keenly aware that Korean companies relied on Japanese and U.S. technologies and were still paying hefty royalties for them, including those for computer and communications equipment. They sharply criticized Japanese and U.S. corporations for abruptly stopping sale of new technologies once Korea became an economic threat in the 1980s—a theme I will return to later in this chapter. Many managers saw this as the true beginning of the economic crisis, particularly in the context of rising labor costs and the growing power of organized labor.

The economic crisis clearly taught these Korean managers that world economic powers would have no mercy on Korea or Korean companies. This created a sense of nationalistic urgency. Time and again, they described their work in Indonesia as part of a broader national effort to build up Korea's dollar reserves by targeting world export markets. Production in Indonesia seemed the natural step for them, because Indonesia needed the development and Korean companies benefited from a cheaper labor force and proximity to cheap materials. Just as the Southeast Korea city of Pohang was home to POSCO, one of the world's largest steel conglomerates, West Java was also the site of such a steel company, Krakatau Steel, just 70 km away from Korean factories.

Korean managers shared a rational, linear view of economic development. They strongly believed that Korean industrial activities were providing Indonesians with modern industrial jobs that would help take their country to the next level of development. They regarded Indonesian workers as quick to learn and very careful in their work. Managers sometimes thought this attention to detail might contribute to their relatively slow pace at work compared to Koreans.

But they also understood that Korean development was an extreme case. During the development decades from 1960 through the 1980s, most Koreans had grown accustomed to working six or seven days a week and fourteen or more hours a day. Meals were taken in less than five minutes, and cigarettes and instant coffee in less than two, so the average mealtime break lasted less than ten minutes. This type of workday was common not just in Indonesian factories, but even in offices employing white-collar workers that I visited in Korea. It was practiced in small and large *chaebol*—the term for Korean conglomerates—alike.

This linear view of economic and social development also influenced managers' views of the more labor-intensive Korean textile, garment, and shoe factories. These factories were technologically less complex than more capital-intensive factories, so their managers tended to have less formal education than their counterparts in more capital-intensive factories. Interestingly, Korean managers from the relatively high-tech chaebol conglomerates often cited this difference to explain managerial problems at the textile factories. They saw textile factory managers as less educated and lower in economic class. They pointed out that these small and medium industries in Korea had very harsh management styles that the managers themselves imported into Indonesia. Unlike chaebol managers, these managers had little to no systematic training and therefore were unprepared to deal with Indonesian customs and traditions. In this way, chaebol managers distinguished themselves from Korean managers in small and medium businesses. Status was always a key variable in comparison.

All chaebol managers had received university education, unlike Indonesian trainees, who on average had had eight years of formal schooling. Still, all of the managers felt some measure of insecurity about their jobs, especially after the 1997 "IMF crisis." Korean labor laws changed because of measures imposed by the IMF, and managers felt that changes to their own employment terms and contracts were imminent. Naturally, not knowing whether they would be able to keep their jobs in the near future made them insecure.

In the context of the financial crisis, the biggest concern affecting Korean managers in Indonesia was the ability to provide for their families and especially their children's education. They worried about their children being unable to adapt, once back in the competitive Korean school setting. They also worried about the ever-increasing cost of educating children in Korea. Even if they attended public school, many children were also sent to private after-school academies that could cost as much as private school tuition or more in extreme cases. The managers therefore felt fortunate to have chaebol jobs. Because of Indonesia's lower cost of living and the perks companies offered those living in Indonesia, many were able to save money for their families.

Koreans in the Jakarta area formed a tightly knit ethnic community, with Protestant churches, schools, stores, and restaurants catering to the community. Chaebol managers socialized almost exclusively with other Koreans. Besides devoting time to family meetings, the men and women both played golf, an affordable luxury in Indonesia that was prohibitively expensive in Korea. Golf was also a means to socialize with other Koreans while engaging in some form of exercise. Aside from children's education, their chief concern was family safety. During the riots in Indonesia in 1998, many families were sent back to Korea because of safety concerns. Factories and residences were fortified with extra security around the clock during the worst days of the violence in May 1998.

In time, like Indonesian trainees in Seoul and Ansan, Korean managers grew accustomed to life in West Java. They adjusted to the pace of life and the different local customs and traditions. The challenge to adjust was arguably greater for Indonesian trainees because basic components of their lives, such as food and dwelling, were structured and determined largely by their companies. Both groups suffered from homesickness, but it was clear that with time, their outlook on the local community usually changed for the better.

Social Institutions: The Role of NGOs and Labor Unions

Nongovernmental organizations (NGOs) in Korea and Indonesia were under duress during the time of my fieldwork. Korean and Indonesian labor NGOs and labor unions were all suffering from the economic downturn, and they faced an uphill battle with bureaucracy, the military, and industry.

After fighting a major battle with government and industrial interests in 1996, Korean groups had had to make major concessions that were required for Korea to enter the OECD that year. The economic downturn further increased their misery, as the IMF imposed strict austerity measures, including changes in labor policies. Labor faced the radical transformation of workers into temporary workers and the concomitant loss of rights and social supports.

Korea's largest independent trade union, the Korea Confederation of Trade Unions (KCTU), had been at the forefront of opposition in 1996 and 1998 but had to make concessions both times. Labor unions found no public sympathy during the IMF era, as the entire country was in a state of grave economic crisis. I noted that labor unions such as KCTU, hit by the economic crisis and its effect on labor, apparently did not assign much priority to international solidarity.

In 1996, KCTU was able to find and maintain strong support from international labor organizations to coordinate its opposition to Korea's entry into the OECD. Its situation was markedly different after successive defeats. Renowned Indonesian labor activist and labor party founder Muchtar Pakpahan's visit to Seoul went largely unnoticed. It did, however, offer me an opportunity to learn about labor politics firsthand.

Migrant labor NGOs faced difficulties immediately after the economic crisis began in November 1997, when the Korean government initiated deportation campaigns, politically driven by the large number of company closures. It followed them with an amnesty period for illegal workers who arranged to leave by April 1998, which was extended to July and then August 1998. Migrant labor NGOs faced the monumental task of supporting thousands of workers who were unsure about how to respond to these policies. But by the end of my research, greater numbers of migrant labor volunteers were contributing to their work.

The Corporate Perspective

Research with corporate executives in Korea, Indonesia, and the United States filled out my vertical slice analysis of the global industrial cycle that ran from workers in Indonesia to Korean subcontracting factories in Indonesia to one of the largest corporate multinationals.

Official Nike corporate press kits expounded a linear view of global economic development: Poor, undeveloped countries gradually develop their industrial base, starting with light manufacturing of simple textiles, which leads to more technical light manufacturing of sports shoes and then to light technical consumer products such as calculators, finally culminating in the heavy industrial production of cars and computers. This linear view of development prevailed among many of my contacts, from corporate executives to bankers, factory managers, and even some labor NGO representatives and workers. Aside from its cultural implications, this view is problematic because it sees the world as a global assembly line without consideration of the local context of development and the class contradictions therein.

Studying Up, Down, and Sideways in the Global Economy: Socio-historical Contexts

A particular form of corporate capitalism that was pervasive in the late twentieth century formed the backdrop to the experiences of the Indonesian and Korean laborers in my study. The contemporary foundation of global economic integration was laid after World War II by the three international financial institutions created following the Bretton Woods agreements in 1944: the World Bank, IMF, and Bank of International Settlements, which throughout the twentieth century were key to the development of the so-called neoliberal capitalist model. These institutions were also significant players in both Korea and Indonesia during the economic crisis of 1997–1998.[7]

Following World War II, when the United States had rushed to curb the rising tide of Soviet communism, the Korean peninsula became the first theater of conflict between the two superpowers. This bloody three-year war, which began on 25 June 1950—and which, some scholars maintain,[8] could have been a much smaller civil war between the predominant union of nationalist, democratic, pro-labor institutions and organizations, and a small U.S.-backed contingent of former Japanese colonial collaborators and sympathizers—resulted in the death of more than 3 million Korean civilians and more than 1 million soldiers. It ended with an armistice signed on 27 July 1953, and with the tragic division of the country along the 38th Parallel. The division remains to this day.

Between the end of the Korean War and the elections of 1987, the United States had strong military and economic relations with three successive military dictatorships in Korea. All three were ended by uncontrollable popular protests by Korean citizens. Throughout this period, however, U.S. corporate and military interests usually ran counter to the democratic aspirations of Korea's population.

Lacking capital and basic infrastructure after the war, Korean economic development was shaped and controlled largely by United States and

Japanese business and military interests.[9] The Japanese normalized relations with Korea and provided grants and loans for exploiting Korea's raw materials and cheap labor—the same rationale behind their colonial annexation of Korea in 1910. U.S. and Japanese corporations provided most of the technology and aid for Korea's development from 1960 to the 1980s, but at a price. Royalty payments caused a negative balance of payments for Korea, increasing its indebtedness to international financial institutions. Korea had to open its markets and change its development policy as a condition for continued assistance.

In the end, however, when Korean exports began to chip away at U.S. and Japanese companies' market share in the 1980s, Korean companies were denied access to technology.[10] These pressures only exacerbated the ongoing labor and student unrest, leading to the downfall of President Chun. The United States, which had supported Chun's rise to power and his massacre of students in Kwangju in 1980, could no longer stem the tide of history. The end of the dictatorship signaled great changes in labor laws and policies. These, together with other macroeconomic factors, led to increased wages in the late 1980s, prompting Korean companies to plan overseas manufacturing.

Facing the prospect of rising wages, U.S. and Japanese manufacturing firms had begun their capital flight to Indonesia well before the end of Chun's dictatorship. Korean firms quickly followed suit. In the case of companies that produced brands such as Nike and Gap for export to the United States, Koreans worked with their U.S. clients to move manufacturing operations to countries with cheaper labor.

Meanwhile, the United States continuously engaged in military and economic trade with Indonesia after the U.S.-supported coup d'état by General Suharto. Even after the atrocities committed by Suharto's military in East Timor were well publicized through Senate hearings, the Clinton administration held to its "constructive engagement" with Suharto's junta. U.S. military and economic interests were too important to permit significant change. Throughout Suharto's brutal New Order junta, this policy prevailed in administrations both Republican and Democratic—Ford, Carter, Reagan, Bush, and Clinton.

Pursuit of U.S. corporate and financial interests, together with the greed of Suharto and his economic monopoly partners, eventually resulted in the collapse of the Indonesian economy.[11] The neoliberal revolution in Indonesia's already open economy in the 1980s led to hyper-development of the financial sector in the 1990s and burgeoning financial debts that Indonesia could no longer pay back. Once Indonesia's heavily skewed balance sheet shattered global investor confidence, global investment pulled out and Suharto's regime could no longer control the economy's free fall.

Further illustrating institutionalized personal greed, Suharto reneged twice on IMF bailouts that could have sustained his regime longer because he was unwilling to adhere to IMF reform measures that would have meant the potential loss of some of his family's businesses.[12] A third bailout offer was impending when the economy finally could no longer sustain itself. Skyrocketing prices in basic commodity prices led to widespread riots. Suharto lost control, and the United States, confronted with global media scrutiny of his military's murder of protesting students, finally ended its 25-year support of the dictator.

Indonesia had provided the United States military-industrial complex with opportunities for lucrative contracts throughout the 1980s and 1990s, so it unsurprising that the United States supported Suharto for so long. Its chief foreign policy architects for many years included Paul Wolfowitz, Dick Cheney, and others who had served on the boards of companies with large investments in Indonesia, including defense contractors.[13]

Studying Up, Down, and Sideways in the Global Economy: Ethnographic Intersections

In 1981, President Chun Doo-hwan made Korea's first-ever presidential visit to Indonesia, and in 1982 President Suharto reciprocated with Indonesia's first state visit to Seoul. Their visits symbolized the two countries' increasing cooperation in the spheres of trade and the economy. President Reagan's embrace of both dictators only made the diplomatic relationship stronger.

Shortly thereafter, in an academic conference held between Korean and Indonesian academics at the Institute for Far Eastern Studies in Seoul—a renowned Korean foreign policy and research institute—policy makers, scholars, and politicians from both countries outlined plans for continued economic and political cooperation between the two countries.

In the closing address, retired Major General Soedjono Hoemardani summed up the goals of greater economic and political cooperation:

> First, Indonesia clearly recognizes South Korea's security concerns and its delicate relations with the major powers in regards to the stability of the Korean peninsula and of Northeast Asia. On the basis of that recognition, Indonesia supports South Korea's efforts and wishes to see greater flexibility in Korea's policies toward the region.
>
> Second, strengthening of bilateral relations between Indonesia and Korea should not be viewed only from an economic perspective by both sides—Indonesia as a source of raw materials only and Korea as a source of capital and technology. In order to broaden this base at this stage, we need to

increase cooperation among mass media in order to enhance mutual understanding about our nations' history, traditions, values and future prospects.

Third, economic complementarity between our two countries, while stages of industrialization differ, may create problems in the future. These problems can be overcome and perhaps even prevented if both sides are sensitive enough about these issues. One important issue relates to that of technology transfer through investments or through training.

Ladies and Gentlemen!

It is my sincere hope that the exchange of views in a frank and open manner as practiced in this dialogue can be exercised in the many contacts between our two countries. When I paid a courtesy call on your President Chun Doo-hwan, we discussed and agreed on the need to publicize the greatest understanding, which had been gained through our dialogue to the wider audiences in both countries.

Cemented by the close diplomatic relations forged between Presidents Reagan, Suharto, and Chun, these concluding sentiments and plans were actualized with numerous Korean manufacturing investments in Indonesia in the 1980s and 1990s. These developments were in line with U.S.-backed economic policies that opened the Indonesian economy to foreign corporations starting in the early 1980s and encouraged the exploitation of resources and cheap labor. Infrastructure developments under these policies led Indonesia to incur considerable foreign debt. The opening of markets also increased indebtedness substantially, as foreign banks were instrumental in developing debt markets in the 1990s.[14]

When the global economic crisis began in 1997, Korea was the second country to be affected (Thailand was the first), followed closely by Indonesia.[15] The financial crisis resulted from inherent contradictions in the neoliberal economic policies in Asia that had caused unsustainable levels of unproductive debt and assets in Asian countries.[16] When these countries could no longer service the debt encouraged by Western financial institutions and banks, their economies risked default. At this point the IMF stepped in, offering bailout packages in exchange for further liberalization and privatization. Therefore Korea and Indonesia today face increasing income disparities and still greater foreign indebtedness, now that Western corporate interests have bought up previously national and local firms. Rather than diminishing, foreign bank indebtedness resumed its growth, to be exposed again in the global financial crisis of 2008.

These larger historical forces definitively shaped the lives of the Indonesian workers and Korean managers I interviewed in my study. Korean managers' stints in Indonesia were an outcome of the liberalization of the Indonesian economy, as were U.S. and Korean industries' move to

Indonesia for resources and cheap labor, and Indonesian workers' search for higher wages in Korea.

The experiences of Indonesian and Korean workers in this global assembly line also illustrate the various ways in which individuals forge their lives within these broader historical and political-economic structures. Both Indonesian migrant workers and Korean factory managers developed strategies for surviving an ever harsher economic environment. Faced with loss of job security due to corporate pressures and the IMF, managers and workers alike planned for an uncertain future by saving earnings and investing in their families and children. Both groups also had aspirations beyond their immediate family. Indonesian workers wanted to return to their country to help build a stronger economic base for their larger communities. Korean managers, for their part, saw themselves as working toward the nationalist goal of keeping Korea safe from outside economic interference, especially from the Japanese and Americans, by earning foreign currency through the export of products. Many also earnestly believed that they were in Indonesia to shoulder a Korean version of the "white man's burden" by helping Indonesians reach higher stages of linear human development.[17]

Korean managers were especially focused on Korea's political independence. All of them had undergone two-plus years of mandatory military service, during which they developed a strong sense of political nationalism. The continued U.S. military occupation of prime real estate in Seoul and, more importantly, U.S. hegemonic military control over South Korea were painful reminders of the legacy of colonialism and U.S. strategic ambitions on the Korean peninsula. Together with U.S. corporate power in Korea and the world at large, these political currents were also strong determinants of Korean managers' views of their work. Korean corporate training and nationalistic media pronouncements further bolstered this sense of patriotic calling.

Meanwhile, Indonesian workers were jubilant upon learning of Suharto's downfall. They shared a strong belief that Suharto and his close network of economic and military elites had controlled the vast majority of the country's economic and natural resources. Now that he was gone, they anticipated changes that would make the country more equitable, allowing them to attain better material conditions. Their experiences in Korea sometimes injured their sense of dignity, but with time, many started to understand the world views of average Koreans.

Indonesian workers who did not come to share something like a Korean worldview of commerce had usually suffered improper treatment from an inhumane boss. They managed to avoid this situation by leaving their jobs, usually at considerable economic and personal cost. Even after revised labor policies were enacted, some companies did not comply with new work hour or wage guidelines, citing economic hardship during the IMF era. By the end of my research in 2000, most workers knew that they had legal recourse though their networks, but recourse was time-consuming and not guaranteed. These were just some of the difficulties and risks migrant workers faced during the economic crises.

Conclusion: Toward an Anthropology of Corporate Capitalism

In *The Sociological Imagination*, C. Wright Mills wrote of global forces' shaping of individual lives:

> Nowadays people often feel that their private lives are a series of traps. They sense that within their everyday worlds, they cannot overcome their troubles, and in this feeling, they are often quite correct. What ordinary people are directly aware of and what they try to do are bounded by the private orbits in which they live; their visions and their powers are limited to the close-up scenes of job, family, neighborhood; in other milieux, they move vicariously and remain spectators. And the more aware they become, however vaguely, of ambitions and of threats which transcend their immediate locales, the more trapped they seem to feel.

For Mills, then, the social scientist's job is to link seemingly impersonal changes to communities, nations, and even the very structure of continent-wide societies:

> The facts of contemporary history are also facts about the success and the failure of individual men and women. When a society is industrialized, a peasant becomes a worker; a feudal lord is liquidated or becomes a businessman. When classes rise or fall, a person is employed or unemployed; when the rate of investment goes up or down, a person takes new heart or goes broke. When wars happen, an insurance salesperson becomes a rocket launcher; a store clerk, a radar operator; a wife or husband lives alone; a child grows up without a parent. Neither the life of an individual nor the history of a society can be understood without understanding both.[18]

Following Mills, this chapter invites the question of how an "anthropological imagination" might contribute to a better understanding of the global economy, contextualizing seemingly individual experiences within macro-economic forces. The research presented here is one attempt to analyze corporate capitalism's social and cultural effects on laborers in Asia in the late twentieth and early twenty-first centuries. Follow-up ethnographic research on Indonesian and other ethnic migrant labor in Korea, and on Korean industrial investments in Indonesia and other Asian countries, should yield valuable comparative perspectives on regional and global political economies. Comparisons with similar movements of capital and labor in the world may provide deeper insights into the nature of corporate capitalism, its relation to economic crises, and successful alternative routes.

More broadly, vertical analysis can inform ethnographic research on the retail and consumer end of corporate capitalism. For example, during my research in Seoul, my Indonesian contacts and I frequently strolled the shop-lined streets of Itaewon, where the mosque was located. When I was growing up in Seoul in the 1980s, these streets were a hub of illicit trade in products from export-oriented factories. Nike, Converse, Members Only, and numerous other branded retail products were sold on store shelves at black-market discounts. In most cases, the products had factory defects and had been surreptitiouslyly routed to hundreds of stores in Itaewon. But by the 1990s, litigation by foreign brands had prompted these stores to stop selling so-called "fake" or "illegal" products.

In 1999, during numerous walks along this street, we noticed consistently large crowds of Chinese, Japanese, Western, and Korean customers lining up at the big three-story Nike store. Curious, I met the owner and learned that for many years running, he had been the biggest retailer of Nike in all of Asia. Upon further investigation, I found that Korea, once the exclusive producer of Nike for the U.S. market, was now one of the largest consumers of Nike in the world.

Some years later, I met a Korean-American entrepreneur whose family was the largest seller of Nike in the United States (but not Korea). Their business had started small in the 1980s in the inner city of a major metropolitan area. It grew exponentially with the growth of Nike, assisted considerably by astronomical sales of the Air Jordan basketball shoes. Most of his consumers were African Americans from lower economic strata. Ethnographic connections inevitably emerge in these different consumption chains in the global economy. For example, consumers of Nike shoes and products made from polyester film are disproportionately individuals in Western societies, but increasingly also citizens in the rest of the world. A comparative study of the cultural and political economic significance of these consumption patterns would add to the larger picture of the global assembly line. Moreover, ethnographic studies of consumption are incomplete without analysis of the distribution and retail industries, including logistics, advertising, marketing, and sales of consumer products.

Perhaps most important, vertical analysis can also be applied to economic crisis. A "longue durée" approach to economic crises and economic catastrophes in different regions is a promising start for this investigation.[19] It could be followed by a detailed look at economic crises in industrial societies. Informed by these historical studies, we could then examine the history of economic crises in the neoliberal era and more specifically the connections between the successive economic crises from 1980 to 2010. There are certain to be ethnographic links, especially between the 1997–1999 crisis and the 2007 global financial crisis. I have made a small attempt to link the 1997–1999 crisis to the neoliberal project writ large, but more detailed study would illuminate the events of that period. Numerous business and economics studies exist,[20] and a historical, ethnographic examination might yield significant findings on the contemporary human condition. In other words, we need sophisticated syntheses. In a world riddled with crises and contradictions, this kind of "committed contingency" would harness the long, significant history of the anthropological imagination to better inform citizens in a global economy.

Notes

1. For example, suppliers for the Korean company FILA have a notorious record of labor abuses in Indonesia. See Oxfam International, "Offside! Labour Rights and Sportswear Production in Asia " (Oxford: Oxfam International, 2006), http://www.oxfam.org/sites/www.oxfam.org/files/OffsideExecSummary.pdf.
2. S.S. Chang et al., "Was the Economic Crisis 1997–1998 Responsible for Rising Suicide Rates in East/Southeast Asia? A Time-Trend Analysis for Japan, Hong Kong, South Korea, Taiwan, Singapore, and Thailand," *Social Science and Medicine* 68, no. 7 (April 2009): 1322–1331.
3. Neil Weinberg, "What Devaluation Hath Wrought," *Forbes*, 5 October 1998, http://www.forbes.com/forbes/1998/1005/6207053a.html.
4. Laura Nader, "Up the Anthropologist: Perspectives Gained from Studying Up," in *Reinventing Anthropology*, ed. Dell H. Hymes (New York: Pantheon, 1972), 151.
5. Laura Nader, "The Vertical Slice: Hierarchies and Children," in *Hierarchy and Society: Anthropological Perspectives on Bureaucracy*, ed. Gerald M. Britan and Ronald Cohen (Philadelphia: Institute for the Study of Human Issues, 1980).
6. See for example, Maria Patricia Fernandez-Kelly, *For We Are Sold, I and My People: Women and Industry in Mexico's Frontier* (Albany: SUNY Press, 1984); Aihwa Ong, *Spirits of Resistance and Capitalist Discipline: Factory Women in Malaysia* (Albany: SUNY Press, 1987).

7. Katie Hunt, "Time to Reform the IMF?" *BBC News*, 9 October 2008, http://news.bbc.co.uk/2/hi/business/7647015.stm.
8. For example, see Bruce Cumings, *The Korean War: A History* (New York: Modern Library, 2011). Cumings argues that the United States's involvement in the war led to a dramatic escalation of violence.
9. Martin Hart-Landsberg, *The Rush to Development: Economic Change and Political Struggle in South Korea* (New York: Monthly Review Press, 1993).
10. Ibid., 155–156.
11. See for example, Naomi Klein, *The Shock Doctrine: The Rise of Disaster Capitalism* (New York: Picador, 2008), 332–354.
12. Richard L. Parry, "Suharto Snubs IMF's Plan to Save Indonesia," *The Independent* (UK), 9 March 1998, http://www.independent.co.uk/news/suharto-snubs-imfs-plan-to-save-indonesia-1149253.html.
13. After serving as U.S. ambassador to Indonesia in the 1980s, Wolfowitz was a board member of the toy company Hasbro (which had large investments there) from 1995 to 2001. He was also a consultant for the weapons manufacturer Northrop Grumman. Cheney famously was the CEO of Halliburton during the period when its Kellogg, Brown, and Root subsidiary used collusive, corrupt methods to secure deals in Indonesia. See Center for Media and Democracy, "Paul Dundes Wolfowitz," last modified 16 March 2012, http://www.sourcewatch.org/index.php?title=Paul_Dundes_Wolfowitz; Jason Leopold, "Shady Background of Dick Cheney's Halliburton," *Centre for Research on Globalisation*, 16 April 2003, http://globalresearch.ca/articles/LEO304B.html.
14. Andrew Sheng, *From Asian to Global Financial Crisis: An Asian Regulator's View of Unfettered Finance in the 1990s and 2000s* (Cambridge: Cambridge University Press, 2009), 243–249.
15. *Frontline* (PBS), "Timeline of the Panic" (1999), http://www.pbs.org/wgbh/pages/frontline/shows/crash/etc/cron.html.
16. Sheng, *From Asian to Global Financial Crisis*.
17. It is historically ironic that this Eastern version of the "white man's burden" was also the Japanese's rationale for their colonial occupation of Korea during and even after the 35-year colonial period. The Japanese believed they were helping Korea develop like a modern Western state. They did this by extracting most of Korea's agricultural and mineral output and exploiting cheap—indeed, virtually free—labor for three and a half decades of colonial occupation. Korea's post-independence dependence on Japanese technology became a form of Japanese economic control, another historical irony that was not lost on Korean managers. It only fueled their desire to work harder for Korea's economic independence.
18. C. Wright Mills, *The Sociological Imagination* (New York: Oxford University Press, 1959).
19. Laura Nader, "Homo Sapiens and the Longue Durée," *Journal of Developing Societies* 24, no. 1 (2008): 83–94.
20. Sheng, *From Asian to Global Financial Crisis*; see also Ha-Joon Chang, Gabriel Palma, and D. Hugh Whittaker, eds., *Financial Liberalization and the Asian Crisis* (New York: Palgrave Macmillan, 2001).

Chapter 3

ON BUREAUCRACY
Excessively Up at the International Labour Organization

Ellen Hertz

As a student of Laura Nader, I know just how much she enjoys and benefits from controversy. Thus, I was disappointed recently to discover that her flagship phrase "studying up" occasions almost none. Many authors seem unaware of the phrase's origin, or worse still, claim that perspectives on studying up are quite common while citing Nader's famous article among numerous "other examples."[1] Moving from sources to content, one finds a similar lack of critical reflection. Many authors (mainly sociologists) have explored the deontological and practical difficulties surrounding the study of powerful people, asking whether researchers are held to the same duties of confidentiality that our ethics codes require for the study of the less powerful[2] or questioning the appropriateness of institutional review board procedures from this perspective.[3] Others point more generally to types of discomfort caused by relations with people who can be categorized or categorize themselves as more powerful than we are.[4] Still others ask whether characterizing science and technology studies (STS) or men's studies as "studying up" might contribute to the very mystification of science or male dominance that STS and feminist studies have tried to undo.[5] Finally, one author writes approvingly of "studying 'up'," putting only "up" in quotes, in a subtle but suggestive modification of the paradigm I wish to explore further here.

Clearly, if there's a wallop in the phrase "studying up", it's the little word "up" that packs it. Yet nowhere does the critical literature on studying up

Notes for this chapter begin on page 80.

simply ask "what's 'up'"? Indeed, the person who has done the most to clarify what "up" is, is Laura Nader herself, in an article titled "The Vertical Slice."[6] As Nader points out there and has repeated elsewhere,[7] the point is not to isolate an "up" to examine as if it were a self-contained unit, but to link ups to downs, looking at the *relations* between different arenas of social power, selected as a function of their differential positions with respect to two key issues: decision-making and responsibility. In rereading "Up the Anthropologist," it is clear that through the notion of "up," Nader is identifying degrees of social and cultural *control*, from which she would like to induce corresponding degrees of social and cultural *responsibility*. As such, her definition of up-ness comes more or less explicitly from C. Wright Mills's definition of the power elite: people, groups, and institutions are "up" when their decisions affect the life conditions of many other people "below" them, and conversely, people are "down" when their decisions do not affect others' lives and when, furthermore, they live in conditions largely structured by others, whether they are fully aware of it or not.[8] In sum, "up" is not a place but a position, and "slicing vertically" means studying the relations between positions by asking how some people's actions asymmetrically affect other people's lives.

Once clarified, this definition of up-ness appears terrifically simple, and I shall retain it here for its gaze-sharpening properties. Let us bear in mind, however, that it is also *too* simple, for if the social sciences had only to study the results of *decision* in a cause-and-effect paradigm, we would have been rolling in clover long before that phrase was coined. Unfortunately, as reflections in social theory have demonstrated for quite some time now, society is shaped as much by drift as by decision. More precisely, because social structures and social change are the not-so-intended outcome of the iteration of institutionalized forms of things, thoughts, and actions, "deciding" is an inappropriate term for what men and women who are arguably "up" can and will do under most circumstances. This is the lesson to be learned, incidentally, from a converse theoretical and methodological move associated with the *Ecole des Annales* that occupied the historical sciences during most of the twentieth century, a move that could be summed up as an exhortation to historians to begin studying down. Fueled by many of the same forms of intellectual dissatisfaction and political engagement that mobilized the radical anthropologists who contributed to *Reinventing Anthropology*, these historians insisted, against generations of venerable predecessors, that we could no longer study social change by simply examining the decisions of this or that great man, or the choices in marriage and alliance between great families, or even the creation and functioning of the great civilizational institutions.[9] Rather, the amorphous mass of smaller, apparently traceless thoughts and deeds performed by those who are "down" had to be included within the material of which history (as a process and as a discipline) was made.

Once again, Nader herself addressed these issues in her discussions of "controlling processes" and "cultural control," but it is unclear whether the implications of these different vocabularies of structuration and change have been fully thought through in the critical literature.[10] Relatively little thought has addressed how "studying up" relates to other major theoretical issues in the social sciences: the structure-agency opposition,[11] for example, or the tension between alienation and resistance in studies of popular culture.[12] "Studying up" can be performed within several theoretical paradigms, and it is no longer sufficient to invoke an "up" without specifying how we believe "up-ness" works to structure social reproduction and change.

As anthropologists James Ferguson and Akhil Gupta have demonstrated, spatialized metaphors have played a central and deceptively simple role in anthropological theorizing since its inception, reinforcing disciplinary belief in discrete territorial-cultural entities and inducing us to think in terms of Russian-doll hierarchies of local to global units. They unpack the various components of up-ness in an article specifically addressing the question of how to conceptualize the nation-state, arguing that the language of verticality and the ranking of social spaces that it makes possible should be examined with great care: "Picturing the state's relation to society through the image of vertical encompassment fuses in a single, powerful image a number of analytically distinct propositions. Is the state's encompassing height a matter of superior rank in a political hierarchy? Of spatial scale? Abstraction? Generality of knowledge and interest? Distance from nature?"[13]

This chapter will explore some of the subtleties of "up-ness" by analyzing a recent experience I had in a context that, at first glance, appears quite full of it. I will analyze a "Meeting," convened 16–18 April 2007 in Geneva by an international organization (IO)—the International Labour Organization (ILO)—on the theme of working conditions in the information and technology (IT) industries.[14] I intend this both as a contribution to the critical literature on studying up and as part of a larger attempt to incorporate IOs as such, and not simply the themes IOs address, into the mainstream of anthropological research topics.[15]

Studying Upper: The ILO

At first glance, IOs might appear to be "higher" than the nation-state, enjoying the same altitude as the largest transnational corporations or international nongovernmental organizations such as the World Wildlife Fund or Amnesty International. In the case of the ILO, this impression is reinforced by the organization's rather remarkable pedigree. The oldest IO, and the only one to have survived the transformation of the League of Nations into the United Nations system, it was founded in 1919 as part of the Treaty of Versailles, and incorporated as the first specialized agency in the UN system in 1946. Samuel Gompers (head of the American Federation of Labor) chaired the commission that drafted its constitution, which included representatives from Belgium, Cuba, Czechoslovakia, France, Italy, Japan, Poland, the UK, and the United States. Its preamble is nothing if not inspiring and, coming out of World War I, reflects a remarkable level of contemporary awareness of global economic interdependence and its consequences for world stability:

> Whereas universal and lasting peace can be established only if it is based upon social justice;
> And whereas conditions of labour exist involving such injustice, hardship and privation to large numbers of people as to produce unrest so great that the peace and harmony of the world are imperiled; and an improvement of those conditions is urgently required
> . . .
> Whereas also the failure of any nation to adopt humane conditions of labour is an obstacle in the way of other nations which desire to improve the conditions in their own countries;
> The High Contracting Parties, moved by sentiments of justice and humanity as well as by the desire to secure the permanent peace of the world, and with a view to attaining the objectives set forth in this Preamble, agree to the following . . . [16]

From its inception, the ILO's principal activity has been to establish Conventions and issue Recommendations governing labor standards. Its first conference, held in Washington, D.C., in 1919, adopted six conventions on working hours, unemployment, maternity protection, night work for women and children, and minimum working ages. In 1944 it enlarged and specified its mission in an annex referred to as the "Declaration of Philadelphia," which states as its first principle: "Labor is not a commodity."

For our purposes here, the significance of this history, best imagined in terms of not height but depth, lies in the nostalgic aura of nobility it lends the ILO (which newer IOs will never quite match). The tone, the vocabulary, even the grammar of its founding documents exude a perfume of history, taking us back to a faraway pre-postcolonial world controlled as much by London, Paris, and Berlin as by New York and Washington. This history is also important in relation to the charged issue of work, the ILO's central concern. A rallying point for the benevolent attention of colonial powers at the beginning of the century, the guarantee of decent working conditions for workers at home and "natives" abroad united Western powers in a display of humanism framed in the evolutionary vocabulary of the "white man's burden."

Though the ILO was awarded the Nobel Peace Prize on the fiftieth anniversary of its founding in 1969, the onset of the Cold War and decolonization radically called into question the entire frame of reference for its civilizing mission, as labor causes became even more tightly associated with Communism and with East-West struggles for influence in the Third World. A more progressive but equally radical shift has been under way since the 1980s with the increased dominance of neoliberal ideology worldwide. Globalization and financialization of corporate capitalism have directly affected national and regional fiscal, investment, and labor policy, undermining both the ILO's possibilities for effective action and much of its ideological legitimacy. The tone of ILO documents has become increasingly subdued, and the Declaration on Fundamental Principles and Rights at Work, which the International Labour Conference (the legislative body of the ILO) adopted in 1998, is mostly toothless in terms of enforcement.

Only traces of this evolution are evident in the very general statement of the ILO's four strategic objectives:

- Promote and realize standards and fundamental principles and rights at work;
- Create greater opportunities for women and men to secure decent employment and income;
- Enhance the coverage and effectiveness of social protection for all;
- Strengthen tripartism and social dialogue.[17]

This last objective points to another unique characteristic of the ILO. The concept of "tripartism," enshrined in ILO founding documents, designates a substantive and procedural commitment to the idea that genuine progress in the area of work and social justice cannot occur unless workers are present to negotiate the relevant instruments with employers and governments. It also represents the commitment to what the ILO calls "social dialogue" within member states by promoting fundamental rights to freedom of association and collective bargaining. Indeed, ILO tripartism reflects an admirable level of sophistication in the operationalization of its mission and principles. The only IO structurally to recognize that the relation between governments and the citizens they are supposed to represent is complex, mediated, and problematic, it folds other large organizations (national and international trade unions, employers' associations, and more recently and in some contexts, NGOs) into its very procedures. Thus, to the height and depth of the ILO's missions and history must be added the breadth of its design, an inclusiveness that it actively promotes as one of its greatest strengths.

Returning to the various attributes of up-ness listed by Ferguson and Gupta above—superior rank in a political hierarchy, spatial scale, abstraction, generality of knowledge and interest, and distance from nature—the ILO seems, at first glance, to possess just about all of them. International law ranks higher than national and local law in a courtroom.[18] In terms of spatial scale, ILO activities covered the globe when the word "globalization" was just a glint in the power elite's randy eyes. The ILO research team commands access to the most thorough and standardized forms of data on working conditions and labor policy in existence, allowing for comparison and generalization at a high level of abstraction. Not beholden to any national territory, the ILO is disengaged from the grimy material conditions of subsistence and governance on the ground. And last but not least, the ILO mission is quite simply lofty, seeking to "elevate" humanity from its "baser" instincts and "lowly" conditions.

The ILO is also "up" in other, more material ways. Housed in a sparkling white building exuding orderly modernist utopianism, on a majestic hill leading away from Lake Geneva to where the rents are high, it offers a splendid view of Mont Blanc from its terrace. Enormous conference rooms and large rectilinear corridors are decorated with oversized wall hangings, sculptures, vases, and other artifacts presented to the ILO as gifts from member states. With a budget of almost $600 million (for 2008–2009), 181 member states, 1,900 employees, and 600 international experts between the Geneva headquarters and regional offices, it is not a large organization by some standards, but neither is it particularly lowly. And most important for me, a concerned anthropologist-lawyer worried about the complex organization of social justice in a globalized world, the ILO offers the promise of precisely the kind of height that Nader singled out in "Up the Anthropologist": a place where the decisions of a few affect the life conditions of the many. Indeed, this is what drew me to the ILO. Now let's see what I found there.

Getting Inside "Up"

Despite this aura of elevation, there are many signs that the ILO may not be as unequivocally up as one might wish. The first of these is undoubtedly the very fact that I was there. This statement is not an exercise in false modesty, for my presence there, and that of many of my colleagues, reveals something about just where we had been parachuted, and the kinds of expertise and representation needed to carry out our functions at this level. To clarify this, I will delve briefly into the many-tiered structure of the ILO and examine how it interacts with its permanent administration, the Secretariat of the International Labour Office (hereinafter "Office") in Geneva.

The Meeting had been convened by the Sectoral Activities Programme, or SECTOR, one of four programs (along with ACT/EMP, DIALOGUE, and ACTRA) of the Social Dialogue Sector (DIALOGUE), which is, somewhat confusingly, one of the four substantive departments of the ILO (along with STANDARDS, EMPLOYMENT, and PROTECTION). SECTOR is something of an oddity in the ILO system, in that it structures its work around specific issues in industry sectors and not around the ILO's four strategic objectives. It thus has what it calls an "integrating agenda" that is unique in the ILO framework. At the bequest of the ILO Governing Body (the ILO's executive arm), SECTOR conducts research, convenes "Meetings," and initiates "action programmes," "standard-related activities," and "cross-sectoral activities," all of which take place on a tripartite basis with representatives of governments, workers' groups, and employers' groups, who usually participate in equal numbers. These meetings and activities are not primarily intended to lead to the formulation of international norms. Conventions and Recommendations—instruments of general or universal applicability with potential binding legal force in international law—are the prerogative of the International Labour Conference, the equivalent of the legislative arm of the ILO. More precisely, the agreements arrived at through SECTOR tend to involve not only state signatories but multiple other actors as well, and are articulated at a lower level of generality. SECTOR works on the assumption that through research, reporting, and social dialogue concerning "best practices," employers, workers, and governments can be brought together to compare experiences, learn from each other's positions, and forward the ILO's agenda in specific areas.

The particular meeting described here pertained to the mechanical and electrical engineering sector, which traditionally encompasses computer hardware production.[19] Participants received a lengthy report titled "The Production of Electronic Components for the IT Industries: Changing Labour Force Requirements in a Global Economy,"[20] researched and written by the Office staff at the request of the Governing Body. It provided participants with an industry overview including global employment trends, subcontracting practices, county and local strategies, training needs, emerging issues for working conditions, and labor and industry responses to these new issues. It was the first ILO report of its kind for the computer manufacturing industry and thus had attracted some attention from the press, attention that intensified in the wake of a campaign that a network of international and national NGOs had launched in the months preceding the Meeting to sensitize consumers to the issue of decent work in the computer industry. This publicity may in turn have been linked to the industry leaders' decision to convene a meeting of the industry-wide standard-setting board in Geneva the following weekend.[21]

This background allows us to take measure of the degree and kinds of expertise that were convened to reflect on these important issues, issues that touch the lives of an estimated 18 million workers worldwide.[22] My own presence was a case in point. Following normal procedure, the ILO invited Switzerland to send a maximum of two government representatives to the Meeting. Since issues of sex discrimination are central to this industry, the Swiss Confederation consulted the Swiss Federal Bureau for Equality, and a friend recommended me for the three-day mandate. I was appointed as a Swiss government "advisor", along with the official Swiss representative, a civil servant from the Federal Office for Communication. Though I was not an expert on working conditions in Asia, I was a China anthropologist, a lawyer, and a feminist active in the area of gender studies. In addition, I had a general understanding of the ILO's workings through previous research on Conventions 107 and 169 concerning indigenous peoples. However, I was in no way an expert in the anthropology of work, or in national and international labor law, and I knew even less at the time about the computer manufacturing industry. And no doubt most important of all, I had never participated in a "Meeting" before.

To my great surprise, many other countries were even less prepared than Switzerland to carry out their jobs. Clearly, expertise was not required of governments at this stage. In fact, the vast majority of states had simply opted out altogether: only nineteen governments in total sent representatives, only a handful of whom—namely Japan, the Philippines, and Indonesia—knew the issues and had taken time to prepare a position. Five of the six largest players in the industry—China (with 35 percent of total employment in the sector at the time), the United States (7 percent), Russia (5 percent), Germany (4 percent), and Korea (4 percent)—honored the Meeting through their absence.[23] Other governments were nominally present but their representatives disappeared after the opening session, materializing again briefly for the wrap-up. Still others seemed to view the meeting as something of a trade fair, and sought to attract direct investment from international firms. The countries that participated most actively in the debates in the end (e.g., Egypt, Spain, and Switzerland) had virtually no stakes in this industry and did so on principled grounds, but with little direction from their respective governments.

Clearly, governments were not the driving force behind the Meeting. Rather, the impetus had come from the Governing Body, no doubt reflecting the concerns and expertise of the permanent staff of the Office. The absenteeism of governments also signaled how distant this Meeting was from the "higher" functions of the ILO, those that take place within the Governing Body or the International Labour Conference during its annual meetings in Geneva. As no binding decisions were to be taken here, many governments simply let the ILO staff do the grunt work, knowing that they would have ample opportunity to participate if activities in this area "rose" to the level of the executive or legislative forums of the ILO.

More encouraging was the level of participation and expertise among labor and employers' representatives. Ten workers' associations or labor unions attended, including the Hungarian Metalworkers' Federation; the Federation of Indonesian Metal Workers; the Japanese Electrical, Electronic and Information Union; and the Alliance at IBM. In addition, members of the International Metalworkers' Federation (IMF) and the International Trade Union Confederation (ITUC) attended in their capacity as representatives of nongovernmental international organizations, for a total of 16 people. These representatives appeared well informed about the issues and unified in their purpose. Their principal objective seemed to be to pressure employer representatives to include unions and workers' associations more systematically in decision-making procedures, and to guarantee that any text resulting from this Meeting included provisions for labor's participation in future discussions.

Employers were represented by ten people officially invited by the Governing Board, including representatives of the Jamaica Employers' Federation; the Belgium Enterprise Federation; the Union des industries et métiers de la métallurgie (France); the Camara Nacional de la Industria Electronica, Telecommunicaciones e Informatica (Mexico); Hewlett-Packard; the Canadian Employers Council; the Employers' Federation of India; and Philips Electrical Industries of Pakistan. Including one technical advisor, this delegation numbered eleven. Twenty other companies were present as members of "other official international organizations," in this case, the International Organization of Employers. Their representatives appeared to be thoroughly informed and prepared, and had a common agenda that, if not negotiated beforehand, fell into place over the course of the three days. This agenda consisted of ensuring that the language of any text that was to come out of this Meeting put their efforts to guarantee good working conditions in the industry in the best possible light while emphasizing the difficulties specific to this sector (high levels of competition; complicated subcontracting schemas that make control over labor conditions in the supply chain difficult; high levels of innovation requiring constant retraining and complex decisions about relocation, etc.).

Finally, the Governing Body had allowed other "official international organizations"—namely, the UN Conference on Trade and Development (UNCTAD)—and NGOs to participate in discussions and distribute materials, but not to vote. The network of NGOs associated with GoodElectronics had one official representative and several more unofficial ones. Of all of the "stakeholders" present at the Meeting, these NGOS were probably the best informed. Their presence and role in the process of "social dialogue" represented an interesting source of tension for other participants.

Other elements defined the particular atmosphere of the Meeting. First, it should be noted that the element of secrecy alluded to in C. Wright Mills' definition of the power elite was entirely absent.[24] All documents were readily available online, depriving participants of the feeling that they were in any way a chosen few. Rows of empty chairs reinforced this sentiment, and the aura of desolation they caused was intensified by behavior that seemed to strike everyone (except my Swiss colleague and me) as normal. All sessions started late—sometimes almost an hour late, with people entering and leaving the room for reasons unknown. Contradicting this apparently casual protocol was the highly formalized nature of some of the procedures, which lent an air of high bureaucracy to much of the three-day encounter, as if going through the motions was not a fallback position but an art to be cultivated. On the one hand, we were confronted with written and unwritten standard procedure determining who spoke when and with what degree of generality. Secretary generals, acting executive directors, deputy secretary generals, executive secretaries, experts, chairpersons, and vice-chairpersons were respectively welcomed, thanked, questioned, and elected in a series of oral interventions lacking anything like verve. On the other hand, certain refreshingly informal moments included sharp criticism of the report we had all received, pointed exchanges between employers' and workers' representatives, implicit threats to leave the Meeting without producing a final text, demands to modify procedures in various ways, and time-outs called by both employers' and workers' representatives to negotiate common positions on language and phrasing. This mixture of formal and informal was rendered all the more poignant by the awkwardness of intercultural communication, miscommunication, and disagreement, intensified in turn by the expert but laborious activities of patient interpreters sitting in booths located somewhere behind wherever one happened to be seated.

Yet despite this ill-assorted collection of individuals, the excessive formalism of certain moments and the frankly amateurish quality of others, and despite my creeping realization that the problems of 18 million workers would not be resolved in these three days, something did happen at the tripartite "Meeting on the Production of Electronic Components for the IT Industries."

The Day I Was Switzerland

The goal of the Meeting was to adopt a document describing what had been accomplished during the Meeting. This statement is not intended to be facetious, and merits elaboration. It is barely an exaggeration to say that the sole "product" of IOs such as the ILO is documents. They come in a wide variety of forms and enshrine many contents, but they remain documents. The extent to which this fact may strike us as disconcerting or disappointing is a measure of the hopes we hold for a direct relationship between "high" and "low," between decisions "at the summit" and conditions "on the ground." In fact, what happened in Geneva over this three-day period in April was that 60–80 people with highly variable degrees of presence, competence and effort produced the papers the International Labour Office staff needed to produce the "Note on the Proceedings TMITI/2007/10."[25]

This accomplishment is more remarkable than it might seem, for the threat of the Meeting adjourning without the desired papers was quite real. As became clear during the plenary discussions scheduled over the first two days, significant differences in tone and emphasis separated workers' and employers' positions. In general, DIALOGUE strives to produce documents that are accepted by consensus. Though the Standing Orders allow acceptance by simple majority vote, this was clearly not a desired outcome in a meeting designed to promote further discussion, inside and outside the ILO context, between workers' and employers' associations in the high-visibility IT sector. Furthermore, time was a key source of pressure, as Meetings are not prolonged beyond their scheduled time slots. Nothing guaranteed the success of this enterprise in advance, and the precise ways in which success came about deserve attention.

The Meeting began at 9:00 A.M. with group meetings to which my Swiss colleague and I were the only ones to arrive on time, a bad habit that we were to repeat on consecutive occasions, with consequences. At approximately 11:30, workers' and employers' representatives joined governments for the opening session, during which we heard statements by the chairperson and the acting executive director of DIALOGUE intended to clarify the formal aspects and set a tone of measured optimism for the Meeting. In the afternoon, we reconvened for the first substantive plenary session, organized around a discussion of the report and specifically of the three broad questions it had highlighted. Three plenary sessions of at least two hours were devoted to substantive tripartite exchanges of views, during which the major fault lines of the discussion became evident, as did the risk of failing to agree on a common statement.

After initial statements thanking the ILO for its role in organizing the Meeting, the three group spokespeople began staking out their respective positions. The first bone of contention was the ILO's definition of "social dialogue." Employers' representatives demanded that this notion be broadened to include all relevant "stakeholders," including, notably, subcontractors, customers, shareholders, and NGOs. Furthermore, they insisted that "employers did not see social dialogue as the solution to all problems"; some decisions had to be made by management alone.[26] The workers' representatives, meanwhile, held that this position was "solely aimed at diluting the role of trade unions in the process" and thus unacceptable.[27] To illustrate this attitude, they cited the absence of worker representatives in the drafting of industry-wide codes of conduct such as the EICC and GeSI initiatives[28] and invoked Martin Luther King's "riotous voices of the unheard" to illustrate the attendant risks in ignoring organized labor. Furthermore, in labor's view, NGOs were all well and good, but nothing could replace trade unions' historical role in vigilant assertion of labor rights and in guaranteeing standards on the floor. This viewpoint was reinforced by the Spanish government and others, who stressed that in the ILO context, social dialogue meant interactions between employers' and workers' organizations. When the employers' spokesperson complained that they "had decided to attend this meeting expecting social dialogue, but found themselves engaged in debate," the secretary-general of the Meeting intervened to "clarify" that "the Meeting and the ongoing debate *were representative* of social dialogue" within the ILO framework.[29] This dialogue on "dialogue" boded ill for subsequent discussions.

The second bone of contention was the role that brand-name manufacturers should play in assuring that their subcontractors respected international labor standards. As a general rule, both sides of the debate agreed this was a problem but disagreed about whether large brand-name companies were making good-faith efforts to tackle it. The workers' spokesperson encouraged employers to adhere to the same standards of transparency in the supply chain currently in practice in the textile industry, and insisted once again that adherence to standards was achievable only through trade unions' active involvement. The employers' spokesperson argued that supply-chain transparency entailed strategic business risks, and that the IT industry differed from other industries in this respect. She reiterated the position that voluntary initiatives set high standards, often higher than those of the ILO, and encouraged the ILO to play a more active role in enforcing existing standards.

The final topic—best practices in the area of lifelong learning—elicited less disagreement. Discussion centered on the proper balance between government, employer, and worker investment in continuing education, with employers taking a guardedly engaged stance and workers a more aggressive one. Overall, the Meeting participants agreed that continued retraining and concentration on competences rather than specific skills were proper policies for avoiding retrenchment and structural unemployment in this fast-changing, highly demanding sector.

This, then, was the discussion that provided the basis for the conclusions of the Meeting, to be adopted on the afternoon of the third and last day. To draft these conclusions, a Working Group on Conclusions was formed of five representatives from each party to the tripartite discussion. Having once again arrived on time to the meeting at which these representatives were chosen, my Swiss colleague and I found ourselves elected. The Working Group was provided with a first draft concocted by the Office's staff members. We then set ourselves to the unlikely task of forging a common statement despite a fair amount of mistrust and disagreement, a task that would occupy us for the next day.

It is important to note that the language being negotiated was anything but technical. The document, which was not binding on anyone, was destined for inclusion in the "Note on the Proceeding," from where it would make its way into the SECTOR's annual report. Producing a potentially binding document can easily take ten years, and requires ratification by member states through their national parliaments. To put this process in further perspective: whereas most governments (with the notable exception of the United States) have ratified all eight conventions that the ILO considers "fundamental," the majority of the ILO's 188 conventions remain unratified by most member states. The stakes involved in determining the language of the paper we were to produce that day were thus indubitably low.

And yet stakes there were. As the working group session progressed, it became evident that the stumbling blocks were not grand principles dividing labor and capital, but rather context-dependent tussles over specific terms, conducted in a climate of both remarkable stubbornness and sudden displays of goodwill on both sides. Both social partners seemed to be aiming not so much to "win" as to guarantee what they saw as a balanced picture, a picture in which the large brand-name companies appeared to be sincerely engaging in the pursuit of higher labor standards in the industry while trade unions were portrayed as key partners in guaranteeing labor justice. Semantic arm-wrestling occurred around apparently negligible nuances: employer representatives insisted, for example, that the word "negative" be systematically replaced by the word "challenging"; and worker representatives demanded that the official ILO definition of "workers' representatives" appear in a footnote. Both sides seemed also to put stock in general opening statements of resounding tone but little applicability.

In short, the Working Group's task was to work through a long series of seemingly minor (yet always threatening) disagreements, negotiated between two groups who fundamentally distrusted each other yet displayed genuine interest in moving forward, as if the threat of failure to produce such a document temporarily overrode more substantive commitments on both sides. Governments played a key mediating role, frequently proposing alternative language and weighing in occasionally on one side or another. To my delight and astonishment, the specific forms of expertise required at this stage were a good command of the English language and tact, two things of which I have a fair amount, making me a key player for this particular phase of the operation. Indeed, my role was considered almost natural, as a palpable mystique surrounds Switzerland's political neutrality and long history of negotiating diplomatic solutions—a mystique all the more hilarious as I am originally from the United States. Nonetheless, this combination of skills and stereotypes compelled the Working Group chairperson to turn to me frequently and ask, "Would Switzerland like to propose alternative language?"

To everyone's obvious relief, the result of this exercise, which lasted for ten hours straight, was a paper that could then be duly adopted in the closing plenary session at 5:00 P.M. Many people were thanked, including "Switzerland," and we all went home, mostly never to see each other again. A few weeks after the Meeting, the Office staff contacted us all once by e-mail, requesting our approval of transcriptions of oral statements we had made that were to be reprinted in the draft "Note." A few months later we received the final version of the Note in the mail. When preparing to write this chapter, I searched the Web to learn the fate of "my" Note and discovered that it had indeed been used to compile the yearly "Report of the Committee on Sectoral and Technical Meetings and Related Issues," submitted to the Governing Body in November 2007 as an attachment to item number 16 of an agenda that comprised a total of twenty-two items (not counting committee work) to be treated over a 15-day period.[30] Reference to my Note appeared on pages 8–9 of document GB 300/16, and the text in these five paragraphs indicates that it elicited little controversy. One employer's representative observed with satisfaction that "real employers" had participated in record numbers, and it was decided, earth-shakingly, that the committee would recommend that the Governing Body authorize the director-general to communicate the Note to governments, international employers' and workers' organizations, and relevant IOs. The committee further requested "that the Director-General bear in mind, when drawing up proposals for the future work of the Office, the wishes expressed by the Meeting in the conclusions."[31]

Instrumentalizing Up-ness

This, then, was the message in the bottle tossed into the sea of a potentially more just world. Put starkly, using Nader's definition of up-ness, nothing was up at this Meeting, or even perhaps at the ILO. More politely, one could say that the ILO is *excessively* up, located "above" the real workings of power and responsibility that interest Nader. In fact, the Naderian notion of up-ness is ill-suited to describe what happened at this Meeting in a number of ways that bear examination.

As my description is intended to demonstrate, nothing in this process is identifiable as a decision, a moment when an individual or group of individuals chose to set the course of events in one direction or another. Rather, the drawn-out procedures, multiple tiers, tripartite structure, and consensual nature of ILO activities all made this particular ILO event look more like an outcome of institutional momentum than any identifiable form of agency. Furthermore, though Nader's (and C. Wright Mills's) aim is to encourage social scientists to examine the *threats* that concentrations of power in modern society pose to social justice, one easily finds oneself wishing the ILO had *more* power and influence, including the force necessary to put its "decisions" into practice. It is no secret that the international arena is seldom equipped with this type of force, and that international law is only "higher" than national law when national law decides to let it be. Nonetheless, it is somewhat troubling to take the full measure of the distance between what goes on in the ILO and the conditions under which 18 million employees labor in the computer manufacturing industry.

If the ILO is not up, and if our efforts over the three days in Geneva were so utterly purposeless, why did we come, and why would anyone return?

Discounting the fact that many will not go back and still more did not attend, it remains the case that such Meetings take place, that documents are produced, and that stakes, energy, intelligence, and even emotions are invested in this production. Clearly, not only the ILO but even the Meeting I attended partook of some of the attributes of height that Gupta and Ferguson teased out—not "superior rank in a political hierarchy," but certainly a level of "generality of knowledge and interest" that lent the whole affair its potentially lofty pretensions. Indeed, it is precisely these lofty generalities that kept social partners at the negotiating table. Employers' representatives sought to benefit from this forum's moral authority to solidify their reputations in the area of corporate social responsibility, while workers' representatives aimed to enshrine in ever more documents the importance of workers' rights and their central role in protecting them. In very concrete ways as well, the levels of linguistic generality that we hammered out together in the working group were what allowed the process to move forward, as conflicts over terms were often resolved by shifting to a higher level of abstraction (or vagueness).

In short, "up-ness" at the ILO is not so much an attribute of the organization as a semantic resource that it and its members can call upon to advance their agendas and defend their causes. (They don't call it the "moral *high* ground" for nothing!) This resource is mobilized by issuing and circulating documents that can then be presented in other international, national, and local arenas: other IOs, the media, boardrooms, national parliaments, and localities. The point here is not to ask how much good faith or cynicism governs the circulation and use of such documents, but to notice that both good faith and cynicism feed on the belief that the ILO is in some senses very much "up." Perceiving up-ness at the ILO is not a simple analytic error; rather, the ILO and its constituencies cultivate this aura of height to accomplish the particular things it is designed to do. Up-ness is a native category.

In the case of the Meeting I attended, this argument can go one step further, for not only was up-ness at stake, but the vertical slice was also at the heart of one of its principal debates: can brand names be held accountable for the labor standards practiced by their subcontractors? At issue here were opposing stances on the degree and kind of control that brand-name manufacturers can exercise over their subcontractors. Predictably, workers' representatives argued that brands were insufficiently serious about exercising influence over subcontractors, and that they refused to acknowledge their own contributions to these violations (e.g., through just-in-time contractual arrangements) and/or the benefits they gained from them (through the lower labor costs they made possible). Employers' representatives, on the other hand, pointed to factors that limited their power to determine conditions on the ground: national governments', particularly China's, lack of commitment to applying international labor standards; poor education of subcontractors, who had not been taught to see "the business case" for investing in better working conditions; the extremely competitive and dynamic nature of the industry; and finally, their own excessive up-ness, that is, the multiple layers of subcontractors that stood between them and knowledge of actual practices on the shop floor.

In sum, key questions of control and responsibility are not simply questions that "we" ask about "them," the social actors we might be studying. Rather, verticality is a stake in an enormously important political debate about who is in charge in a globalizing world. Issues of traceability are central for actors and analysts alike, as the length of command chains and the complexity of the networks that define globalization inevitably dilute both the power to determine the direction of change and the kinds of responsibility one can hold people to as a consequence.

Conclusion

Based on my participation in a three-day Meeting at the ILO, I have argued that the aura of height that we associate with international organizations—their institutionalized ethereality—deserves to be taken seriously, but not at face value. Clearly, more is needed to gain a full understanding of the raison d'être of such Meetings, and to trace their direct and indirect influence on social justice in work over five, ten, twenty, or fifty years to come. The geography and temporality of these studies must mirror that of the ILO itself, with periodic short visits to other meetings at which collective energy is mobilized around still more documents. Practitioners of the anthropology of IOs must follow the paper trail wherever it leads, deep into the bowels of many other organizations (national and international federations of workers, of employers, other IOs, corporate boardrooms and forums, state administrations), to thoroughly document the diverse processes of digestion and regurgitation at work. Ideally, these studies would also be of some interest to the analyzed IOs, creating a scholarly dialogue between international administrations and anthropologists. This is the work to be done if we wish to transpose into the 21st century the crucial questions of power and responsibility raised by Laura Nader in her 1969 article.

Acknowledgments

I would like to thank Irène Bellier and Birgit Müller from the *Ecole des hautes etudes en sciences sociales* for organizing a very fruitful symposium on this subject; Paul Bailey, Marion Fresia, and Hans Steinmüller for their helpful comments and criticism on this chapter; and Rachael Stryker and Roberto González for their determination, intelligence, and patience while steering this volume to publication.

Notes

1. See Pamela Moss and Margo L. Matwychuk, "Beyond Speaking as an 'As a' and Stating the 'Etc.': Engaging in a Praxis of Difference," *Frontiers: A Journal of Women's Studies* 21, no. 3 (2000): 101.
2. For example, see John F. Galliher, "Social Scientists' Ethical Responsibilities to Superordinates: Looking Upward Meekly," *Social Problems* 27, no. 3 (1980): 298–308. See also Murray Wax, "Paradoxes of 'Consent' to the Practice of Fieldwork," *Social Problems* 27, no. 3 (1980): 272–283.
3. See for example Joan E. Sieber, "On Studying the Powerful (Or Fearing to Do So): A Vital Role for IRBs" *IRB: Ethics and Human Research* 11, no. 5 (1989): 1–6.
4. Monica J. Casper, "Feminist Politics and Fetal Surgery: Adventures of a Research Cowgirl on the Reproductive Frontier," *Feminist Studies* 23, no. 2 (1997): 232–262.
5. Linda L. Layne, "Introduction," *Science, Technology, and Human Values* 23, no. 1 (1998): 12.
6. Laura Nader, "The Vertical Slice: Hierarchies and Children," in *Hierarchy and Society*, ed. Gerald M. Britan and Ronald Cohen (Philadelphia: Institute for the Study of Human Issues, 1980).
7. Laura Nader, "Controlling Processes: Tracing the Dynamic Components of Power," *Current Anthropology* 38, no. 5 (1997): 711–739.
8. Mills begins *The Power Elite* with the following passage: "The powers of ordinary men are circumscribed by the everyday worlds in which they live, yet even in these rounds of job, family, and neighborhood they often seem driven by forces they can neither understand nor govern. 'Great changes' are beyond their control, but affect their conduct and outlook none the less. The very framework of modern society confines them to projects not their own, but from every side, such changes now press upon the men and women of the mass society, who accordingly feel that they are without purpose in an epoch in which they are without power. But not all men are in this sense ordinary. As the means of information and of power are centralized, some men come to occupy positions in American society from which they can look down upon, so to speak, and by their decisions mightily affect, the everyday worlds of ordinary men and women." Later, Mills goes on to more precisely define the group he is analyzing in the following terms: "By the power elite, we refer to those political, economic, and military circles which as an intricate set of overlapping cliques share decisions having at least national consequences. In so far as national events are decided, the power elite are those who

decide them." See C. Wright Mills, *The Power Elite* (New York: Oxford University Press, 1972 [1956]).
9. Peter Burke, *The French Historical Revolution: The Annales School, 1929–1989*, (Cambridge: Polity Press, 1990).
10. Nader, "Controlling Processes."
11. Anthony Giddens, *Central Problems in Social Theory: Action, Structure and Contradiction in Social Analysis* (Los Angeles: University of California Press, 1990).
12. Claude Grignon and Jean-Claude Passeron, *Le Savant et le Populaire : Misérabilisme et Populisme en Sociologie et en Litérature* (Paris: Gallimard, 1989).
13. James Ferguson and Akhil Gupta, "Spatializing States: Toward an Ethnography of Neoliberal Governmentality," *American Ethnologist* 29, no. 4 (2002): 983. See also Simon Coleman and Peter Collins (eds.): *Locating the Field: Space, Place and Context in Anthropology* (Oxford: Berg, 2006).
14. This sentence is intentionally awkward. I wish to underscore how terms represent the greater part of what we (and they) have to work with within IOs, rendering an approach that we might label "the social life of terms" perspective virtually inescapable. The word "Meeting," for example, properly takes a capital letter here, as "Meetings" are one of the things the ILO is organized and authorized to do. To understand the particular ways in which IOs are "up," we must pay great attention to the creation of acronyms, circulation of phrases, and selective institutional hardening—or "coining"—of terms. See Barbara Czarniawska et al., *Global Ideas: How Ideas, Objects, and Practices Travel in the Global Economy* (Malmö: Liber, 2005).
15. Several anthropologists have undertaken fieldwork and document-based research more or less directly on IOs, but no body of positions has yet emerged from these various studies. See generally Birgit Müller (ed.), *The Gloss of Harmony. The Politics of Policy-Making in Multilateral Organisations* (London: Pluto Press, 2013). On the World Bank, see Susan George and Fabrizio Sabelli, *Faith and Credit: The World Bank's Secular Empire* (London: Penguin Books, 1994); Scott Guggenheim, "Crises and Contradictions: Understanding the Origins of a Community Development Project in Indonesia," in *The Search for Empowerment: Social Capital as Idea and Practice at the World Bank*, ed. Arthur Bebbington et al. (Kumarian Press, 2006); David Mosse, "Anthropologists at Work at the World Bank: An Institutional Ethnography," in *Terms of Reference: The Anthropology of Expert Knowledge and Professionals in International Development*, ed. David Mosse (Oxford: Berghahn Books, 2008). On the UN Working Group on Indigenous Peoples, see Andrea Muehlebach, "'Making Place' at the United Nations: Indigenous Cultural Politics at the UN Working Group on Indigenous Populations," *Cultural Anthropology* 16, no. 3 (2001): 415–448; Irène Bellier, "Dernières nouvelles du Groupe de travail sur le projet de Déclaration des droits des peuples autochtones à l'ONU," *Recherches amérindiennes au Québec* 33, no. 3 (2003): 93–99. On the UNHCR, see Liisa H. Malkki, "Citizens of Humanity: Internationalism and the Imagined Community of Nations," *Diaspora* 3, no. 1 (1994): 41–68; Marion Fresia, "Une élite transnationale: la fabrique d'une identité professionnelle chez les fonctionnaires du Haut Commissariat aux réfugiés", *Revue Européenne des Migrations internationales* 25, no. 3 (2010). On the UN Global Compact, see Christina Garsten, "The United Nations—Soft and Hard: Regulating Social Accountability for Global Business," in *Organizing Transnational Accountability*, ed. Magnus Boström and Christina Garsten (Edward Elgar Publishing, 2008). On the ILO, see Phillipe Geslin and Ellen Hertz, "Public International Indigenes," in *Making Things Public: Atmospheres of Democracy*, ed. Bruno Latour and Peter Weibel (Cambridge, MA: MIT Press, 2008). On the World Intellectual Property Organization, see Stefan Groth, *Negotiating Tradition:*

The Pragmatics of International Deliberations on Cultural Property (Göttingen: Universitätsverlag Göttingen (Göttingen Studies in Cultural Property), vol. 4 (2012).
16. This quote is taken from the ILO Constitution. This and other basic information on the ILO is available at http://www.ilo.org.
17. For the full inventory and texts of ILO Conventions and Recommendations, see http://www.ilo.org/ilolex. Other areas of activity include technical cooperation, dissemination of "best practices," and research and publications in the areas of vocational training, employment policy and law, working conditions and health, social security, and labor statistics.
18. We will return to this very problematic assertion below; for our purposes here, let us simply retain that it is not entirely false.
19. See http://www.ilo.org/public/english/dialogue/sector/techmeet/tmiti07/index.htm.
20. International Labour Organization, "The Production of Electronic Components for the IT Industries: Changing Labour Force Requirements in a Global Economy," (Geneva: International Labour Office, 2007), http://www.ilo.org/public/english/dialogue/sector/techmeet/tmiti07/report.pdf.
21. See http://goodelectronics.org, the website of a well-known international coalition of NGOs active in this area.
22. International Labour Organization, "Production of Electronic Components," 6.
23. Ibid., 7.
24. Mills, *The Power Elite*, 363.
25. International Labour Organization, "Note on the Proceedings: Tripartite Meeting on the Production of Electronic Components for the ITC Industries: Changing Labour Force Requirements in a Global Economy," (Geneva: International Labour Office, 2007), http://www.ilo.org/public/english/dialogue/sector/.
26. Ibid., 10.
27. Ibid., 11.
28. The EICC (Electronic Industry Code of Conduct) initiative unites more than eighty brand-name and contract manufacturers committed to adopting common standards in the areas of labor, health and safety, the environment, management systems, and ethics (see http://www.eicc.info/). GeSI (the Global e-Sustainability Initiative) is currently composed of more than thirty companies in the IT sector working to promote sustainable development through activities in the areas of supply chains, climate change, accountability, e-waste, materiality, and sustainability (see http://www.gesi.org).
29. International Labour Organization, "Notes on the Proceedings," 16, 17.
30. International Labour Organization, "Report on the Committee on Sectoral and Technical Meetings and Related Issues," (Geneva: International Labour Office, 2007), http://www.ilo.org/wcmsp5/groups/public/—ed_norm/—relconf/documents/meetingdocument/wcms_087418.pdf.
31. Ibid., 9.

Part II

Studying Environment and Subsistence

Chapter 4

ON DISPOSSESSION

The Work of Studying Up, Down, and Sideways in
Guatemala's Indigenous Land Rights Movements

—⊗⊗⊗—

Liza Grandia

Dispossession: *The expulsion of someone (such as a tenant) from the possession of land by process of law.*

—thefreedictionary.com

In late 2009, director James Cameron released *Avatar*, which eventually became the highest-grossing film of all time. It is set in the year 2154 on the ecologically exquisite planet of Pandora, where the RDA corporation has established a small outpost. The atmosphere is inhospitable to humans, but Pandora is home to the Na'vi, ethereally blue sentient beings living in close harmony with nature. RDA's mission is to extract a mineral ironically called "unobtanium," worth $20 million per ounce. To explore the planet, RDA contracts with a private security force called Sec-Ops and a scientist, Dr. Grace Augustine (played by Sigourney Weaver), who is familiar with the language and customs of the Na'vi. Conducting her scientific research through a human-hybrid body called an "avatar," Grace reluctantly allows ex-marine Jake Sully to take the place of his deceased twin as her research assistant. Once Sully's avatar discovers that the Na'vi would never voluntarily relocate from their ancestral lands, under which the main deposit of unobtanium lies, the brutal Sec-Ops commander, Colonel Miles Quaritch, persuades the RDA company administrator to destroy the Na'vi's home, including their most sacred Tree of Souls. Having fallen in love with the

---

Notes for this chapter begin on page 104.

Na'vi princess Neytiri, Sully decides to help the Na'vi defend their homeland through guerrilla warfare against Colonel Quaritch.

While some U.S. viewers embraced *Avatar* for its thinly veiled critique of private security operations such as Blackwater in Iraq, others rightly criticized the film for its simplistic, "white messiah" narrative of native peoples appealing to a white man to rescue them from outsiders. The film nevertheless provoked an unusual level of mainstream media attention to the dispossession of native peoples across our own planetary biosphere. From the Ecuadorian Amazon to the Navajo Nation, indigenous leaders cleverly leveraged the film to raise the media profile of ongoing campaigns against resource extraction on their homelands. Canadian First Nations convinced James Cameron to join them in a campaign to stop the mining of coal tar sands in their territory. Even Palestinian activists dressed in Na'vi costumes to attract attention to a demonstration. Attending the cinema for only the third time in his life to view *Avatar*, Bolivia's first indigenous president, Evo Morales, publicly praised the film as a "profound example of resistance to capitalism and the struggle for the defense of nature." Perhaps for the same reason, the Chinese government curtailed its distribution.

As an anthropologist, I too saw *Avatar* as a way to draw attention to my years of work as an anthropological ally of Q'eqchi' Maya resistance against land dispossession—a role I hope I have conducted less paternalistically than Dr. Grace Augustine. Like the Na'vi, Q'eqchi' people have had the repeated bad luck of living in places coveted by outsiders. Displaced multiple times over the colonial, liberal, developmentalist, and neoliberal periods, Q'eqchi' people have nonetheless claimed new lands with a tenacious resistance no less epic than *Avatar's* plotline. Although epidemics reduced the Q'eqchi' population to just a few thousand people after the Spanish invasion of Mesoamerica, their numbers have rebounded to more than a million people today. Once forcibly relocated during the colonial period to fifteen Spanish towns in a mountainous region of North-Central Guatemala, through adaptive migration Q'eqchi' people have regained much of their original territory stretching from Chiapas to the coasts of Belize. Yet in another tragically short span of little more than a decade, they have lost more than half their farmlands, largely as a consequence of an ill-conceived World Bank land-titling project that I critiqued in my dissertation and first two books (see Map 1).

While Q'eqchi' peoples have demonstrated remarkable resilience over the last five hundred years, the spectacular scale and pace of land grabbing occurring now in northern Guatemala, and indeed across much of the Americas and large swaths of Africa and Asian farmlands, is worrisome.

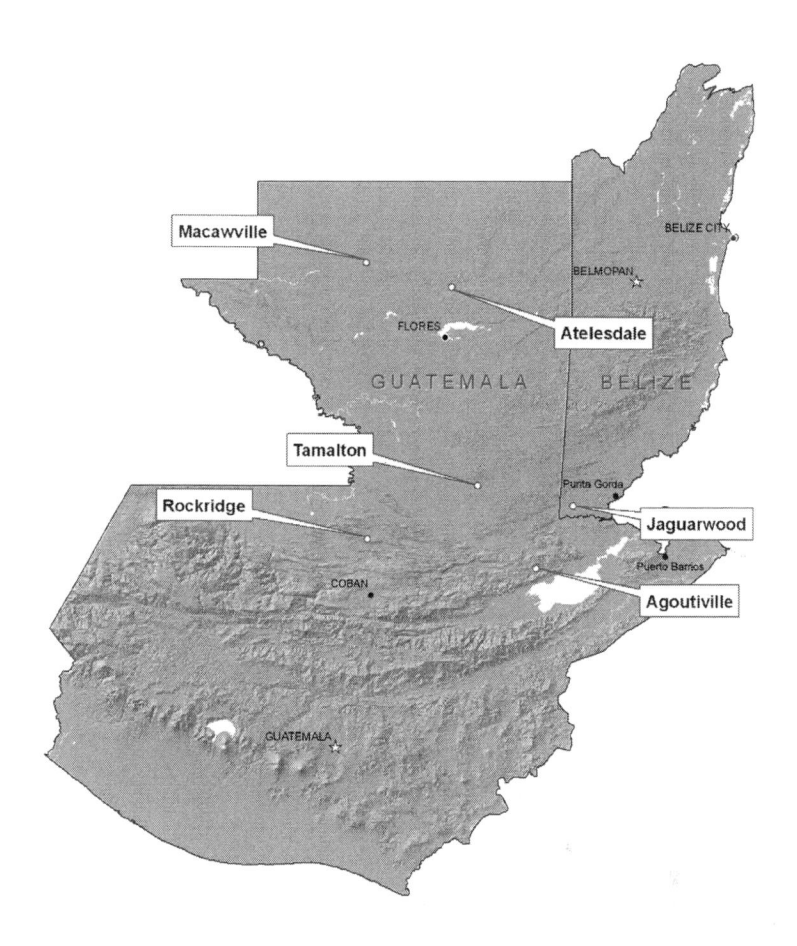

Map 1. Approximate field site locations. *Source:* Jason Arnold and Daniel Irwin, NASA/SERVIR 2010.

The Land Matrix, an independent monitoring initiative, conservatively estimates that since 2000, transnational corporations, elites, and states like China and Saudi Arabia have made land deals worldwide for at least 35 million hectares of arable farmland. Development projects displace another fifteen million or more annually.[1] It is little wonder that *Avatar's* narrative has resonated with so many indigenous groups worldwide.

Lest the reader dismiss this chapter as yet another anthropological tale of a beleaguered indigenous group, my central argument is that "what goes around comes around"—a concept succinctly expressed in the Q'eqchi' Mayan language with the elegant verb *q'oq'onk*. To explore the potential boomerang effect of the neoliberalization of land and other aspects of life, later in the chapter I turn to five important academic voices about global economic transformations: Michael Hardt and Antonio Negri on "Empire," David Harvey on "The New Imperialism," and Ugo Mattei and Laura Nader on "Plunder." In different ways, these authors challenge us to consider how the perils of progress on the periphery for peoples such as the Q'eqchi may be prelude to intensified corporate profiteering at the expense of our own lives and livelihoods at home, as exemplified by the 2010 British Petroleum (BP) oil spill.

Five Centuries of Plunder

Renowned in the sixteenth century as one of the few indigenous groups to successfully resist Spanish military conquest, the Q'eqchi' Maya were eventually "pacified" in 1547 by Bartolomé de las Casas, a Catholic priest and proto-human rights advocate who convinced Charles V to allow him to experiment with a new method of religious conquest in what would become northern Guatemala. After nominally converting Q'eqchi' leaders to Christianity, his Dominican order administered Q'eqchi' lands in the name of the Spanish Crown for two centuries. In this first dispossession, Q'eqchi' people lost their right to cultivate land except as tribute-paying subjects of the Catholic Church. They also lost the opportunity to initiate property claims in the colonial land registries as other highland Maya groups did to protect their communal lands against the expansion of Spanish plantations known as "haciendas."

For a short period after Guatemala's independence from Spain in 1821, Q'eqchi' people nonetheless regained de facto control of their village farmlands. Some even experimentally cultivated coffee, an export crop that proved unusually suited to their highland cloud forests. However, the economic "liberals" who gained political dominance in Guatemala by the late nineteenth century argued that large coffee plantations managed by Europeans and North Americans for export would bring greater "progress" to the country than Guatemalan smallholder agriculture. Through a series of laws passed in the late 1870s, the Guatemalan state seized untitled indigenous territories (reclassified as "baldíos" or wastelands) in order to award vast land concessions to foreign colonists and companies, including the United Fruit Company. By the end of the nineteenth century, Q'eqchi' communities had again lost most of their territory to foreigners. Vagrancy and other coercive laws compelled them to work as serfs and sharecroppers on these same plantations.

Risking corporal and other harsh punishments, many nevertheless fled plantation bondage by fleeing northward into the lowland forests of Petén. Depopulated by a colonial-period Spanish genocide of neighboring Maya groups, this hinterland provided Q'eqchi' people with what Mexican anthropologist Aguirre-Beltrán termed a "region of refuge."[2] Covering nearly a third of Guatemala's area, the department of Petén had a population of less than 5,000 before 1950. Dense tropical forest covered more than 90 percent of it, concealing dozens of archaeological sites, such as the ancient Maya city of Tikal. The Petén's surviving inhabitants practiced small-scale subsistence agriculture and earned cash from the harvesting of timber and non-timber products, such as a tree resin used to make chewing gum, palm fronds for export to floral companies, and allspice berries. Countless Q'eqchi' immigrants to Petén told me that after working as coffee laborers or sharecroppers with plots smaller than a couple of acres, these lush but sparsely populated tropical forests seemed like "paradise." Their pioneer optimism is reflected in the many Biblical names they chose for their new lowland villages, like La Nueva Eden (New Eden) or simply La Gloria (Heaven).

Other Q'eqchi' people migrated back into what is now the Toledo District of southern Belize. With little interference from the British colonial government, these Belizean Q'eqchi' villages kept their customary land governance systems relatively intact. Whereas Guatemalan Q'eqchi' agricultural practices have been degraded by decades of sharecropping rules that promoted monocropping, Belizean Q'eqchi' communities still manage extraordinarily diverse, ecologically balanced agro-forestry systems, as I have documented in publications and court testimony to help these communities defend their community lands from government and corporate incursion.[3]

In this socially and ecologically beneficial land management system, Q'eqchi' families customarily retain long-term usufruct of their own fallowed fields but share access to forest areas, sacred sites, and village infrastructure. Although this family farmland might seem to resemble private property, no one may sell an agricultural plot without the entire village's approval. Likewise, newcomers must obtain the village's consent to settle there and claim land. The fields of a retired or deceased Q'eqchi' farmer usually return to the village common for the use of a younger family. The community might also assign lands closest to the village center to its most vulnerable members, such as women-headed households or elderly and disabled farmers. By allowing villagers to claim only as much land as they could actively use, this system tended to reinforce socioeconomic equity and ethics of mutual aid and labor exchange.

Setting up hearth and homesteads in these dense and often swampy lowland Maya forests was not easy, but Q'eqchi' pioneers proved highly successful migrants for various cultural reasons (e.g., strong but not binding kinship systems, flexible spiritual beliefs, and remarkable egalitarian leadership structures). Little by little, they transformed Petén's open-access forests into managed commons and expanded their territory almost threefold over the centuries. Migratory success may also have been their Achilles' heel. Believing they would be able to claim land further on the frontier, many Q'eqchi' settlers began to sell the lowland homesteads they worked hard to claim, only to discover that the remaining "free" land in Guatemala was turned into protected areas for biodiversity conservation during the 1990s or claimed by large landholders.

Determined to remain farmers and cultivate maize crops they consider sacred, Q'eqchi' people are now responsible for the highest rates of private land occupations and the most numerous invasions of protected areas of any ethnic group in Guatemala. With thinly veiled racism, government and NGO officials routinely characterize Q'eqchi' as environmentally destructive, calling them derogatory names such as "leaf cutter ants," "termites," or "nomads." Yet, compared to other ethnic groups, Q'eqchi' people have had to contend with a disproportionate conservation burden in their territory.[4] Constituting less than one-tenth of Guatemala's population, Q'eqchi' people are surrounded by one-fourth (by number) and one-fifth (by area) of Guatemala's parks. Some Q'eqchi' communities were already legally settled in these buffer zones before parks were established in the 1990s, but others "invaded" after it became illegal to settle there, thereby acquiring a negative reputation for environmental conflict. Many migrated into parks after the end of Guatemala's civil war in 1996 in response to false rumors spread among indigenous communities that the Peace Accords authorized them to claim land anywhere, regardless of its conservation status.

With Guatemala's northernmost region now protected as the 1.6 million hectare Maya Biosphere Reserve, there is no longer a northern frontier into which to flee. Nor are there many opportunities to return to their highland places of origin. Aside from illegal migration to the United States or to urban slums, the only recourse for landless Q'eqchi' farmers is to invade private properties. The choice between confronting cattle guards armed with AK-47s or poorly paid, unmotivated, unarmed park rangers seems obvious.[5]

To help biodiversity conservationists prevent invasions of Petén's extensive protected areas by the rural poor, the World Bank loaned the Guatemalan government $31 million to improve and "order" what they perceived as a chaotic land system in Petén. Implemented between 1998 and 2007, this cadastre and land titling project offered Q'eqchi' farmers and other smallholders living in Petén the chance to title their frontier land claims as private parcels. Although they might have preferred communal titles to support customary land management, Q'eqchi' people initially cooperated with the project, perceiving private titling to be the most expeditious path to tenure security in Guatemala's recent postwar context.

Given their unique colonial history, Q'eqchi' people have little to no experience with private land ownership or the intricate legal procedures required by Guatemalan property inheritance law. In fact, the concept of "owning" land cannot be directly expressed in the language, as I learned when I first began my dissertation research in 2002. My Q'eqchi' language skills were then still rudimentary and, based on a direct translation from my Spanish-Q'eqchi' dictionary, I started to ask farmers "Do you have any land (*Ma wan laa ch'och'*)?" I would repeat the question, but still no one seemed to understand. Don Manuel Xuc, a catechist from Agoutiville, later explained to me that land is sacred and cannot be owned: "*Chiru li ch'och' noqo wa. Chiru yooko chi waak* (By the land, we eat. By it, we are living)." Eventually I corrected my question using a Spanish-derived word, *parseel* (from "parcel"), to approximate the idea of private property. This elicited animated tales of dispossession.

With tragically repetitive stories, Q'eqchi' farmers explained how the geometric plots allotted to them provide insufficient access to the variety of ecological niches needed to subsist in this harsh tropical landscape. Many farmers were assigned a square lot of marshy land or a rectangle of rocky hills. While quadrangular parcels plots might look neat on a survey map (what is known as a "cadastre" in Guatemala), as Sebastian Tiul explained, through the luck of the draw, "You might get some broken ridges or swamp and there would not be enough fertile land to lay fallow and the land will harden." He also thought it challenging to plant permanent crops on a single square parcel because of the risk of fire spreading from cornfields to fruit orchards. Hundreds of farming families who received substandard plots willingly sold them for abysmal prices to the first wave of land speculators in the hopes of claiming another parcel further north that would be more conducive to swidden agriculture. In other instances, small landholders were so bewildered by the complex legal steps required to register their parcels with the government and later bequeath them to the next generation that many parents decided to avoid family conflicts by selling.

Increasingly, however, land sales are more coercive than voluntary. In addition to the ranchers who have long coveted their lands, medleys of ex–military officers, agribusiness companies (especially African palm planters), narco-traffickers, transnational nickel mining companies, and other investors who covet Q'eqchi' land are now forcibly dispossessing Q'eqchi' peasants of their farms. During Guatemala's civil war (1960–1996), the physically powerful, expansive nature of free-range cattle ranching allowed elites to claim large plantations with low overhead costs until opportunities for alternative investments arose. Soon into the postwar period, cattle ranchers began converting their pastures to African palm or even reforesting them to capture carbon credits. Many new investors are simultaneously purchasing and often stealing Q'eqchi' land for similar purposes. Various informants report that pistol-toting intermediaries convince Q'eqchi' farmers to relinquish newly titled parcels with thinly veiled threats like: "*You* can sell to me now or *your widow* will sell to me later."

The wealthy also are buying land simply for its speculative value in anticipation of highways and other economic infrastructure planned under the Mesoamerican Project (formerly, the Puebla to Panamá Plan), a multibillion dollar regional initiative to make Central America and southern Mexico more attractive to corporate investors through the construction of highways, electric grids, hydroelectric dams, and other big development projects, as well as administrative and legislative reforms to "harmonize" border crossing procedures and regional regulations.[6] Under these pressures, thousands of Q'eqchi' farmers have sold their parcels to outsiders for paltry sums. Without urban and professional connections to move into off-farm employment, most of the families that sold now lack stable means to grow or acquire food. As more than one Q'eqchi' villager remarked to me, "cash is like water"; it disappears before one realizes it is gone.

The bi-ethnic (Q'eqchi' and mixed Spanish background, known in Guatemala as "Ladino") village of Atelesdale, located in the Maya Biosphere Reserve, exemplifies the dispossession suffered after a state-sponsored land survey. Within two years of receiving permanency rights from the national park service and GPS-measured blueprints of their parcels, almost a quarter of residents sold their holdings to cattle ranchers—in some cases, for prices less than one-fifth of 1 percent of the real value of comparable parcels south of the reserve. More worrisome is that many more would consider selling if offered even a slightly larger fraction of the land's worth. In door-to-door interviews with all 175 Q'eqchi' village households in Atelesdale in 2003, I found that of 109 (61 percent) who had parcels, only 55 would not sell. The rest had already sold (13), might sell (13), or would definitely sell (14).[7]

I also learned that many sellers who had attempted to become city residents had moved back to the village once the land sale cash was exhausted, because they could not pay for rent, firewood, water, and food on an urban day laborer's salary. As Atelesdale farmer Vicente Ax lamented, "Although I used to work in construction in the city, my wife prefers the country. She doesn't want to have to buy corn this week and then buy some more next week. She likes having a full corn bin in the house, so she can grab what she needs for making tortillas, feeding the animals, whatever. Plus we have firewood nearby." Many landless families who had moved back to the village were paying rents of $45/hectare to the new ranch owners for small parcels from which they might hope to earn only $110/hectare for a typical corn harvest.

The story was virtually the same in all five Q'eqchi' villages in which I lived during twenty months of fieldwork between 2002 and 2004 and across another forty-six communities my research team surveyed in 2011. In Agoutiville, for instance, over 70 percent of farmers had sold their parcels within ten years of the government encouraging them to abandon their customary communal management and divide their lands into private plots. Wealthy outsiders began to arrive via a new dirt road. Parcel by parcel, they bought up the best farmland, especially fertile areas alongside the river and convenient parcels next to the road and near the village. Only a few farmers, like Don Nicolas, managed to keep less desirable plots located two or more hours by foot from the village. He still has five and a half hectares of land and a horse for transporting crops, which saves him the daily $3.25 fee to rent a beast of burden. Squeezed into his small plot are various foods for his family, some pasture for his horse, and an area fallowed in green mulch. Though he knows something about raising vegetables that could be marketed in town, transportation remains an irresolvable obstacle to further crop diversification. Cattle ranchers have already purchased all the irrigable land near the river and closed off most of the farmers' footpaths to their farms with barbed-wire fences. Don Nicolas can reach his own parcel only via a treacherous two-hour walk over a mountain—a journey ill suited to carrying heavy, perishable produce. Though his children are the brightest pupils in the village, Nicolas wonders how he will ever raise enough money to pay their tuition and expenses for middle and high school. With more cattle barons entering the village each year, Nicolas's sons will instead likely become poorly paid cowboys and ranch hands. Nicolas's neighbor Sebastian Yaxcal described these pressures with a prophetic declaration: "We're all caged up (*Estamos enjaulados*)."

Having been involved with environmental organizations in northern Petén since 1993, for my dissertation research[8] I originally intended to study migration patterns and communities' relationship with national parks. In hearing comments such as Sebastian Yaxcal's about the spectacular process of enclosure underway, I quickly learned that what was of most concern to Q'eqchi' communities were more pressing issues surrounding land ownership, cattle and oil palm plantation encroachment, and the World Bank land administration project. As Laura Nader once asked in her revolutionary 1969 essay, "Up the Anthropologist":

> How has it come to be, we might ask, that anthropologists are more interested in why peasants don't change than why the auto industry doesn't innovate, or why the Pentagon or universities cannot be more organizationally creative? The conservatism of such major institutions and bureaucratic organizations probably has wider implications for the species and for theories of change than does the conservatism of the peasantry.[9]

Hence, rather than just asking why Q'eqchi' communities were stubbornly squatting in national parks, I realized I also needed to ask why international donors so stubbornly continued to promote projects that were obviously leading to smallholder land dispossession. This led me to "study up" to the World Bank.

Banking Land

Territorial administration was once considered the sacrosanct domain of nation-states. Even the International Fund's most aggressive structural adjustment programs in the 1980s left land policy untouched. Deterred by indigenous and environmental protests against big development projects like dams and highways in the 1990s, the World Bank quietly began to explore projects in the more discreet but no less consequential realm of agrarian policy and law. As neoliberal ideology acquired greater momentum, key World Bank economists like Klaus Deininger began to publish a series of policy papers arguing that state-led land reform was outmoded and that land distribution could be more efficiently managed by the invisible hand of the market, with governments becoming passive agents mediating between "willing sellers" and "willing buyers."[10]

The World Bank experimented with different names for this initiative, first calling it "market-assisted agrarian reform," then "land administration," and more recently "land governance." For pilot projects, the World Bank first targeted countries with some of the most inequitable agrarian regimes in the world: Colombia, Brazil, South Africa, and Guatemala, where less than 2 percent of the population has consistently owned more than two-thirds of the country's arable land. Projects were to focus on establishing tenure security for the land people already claimed, but notably not on helping the poor secure *more* land.[11]

The first step in justifying these land projects was to portray local land administration in a negative light. In so doing, project designers effectively substituted the old colonial justification for land seizures, *terra nullius* (imagining lands were empty), with a neocolonial justification of *lex nullius* (imagining places lacked the rule of law).[12] World Bank planning documents derided state systems as legally "insecure," "supply-driven," "conflictive," "inefficient," or "corrupt." Of course, many countries do have outmoded land administration systems. In Guatemala, people joke that they need land with three floors because there are so many conflicts among multiple parties claiming the same parcel. However, these same land conflicts and "inefficiencies" also served to protect local people from external land grabs, as the force of possession and occupancy could often override paper transactions.

Beyond undermining states' fundamental power to administer their own territories, another insidious aspect of these early land administration projects was the seemingly innocuous alignment of diverse land systems to a singular registry model. For foreigners, purchasing or leasing land was once one of the most opaque, complicated business transactions imaginable, typically requiring intermediaries, bribes, and other complex legal maneuvers. Standardization of land administration, however, does away with the red tape that once limited corporations' and wealthy investors' ability to purchase large tracts of land for mechanized agriculture. Many Third World countries, already weakened by structural adjustment programs, have thus become targets of substantial land grabs by big agribusiness.

More than any other institution on earth, the World Bank understands how the power of an idea can set in motion profound institutional and legal transformations far beyond the project cycle.[13] Bank project managers soon discovered they could enhance their institutional impact on agrarian policy by financing small field projects in tandem with efforts to reform and standardize national land laws. As land activist Héctor Mondragón points out, the World Bank's project in Colombia affected very few families directly, but it had far-reaching impacts on national agrarian policy.[14] This clearly was also the strategy for Guatemala. Selecting the northernmost department of Petén for the first phase of the land administration project (1997–2002), the World Bank worked simultaneously to shape the National Cadastre Law of 2005 largely according to methodologies developed through land titling in Q'eqchi' territory.

Initially, Guatemala's peasant organizations and leftist activists supported the World Bank's efforts for land reform and passage of the cadastre law. In a country where, twenty years ago, people risked execution by death squad for visiting the land archive or publicly discussing land reform, peasant rights organizations hoped that greater administrative transparency would provide them with historical information to resolve long-standing conflicts with large landholders. However, project implementation soon shifted from the World Bank's stated social goal of resolving land conflicts to a more narrow set of technical indicators (raw numbers of parcels measured and registered). Land project employees found it more expedient, and perhaps personally safer, to focus on the accuracy of GPS coordinates instead of the fairness of the allotment process. As peasant leader Rigoberto Tec commented to me recently on Skype, he and his comrades had imagined the new land institutions would be "discovery entities" to document land grabs initiated by military officers and other elites during the civil war, but to his dismay, the process became "technified" and "presentist," freezing land distribution as it was. "It's dispossession through the political system now," Rigoberto lamented.

To give a quantitative example of the injustice of titling land "as is," in a data set I collected of soil studies of 600 parcels legalized in Petén between 1999–2003, the average size allotted to Ladinos was 74.2 hectares versus just 44.2 hectares for Q'eqchi' parcels. A young Q'eqchi' farmer, Floricelda Mo, vividly remembered these gross historical inequities, explaining, "In San Luis, the rich people—the ones that know the system—got their parcels first and when everything was almost distributed, we Q'eqchi' people received the remainder. So it was mostly the ranchers and the southerners (*sureños*) who got land. Since a Q'eqchi' person doesn't know how to enjoy [private] land, we can be easily tricked" (field notes 2003).

Ignoring or perhaps just oblivious to these inequities, the World Bank project designers who traveled to Guatemala in the early 1990s considered Petén an ideal place for a pilot land program because they wrongly presumed that (1) it would have fewer boundary conflicts than other places, (2) no indigenous groups would claim communal lands, and (3) private land titling would generate collateral environmental benefits. The World Bank's hypothesis was that by finishing the frontier titling process and eliminating informal land markets, the project would slow the expansion of slash-and-burn agriculture into Petén's protected areas by inspiring settlers to seek credit and invest in more sustainable sedentary agriculture, leading also to greater economic development. Most of these a priori assumptions proved unfounded. Petén had at least as many latent land conflicts as other areas of the country. Most Q'eqchi' villages also had, unbeknownst to state authorities, maintained communal management of certain forests and sacred places, whose continued privatization and expropriation constitutes a serious violation of World Bank policies toward indigenous people. Finally, as my research has shown, the project led to rampant land speculation and dispossession that accelerated rather than diminished invasions of protected areas.[15]

Because many rural property sales are never documented in the land registry, exact numbers are hard to calculate. From observation and interviews with dozens of people involved with the project, however, I estimated in 2006 that a quarter of parcels were sold immediately after the project passed through to survey them. By 2011, a survey of 46 representative communities across Petén documented that almost half had sold.[16] Without associated projects for integrated agrarian development (e.g., feeder road access for transporting crops to market, irrigation systems, storage facilities to minimize post-harvest losses, secure markets for new crops, and agricultural extension services), few farmers have risked applying for credit to intensify or improve their production. Bureaucratic inefficiencies within the design of the project rendered land technicians barely able to complete 3 percent of the original titling goal in Petén's rural areas. Moreover, absent a plan to update the land registry for inheritance transactions or land sales (whether voluntary or illicit), many of the parcels measured by the project are uselessly outdated due to a lack of inter-institutional coordination between the cadastre and registry offices.

The World Bank's strategic choice to test its new approach to land administration in the most remote region of Guatemala meant problems with the project could be contained or dismissed as peculiar to this lowland frontier. Had the World Bank chosen a location near the capital or in the densely settled Western highlands, it likely would have faced extensive social protest about the denial of communal tenure for indigenous lands, as well as heightened scrutiny from reporters, academics, and Guatemalan public servants. As it was, the government agreed to accept another $62 million World Bank loan in December 2007 to expand the project to six other departments, including all the rest of the Q'eqchi' territory in Alta Verapaz and Izabal—*without ever having evaluated the Petén project*. Hence, although even ex-directors of the Petén project now admit with dismay that their efforts led to rampant land speculation, very few of the lessons learned (whether social, environmental, or administrative) are informing the second, ongoing World Bank project just south of Petén. Having fired most of the original Petén project staff, those in the higher echelons of power in Guatemala City consider the first phase an unqualified success and may even be negotiating with the World Bank for a third and fourth loan to expand this cadastral process to the entire country.

Empire, Neoliberalism, and Plunder

The plight of Q'eqchi' and other Maya peoples in Guatemala is, unfortunately, not unique. Their dispossession exemplifies a worldwide surge of accumulation by global elites. Some academics describe this trend as a resurgence of "empire" or "accumulation by dispossession," while others more candidly portray it as "plunder."

In their starkly titled book *Empire*, Antonio Negri and Michael Hardt argue that humanity is passing through a critical transition from classical imperialism (or empire with a lowercase "e") based on the power of nation-states to a postmodern system of de-centered international hegemony that they call Empire (with a capital "E").[17] This new, sprawling form of Empire combines economic, political, and cultural power into something akin to what other scholars loosely term "globalization." Sovereignty and political hegemony are no longer based on the power of nation-states and their interests, they argue, but upon a multinational class-based rule by economic elites through global institutions such as the World Bank, the G8, NATO, and the IMF. The enemies of this finely tuned system can no longer be classified by place or ethnicity: now they are anyone who threatens the engine of economic growth—for instance, Q'eqchi' peasants who invade private plantations or ecotourism parks to pursue subsistence agriculture.

Following a Gramscian perspective on power, Hardt and Negri theorize that Empire is legitimated via social communication as much as force. Empire, they note, is bathed in blood but speaks of peace. With similar rhetorical disjunction, the World Bank's highly paid multicultural workforce conducts regular inspections or "mission trips" to document project advances, yet fails to speak to civil society or peasant leaders who might report a different reality. They write cookie-cutter reports with sophisticated cost-benefit analyses based on faulty data. Although on paper the World Bank now funds more "social communication" efforts in land project implementation, this is more a top-down process of manufacturing consent than veritable democratic consultation. To give but one example of the superficial preparation of the second land administration loan in 2006, World Bank managers fulfilled their "indigenous participation" protocols by convening six half-day workshops with Maya leaders—hardly time for real citizen input into an initiative that will radically transform the entire country's territorial administration. Recognizing that this was not a serious consultative process, some Maya leaders, in fact, refused to comment, as documented by workshop transcripts leaked to me.

Yet such spectacles of inclusion may also be Empire's greatest weakness. Just as anti-colonial leaders like Haiti's Toussaint L'ouverture used the rhetoric of the French Revolution to lead his liberation struggles against France, Hardt and Negri emphasize the utopian potential of increasing global interaction among "the multitude" and the transformation of transnational alliances of people no longer bound by identities tied exclusively to nation-states into a kind of postmodern proletariat that rebels by necessity against the geographically expansive and socially penetrative power of Empire.

In *The New Imperialism*, geographer David Harvey makes a similar intellectual argument that distinguishes between an older imperialism operating via direct territorial control and contemporary capitalist exploitation operating through global financial markets.[18] To translate Harvey's argument into anthropological terms, dispossession can be a "synchronic" spatial process that weaves new geographic areas into the orbits of capitalism (classic imperialism), or a "diachronic" temporal process that deepens people's dependence on wages and undermines their ability to live and enjoy life outside the market (Empire). As a geographer attuned to space and place, he notes that these two processes tend to be most dramatic in frontiers because the brutal facts of dispossession remain unknown to those in the center.

For Harvey, the most threatening institutional tool of global capitalism is incremental privatization—the transfer of property from the public realm to private ownership—usually at subsidized prices far below what these goods, spaces, places, and institutions are worth. Many refer to this process as "neoliberalism," which Harvey defines elsewhere as "a theory of political economic practices that proposes that human well-being can best be advanced by liberating individual entrepreneurial freedoms and skills within an institutional framework characterized by strong private property rights, free markets, and free trade."[19] If markets do not yet exist (for water, education, health care, social security, or land administration), then according to neoliberal logic, states must help facilitate their creation but relinquish regulatory power over their long-term operations. In this spirit, the Guatemalan state willingly borrowed more than $90 *million* from the World Bank to establish new land registration systems, but then reduced itself to absentee landlordism by relegating territorial distribution to the market.

Contrary to those social scientists who argued in the 1980s and 1990s that neoliberalism signaled the demise of state power, Harvey shows how states (or rather, government officials lured by profit and progress) continue to play a critical role in dispossession through deregulation or, worse, repression of their own citizens to protect private property and create space for the so-called free market. For example, shortly before police attacked Maya protesters during a 2005 conflict with the Glamis Gold mining company, Guatemala's former President Berger explained to CNN, "We have to protect the investors." Albeit fragmented by privatization (turned into "governments by contract," in Margaret Thatcher's words), states nonetheless continue to provide business elites with critical protection.

While Keynesian economics ("embedded liberalism") emphasized government leadership in protecting citizens' well-being, the new "Washington consensus" focuses on developing markets rather than humans. The devastating effects were perhaps more visible in the Third World, but privatization in the global North led to growing inequities exposed by the recent financial recession. Employing clever rhetoric that endowed privatization with almost religious virtue, Ronald Reagan and Margaret Thatcher replaced so-called "Big Government" with "McGovernment" by cutting taxes, liberalizing regulations, and busting unions. They ripped apart social safety nets painstakingly earned by previous generations, reopening domains that democratic societies had once decided should be protected from the market—education, health, social security, even the military—to corporate profiteering.[20]

Cognizant of this recent and potentially reversible political history, in their co-authored book, *Plunder: When the Rule of Law Is Illegal*, Laura Nader and Ugo Mattei refocus our attention on the juggernaut of rapidly expanding corporate power. Of the largest 100 economies worldwide, 53 are corporations; only 47 are nation-states.[21] Eighty-three of the 100 largest corporations operate with subsidiaries in nations judged by the United States to be tax havens, according to a January 2009 Government Accountability Office report. In the Cayman Islands, one mailing address alone houses 18,857 corporations. Having incrementally gained the legal standing of a person through a bizarre series of court cases dating back to the late 1800s, corporations are peculiar legal creatures that the courts continue to aid and abet. Like Hardt and Negri, Mattei and Nader weigh the dark side of the rule of law against its liberatory potential. In case after case, they show how corporate elites have justified Western legal expansion over the planet's resources through institutions like the World Bank by depicting non-Western forms of law as "lacking" or simply inefficient. Then, to legitimize new property claims, usurpers assert the civilizational superiority of legal systems that work to the invisible advantage of elites.

Mattei and Nader's arguments resonate strongly with how many Q'eqchi' activists have traced the roots of their agrarian dispossession. In a 2010 video conference about our campaign to persuade the World Bank to reopen Petén's land administration project to an external evaluation, Q'eqchi' leader Rigoberto Tec was outraged by two key illegalities of the new agrarian law, which ignores: (1) the government's willful lack of historical investigation into community claims against large holders, and (2) the vast acreage legally claimed by military officers through their government connections during the civil war. That morning he had returned from a meeting of hundreds of Q'eqchi' farming families evicted from their homesteads by an absentee landlord who sent legal papers through an intermediary. Despite having lived on the land for two decades, the people had never seen or heard of this person.

The forces of dispossession are increasingly remote and all the more difficult to hold accountable. Novelist and essayist Arundhati Roy quips that Rumpelstiltskin, the gnome who transforms straw into gold, has returned, now "metamorphosed into an accretion, a cabal, an assemblage, a malevolent, incorporeal, transnational multignome."[22] Rumpelstiltskin Inc., though no less ruthless today, has a shinier, happier face, scrubbed carefully by public relations managers in faraway cubicles. In Laura Nader's terminology, Q'eqchi' people are experiencing a transition from "face-to-face" plunder (as in the cattle economy) to "face-to faceless" plunder (by distant corporations). As global elites float ever higher through the clouds in private jets far removed from any contact with squalor, they remain blissfully unaware of acts their legal mercenaries commit far away.

To summarize: Hardt and Negri show that Empire is less about territory than about opening places up to markets. Harvey teaches us about the state's continued importance as facilitator of processes of dispossession through privatization. Finally, Mattei and Nader provide concrete suggestions about holding accountable corporations by critiquing the legal philosophy that professionalizes and legitimizes plunder.

Blowback

While dispossession is often seen as something that happens to exotic people who have the misfortune to live in peripheral places with coveted natural resources, exploitation often boomerangs back to its source. Indeed, the CIA has a special term, "blowback," to describe the unintended consequences or retaliation at home that can result from its geopolitical power manipulations—a prime example being the spectacular 9/11 attacks orchestrated by a former member of the CIA payroll, Osama bin Laden.[23] As Hannah Arendt observed, the building of empire abroad also brings tyranny at home.

Law may be the legitimizing channel of dispossession, but economic growth is typically the rationale. Outsider investors claim they can use a particular resource, such as land, more efficiently, creating more monetary value than those who have traditionally used the same resource for subsistence outside the market economy.[24] This argument is supported by political systems organized around reductive economic measurements such as the GNP or the NASDAQ that place little to no value on local lifeways, knowledge, and happiness — whether that be the value of having enough corn in the corn bin to make as many tortillas as one wants or the ability to fish along the sugar sands of the Gulf Coast.

Although dispossession is a continuous feature of corporate capitalism both home and abroad, resistance is often muted because, as Laura Nader has noted in her theory of legal drift, even the most radical processes of social transformation can pass unnoticed if they happen little by little. In the United States, for example, deregulation over both Democratic and Republican administrations alike gutted agencies like the Minerals Management Service (MMS), meant to oversee oil companies. As former White House Supervisor of Offshore Programs David Abraham detailed in a July 2010 *New York Times* op-ed, over the last two decades Congress repeatedly cut government royalties on deep-water wells to encourage more offshore drilling, simultaneously approving budgets that chopped regulatory staff by more than 15 percent between 2002 and 2008, despite internal MMS concerns about deep water drilling. This might be characterized as a "sea grab."

Though British Petroleum (BP) has tried to portray its 2010 Deepwater Horizon rig disaster as an anomaly, this accident was in the making amid at least a decade of relentless deregulation and consequent corporate disdain of basic precautionary measures. In fact, the entire industry has apparently forgotten an almost identical disaster, the 1979 Ixtoc spill, which spewed 140 million gallons over ten months into the Gulf of Mexico near Campeche. In their testimony of 15 June 2010 before Congress, executives from Exxon, Chevron, Conoco-Philips, Shell, and BP-America could only stare blankly when Rep. Ed Whitfield (R-Kentucky) questioned them about their knowledge of the Ixtoc spill. Apparently "top kill," "junk shot," containment dome, booms, burn-offs, and dispersants — all the aborted tricks BP tried to halt the Horizon disaster — had also all failed to contain the previous Ixtoc disaster.[25]

When historical ignorance and indifference so thoroughly numb citizen and government oversight of corporations, sometimes only a big crisis can wake them from the slumber of apathy. If BP's 2010 Gulf oil disaster had one welcome aspect, it was its vivid demonstration of the need for greater regulation of corporate activities, especially those of foreign oil companies.[26] Perhaps it may also free or "dispossess" North Americans of their illusory faith in the benevolence of corporations—what Laura Nader aptly calls "trustanoia," or the mistaken belief that institutions will protect us from the oil industry and others that threaten human health and planetary well-being.

Indeed, I have noticed small but important changes in discourse among my parents' neighbors in southern Alabama. These Gulf Coast residents from the politically conservative "redneck Riviera" learned the hard way that unaccountable corporate managers made ghastly cost-benefit analyses for drilling below 5,000 feet of ocean and decided their own profits were worth risking the entire ecosystem and regional economy. Press coverage of the disaster included unusually insightful pieces about the long-term impacts of the spill on the livelihoods and culture of the coast. Fishermen spoke eloquently of their hard-earned firsthand knowledge of the marine environment, suddenly made worthless by the ruination of the fishing industry. Thousands, from the Louisiana bayou shrimpers to the oyster farmers of Alabama, lost their livelihoods for years to come— perhaps forever, as their children will be forced to seek other careers. Having carefully stewarded marine resources to prevent overharvesting, they are understandably bitter. Many resented placing their boats in BP's cleanup—an operation under the Orwellian name "Vessels of Opportunity"—or refused to do so. A crabber, Jeff Ussury, responded with understandable sarcasm to the news that BP had finally capped the well after eighty-six days: "It's like putting a Band-Aid on a dead man in my opinion." The wife of a shrimper added, "My way of life's over, they've destroyed everything I know and love."[27]

Though not technically "displaced" like Q'eqchi' villagers whose farmlands are coercively purchased for African palm plantations, Gulf residents have suffered indirect displacement akin to what happens when a factory closes in a company town. Though not technically compelled to leave the region, many able-bodied workers facing a collapsed local economy had no alternative but to move elsewhere in search of a new job. BP offered some compensation, but money cannot replace the culture, friendships, family ties, and sense of belonging that come from living in one place for a long time.[28] Nor will it bring back the rising numbers of those diagnosed with cancers after the spill whose illnesses regional oncologists suspect may be related to the unusually high levels of benzene found in residents' bloodstreams from the oil and/or other toxic chemicals in the millions of gallons of dispersants sprayed along the seashore.

Unfortunately, leftist discourse often presumes that resistance to the contemporary corporate order will come from urban progressive sectors. As Gillian Hart observes, "many activists and intellectuals have taken for granted the vanguard role of the urban industrial working class in paving the way toward socialism."[29] They presume that people who, like many Gulf coast residents, subscribe to fundamentalist religions must also necessarily subscribe to free-market fundamentalism. Having absorbed Marx's own prejudice against peasants (whom he once referred to as "potatoes in a sack"[30]), many urban intellectuals in Guatemala also view Q'eqchi' farmers with suspicion. Yet the success of anti-dispossession struggles depends on resolution of the historic division between urban-based liberation movements and agrarian issues, and on new creative alliances and linkages ("historical blocs," in Gramscian terminology) built among unlikely allies struggling against a corporate order.

Were "conservative" First World citizens "dispossessed" of their allegiance to corporate America and inspired to empathize with oil companies' plunder of indigenous lands from Nigeria to Ecuador, perhaps even the most powerful polluters might be held accountable for their actions. And should even a fraction of the millions of *Avatar* viewers develop an interest in the Q'eqchi' and other indigenous peoples' struggles against dispossession, new social movements might bring down empires—both old and new.

Notes

1. Anthony Oliver Smith, *Defying Displacement: Grassroots Resistance and the Critique of Development* (Austin: University of Texas Press, 2010). This figure comes from Michael Cernea, former chief sociologist for the World Bank.
2. Gonzalo Aguirre Beltran, *Regions of Refuge* (Washington, D.C.: Society for Applied Anthropology, 1979).
3. Due to greater repression (following nearly four decades of CIA-induced civil war), Guatemalan Q'eqchi' people have had less success resisting outsiders seeking to privatize their land than Belizean Q'eqchi'.
4. Guatemala boasts more than ninety protected areas covering three million hectares or 28 percent of national territory. The centerpiece is Petén's 1.6 million hectare Maya Biosphere Reserve (roughly twice the size of Yellowstone), connecting a tri-national arc of parks in Belize, Mexico, and Guatemala known as the "Maya Forest." Adding the smaller parks established in southern Petén in the mid 1990s, roughly half the department falls under protected status.
5. Private property owners can sometimes mobilize support from political cronies to evict squatters, but the national park service has little political will to remove invaders from protected areas, much less relocate them to new land.
6. What appears to be "harmonious" is not necessarily so. See Laura Nader's discussion of "coercive harmony" in *Harmony Ideology: Justice and Control in a Zapotec Mountain Village* (Stanford: Stanford University Press, 1990).

7. Of 178 households, 14 did not respond. Women, significantly, were more likely than their husbands to worry about inheritance for their children and warn their spouses not to sell. Yet women's input is usually ignored because state land representatives tend to hold meetings with men in Spanish, thereby implicitly deferring land inheritance decisions to men alone.
8. See Liza Grandia, *Unsettling: Land Dispossession and Enduring Inequity for the Q'eqchi' Maya in the Guatemalan and Belizean Frontier Colonization Process*, Ph.D. dissertation (University of California-Berkeley, 2006).
9. See Laura Nader, "Up the Anthropologist: Perspectives Gained from Studying Up," in *Reinventing Anthropology*, ed. Dell H. Hymes (New York: Pantheon Books, 1972), 289.
10. The key architect of these papers is Klaus Deininger. See his *Land Rights for Poor People Key to Poverty Reduction, Growth: Summary of a World Bank Policy Research Report* (Washington, D.C.: Center for International Private Enterprise, 2003).
11. Central to World Bank logic on agrarian reform is the argument of Peruvian economist Hernando de Soto in his 2000 book, *The Mystery of Capital*, that without formal property titles, the hardworking poor will be unable to prosper within a capitalist system. His solution—to lift poor people out of the informal economy by helping them gain property rights—is almost a mirror image of Locke's portrayal of property and profits as mutually interdependent. Whereas de Soto argues that people cannot profit without property, Locke argued that without profit, people cannot claim property.
12. See Ugo Mattei and Laura Nader, *Plunder: When the Rule of Law is Illegal* (Malden, MA: Blackwell, 2008), 110.
13. See Michael Goldman, *Imperial Nature: The World Bank and Struggles for Social Justice in the Age of Globalization* (New Haven: Yale University Press, 2006).
14. See Héctor Mondragón, "Colombia: Agrarian Reform, Fake and Genuine," in *Promised Land: Competing Visions of Agrarian Reform*, ed. Peter Rosset, Raj Patel, and Michael Courville (Oakland, CA: Food First Books, 2006), 165–76.
15. See my 2009 Spanish ethnography titled *Tz'aptzooqeb'*, a Q'eqchi' word meaning "enclosed" or "dispossessed" (AVANCSO: Guatemala City). This was published in English as *Enclosed: Conservation, Cattle, and Commerce among the Q'eqchi' Maya Lowlanders* (Seattle: University of Washington Press, 2012).
16. See Jorge Grünberg, Liza Grandia and Bayron Milian, *Tierra e Igualdad: Desafíos para la Administración de Tierras en Petén, Guatemala* (Guatemala City: World Bank, 2012), xviii.
17. Michael Hardt and Antonio Negri. *Empire* (Cambridge, MA: Harvard University Press, 2000).
18. David Harvey, *The New Imperialism* (Oxford: Oxford University Press, 2003), 173.
19. David Harvey, *A Brief History of Neoliberalism* (Oxford: Oxford University Press, 2005), 2.
20. Ken Worthy, "Biotechnology, Enclosures, and the Privatization of Life." May 15, 2001, http://nature.berkeley.edu/kenw/maize/biotech_exclosures.htm: 12.
21. Medard Gabel and Henry Bruner, *Global Inc.: An Atlas of the Multinational Corporation* (New York: The New Press, 2003).
22. Arundhati Roy, *The Algebra of Infinite Justice* (London: HarperCollins, 2001), 129.
23. Chalmers Johnson. *Blowback: The Costs and Consequences of American Empire* (New York: Metropolitan/Owl Book, 2004).
24. Smith, *Defying Displacement*.
25. See the *Rachel Maddow Show* archives for both these stories, 26 May and 15 June 2010.
26. After all, BP is a foreign corporation whose oil gets exported into the world oil supply and does little to lower U.S. gasoline prices. Oil prices have remained stable since the

Obama administration suspended drilling in the Gulf, showing that risky offshore drilling is less essential to U.S. domestic oil security than previously assumed.

27. Campbell Robertson and Henry Fountain, "BP Caps Its Leaking Well, Stopping the Oil after 86 Days," *New York Times*, 16 July 2010, A16.
28. Commercial fishermen may be compensated, but BP has declined to reimburse the grocery bills of people who caught fish to eat. See John Schwartz, "Claims to BP Fund Attract Scrutiny," *New York Times*, 2 October 2010, A21. Similarly, absentee landlords who rented condominiums to tourists may claim lost income, but people who make the beach their home will not be compensated for lost quality of life or real estate values.
29. Gillian Hart, "Denaturalizing Dispossession: Critical Ethnography in the Age of Resurgent Imperialism," *Antipode* 38 (2006): 989.
30. See Karl Marx, *The Eighteenth Brumaire of Louis Bonaparte* (New York: International Publishers, 1963).

Chapter 5

ON FOOD
Manufacturing Food Insecurity in Oaxaca, Mexico

Roberto J. González

> A human being is primarily a bag for putting food into; the other functions and faculties may be more godlike, but in point of time they come afterwards.... It could be plausibly argued that changes of diet are more important than changes of dynasty or even of religion.... Yet it is curious how seldom the all-importance of food is recognized. You see statues everywhere to politicians, poets, bishops, but none to cooks or bacon-curers or market gardeners.
>
> —George Orwell, *The Road to Wigan Pier* (1937)

Imagine for a moment that you are eating a substantial breakfast of fried eggs, bacon, hash browns, buttered toast, and sweet coffee.

Now imagine that you know where every part of the breakfast originated, and that you personally know everyone involved in preparing its ingredients: the farmers who raised the pigs and chickens that provided the bacon and eggs; the people who cultivated and harvested the potatoes and the wheat that became hash browns and toast; the workers who picked the coffee beans and the sugarcane that went into your steaming cup of coffee.

Few people in the United States have this depth of knowledge about their meals.

However, among the indigenous people of northern Oaxaca, Mexico, such knowledge is commonplace. A typical breakfast is hearty and

---

Notes for this chapter begin on page 124.

complex: it would likely consist of corn tortillas and black beans, accompanied by a side dish of chorizo (spicy pork sausage), string cheese, scrambled eggs, and chili sauce. It would probably also include a cup of heavily sweetened coffee. Nearly all of this food would have been produced within five miles of where it was consumed.

Most Rincón Zapotec people live in villages with fewer than 2,000 inhabitants. The vast majority are family farmers who grow their own corn, beans, tomatoes, onions, and chilies. They often raise chickens and turkeys, and a smaller number raise pigs and even cattle. In some parts of the region (which enjoys a tropical climate), farmers grow coffee and sugarcane to sell at the market, reserving some for the family's pantry. Consequently, the Rincón Zapotec breakfast is usually a local affair in the strict sense of the term. It impressively illustrates how food security—that is, access to sufficient and nutritious food that comes from known sources—continues to thrive in some societies today. And whereas it contrasts strikingly with our own food system in many ways, it has increasingly become interconnected with it.

This chapter is about food security and its future in Mexico and beyond. It is based on two years spent learning about farming and food in the mountains of the Rincón,[1] as well as on observations and reflections on food and diet in our own society. It aims to realize the insight that can come from comparing different lifeways, and to show how seemingly disparate institutions and organizations, viewed through an anthropological lens, are connected to one another. Anthropologist Clyde Kluckhohn once noted that learning about other cultures and customs can serve as a *Mirror for Man*—a means of reflecting on one's own society and perhaps even a tool for critical self-awareness.[2] Exploring food can improve understanding of how one's own situation may be developing and how it compares to other human experiences.

Subsistence and Abundance

Rincón Zapotec farmers—and for that matter, peasant farmers everywhere—are often described as subsistence farmers. But there is something misleading about the term "subsistence." The term implies a meager existence, a situation in which there is barely enough food for survival. In the Rincón, subsistence farmers would be more accurately called "abundance farmers" because most villagers are very well fed. Adults commonly consume more than 3,000 calories a day, as is necessary for people engaged in physically demanding work. Besides maize, beans, sugarcane, and coffee, many households cultivate squash, avocados, citrus fruits, mangoes, pineapples, bananas, guavas, and other crops. By combining subsistence and cash crops, villagers can provide food for themselves while earning money for expenses such as steel tools or school uniforms and textbooks for their children.

Everyday life in the Rincón is easy to romanticize, but it can be difficult. In the village of Talea, for example, some farmers walk two hours or more to get to their farms, hiking 600 meters down one winding mountain trail and then up another, sometimes carrying heavy loads. For four months out of the year (May through August), frequent rains turn steep mountain trails into muddy, slippery chutes. Even so, most farmers do not consider the morning commute to be work—*real* work involves clearing brush with machetes and axes, plowing with oxen and a wooden plow, planting with digging sticks, weeding with short-handled hoes, harvesting with straw baskets, and transporting food back to the village. A typical farmer can easily work from ten to twelve hours, six days a week. Women's work is at least as strenuous as men's, perhaps more so. Women select and cut firewood from the forest above the village and carry it home on their backs. They also maintain the house, children, chickens, and turkeys, and grow spices, flowers, and medicinal herbs in the kitchen garden.

A visitor to the Rincón would probably be impressed by the region's cuisine and the way food is served. In Talea, women prepare corn by transforming it into huge tortillas (nearly 18 inches across) that are stacked in the middle of the table. Each person receives a bowl of food. Utensils are not common; instead, the tortilla functions as both fork and spoon. Villagers skillfully ladle soups and sauces with folded tortilla strips, and expertly draw chunks of meat and vegetables out in this way as well.

Corn is the culinary core, with a wide variety of rich relishes—bean dishes, soups, chili sauces, mole, or meat—at its periphery. On special occasions and festival days, villagers make tamales filled with savory sauces. Many other delicacies are prepared from the grain, including atole (a gruel sweetened with chocolate or sugar), *memelas* (toasted maize cakes flavored with herbs and beans), *chilaquiles* (a layered casserole similar to lasagna), and *yht za'a* (sweet corn tortillas), to name a few. A meal is considered a meal only if maize is present in some form.

A handful of bakers in Talea prepare fresh, lightly sweetened bread sometimes eaten in small pieces soaked in coffee as an appetizer, especially on cold mornings. However, farmers often eschew this practice, claiming that bread "inflates" the stomach and takes away one's appetite for "legitimate" food—tortillas and beans. Many also describe snacking or eating between meals as a "vice" and an unnecessary indulgence.

Black beans, the most common complement to corn tortillas, are seasoned with salt, garlic, chiles, and the leaves of a fragrant herb called *epazote*. People in Talea frequently add other ingredients such as diced squash, squash blossoms, string beans, bananas, diced cactus, or chayotes. Different condiments used to vary the taste include six varieties of chiles, onions, chives, and lime juice. Many other foods round out the culinary repertoire. For two or three months a year, avocados are eaten as a side dish. Sauces made with toasted chiles, tomatoes, garlic, and onions are as common on kitchen tables as salt and pepper shakers are in the United States. And farmers grow dozens of kinds of fruits: oranges, limes, lemons, apples, peaches, loquats, pineapples, bananas, blackberries, mangoes.

People in the Rincón eat meat sparingly, usually on weekends or fiesta days, and forgo it entirely when money is scarce (especially before the coffee harvest). They most commonly eat poultry (chickens or turkeys), which is usually prepared in soups. They slaughter pigs and cattle on special occasions. Cattle are without exception the same muscular draft animals used to plow the fields, so beef is relatively low in fat. Young men spend some of their leisure time hunting wild game for the table, especially deer, armadillos, weasels, peccaries, doves, and quail.

Some anthropologists have called maize, beans, and squash the "American trinity."[3] When seasoned with chiles (rich in vitamin C) and supplemented with small amounts of animal-based proteins, these three plants supply a nearly perfect combination of vitamins and minerals. The traditional Mesoamerican diet of tortillas, boiled beans, and squash—high in protein and fiber and low in fat and cholesterol—would be difficult to improve upon, in nutritional terms. In fact, some food activists in the United States argue that the Mesoamerican diet might serve as a nutritionally sound, ecologically sustainable example for other societies to follow.[4]

In Talea, wild greens play an essential nutritional role. Collected in maize fields, in forests, or along the banks of streams, they are rich in the riboflavin, niacin, and vitamin C that are deficient in a diet of maize and beans alone. Farming families often relish boiled greens seasoned with chili and salt, especially in hot weather. Such meals are considered light and refreshing compared to heavier dishes prepared from beans.

On average, men eat five or six tortillas daily and women eat slightly less, approximately four or five. About 75 percent of Talean campesinos' daily caloric intake comes from maize. Nearly all the rest comes from plant sources, especially beans and unrefined sugar. Total caloric intake was high (for adults, approximately 3,500 calories a day), but most villagers burned much of this energy in their daily work.

Rincón Zapotec villages exemplify what anthropologist Sidney Mintz has called "starch-based" societies, "built on the cultivation of a particular complex carbohydrate, such as maize or potatoes or rice or millet or wheat ... [supplemented by] other plant foods, oils, flesh, fish, fowl, fruits, nuts and seasonings—many of the ingredients of which are nutritively essential."[5] Mintz observes that "[t]his fitting together of core complex carbohydrate and flavor-fringe supplement is a fundamental feature of the human diet—not of *all* human diets, but certainly enough of them in our history to serve as the basis for important generalizations."[6] Though *Homo sapiens* only began farming 10,000 years ago, combinations of core carbohydrate and "flavor-fringe supplement" have dominated human diets since that time. Mintz summarizes these general features:

> People subsist on some principal complex carbohydrate, usually a grain or root crop, around which their lives are built. Its calendar of growth fits with their calendar of the year; its needs are, in some curious ways, their needs. It provides the raw materials out of which much of the meaning in life is given voice. Its character, names, distinctive tastes and textures, the difficulties associated with its cultivation, its history, mythical or not, are projected on the human affairs of a people who consider what they eat to be the basic food, to be *the* definition of food.[7]

The variety of "starch-based" societies is impressive. Many East Asian societies have relied for centuries on a "core" of rice or millet and a "flavor-fringe" of fish, bean pastes and soy, greens, and other plant foods. In West and Central Africa, many diets are built around cassava dumplings, accompanied by stews made with okra, peanuts, tomatoes, or meats. In parts of Europe, peasant families typically subsisted on black bread eaten with fatty, salty soups. Many Pacific Island societies prospered on either breadfruit—baked, boiled, or roasted—or taro root. These starchy staples were often prepared with coconut milk and eaten with salted fish, vegetables, or greens. Middle Eastern farmers' diets consist of a "core" of unleavened wheat breads and a rich variety of "fringe" foods such as mashed garbanzo beans, eggplant, peppers, garlic, onions, olive oil, and dishes prepared with chicken, lamb, goat, or fish.

Soul Food

It would be an understatement to say that corn has dramatic significance for the Rincón Zapotec people, for they and their Mesoamerican ancestors have continuously cultivated corn (maize), beans, squash, and other crops for nearly 10,000 years. Biologist Walton Galinat has described its domestication from teosinte, a grass native to central and southern Mexico, as "the most remarkable plant breeding accomplishment of all time" because of the crop's highly adaptable nature.[8]

Over this period, techniques for producing, processing, preserving, and preparing corn evolved to the point that agricultural surpluses supported great Mesoamerican civilizations, including those of the Olmec, Maya, Toltec, Zapotec, Mixtec, and Aztec. Therefore, humans and corn have been in an intimate relationship from the beginning. Humans produced corn by domesticating it, but corn also produced human societies by providing the nutritional base for the development of large urban centers such as Teotihuacan and Tenochtitlan, which each had hundreds of thousands of inhabitants in ancient times. This close connection between corn and people is evident in Mesoamerican origin myths. For example, in the great Mayan epic *Popol Vuh*, the gods succeed in creating humans only by fashioning them from tortilla dough.

In the Rincón region, cornfields are always planted with local maize varieties saved from the previous year's harvest. Seed is never purchased among the Rincón Zapotec, but freely given as a gift: a farmer who wishes to plant a particular variety of seed trades a portion of his own with that of another farmer—a friend, neighbor, or relative. Knowledge about farming and food has traditionally been passed down from generation to generation as children emulate their parents. By the age of three, many Rincón children have planted seeds in the household garden under their mothers' supervision and possess detailed knowledge about local crops. For example, most children are able to recognize the different leaf patterns that distinguish squash varieties before they have entered kindergarten. Anthropologist Eugene Hunn, who has written extensively about the traditional ecological knowledge of Zapotec farmers in the southern sierra of Oaxaca, notes that Zapotec children in the village of San Juan Gbëë are "precocious" learners who quickly master vast amounts of knowledge about the natural world. Girls and boys, some as young as seven, are able to identify dozens (and sometimes hundreds) of different plants, the basic vocabulary associated with them, and their practical uses. Hunn observes that

> perhaps it is not the children of San Juan whose precocious acquisition needs to be explained, but the persistent ignorance of our own children, who very often, college degree in hand, are at a loss to see the difference between an oak and a maple, a thrush and a wren, or a bee and a wasp, the intellectual complement to Richard Louv's provocatively named "nature deficit disorder."[9]

The importance of corn extends far beyond the kitchen table. For many Rincón Zapotec farmers, maize is no ordinary plant but might more accurately be called a plant-person with a heart, a soul, a memory, a strong will, and the ability to punish people. A few accounts illustrate corn's status as a plant-person. In January 1997, a farmer from Talea related the following incident as we husked corn in a frigid ranch house:

> Pablo was a Talean campesino who was a successful farmer and every year he harvested more than enough to feed his family. But one year his widowed mother fell ill and was unable to purchase maize at the market. Pablo secretly took some maize from his family's granary for his mother next door. But his wife, a jealous and miserly woman, found out, scolded him, and took the maize from the widow. Pablo was a tranquil man and did not dare contradict his wife. That night Pablo and his neighbors awoke to a terrible sound, like that of a waterfall. It seemed to come from a corner of the house, but it ended before he was able to light a candle. Thinking that perhaps he had been dreaming, he went back to sleep. In the morning, however, he discovered that every last kernel of maize was gone. It had punished him.[10]

After telling the story, the farmer paused reflectively for a moment and then said, "That's why we say 'corn has a heart.'"

This is biologically correct. A maize kernel does have a heart (the "embryo" or "nucleus") from which the plant germinates, once it is in the ground. But the farmer meant something more: he was assigning human qualities to something that we consider to be a mere plant. In the Rincón, corn can be vengeful, and it has a memory. In a recently published accocount, a man from a village near Talea tells of how corn punished him as a child. Over the boy's objections, his mother insisted that he help her harvest maize. Grudgingly, he went to the cornfield and helped, maintaining a foul mood throughout the day. They returned home that evening, each carrying a heavy basket of maize. Grouchy and tired, the youngster stormed angrily away from his mother, intentionally letting some ears drop to the ground, knowing she would pick up after him. Then, inexplicably, he tripped on a smooth, well-trodden part of the familiar path home. Even though the fall was not a bad one, his leg hurt for months. He learned a valuable lesson: "Later I knew that it wasn't the fall that had injured me, it was the corn, which I had scorned. That's what punished me. That's why I've never despised corn since."[11]

Corn also has intrinsic moral value. Respectful of its ability to punish those who treat it disrespectfully, villagers avoid wasting it, spilling it, burning it, or letting dough spoil. Stale or dry tortillas are soaked in tomato sauce or black bean sauce to make *chilaquiles*, used in soups, or put in cups of sweet coffee as a cereal. Should tortillas begin to mold, Taleans place them directly on hot coals, turning spores into specks of dust that are easily brushed away. Old tortillas go back into the food cycle when they are fed to pigs, chickens, and turkeys.

Finally, corn is an important medium of ritual exchange. For example, when Taleans hold festivals, visitors from nearby villages who ask for food are freely given tortillas. Withholding corn from the unfortunate or needy violates the plant-person's moral sensibilities. Corn is also the preferred medium for reciprocal exchanges at key social events like weddings, funerals, and village fiestas, where visitors present hosts with foodstuffs typically including several kilograms of maize.

Corn is thus no mere crop but a powerful living being amidst humans at all times. It is present at festivals, baptisms, weddings, and funerals; inside churches, homes, and human bodies; surrounding ranch houses and villages. Corn is a wonderful plant-person with a long memory, a strict moral code, and an unshakable will. It serves as a medium connecting peasant families to their kin, their neighbors, their village, their region, and their deities.

How did a science premised on the idea that maize and the earth are alive and have souls, memories, feelings, and willfulness lead to maize's domestication and improvement? Zapotec farming is effective at solving certain practical problems, likely not despite but because of fundamental assumptions—particularly the personhood of maize—that many Western scientists would consider false or superstitious. In other words, it may well be that the remarkable plant breeding accomplished by ancient Oaxacans and continued by their contemporary Zapotec descendants relates directly to maize's status as a plant-person, and the stunning achievement of domesticating and improving the crop was probably stimulated by the very assumptions that are incorrect by the standards of cosmopolitan science. The intense symbolic, religious, and emotional significance attached to maize—the passion, fear, respect, and love that farmers had (and still have, in many places) for maize the plant-person—likely spurred them to spend more time and effort tending, improving, nurturing, strengthening, and adapting it to different ecological niches over the course of generations. Eugene Anderson's book *Ecologies of the Heart* more fully explores the connection between sustainable ecosystems, biodiversity, and human emotion.[12] It is small wonder that today, southern Mexico boasts the world's greatest maize diversity, growing more than 20,000 varieties.

Perhaps the most impressive of the many remarkable aspects of Rincón Zapotec food is the strong sense of control that people maintain over their food supply. Over hundreds of centuries, they and their ancestors managed to create and maintain a sustainable, nutritious, varied cuisine based on local ingredients and indigenous crops, and enriched over the past 500 years by plant and animal foods from other parts of the world.

Modern Tragedies

Profound, interrelated changes that are underway in the Rincón have accelerated in the twenty-first century, so dramatically transforming the texture of daily life in so many villages that they are in some ways unprecedented. One source of many changes is modernization—what some might call economic "development." Beginning in the late 1940s and 1950s, the Mexican government undertook massive modernization schemes to bring electricity to urban and rural areas by building massive hydroelectric dams along several rivers. Most of these projects included initiatives for improving communication and transportation between geographically remote regions and cities. The Papaloapan Commission, one of the most ambitious of these projects, aimed at modernizing villages and towns in the Papaloapan River Basin (which includes the Rincón).[13]

Among the most sweeping changes was the construction of a road linking Talea (and eventually other Rincón villages) to the central valley of Oaxaca, site of the state capital. Even today, elders in Talea say, "When the road arrived, *everything* changed." And the transformations were indeed profound. Before the road, Talea had many small industries that produced matches, carbonated fruit juices, soap, fireworks, shoes, boots, sandals, hats, rifles, machetes, and many other things; and carpenters, blacksmiths, weavers, tailors, butchers, and farmers did brisk business at the town's Monday market. By the late 1960s, however, many of these businesses had disappeared. The new road allowed merchants from the state capital to more easily supply villages with factory-made goods (including state-subsidized foodstuffs), thus encroaching on local farmers' and artisans' livelihoods. Furthermore, the Mexican government began to strictly enforce laws requiring small business owners, even in remote parts of the country, to pay taxes and licensing fees. These changes severely diminished villagers' ability to provide for themselves. In addition, in the 1960s the government opened a nationwide chain of subsidized food stores, making it easier for many Rincón Zapotec people to abandon farming, migrate to cities, and send wages home to feed children and the elderly. Within a generation, it seemed that the largely autonomous and self-sufficient people of the Rincón might become dependent on others.

Another set of changes took effect in 1994, when the governments of the United States, Canada, and Mexico began implementing the North

American Free Trade Agreement (NAFTA), a trade treaty that committed the three countries to lowering tariffs. In Mexico, NAFTA paved the way for the expansion and consolidation of factory farms. As a result, U.S.-based multinational corporations—Archer Daniels Midland; Ralston Purina; Anderson, Clayton; ConAgra; and others—began entering into joint ventures with Mexican food conglomerates. Some began importing hybrid corn varieties produced on factory farms in the Midwestern United States to Mexican subsidiaries. Unlike corn farming in the Rincón, U.S. corn production requires machinery (tractors, harvesters, crop dusters), chemical fertilizers, pesticides, herbicides, fungicides, and irrigation systems. Since hybrids are effectively sterile, farmers have to purchase them annually; hence a seed industry was created and grew rapidly. Agribusiness and chemical companies are therefore among NAFTA's greatest beneficiaries.

Ironically, imported corn began flooding government-subsidized stores in regions whose inhabitants descended from the original creators of modern corn. Mexican government officials made the problematic assumption that small-scale farmers in the countryside were "inefficient" or "underdeveloped." They ignored the fact that U.S. corn is cheap because it is heavily subsidized by U.S. taxpayers. They also neglected to consider the hidden costs of factory farming. As Peter Canby recently noted:

> Comparisons of small-scale and industrial productivity can be deceptive. Each bushel of industrial corn in the United States requires between a quarter and a third of a gallon of oil for fuel, fertilizer and other applications. This can add up to fifty gallons or more of oil per acre, a level of consumption that is practicable only as long as fossil fuel is cheap. . . . Industrial agriculture can also have steep "external costs." Timothy Wise, research director of the Global Development and Environment Institute at Tufts University, points out that corn is one of the most chemically dependent crops. Moreover, the prices at which it is sold fail to account for the associated environmental damage caused by chemicals. High on the list of damages is the growing "dead zone" at the mouth of the Mississippi River in the Gulf of Mexico; roughly the size of New Jersey, the area is almost devoid of marine life as a result of nitrogen runoff.[14]

Not only did NAFTA have a devastating impact on Rincón Zapotec farmers dependent on selling surplus corn to people outside the region; it also accelerated the process of urban migration. Recently, however, these migrants have increasingly traveled to the United States (particularly Los Angeles) and seldom returned to the Rincón.

The last twenty years—the "free trade" era—brought the elimination of trade tariffs, privatization of communal lands, and Mexico's entry into international trade regimes such as the World Trade Organization and NAFTA. Heavily subsidized U.S. corn flooded the market, increasing corn imports from the U.S. to Mexico nearly twentyfold between 1994 and 2002 and radically depressing the price of corn. Throughout the country, subsistence farming became increasingly unprofitable—and rare. Within a decade, a large proportion of the peasantry was literally driven out of the fields. The heaviest migration into the United States was from precisely those regions most devastated by this process.

The fallout from NAFTA negatively impacted nutrition among some families in the Rincón. Parents with extra spending money sometimes indulged their children by giving them a peso or two for candy, potato chips, artificial fruit drinks, or Coca-Cola. In the 1990s this was rare in most homes, but members of some families—of merchants in particular—were clearly overweight. Many of these households had televisions, and family members engaged in little or no farm work or strenuous activity. A strong correlation seemed to hold between farming work and physical fitness—those who worked in the fields, ate tortillas and beans, and walked to and from the farm were much more likely to be healthy.

NAFTA's dietary effects probably hit Rincón Zapotec immigrants to the United States hardest of all. One 29-year-old man had left Talea at seventeen to work in the United States, crossed the border at Tijuana with a group of Mixtec friends, and accompanied them to New York. After working as a busboy at the Hard Rock Café for several years, he moved to Los Angeles and got a job in the kitchen of an all-you-can-eat buffet restaurant. Descriptions of the Los Angeles fast-food scene were among his most vivid recollections of life in the United States. Hamburgers were his favorite American food, especially those served at a restaurant called Fatburger. The young man returned to Talea after nine years, but the effects of the Fatburgers and the all-you-can-eat dinners apparently lingered: at more than 220 pounds, he was one of the largest people in the village and a likely candidate for diabetes.

Engineering Corn

Yet another change in the Rincón (and across the Mexican countryside) came about at the turn of the twenty-first century. It involved the diffusion of genetically modified corn—seed corn whose genes have been altered through transference of DNA from another species. Biotechnology companies have portrayed genetically modified organisms (GMOs) as the solution to world hunger. (E.g., one of Monsanto's recent ads is headlined:

"9 billion people to feed. A changing climate. NOW WHAT?"[15]) Such claims are premised on the notion that world hunger is simply a technological issue, not a social one—a dubious argument, as Francis Moore Lappé demonstrated more than a generation ago. The problem is not lack of food production, but rather the inequitable way in which food is distributed globally.[16]

Among the most common genetically modified (GM) crops is "Bt corn," named after *Bacillus thuringiensis*, a microorganism that destroys the intestinal walls of the corn borer (a pest that munches on various parts of the maize plant). Monsanto is not the only company with GM corn: Novartis, DuPont, Bayer, and Dow are also leaders in the GM seed industry. Corn is not a plant-person to these companies—it is a commodity. They have desperately sought to boost GM seed sales worldwide to recoup at least some of the $8 billion they spent acquiring seed companies in recent years—and the billions more invested in scientific research to develop GMOs.

This commercial drive led to one of the most rapid transformations ever in the U.S. food supply. Bt corn—which was only introduced in 1995—now accounts for nearly one-half of the corn harvested in the United States.[17] Maize-based products from corn sweeteners to corn oil to corn chips are so common that all Americans are likely to have consumed at least some Bt corn. Yet very little is known about the long-term health and environmental effects of GM crops. In 1999, respected journals such as *Nature* and *Lancet* published reports about the deleterious health effects of Bt corn pollen and transgenic foods on monarch butterflies and rats, respectively.[18] Other reports suggested that some people may have allergic reactions to the new crops.[19]

In late November 2001, a report published in *Nature* by Ignacio Chapela and David Quist of the University of California, Berkeley, confirmed that transgenic material from GM corn had cross-pollinated with native maize varieties in Oaxaca.[20] Their discovery, made less than twenty miles from Talea in the Zapotec village of Capulalpan, was especially worrisome because it occurred near the center of origin of maize, where biodiversity of the crop is highest. Scientists working in the region—not to mention its inhabitants—are greatly concerned about what such cross-pollination might mean for the health of the Rincón Zapotec, for people's living environment, and for the corn they consume. Bt corn most likely arrived in northern Oaxaca in shipments to government-subsidized food stores throughout rural Mexico.

Among the most revealing (and troubling) outcomes of these developments was the apparent lack of interest on the part of many Mexican government officials. Top officials in the Secretariat of Agriculture displayed either ignorance or callous indifference. For example, Assistant Secretary of Agriculture Victor Villalobos claimed that GMO corn presented no threat because it was "just another hybrid." Villalobos's boss, Minister of Agriculture Javier Usabiaga, said, "A farmer who cannot survive in the twenty-first century is simply going to have to get another job."[21]

As these events played out, the Zapotec people of northern Oaxaca did not stand by waiting for Mexican officials to take action. Miguel Ramírez, head of Capulalpan's Communal Lands Committee, attended an intergovernmental conference at The Hague on the implementation of the UN Biosafety Protocol (the so-called Cartagena Protocol). Ramírez had served as an officer in the Union of Zapotec and Chinantec Communities, a grassroots organization that plans and coordinates economic programs for nearly three dozen villages in a region called the Sierra, near the Rincón. He and others have been informing Sierra villagers about the importance of not planting imported corn and the need to monitor individual fields. In an interview, he noted that whereas the most important long-term effect could be the loss of pure "criollo" or local varieties, there might also be more urgent consequences, such as harmful physical effects (especially on children) and unforeseen consequences down the food chain.

Ramírez was also concerned about the possibility that biotechnology companies like Monsanto or DuPont might seek royalties from local farmers. Will big biotech firms one day decide to sue Oaxaca farmers for illegally "using" their patented crops without paying licensing fees? This scenario is not implausible, as the World Trade Organization's Agreement on Trade Related Aspects of Intellectual Property (TRIP) establishes global property rights covering GMOs, among other things. The TRIP agreement could allow corporations that hold patents over GMO seeds to demand user fees from local farmers whose corn has been contaminated, even if the crop itself is the product of generations of selective breeding by the farmers' ancestors—as in the case of the Mesoamericans, who accomplished "the most sophisticated plant breeding accomplishment of all time." GM material represents a kind of "brand," indicating a real possibility that under TRIP, corporations could take legal action against Zapotec farmers whose crops have been contaminated by GM pollen. The case of Percy Schmeiser, a Canadian canola farmer Monsanto sued for this reason, demonstrates the plausibility of such a scenario.[22]

Ramírez and dozens of other Zapotec officials were so concerned about the possible consequences of GM corn that they requested a thorough investigation into transgenes in Mexican native maize varieties and the development of effective remedial measures. They appealed to the Commission for Environmental Cooperation (CEC), a body formed to address environmental problems under the NAFTA regime. Ramírez and the others urgently called for immediate assessment of the damage caused by GM maize contamination. When the CEC issued its report in November 2004, it recommended a ban on U.S. maize into Mexico and suggested that the "Mexican government should strengthen the moratorium on commercial planting of transgenic maize by minimizing the import of living transgenic maize grain from countries that grow transgenic maize commercially," potentially by milling transgenic grain at the point of entry.[23] George W. Bush administration officials were outraged by the CEC report, and consequently some sections of the report were effectively suppressed.[24] Though the Mexican government had banned cultivation of genetically modified crops in 1999, its policy had changed by October 2009, when the Mexican agriculture ministry issued two permits to grow GM corn.[25]

Another indigenous organization based in the Sierra, the Union of Organizations of the Sierra Juárez (UNOSJO), represents more than twenty Zapotec, Mixe, and Chinantec villages in the Sierra and Rincón regions. The programs that UNOSJO coordinates traditionally target concerns like road construction and organic coffee, but they also attempted to confront the GMO issue. UNOSJO worked directly with Sierra and Rincón campesinos in January and November 2002 to organize workshops to share information with local farmers about the risks posed by GMOs. The organization did this through traditional forums like citizen assemblies and meetings with representatives of communal land committees. When I left, UNOSJO officials were also about to launch a series of public service announcements over a community radio station that broadcasts across the northern Sierra in the Zapotec, Chinantec, and Mixe languages to raise consciousness about GMOs and the need to protect local varieties. An UNOSJO official, Aldo González, noted that the organization also hopes to create a seed bank over the long term.

UNOSJO has also worked with international NGOs to draw global attention to GMOs in Oaxaca and develop strategies to halt the contamination. For example, UNOSJO representatives have cultivated relationships with Greenpeace, Food First, and the Rural Advancement Fund International (now the ETC Group) and participated in a UN Food and Agriculture Organization meeting on crop biodiversity. UNOSJO has also participated in workshops and forums across Latin America (including the World Social Forum in Porto Alegre, Brazil) to inform other civil society organizations about the potential consequences of GMO contamination. And in 2002, UNOSJO representatives received several dozen GMO test kits from the San Francisco–based NGO Global Exchange to begin screening fields in the region for GM corn. In short, indigenous organizations are confronting the problem of GMO corn by appealing to global organizations, notably the CEC, the United Nations Food and Agriculture Organization, and NGOs.

Reflecting upon the appearance of GM corn in a historical context, we might consider how it is part of a broader process that stretches back decades. In the Sierra it began with the federal government's "rural schools" in the 1930, which brought forced assimilation and declining use of the Zapotec language, to be followed by government-initiated logging projects in the 1950s that drew villagers away from subsistence farming and into the cash economy, the introduction of government-subsidized food stores in the early 1970s, and finally the neoliberal reforms of the late 1980s and 1990s, which led to privatization of common resources and a decline in subsistence farming nationwide. This trajectory is rapidly leading to the destruction of what remains of regional self-sufficiency.

Many Zapotec farmers have observed that altogether, these changes jeopardize the viability of their food system—and of their land-based culture. From their perspective, GMOs' transgression into native corn varieties is part of a larger process undermining the very foundations of their societies: the self-provisioning household, the autonomous village, and the land itself. Not only GMO corn, but the entire set of transformations that foreshadowed it threaten the ability of these farmers—who have also been stewards of biodiversity—to continue their work of maintaining a rich genetic pool, a critical task and service that, though unrecognized by many, has benefited the world, as David Quist and Ignacio Chapela have stated.[26]

Losing Control—and Regaining It

The Rincón Zapotec are still mostly in command of what they eat, but they are increasingly embroiled in a struggle to maintain control over their farmland, crops, and diets. In many ways, their society differs little from our own. In the United States, the process of losing control over food was under way throughout the twentieth century. It began when agribusiness firms—beneficiaries of generous government subsidies and favorable tax policies—rose to prominence and drove small farmers out of business.[27] As the United States became less agricultural and more industrial, families increasingly relied on food companies to provide the necessities of daily life: Pet Milk, Kraft Foods, General Mills, Frito-Lay, Armour Meats, Tyson Farms, and other firms gained ever more influence in creating a new American diet.[28] The rise of fast food restaurants was another step toward loss of control over food. Fewer and fewer people had any idea who was producing their food, and more and more people lacked basic knowledge about preparing nutritious meals. Within a century, the United States had gone from a farm-based culture to a microwave culture.

This shift was gradual—as is typical when mechanisms of cultural control operate—but profound. For example, in a recent survey of children in the United States, 96 percent could identify Ronald McDonald; the only fictional character with a higher degree of recognition was Santa Claus. In many neighborhoods, McDonald's is the safest place for a child to play. The company now owns and operates more playgrounds than any other organization in the United States, public or private.[29] No wonder one public health specialist recently stated that "becoming obese is a normal response to the American environment."[30]

Now, it seems, our society has reached a stage in which many have lost control of knowing what they eat. Given the biological and cultural significance of food over many hundreds of centuries, the following lines, published in a recent edition of a leading American culinary magazine, are worth contemplating: "If you have an iPhone, chances are you have enough apps installed to run your whole life from the palm of your hand. That includes keeping your diet on track, too. Here are our favorite apps that let you take control of what you're eating and drinking. All of them are available for download at the iTunes store."[31] This passage is followed by descriptions of several "apps" (applications for hand-held personal computing devices) including "Eatright" ("a super-simple interface that lets you quickly check off how many servings of the main food groups you've eaten each day . . . you probably need to eat a lot more veggies and a lot less meat") and "Shelflife" (a "handy app [that] tracks your perishables, letting you know how long they will last with color codes for fresh, past prime, and inedible").[32]

In the minds of observers who are unfamiliar with our society, such phenomena might raise questions: How do some people lose track of how many servings of food they eat in a day? Why do some humans need color-coded computer programs to determine whether or not their foodstuffs have spoiled? What is the cultural significance of transforming material objects like food and drink into numbers: calories, grams of fat, serving sizes, expiration dates, and the like? And when did some people begin relying upon computer technologies to intermediate between the very human act of eating and providing sustenance for their own bodies?[33]

Does the idea that people have become alienated from their own physical selves in an increasingly mechanized and computerized world have some basis in reality? Few adults have completely surrendered control over eating and drinking; however, such notions seem to express deeply rooted anxieties about losing autonomy over this basic human function. At least since Charlie Chaplin produced the 1936 movie *Modern Times*—featuring an unforgettable scene in which the protagonist is force-fed at accelerating speeds by a mechanized turntable—such concerns have been a common theme in American life.

Another significant change in the United States is the widespread loss of self-perception. The obesity epidemic still spreading unabated through the United States seems to indicate that many people have lost any sense of being able to control the fate of their bodies. Meals laden with fats and sugars take on the characteristics of addictive substances. Some marketers refer to those who purchase four or five meals a week at fast food restaurants not as regular customers but as "heavy users."[34] Incredibly, disturbingly, we are witnessing the normalization of the unthinkable as a full-blown public health crisis of overeating becomes a reality before our very eyes.

Food in a global context has been subjected to "controlling processes," dynamic components of power that anthropologist Laura Nader has proposed for closer analysis, understanding, and action. Controlling processes refers to "the transformative nature of central ideas ... that emanate from institutions operating as dynamic components of power. ... [It] is the study of how individuals and groups are influenced and persuaded to participate in their own domination or, alternatively, to resist it."[35] One example is the work of historian Stuart Ewen, who uncovers the ways in which the *Captains of Consciousness*—advertising men, bankers issuing credit and installment plans, and multinational corporations—worked to create "fancied needs" among working people where few had existed before. Quite suddenly, millions of Americans felt that they *needed* mouthwash, cosmetics, automobiles, kitchen appliances, and other gadgets. The captains of consciousness transformed citizens into mass consumers—an entire country was persuaded to need new things.[36] Ewen illustrates a special type of controlling process that Laura Nader has called "ideological control":

> Ideological control deals with pressures outside of individuals or groups that result in the formation of a control that becomes culturally set over time. Ideals and principles affecting the behavior of individuals are developed, penetrating and linking together different social domains and spheres of action, thought, and influence ... [I]deological controls are the most indirect and pervasive in modern society ... they are less vulnerable to abrupt change.[37]

Understanding how food and farming have changed among the Rincón Zapotec reveals much about how the United States food system has been similarly transformed, perhaps through parallel processes. Yet alongside these realities are clear signs that many people in our society are reasserting control over food. Urban farms and "backyard homesteads," though not yet a truly nationwide phenomenon, are popular in many cities. Most regions of the country have benefited from community gardens, farmer's markets, and community-supported agriculture initiatives over the past decade. As the recession enters its third year, some people are talking about "victory gardens" as a way of dealing with high food prices and unemployment. Heightened awareness about food has led to a boom in organic and sustainably produced foods, prompting even Walmart and other huge retail chains to offer organic products. In places like Hamden, Connecticut; Evanston, Illinois; Madison, Wisconsin; and Salem, Oregon, it is now legal to keep hens thanks to the efforts of "egg-gathering activists" who successfully lobbied their city governments.[38]

The multiple benefits of these projects—a safer diet in a time of massive food recalls, self-reliance in a period of economic recession, fresh nutritious food in an era of packaged supermarket products—are motivating more and more Americans to retake control of their diets. Are these shifts just a bizarre series of anomalies in a broader history of agricultural consolidation and food industrialization, or the beginnings of a genuine food revolution? It is too early to know, but one thing is clear: studying up, down, and across the food chain can help people create a less centralized, more democratic, more palatable future.

Notes

1. For a more comprehensive analysis of Rincón Zapotec farming and foodways, see Roberto J. González, *Zapotec Science: Farming and Food in the Northern Sierra of Oaxaca* (Austin: University of Texas Press, 2001).
2. Clyde Kluckhohn, *Mirror for Man: The Relationship of Anthropology to Everyday Life* (New York: Whittlesey House, 1949).
3. Eric Wolf, *Sons of the Shaking Earth* (Chicago: University of Chicago Press, 1959), 63.
4. Frances Moore Lappé, *Diet for a Small Planet* (New York: Ballantine Books, 1971).
5. Sidney Mintz, *Sweetness and Power: The Place of Sugar in Modern History* (New York: Viking, 1985), 9–10.
6. Ibid., 9.
7. Ibid., 10.
8. Walton C. Galinat, "El Origen del Maiz: El Grano de la Humanidad," *Economic Botany* 49, no. 1 (1995): 3–12. See also Laura Nader (ed.), *Naked Science: Anthropological Inquiry into Boundaries, Power, and Knowledge* (New York: Routledge, 1996).
9. Eugene S. Hunn, *A Zapotec Natural History* (Tucson: University of Arizona Press, 2008), 224–225.

10. González, *Zapotec Science*, 103–105.
11. Javier Castellanos, *El Maiz en Yojovi, Villa Alta, Oaxaca* (Mexico City: Primer Lugar, 1988), 245.
12. Eugene Anderson, *Ecologies of the Heart: Emotion, Belief, and the Environment* (Oxford: Oxford University Press, 1996).
13. Thomas Poleman, *The Papaloapan Project: Agricultural Development in the Mexican Tropics* (Stanford, CA: Stanford University Press, 1964).
14. Peter Canby, "Retreat to Subsistence," *The Nation*, 16 June 2010, 30–36.
15. Monsanto, "Now What?" accessed 8 February 2014, http://www.elephantjournal.com/wp-content/uploads/2010/05/Picture-681.png .
16. Lappé, *Diet for a Small Planet*.
17. Center for Food Safety, "Genetically Modified Food," accessed 29 October 2010, http://centerforfoodsafety.org/geneticall7.cfm.
18. Stanley Ewen and Arpad Pusztai, "Effect of Diets Containing Genetically Modified Potatoes Expressing *Galanthus nivalis lectin* on Rat Small Intestine," *Lancet* 354 (1999): 1353; John Losey, Linda Rayor, and Maureen Carter, "Transgenic Pollen Harms Monarch Larvae," *Nature* (20 May 1999): 214.
19. Clare Mills, "Could Genetically Modified Foods Be a New Source of Allergens?" *SciDevNet* (1 March 2005), accessed 2 November 2010, http://www.scidev.net/en/policy-briefs/could-genetically-modified-foods-be-a-new-source-o.html.
20. David Quist and Ignacio Chapela, "Transgenic DNA Introgressed into Traditional Maize Landraces in Oaxaca, Mexico," *Nature* (29 November 2001): 541–542. The study by Chapela and Quist generated further studies, and although a few did not confirm genetic transgression, others did, including one by the Mexican Secretariat of the Environment and Natural Resources and another by an international team led by Elena Alvarez-Buylla (see A. Pineyro-Nelson et al., "Transgenes in Mexican Maize: Molecular Evidence and Considerations for GMO Detection in Landrace Populations," *Molecular Ecology* 18 (18 December 2008): 750–761.
21. Javier Usabiaga, quoted in Claire Hope Cummings, "Risking Corn, Risking Culture," *WorldWatch* (15 October 2002), accessed 2 November 2010, http://www.worldwatch.org/node/525.
22. Matt Hartley, "Grain Farmer Claims Moral Victory in Seed Battle against Monsanto," *Globe and Mail* (Canada), 20 March 2008, A3.
23. Center for Environmental Cooperation, *Maize and Biodiversity: The Effects of Transgenic Maize in Mexico* (Montreal: CEC, 2004), accessed 22 August 2010, http://www.cec.org/Storage/56/4837_Maize-and-Biodiversity_en.pdf.
24. See Canby, "Retreat to Subsistence."
25. "Mexico Issues First Permits to Grow GM Corn," *Reuters* (U.S.), 15 October 2009, accessed 30 October 2010, http://www.reuters.com/article/idUSN1527085220091016.
26. Quist and Chapela, "Transgenic DNA," 542.
27. E. C. Pasour and Randal Rucker, *Plowshares and Pork Barrels: The Political Economy of Agriculture* (Oakland, CA: Independent Institute, 2005).
28. Naomi Aronson, "Working Up an Appetite," in *A Woman's Conflict: The Special Relationship between Women and Food*, ed. J. R. Kaplan (New York: Prentice-Hall, 1980).
29. Eric Schlosser, *Fast Food Nation* (Boston: Houghton-Mifflin, 2001).
30. Greg Critser, *Fat Land: How Americans Became the Fattest People in the World* (Boston: Houghton-Mifflin, 2003).
31. Victoria Von Biel, "The iPhone Health Plan," *Bon Appetit* (January 2010): 32.
32. Ibid.

33. For other examples of "apps" designed to help humans track, monitor, and regulate the basic bodily functions of sleeping and ovulating, see Excelltech Inc., "Sleep Analyzer," accessed 31 August 2010, http://itunes.apple.com/us/app/sleep-analyzer/id296266786?mt=8; and AreitoSoft, "iOvulate" accessed 31 August 2010, http://www.iovulate.com.
34. Jennifer Ordonez, "Hamburger Joints Call Them 'Heavy Users'—But Not to Their Faces," *Wall Street Journal*, 12 January 2000, A1.
35. Laura Nader, "Controlling Processes: Tracing the Dynamic Components of Power," *Current Anthropology* 38, no. 5 (1997): 711–737.
36. Stuart Ewen, *Captains of Consciousness* (New York: McGraw-Hill, 1976).
37. Laura Nader, "1984 and Brave New World: The Insidious Threat of Covert Control," Radcliffe Quarterly (December 1983), 2–3.
38. For an exploration of urban farming, food, and related topics, see Novella Carpenter, *Farm City: The Education of an Urban Farmer* (New York: Penguin, 2010); Manny Howard, *My Empire of Dirt* (New York: Scribner, 2010); Carleen Madigan, *The Backyard Homestead* (North Adams, MA: Storey Publishing, 2009); Michael Pollan, *In Defense of Food* (New York: Penguin, 2008).

Chapter 6

ON ENVIRONMENT

The "Broker State," Peruvian Hydrocarbons Policy, and the Camisea Gas Project

Patricia Urteaga-Crovetto

Like many societies around the world, over the past thirty years Peru has faced a multidimensional matrix of controlling processes. Slow-motion transformations in the country's economic, political, and ideological systems have had an accelerating impact upon the vast majority of Peruvians—and their environment. This chapter will focus upon one region of the Peruvian Amazon that has been dramatically affected by these processes. Numerous indigenous peoples have inhabited this biologically diverse region for millennia, but recently it has gained prominence internationally as the site of the Camisea Gas Project, a multinational consortium of petroleum companies from Argentina, Spain, and the United States.

The history of petroleum over the past century in Peru reflects the country's dependent position vis-à-vis transnational oil corporations, multilateral financial institutions, and First World countries. Except for a short period between 1968 and 1978, when Juan Velasco Alvarado's military regime attempted to nationalize the oil industry, most of the republican period was characterized by the subordination of national interests to foreign gas and oil companies. During the 1990s, state institutions were transformed by the Fujimori administration's neoliberal dictates, a response to "structural adjustment" policies dictated by the World Bank and IMF. Reasserting the assumption that foreign capital was necessary to fuel the national economy, the government privatized public companies and drew up legal

Notes for this chapter begin on page 142.

frameworks to attract foreign investment.[1] The energy sector was no exception, and the World Bank was an essential player in this process.

In this context, the Camisea gas field was depicted as one of the most promising and successful mega-projects ever carried out in Peru. Successive governments continuously emphasized its potential to promote economic development. Camisea would reduce the negative balance of hydrocarbons and lessen the country's dependence on gas. In addition to covering domestic needs, surpluses from Camisea would allow Peru to export gas. Development rhetoric veiled not only unethical links between state officials, Camisea multinational corporations, and the Inter-American Development Bank (IDB), but also, and most importantly, the project's pervasive negative consequences for indigenous peoples.

The Camisea project is emblematic of mega-projects' frequent basis in flawed assumptions about development and indigenous peoples. It demonstrates how these assumptions formed historically and shows how they function intrinsically within neoliberal projects. Here, I borrow anthropologist James Bodley's idea of the "inevitability argument" to explain how Camisea was portrayed as a vehicle for the inevitable drive toward "progress."[2] The alleged inevitability of Camisea facilitated its imposition on indigenous peoples, many of whom eventually came to think that it was useless to oppose the project.

In this chapter I will trace the processes that reinforce state rhetoric on Camisea with a focus on its users and its beneficiaries that also shows how the parties involved fulfill roles that gradually change their identities. I will particularly scrutinize the role of the Peruvian state and the gradual transformation of its identity from a public one into that of a broker—a process that benefits both multinational corporations (MNCs) and state elites. In analyzing these transformations, I will rely on the concept of controlling processes—"the mechanisms by which ideas take hold and become institutional in relation to power"[3]—devoting special attention to the ways in which elites aggressively promoted ideologies of progress, inevitability, and neoliberal economics to create new legal, economic, and bureaucratic institutions that facilitated environmental degradation, cultural control, and plunder.

Notes on the Ethnography of Corporations and Studying Up

Anthropological research on corporations has achieved relevance in the last forty years, but much of this research is not vertically integrated and cannot be labeled "cultural critique."[4] One apparent explanation for anthropological self-limitation is the recurring idea that anthropologists should study the exotic, travel to secluded locations, learn other languages, and live together with people of cultures different from one's own. Methods have also been a significant limitation, with ethnographic research often perceived as a long-term, systematic process of data collection over years spent building rapport and carrying out participant observation.

Globalization, including the rise of global business enterprises, definitely challenges these disciplinary assumptions. Laura Nader observed that transnational companies usually are headquartered in secluded locations, use a rather complex technical language, and have a staff whose culture differs from that of laypeople.[5] In the early 1970s, Nader challenged the underlying politics in classic anthropology, which tended to focus upon the most powerless social groups, by proposing that anthropology widen its scope of study. Subsequently, and from a purely critical standpoint, anthropologists George Marcus and Michael Fischer targeted the representations that anthropologists created of other societies through their ethnographic writing.[6] Since then, anthropology's object of study has broadened to include work focused on the activities of the Atlantic Richfield Company (ARCO) in Ecuador's tropical rainforest; the labor organization of corporations such as General Electric; negotiations between the U.S. government and Native American peoples on nuclear wastes; and science, its practitioners, and their influence in American society.[7] Common to all of these studies is the idea that corporations are social actors that significantly influence our lives. Like the state, corporations carry out processes of subject formation, and this is where anthropology's interest lies: in understanding political processes intertwined with cultures and ideologies that emerge in specific historical contexts.

The 1990s oil boom in Peru primarily affected the lives of indigenous peoples. Richard Lee's statement regarding Africa's nomadic peoples is appropriate to the situation of Peru's indigenous peoples, particularly during the boom: "the future of the hunting-gathering peoples is more closely bound up with the behavior of the multinationals than it is with the behavior of the seal and the antelope population."[8] During this period dozens of MNCs obtained grants of indigenous lands in the Amazon. The Indians who were forced to deal with corporate representatives lacked adequate information about them. In 1999 and 2000, when I carried out doctoral research, indigenous leaders were particularly interested in studies that would improve their understanding of corporate logic and functioning. They also emphatically challenged and coherently resisted the classic anthropology that had made them into objects of study. "This kind of anthropological research is only of use to transnational companies," they said, quite rightly.

Data gathering in indigenous communities was easier than data collection involving corporations. In 2006 and 2007, I collected information from Machiguenga communities regarding the consequences of the Camisea project. This research also, however, required me to study up to gain understanding of the ideology and performance of gas and oil companies, the Peruvian state's subordinate position vis-à-vis corporate power, and the role of international financial institutions (IFIs) in national economic policies. I wanted to expose the indigenous peoples' enormous social and political inequality, and the ways that gas and oil extraction reinforced it.

Methodological problems that arose in dealing with corporations and state institutions meant participant observation was not always possible. Certain public officials tried to dissuade me from studying the issue. In 2006, high-ranking officials publicly declared that opponents of the detrimental impacts of the oil, gas, or mining industry were extremists or terrorists who threatened the nation itself. Firsthand information on gas corporations was hard to obtain, mostly because of the corporations' characteristic secretiveness and the confidentiality clauses they impose on workers and the documents they work with. Thus I resorted to documents and archival work, research done by journalists and lawyers especially, informal conversations with people involved, depositions before international trials, and other eclectic methods. I gathered information via colleagues who conducted interviews and provided information. State officials also gave me access to information on public businesses. Private archives held information of more restricted scope. Although most of this information is public, Peru has done little to formally investigate and prosecute corporate crime in the courts. The sense of indignation this situation created as I conducted my research became an intellectually valuable resource.

An Overview of Camisea

During the 1980s, oil and gas extraction became concentrated in the central and southern Amazon. In 1981, Shell signed contracts for exploration and extraction of liquid hydrocarbon from Blocks 38 and 42, which entailed disbursing $30 million to the state in bank guarantees for the first stage and $50 million for the second.[9] Soon afterward, Shell began exploration in Manu National Park. When negotiations with President Alan García (1985–1990) commenced, Shell had already explored 3,400 km of seismic lines and drilled six exploratory wells; by 1987, it had discovered significant gas reserves in the upper Ucayali River. Shell's plan was to secure control over a region extending from southeast Peru to northeast Bolivia, where it also held petroleum and gas concessions.[10] Because Shell's exploration and extraction agreement covered only liquids, not gas, Shell and the government signed an agreement to negotiate a contract for gas exploration and extraction.

However, the Senate's Hydrocarbons Commission advised against this exploration and extraction contract with Shell.[11] Despite Shell's interest, its agreement with the Peruvian government to develop the Camisea gas field broke down in August 1988, ushering in a period of less oil production than in the 1970s and early 1980s.[12] Then, in 1990, President-Elect Alberto Fujimori promised to bring back MNCs and boost oil and gas investment. Fujimori's administration reformed state institutions and legislation to facilitate commercial goals. When Fujimori's second term (1995–2000) began, the recently created state-owned company Perupetro offered several oil concessions in the Amazon. Foreign companies like Murphy Oil, Great Western Resources, Quintana Minerals Corporation, IPF, Mobil, Chevron, ARCO, and Atlantic Resources International signed contracts.

In 1996, Peru's government and the Shell-Mobil consortium signed the "contract of the century," under which Shell could explore and extract gas from the Camisea area. Three blocks were granted in concession (88A, 88B, and 75); one overlapped with the territory of myriad indigenous peoples—Nanty, Yora, Machiguenga, and others.[13] In terms of liquid hydrocarbons, the Camisea fields' potential was now 2.5 billion barrels, seven times the reserves available at the time. Approximately twenty wells would each produce 80 million cubic feet of gas on a daily basis. By October 1997, Shell had invested nearly $2.5 billion in the project. Even the government thought that the second phase would proceed without a hitch. However, disagreements between the government and Shell put an end to the agreement in July 1998. Shell claimed that the weakness and limits of the Peruvian market necessitated state intervention to develop internal demand for gas and allow gas exports to Brazil. Shell also required the government to guarantee that the electricity generation sector would use gas. The government, for its part, did not agree to any of Shell's demands.[14]

Peru's critical hydrocarbon condition forced the state not only to further ease its own investment laws, but also to create new public entities to promote Camisea abroad. Several international and domestic firms were hired to design the legal, technical, economic, and bidding conditions of the Camisea project.[15] In 1999, a special committee appointed by the government called for international public bidding for concessions to extract hydrocarbons in Camisea and transport liquid and natural gas to Lima. The winning bid would be the one offering the greatest royalties. Of the several interested consortiums, a middle-sized company offered the highest royalty—37.42 percent—and won the bid. In February 2000, the Fujimori administration granted extraction rights over Block 88 to this consortium, formed by Pluspetrol Peru Corporation, the Peruvian subsidiary of the Texas-based Hunt Oil Company, South Korean conglomerate's subsidiary SK Corporation, and Tecpetrol del Perú (a property of the Argentine company Techint).

In 2000, the media exposed corruption within the Fujimori regime, and Fujimori resigned by fax and fled the country. Valentín Paniagua was chosen Speaker of Congress and then appointed Interim President of Peru until new elections were held in 2001. The Paniagua administration opted to create new incentives to promote oil and gas investment. In December 2000, the government authorized Perupetro to sign a contract with the Camisea Consortium with the aim of modifying energy consumption pattern to favor gas over oil.[16] In 2001, Alejandro Toledo was elected president. His political rhetoric centered on two issues: fighting corruption, and a vigorous but messianic *indigenismo*. Lacking a substantial political and economic program, Toledo needed to legitimize his government, so he sought out Pedro Pablo Kuczynski, a well-known, foreign-educated economist whose first-rate contacts in IFIs and MNCs had potential to redress the gradual deterioration of his administration's standing. Once in office, Kuczynski lobbied IDB officials to grant the Camisea Consortium a loan to develop, transport, and distribute gas.

By 2003, Pluspetrol had drilled 15,158 holes, built 2,022 km of seismic lines, developed four gas fields, built a refinery, and installed two pipelines, for which it paved 700 km of road.[17] Soon, environmentalists and indigenous organizations organized an international campaign to publicize the negative effects of Transportadora de Gas del Perú (TGP) and Pluspetrol's activities on indigenous peoples and the environment. The IDB, upon being informed of the environmental and human rights risks of the project, consequently granted a $5 million loan to the Peruvian government in December 2002 for the so-called Program for Institutional Strengthening and Support for the Environmental and Social Management of the Camisea Project. The Technical Group for Inter-institutional Coordination (GTCI), created by the Ministry of Energy and Mines to implement the institutional strengthening program, was in charge of developing and reinforcing mechanisms to supervise, monitor, and control environmental and social issues pertaining to Camisea's development. In August 2003, the directors of IDB and the Export-Import Bank of the United States again postponed granting the loan to the Camisea Consortium due to environmental concerns. But in September 2003, IDB approved a $135 million loan to the multinational TGP for gas transportation.[18]

From 2005 to 2009, three more concessions were granted in the area. Block 56, located in the Echarate district of Cusco, was granted to a consortium comprising Pluspetrol, Hunt Oil, SK Corporation, Tecpetrol del Perú, Sonatrach Peru, and Repsol Exploración Perú. Block 58, also in Cusco, was granted to Petrobras Energía Perú. Block 57, positioned between the departments of Junín, Ucayali, and Cusco, was granted to Repsol Exploración Perú, Burlington Resources Peru, and Petrobras Energía Perú. The area of these concessions essentially overlaps the whole of the Machiguenga territory.

Camisea Como Sea, or the Inevitability of "Progress"

State and corporate campaigns to promote the Camisea project reinforced the idea that both a national pro-market economy and neoliberalism itself are inevitable. Some contend that the principle of inevitability is a rhetorical device that market defenders use to assert that "there is no alternative to corporate globalization." This serves to "conceal the political forces and institutions that govern them" and to control social agency.[19] Laura Nader has noted that ideas like the inevitability argument serve as controlling mechanisms that are often "naturalized," reinforcing existing power structures.[20] In the context of development projects, Bodley argues, "progress"—understood as economic development—is portrayed as inevitable, unidirectional, and led by the economic market. The "inevitability argument" obscures the causes of change and veils the people (or institutions) who set those changes in motion. Once the assumption of inevitability is institutionalized, it becomes self-fulfilling and might weaken or erode indigenous autonomy.[21]

The ideology of inevitability is not new. In the 1950s, it undergirded Peruvian President General Manuel Odría's assertion (along with that of some U.S. officials) that indigenous peoples had to be assimilated into national society and should share their lands' riches with the rest of the world. Odría encouraged U.S. investment in the Amazon, including oil projects, cattle ranching, and logging.[22]

In the neoliberal era, multilateral banks, governments, and MNCs have seized upon inevitability anew, assuming that nation-states must engage in a globalized economy facilitating corporations' entry into Peru's national economy because investment boosts development. From this perspective, neoliberalism is inevitable, leaving those exposed to it—such as indigenous peoples—few options other than assimilation into the hegemonic economic trend. The "inevitability" of Camisea was artfully contrived through several discursive devices and illegal means that highlighted the potential benefits of the project for people themselves as well as the national economy.

Social compliance with the Camisea project was carefully designed through a twofold promotional campaign. In the first phase (1990s–2003), the government emphasized Camisea's domestic importance by discursively evoking the "national interest" in terms geared to achieve social legitimacy for the project. The government attempted to show that Camisea was a lifesaver amidst worrisome statistics on hydrocarbon imports: between 1990 and 1999, petroleum imports had reached almost $4.6 billion.[23] By 1997, hydrocarbon imports exceeded exports by $407 million.[24]

Camisea gas was earmarked to cover internal Peruvian demand first and be used for export thereafter. If gas reserves were insufficient for export, new sources would have to be found: "the aim was independence with respect to energy sources."[25] The Camisea promotional campaign stressed that the project would also promote foreign investment, increase state revenues, distribute revenues to regional governments, create jobs, diversify energy sources, reduce environmental pollution, increase the competitiveness of the electricity sector, bring about economic development (through a "trickle-down effect"), and reinforce Peru's image as an excellent place for foreign investment. The media promoted the idea that Camisea's arrival would benefit everybody by lowering gas and electricity prices, and continued to support the project even after frequent spills provoked criticism. The press apparently kept quiet about the spills or minimized their impacts; for example, media did not react when state officials responsible for Camisea stated that gas leaks were "normal."[26]

Gradually, the goal of covering internal demand was replaced by another: exporting Camisea's gas. The rhetoric in the second phase of the state's promotional campaign (2003–2008) emphasized the country's need to export gas. Gas exports would boost GDP by 1.3 percent per year, generate $3 billion in direct investment and $10 billion in state revenues, create jobs, and reinforce Peru's image as an energy exporter.[27] In September 2006, President Alan García promised to commence gas exports in January 2010. The companies involved in this process proceeded to benefit from exports before meeting domestic demand by devising a legal strategy and resorting to deceptive means. The Camisea contract could not be changed unless the Gas Law (27133) was modified, so key state officials argued in favor of amendments to Article 4 of the law. In 2005, they enabled the necessary changes and also deleted part of a sub-point that prohibited gas exports unless new sources of gas were discovered.[28] Following these changes (implemented by Supreme Decrees), the Executive modified the contract to allow the Camisea Consortium to export reserves that had originally been earmarked for domestic consumers. Additionally, special bills passed for oil companies working on Block 56 allowed them to give the Peruvian government only 5–6 percent (rather than 38 percent) royalties. Gas extracted from Block 56 would be exported.

The contract signed between Perupetro and the Camisea Consortium in 2000 outlined several obligations for the consortium, which were later changed. State officials' intention to reduce the established royalty percentage faced decisive opposition in high-ranking spheres. Nonetheless, the government financed the construction of a pipeline by the Camisea companies with subsidies of approximately $300 million dollars, which were borne by consumers.[29] In addition; electricity fares and liquefied petroleum gas (LPG) prices were increased, despite promises by the government and the consortium to lower them. Residential rates for gas were 40 percent higher than the amount established in the gas distribution contract. Meanwhile, changes in the contract replaced the minimum number of *actual* gas connections with an offer of *potential* connections. The mechanisms the Toledo administration used to pave the way for the Camisea project led some journalists to call the process *Camisea como sea* (Camisea by whatever means necessary).

The Vanishing "Public" Sector: The Peruvian State as Broker

Many authors have analyzed the gradual loss of sovereignty of the nation-state and transformation of state function in an era of neoliberalism.[30] The Camisea project illustrates how the formation of Peru's neoliberal identity led to the emergence of a new form of state sovereignty. The state practices that facilitated the Camisea project reveal numerous connections between the "private" (national and international) and "public" sectors that blur the margins of the public. By assuming the role of a broker—an intermediary or agent who negotiates contracts and facilitates the entry of corporate capital into the national economy—the state disavowed its theoretically neutral public status as guardian of its people's well-being. Government officials directly or indirectly representing private interests directed certain branches of the state to assume this blurred neoliberal stance.

In his 2002 analysis of IMF policies, economist Joseph Stiglitz raised an important question: "Who decides what countries do?" Institutions such as the IMF, he says, are not run by the richest industrialized countries alone, but also by their commercial and financial interests. The commerce and economy ministers who attend IMF and World Bank meetings represent the economic interests of specific groups within their own countries. Ministers and multilateral development bank staff usually are inextricably linked to the financial community: " . . . many of [the IMF's] key personnel came from the financial community, and many of its key personnel, having served these interests well, left to well-paying jobs in the financial community."[31] This intermingling is important because these individuals see the world through the eyes of the financial community. Together they produce particular knowledge and expertise about how the world should work, what it should look like, and what processes are convenient for creating that world.

The "revolving door" is a global phenomenon with historical roots.[32] In Peru since the 1990s, relations between the private-capital sector, IFIs, and the state have been reinforced and naturalized to shape the state as a nebulous public entity and allow the development of neoliberalism. Structural adjustment in the 1990s was an opportunity for powerful economic groups to control the state and profit from it: "It could be said that the ministers of economy actually worked for the main [entrepreneurs] . . . thus, the Ministers of Economy and others ended up in the board of directors of important private companies when their mandate was over."[33]

Pedro Pablo Kuczynski had ties to the international financial community and also to corporations involved in Camisea. He began his career at the World Bank in the 1960s and eventually held senior positions there, but he has constantly switched between the state and private sector throughout his professional life. As mentioned earlier, the Toledo administration appointed him Minister of Economy and Finance. Kuczynski left this post to work as a private investor and then, in 2002–2003, was appointed to a high post at IDB.[34] These were key years for the Camisea corporation TGP, as it fell to IDB to decide whether to approve a loan to it (see above).

Kuczynski's ties extend to other oil corporations as well. In 2003 and 2004, he was a financial advisor for Ray Hunt, president of Hunt Oil.[35] He has also been affiliated with Techint, owner of Tenaris. From December 2002 to February 2004 Kuczynski was the director of Tenaris, which sold steel pipes for Camisea pipelines, six of which spilled between 2004 and 2007. In August 2003 Kuczynski—still working as a private consultant for Pluspetrol, partner of Hunt Oil and Techint—prepared a financial proposal to obtain $225 million for Camisea via a $75 million loan and internal bonds for $150 million.[36]

In 2004 and 2005, Kuczynski went back to working for the Toledo administration. Reappointed Minister of Economy in February 2004, he served in that post until his July 2005 appointment as Prime Minister of Peru. His intervention in favor of Camisea was well known by the press.[37] After his ties to Camisea were made public, Congress initially wanted to impeach him; however, these efforts were curtailed by lobbying, orchestrated deep within the administration, that sought to convince each congressional representative to halt the impeachment process. Soon afterward, the scandal about the government's connections to Camisea corporations and the IDB was silenced.[38] Congressional officials declared to the media requesting an impeachment process posed a serious risk in the midst of an electoral period.

This was not the only case of the state playing the role of broker. The year 2003 was key for the Camisea Consortium, thanks in part to then Minister of Energy and Mines Jaime Quijandría, whose term witnessed the passage of many bills and decrees facilitating the development of Camisea. Later, press reports revealed that Quijandría had been a private consultant for TGP in 2001, and that his son was general manager of Sodexho, a corporation that provided food services for mining and hydrocarbon companies. When his term ended in 2004, the World Bank hired the former minister.[39] For several years, Pedro Gamio, vice minister of energy from 2006 to 2008, worked as a lawyer for the National Society of Mining and Petroleum. Humberto Cabrera, a manager for the Yanacocha mining company, was also chief of staff to Interior Minister Luis Alva Castro (2007–2008). Other officials at the Ministry of Energy and Mines have likewise worked for mining or petroleum corporations. Even President García made his commitment to Camisea public in September 2006, shortly after winning the presidential elections, when he told Ray Hunt he would back Hunt Oil and the Camisea Consortium and stressed that Camisea was a strategic project for the government.

In promoting Camisea abroad, the state played the role of broker, bringing together the international financial community and hydrocarbon corporations, and lobbying for the loans the Camisea Consortium needed. State officials enabled this process while cycling through a "revolving door" between private capital and the public sector, using their ties to benefit Camisea MNCs. The international financial community naturalized the unethical role of these state officials, who not only set up an alliance between the state and MNCs but also were *part of* the MNCs and IFIs, thus blending corporate and public interests. Captured by corporate capital, the state became simultaneously judge and party, which affected its legitimacy by subordinating it to the private sector.[40]

Sovereignty was porous when it came to the interests of powerful local groups, MNCs and IFIs, yet it was strongly imposed upon underrepresented groups (such as indigenous peoples) and outspoken opponents of Camisea's detrimental impacts, who included state actors. Relatively powerless vis-à-vis the executive branch of government, state institutions like the Ombudsman's Office and the Congress unsuccessfully attempted to regulate the harmful activities of the Camisea Consortium. Ultimately, however, they were thwarted by the different legal, administrative, and informal mechanisms at the disposal of an executive branch convinced that regulation impedes investment.

Controlling Dissidents within the State

The Energy Regulator Institution (formerly, Organismo Supervisor de la Inversión en Energía, or OSINERG, and now known as Organismo Supervisor de la Inversión en Energía y Minería, or OSINERGMIN), a state institution created in 1996 to monitor gas and oil activities, has only meekly exercised its powers. For example, regarding the claim, made by the indigenous organization Interethnic Association for Development of the Peruvian Forest (AIDESEP) and the NGO Shinai Serjali,[41] that in 2003 influenza had caused seventeen deaths in several Nanti communities, OSINERG replied that "there were really 22 deaths, of whom 82 percent were under 12 years old and the cause of death was diarrhoea due to a deficient nutritional state of the children, especially in their first year of life . . . there is no evidence that the deaths were due to contagious diseases from the workers of the companies operating in the area."[42]

On 24 November 2005, a pipeline breach in the area of the Camisea project—the fourth—spilled natural gas for several hours, contaminating the Parotori, Picha, and Bajo Urubamba Rivers, the Machiguenga Communal Reserve, and the Camaná, Mayapo, Puerto Huallana, and Kirigueti communities. Indigenous Camisea project monitors found a tapir and several fish that had died from the pollution. An intense hydrocarbon stench spread throughout the area, and people from the Camaná, Puerto Huallana, and Nueva Vida fell ill. OSINERG officials, who arrived four days after the spill, offered no explanation to the communities. Three months later, OSINERG and TGP officials visited Bajo Urubamba communities to report on the causes of the spill, identify responsibilities, and discuss compensation. According to OSINERG, the broken pipeline had spilled approximately 6,000 barrels, polluting water and soil. Each family in the

Nueva Vida community received $29 as compensation. In Kirigueti, by contrast, each family received $100.[43]

Multiple cracks and spills in the gas pipeline are undeniable evidence of the environmental and social impacts of TGP's irresponsible activities in the region. In a report to the Peruvian Congress, the independent environmental firm E-Tech International noted that TGP was culpable in that it had traced a perilous route for the pipeline, used defective pipes, and fastened them inadequately, hastily completing the pipeline to avoid contractual sanctions for missing deadlines. OSINERG levied fines of $3.5 million against TGP, but only $2 million has been paid. A sound critique of OSINERG is that whereas indigenous communities suffer the consequences of gas production, it is the state, not communities, that receives the money.[44] So little time elapsed between spills that before OSINERG reported the causes of one spill, another had occurred. In view of the numerous spills caused by TGP's flawed pipelines, the Executive ordered that TGP bear the costs of an inquiry. Legally, OSINERG should have supervised this inquiry, but in 2006 the Ministry of Energy and Mines approved a Supreme Decree assigning supervision to itself, not OSINERG.[45]

The government overtly attempted to control any obstacle to the project. It not only dismantled and/or blocked state institutions, but also left bilateral agreements—such as the one with the IDB—unfulfilled, for which no institution or state official was even sanctioned. The Ombudsman's Office created for the Camisea project in September 2002 was dismantled in December 2006. Likewise, the government dismissed a former chief of the National Institute of Natural Resources (INRENA) who opposed construction of underwater pipelines because of potential risks to the marine ecosystem.[46]

The state's 2003 agreement with IDB stipulates compliance with 104 points related to environmental and social mitigation. So far, however, little effort has been made to honor these commitments. INRENA and the National Institute of Development of Andean, Amazonian and African-Peruvian Peoples (INDEPA) are the public entities charged with coordinating installation of control posts in the Kugapakori Nahua Reserve close to the Camisea area to protect isolated indigenous peoples from outsiders, especially loggers. The former is responsible for environmental and forest protection; the latter, for the protection of indigenous peoples. INRENA argued that installing posts in the reserve was not its responsibility,[47] whereas INDEPA lacked the staff to do so. In September and October 2006, INDEPA finally repaired a control post that the Yora had built in the reserve and built another one, but neither INDEPA nor INRENA is involved in activities there.[48]

In March 2006, the Peruvian Congress appointed a committee to investigate the causes of the numerous spills. The committee concluded that officials from the Ministry of Energy and Mines, General Bureau of Hydrocarbons, and OSINERG had systematically evaded monitoring the design and construction of the Camisea infrastructure. Consequently, the zones of Atalaya (in the Ucayali region), Las Malvinas (in the Camisea area, Cusco region), the route of the pipeline, and the surrounding communities were polluted.[49]

The IDB-financed GTCI had been charged with distributing funds to state agencies, including the National Commission of Andean, Amazonian, and Afro-Peruvian Peoples (CONAPA). But the executive branch had covertly conditioned the portion of the IDB budget assigned to CONAPA to force its officials to support GTCI's activities related to Camisea. I attended a meeting where GTCI's director, Carlos Garaycochea, suggested that the portion of the IDB loan assigned to fund CONAPA activities depended on CONAPA's backing GTCI activities.

Other state agencies' efforts to publicize Camisea's impacts on local communities were systematically ignored. Reports from the Ministry of Health, the Ombudsman's Office, and officials from its decentralized offices in Ayacucho, Cusco, Huancavelica, and Ica described Camisea's tremendous environmental, social, and political impacts but were disregarded by the Executive. Meanwhile, TGP, Pluspetrol, and subcontracted companies pressured state officials to suppress reports harmful to their image.[50] In 2006, an Ombudsman's Office report questioned the Camisea Consortium's harmful activities vis-à-vis indigenous peoples and settlers, arguing that no legal framework existed to protect them from arbitrary negotiations with the Camisea corporations. The office recommended a halt to state concessions for hydrocarbon development activities that risked the rights of indigenous or other particularly vulnerable people.[51]

Many state officials do not even know whether indigenous peoples inhabit the area of the proposed blocks before they grant concessions, and once made aware of these peoples' existence, they favor hydrocarbon projects.[52] The assumption is that indigenous peoples are less important than national "development." For instance, Ministry of Energy and Mines officials arbitrarily interpret the rights of indigenous peoples established in ILO Convention 169. The officials assume that consultation should occur after concessions have been granted, whereas indigenous organizations claim, according to ILO Convention 169, that it should take place before, as otherwise consultation would be absolutely pointless. The Ombudsman Office's report outlines the reasons for Energy Sector officials' indifference to the situation of the local population: "We must call attention to the attitude of some officials of the Ministry of Energy and Mines, which seems to reflect the perception that there is a contradiction between the protection of human rights and the promotion of the Camisea project, and that, in view of that contradiction, they have chosen to give preference to the project."[53]

The state is not a homogenous entity. Rather, it is composed of several institutions acting in a disarticulated fashion, especially vis-à-vis the social and environmental impacts of the Camisea project. However, it is also evident that the executive branch, through the Ministry of Energy and Mines, is more powerful than other state agencies. In this case, the state acted as a broker for multilateral banks, favoring the Camisea corporations and thus abandoning its regulatory obligations toward indigenous peoples and the environment. Today, the state's role as a broker is key to neoliberalism's functioning. Its advocates know this premise well and act accordingly, expecting eventual benefits for performing their role. In the end, the state's new corporate identity leaves indigenous communities unprotected, which in turn strengthens the Camisea Consortium's role as donor and benefactor. Thus, the idea of Camisea as inevitable becomes a self-fulfilling prophecy.

Conclusion

Laura Nader's ideas—of studying up, down, and sideways, and of controlling processes—are key to analyzing the Camisea project. Structural conditions, such as the country's dependence upon hydrocarbon imports and the extreme poverty of the Camisea region, partly explain why the gas project initially won national consensus, but at the same time this consensus was artfully crafted by government officials who portrayed Camisea as a win-win investment for all. The project was financed through the efforts of state officials who cycled in and out of financial institutions, MNCs, and the state, working for the private sector at one time and for the state at another, thus mixing corporate and state interests via a "revolving door." The Peruvian state, ultimately transformed into a broker, representing the interests of private capital, and subordinating its public role as the defender of legality, human rights, and the environment to its role as intermediary between MNCs and IFIs. Privatization of public goods, hardly restricted to Peru, is a neoliberal pattern evident in many countries, including the United States.[54]

Camisea como sea expresses not only the inevitability attributed to Camisea, but also state officials' unethical practices in pushing its development and, most importantly, the "inevitability" of neoliberalism itself. Local and international claims denouncing environmental and social damage caused by six consecutive gas pipeline spills were given undue attention by the executive branch's Ministry of Energy and Mines. Although the state is not a homogenous entity, this ministry controlled the relatively powerless agencies that expressed concerns about the project. Despite significant concerns about the project, high-ranking officials representing the Peruvian state established links between Camisea corporations and IDB. The state acted as a broker lobbying multilateral banks on behalf of Camisea corporations. Ultimately, it surrendered its regulatory role and its obligation to protect indigenous peoples and the environment.

Acknowledgments

This chapter draws on research carried out for the United Nations Research Institute for Social Development. Those further interested in the history of petroleum in Peru may want to refer to my earlier work. See Patricia Urteaga-Crovetto, *Negotiating Identities and Hydrocarbons: Territorial Claims in the Southeastern Peruvian Amazon*, unpublished Ph.D. dissertation, University of California, Berkeley (2005). I thank Suzana Sawyer, Terence Gomez, Thomas Perrault, and Jon Altman for their insightful comments. I am also grateful to Rachael Stryker and Roberto González, who invited me to participate in this project and made suggestions that are very much appreciated, and to Iván Vera, who kindly helped me obtain important information. Finally, I thank Armando and Sebastián Guevara for their infinite patience.

Notes

1. Although defenders of privatization in Peru contend that this was necessary in a time of economic globalization, many Latin American countries did not privatize their oil companies; instead, they promoted the free market while preserving state enterprise.
2. See James Bodley, "Alternatives to Ethnocide: Human Zoos, Living Museums, and Real People," in *Western Expansion and Indigenous People*, ed. Elias Sevilla-Casas (The Hague and Paris: Mouton, 1977).
3. Laura Nader, "Controlling Processes: Tracing the Dynamic Components of Power," *Current Anthropology* 38, no. 5 (1997): 711–339.
4. George Marcus and Michael M. J. Fischer, eds., *Anthropology as Cultural Critique* (Los Angeles and Berkeley: University of California Press, 1986).

5. Laura Nader, "Up the Anthropologist: Perspectives Gained from Studying Up," in *Reinventing Anthropology*, ed. Dell H. Hymes (New York: Pantheon Books, 1972).
6. Marcus and Fischer, *Anthropology as Cultural Critique*.
7. See for example June Nash, "Anthropology of the Multinational Corporations," in *New Directions in Political Economy: An Approach from Anthropology*, ed. Madeleine Barbara Leons and Frances Rothstein (Westport, CT: Greenwood Press, 1979); Suzana Sawyer, *Crude Chronicles: Indigenous Politics, Multinational Oil, and Neoliberalism in Ecuador* (Durham, NC: Duke University Press, 2004); Roberto González, "Brave New Workplace," and Jay Ou, "Native Americans and the Monitored Retrievable Storage Plan for Nuclear Wastes," both in *Essays on Controlling Processes*, ed. Laura Nader, special issue, *Kroeber Anthropological Society Papers* 80 (1996): 14–31 and 32–89 respectively.
8. Richard B. Lee, 1982 "The Impact of Development on Foraging Peoples: A World Survey." In *Tribal Peoples and Development Issues: A Global Overview*, ed. John Bodley (Mountain View, CA: Mayfield Publishing, 1982).
9. Humberto Campodónico, *La Política Petrolera 1970–1985: El Estado, las Contratistas y Petroperú*. (Lima: Desco, 1986).
10. One project included an IDB-financed duct linking the coast and the rain forest at an estimated cost of $700 million. See Koy Thomson and Nigel Dudley, "Transnationals and Oil in Amazonia," *The Ecologist* 19, no. 6 (November/December 1989): 219–224.
11. The Hydrocarbons Commission declared that the basic agreement between Shell and the state was void because their legal relationship had already ended, and in fact, the exploration contract between Shell and the state ended in January 1988 because Shell had not discovered any oil. Moreover, Blocks 38 and 42 had been returned to the state. The agreement, signed in March 1988, did not have the binding force of a contract. It established conditions pertaining to the extraction, development, and production of the discovered gas field not included in the contract. The commission also declared that the economic conditions of the deal were unclear and held the agreement to be legally, economically, financially, technically, and commercially ambiguous. The Peruvian government, it suggested, should seek more convenient proposals according to its interests. See Carlos Malpica, *La Verdad sobre el Gas de Camisea* (Lima: Ediciones La Escena Contemporánea, 1989).
12. Juan de Onis, *The Green Cathedral: Sustainable Development of Amazonia* (New York: Oxford University Press, 1992).
13. Beatriz Huertas, "El proyecto Camisea y los derechos de los pueblos indígenas," in *Asuntos Indígenas 3/03: Terrorismo, Conflictos y Derechos*. (Copenhagen: International Work Group for Indigenous Affairs, 2002); see also Roberto Espinoza and Beatriz Huertas, *Evaluación social del proyecto Camisea y defensa de los pueblos indígenas auto aislados* (Informe presentado por encargo de Aprodeh), unpublished manuscript, 2003.
14. Jorge Eusebio Manco, *Privatización e Hidrocarburos: Mito y Realidad, Perú 1991–2002*. (Lima: Fondo Editorial, Universidad Nacional Mayor de San Marcos, 2002).
15. Hernán Tello, "Actividad Petrolera," in *Amazonia Hoy, Politicas Publicas, Actores Sociales y Desarrollo Sostenible*, ed. Martha Rodríguez Achung (Lima: IIAP, PUCP, 1994).
16. Manco, *Privatización e Hidrocarburos*.
17. See Carlos Herrera Descalzi, "Assessment on the Camisea Pipeline Project in Peru," testimony presented before the U.S. Senate Committee on Foreign Relations hearing on "Multilateral Development Banks: Development Effectiveness of Infrastructure Projects," 12 July 2006, accessed 18 October 2010, http://www.etechinternational.org/07–13–06_Carlos percent20Herrera percent20Descalzi_testimony_US_senate.pdf.
18. Espinoza and Huertas, *Evaluación social*.

19. Peter Shorett, "Dogmas of Inevitability: Tracking Symbolic Power in the Global Marketplace," in *Controlling Processes—Selected Essays 1994–2005*, ed. Laura Nader, special issue, *Kroeber Anthropological Society Papers* 92/93 (2005): 335, 339.
20. Nader, "Controlling Processes," 711.
21. John Bodley, "The World Bank Tribal Policy: Criticisms and Recommendations," testimony presented before U.S. House Committee on Banking, Finance, and Urban Affairs and U.S. House Subcommittee on International Development, Institutions, and Finance, 29 June 1983; see also John Bodley, *Victims of Progress* (Menlo Park, NJ: Cummings, 1975).
22. See Gerard Colby and Charlotte Dennett, *Thy Will Be Done: The Conquest of the Amazon, Nelson Rockefeller, and Evangelism in the Age of Oil* (New York: HarperCollins, 1995); Norconsult, *Social and Economic Effects of Petroleum Development Programmes: Consultant's Report* (Geneva: ILO, 1984); Eleodoro Mayorga, *The Social and Economic Effects of Petroleum Development in Peru* (Geneva: ILO, 1987), 116.
23. Manco, *Privatización e Hidrocarburos*.
24. Instituto Nacional de Estadística e Informática, *Perú: Compendio Estadístico 1996–1997* (Lima: Instituto Nacional de Estadística e Informática, 1997).
25. Descalzi, "Assessment on the Camisea Pipeline," 2.
26. Espinoza and Huertas, *Evaluación social*; Manco, *Privatización e Hidrocarburos*.
27. Descalzi, "Assessment on the Camisea Pipeline," 4, 5.
28. Descalzi, "Assessment on the Camisea Pipeline," 6.
29. Juan Valdivia, 03/27/07, *La República*; see also Descalzi, "Assessment on the Camisea Pipeline."
30. See Sol Picciotto, "Fragmented States and International Rules of Law," *Social & Legal Studies: An International Journal* 6, no. 2 (1997): 259–279; Joseph E. Stiglitz, *Globalization and Its Discontents* (New York: W.W. Norton, 2002); Boaventura de Sousa Santos, *Toward a Common Sense: Law, Science and Politics in the Paradigmatic Transition* (New York: Routledge, 1995); Shalini Randeria, "Protecting the Rights of Indigenous Communities in the New Architecture of Global Governance: The Interplay of International Institutions and Post-Colonial States" and Gerhard Anders, "The 'Trickle-Down' Effects of the Civil Service Reform in Malawi: Studying Up," both in *Legal Pluralism and Unofficial Law in Social, Economic and Political Development. Papers of the XIII International Congress, 7–10 April 2002, Chiang Mai, Thailand*, Ed. Pradhan, Rajendra, Kathmandu: The International Centre for the Study of Nature, Environment and Culture; Sawyer, *Crude Chronicles*.
31. Stiglitz, *Globalization and Its Discontents*, 207.
32. C. Wright Mills, *The Power Elite* (New York: Oxford University Press, 1956).
33. Óscar Ugarteche, *Adiós Estado Bienvenido Mercado* (Lima: Friedrich Ebert Stiftung, UNMSM, 2004).
34. During the first term of Fernando Belaúnde Terry (1963–1968), Kuczynski was a state official who helped the International Petroleum Company; during Terry's second term (1980–1985) Kuczynski, now Minister of Energy and Mines, sent Congress a bill that created tax breaks for petroleum corporations. See Malpica, *La Verdad sobre*; Ángel Páez and Milagros Salazar, "Kuczinski y la red financiera de las Empreseas de Camisea," *La República*, 10 March 2006.
35. Members of the Upstream Consortium, which conducts gas exploration and extraction, include Pluspetrol, Hunt Oil, SK Corporation, Tecpetrol del Perú, Sonatrach Perú, and Repsol Exploración Perú. TGP heads the Downstream Consortium, which transports gas from Camisea to the coast.
36. Páez and Salazar, "Kuczinski y la red financiera."

37. When the fifth spill occurred in March 2006, Kuczynski first called it an act of sabotage, then argued it had been blown out of proportion. Stressing that many spills happen worldwide, he said geological conditions—not defective pipes—had caused the spills. Media and government officials repeated this explanation verbatim. For instance, Cecilia Blume, Kuczynski's main adviser, told reporters that spills were "normal." See Cecilia Blume, "Que se rompan los ductos es algo normal," *La República*, 7 March 2006. Such instances illustrate the Peruvian government's capacity for "damage control."
38. Manuel Dammert publicly denounced the conflict of interests in Kuczynski's involvement as a state official linked to Camisea corporations. Kuczynski, in turn, sued Dammert for calling him a "lobbyist." See Dammert, *La República Lobbysta: Amenaza contra la Democracia Peruana en el siglo XXI* (Lima: Medios y Enlaces SRL, 2009).
39. Other former ministers are working at the IMF or the World Bank at this time of writing. For instance, Javier Silva Ruete, former Peruvian Minister of Economy, was part of the IMF staff.
40. Descalzi concluded that these issues rendered the project illegitimate and illegal, and would also cause future credibility problems for the government and IDB, and affect other mining and energy projects in Peru, which is actually happening. Descalzi, "Assessment on the Camisea Pipeline."
41. Shinai is a Peruvian NGO whose members are mostly English professionals working in the Peruvian Southeastern Amazon Basin. It was founded in 2003 to investigate and share information about indigenous peoples' situations, and to help them defend natural resource rights. In the Nahua language, *shinai* means to remember, love, or care.
42. OSINERG, official letter no. 7514, 24 September 2004; see Dirección General de Salud Ambiental, *Informe de Ensayo Hidrobiológico No. 0463, Laboratorio de Hidrobiología, Microbiología de Aguas*, 18 July 2006.
43. See Dirección General de Salud Ambiental, *Informe*. When explaining the gravity of the fifth spill (300,000 gallons) to the Peruvian Congress, engineer Bill Powers of E-Tech mentioned that 300,000 gallons was enough to fill the tanks of 30,000 cars. See Peru Congreso de la República, *Informe Final de la Comisión Investigadora Encargada de la Investigación del Transporte del Gas (Gasoducto) del Proyecto Camisea, las Causas y Consecuencias de los Reiterados Accidentes Producidos en el Mismo y la Determinación de las Responsabilidades Políticas, Administrativas y Penales a que Hubiere Lugar, así como el Estudio y Evaluación de los Compromisos Asumidos en los Contratos Suscritos*, 20 June 2006, http://www.amazonwatch.org/newsroom/view_news.php?id=1173 (accessed 18 October 2010). For information on compensation to Nueva Vida families, see David Martínez de Aguirre, "Situación, oportunidades y riesgos del Proyecto Camisea," *Estudios Amazónicos* 2, no. 2 (2005): 71–89.
44. The administration of the money generated by the Camisea project, be it fines or royalties, is questionable. A share of the Camisea royalties was earmarked for creation of a National Defense Fund to obtain weapons for the Peruvian military. In July 2006, at a U.S. Senate Foreign Relations Committee hearing on the effectiveness of infrastructure projects funded by multilateral development banks, U.S. Senator Richard Lugar expressed concern over Toledo's decision to channel Camisea royalties toward national defense.
45. The Germanischer Lloyd Company concluded that the annual frequency of fractures in the pipeline is 3 per 1,000 km, which is comparable to the frequency of accidents of pipelines constructed before 1982. Pipelines built after 1982 with the best modern geological engineering practices show an annual frequency of accidents of 0.33 per 1,000 km. The selection of the tubes and the welding procedures were flawed. See Gustavo Gorriti, "Camisea ¿Cómo sea?" *Ilustración Peruana Caretas*, 14 June 2007.

46. See also Soria, Carlos "Camisea: ¿Por qué cuesta tanto el gas barato?" *ICONOS: Revista de Ciencias Sociales* (Quito) 21 (January 2005): 47–55.
47. State official, Aráoz, pers. comm., 2006.
48. Anthropologist working in the region, Gregor MacLellan, pers. comm., 2007.
49. Peru Congreso de la República, *Informe Final.*
50. Soria, "Camisea."
51. See Peru Defensoria del Pueblo, "Superposición de lotes de hidrocarburos con áreas naturales protegidas y reservas territoriales en la Amazonía Peruana," Report No. 009–2007-DP/ASPMA.CN (2007), http://www.petronoticias.com/noticias.php?op=NoticiaCompleta&id=152.
52. Daniel Saba, former director of Perupetro, stated that there is no evidence that isolated Indigenous Peoples are present in the areas where Perupetro will be granted concessions. He also challenged the Ombudsman's Office's report that hydrocarbon activities in these areas would harm the lives of isolated Indians, accusing the office of risking petroleum and gas investment. See petroleumworld.com, "Out of Order," *Petroleumworld News*, 26 September 2008, http://www.petroleumworld.com/issues08092601.htm
53. Peru Defensoría del Pueblo, "El Proyecto Camisea y sus efectos en los derechos de las persona," Report No. 103 (2006), http://www.eclac.cl/dmaah/noticias/paginas/7/27987/DEFENSORIA_PUEBLO_CAMISEA.pdf.
54. E.g., the recent debate on the merits of a public vs. private health insurance system in the United States.

Part III

Studying Relationships and Bureaucracies

Chapter 7

ON FAMILY
Adoptive Parenting Up, Down, and Sideways

Rachael Stryker

On American culture, Margaret Mead has been paraphrased: "Nobody has ever before asked the nuclear family to live all by itself in a box the way we do. With no relatives and no support, we've put it in an impossible situation."[1] Some have interpreted Mead's sentiments as inviting more institutional intervention into families, but when Mead said this in 1963, she was actually referring to Americans' tendency to promote the nuclear family at the expense of extended, intergenerational, and non-sanguine families forged in local communities. She was also concerned that this tendency would pave the way for out-of-touch politicians, businesspeople, and experts to make important personal and local decisions for people, disrupting the flows of organic and local knowledges that enable families to act on their own behalves.

In an essay titled "The Vertical Slice: Hierarchies and Children," Laura Nader elaborated similar points but added that institutions of *all* stripes in the United States were telling families how to think and act. For example, she linked the U.S. real estate development industry's construction of housing tracts for the young and nursing homes for the elderly to age segregation and to children's lack of a sense of history. She also observed many such linkages and hierarchies affect child rearing, even when they seem hidden or distant: "When we ask the same questions we would ask in smaller societies—who is feeding the children, who is clothing them, who is sheltering them, who is entertaining them, and who is determining their genetic

---

Notes for this chapter begin on page 168.

legacy—the answer depends upon what part of the institutional hierarchy we are looking at: the family, McDonald's, or General Foods."[2]

Anthropologists know that the family expresses itself differently across time and space—there are families of all sizes and compositions, with children and without—and that most family forms around the world have undergone much transformation in the last 200 years as territorial nation-states have replaced kin groups in organizing social, political, and economic life.[3] Yet from a socio-biological perspective, the family's function is fairly universal. Family, a culturally specific, elastic unit that can present in a range of ways, from "blood" to non-sanguine relations, and from households to villages, is the primary site for the generation of relationships that promote the birth, care, and enculturation of children.[4]

Anthropologists also know that *how* the family invests in children differs across cultures. Again from a socio-biological perspective, some families include many offspring while investing little energy in keeping each alive and raising them, in the hope that some will survive and carry on the genetic inheritance. Such families are typically found in cultures marked by high youth mortality and large extended family interaction in pastoral or agrarian contexts. In other cultures—usually industrialized and capitalist, with a low youth mortality rate—adults take their chances on a low number of children and invest considerably in them, attempting to assure these offspring a long life expectancy. In these cultures, the nuclear family is the most common expression of family, and experts and professionals often replace biological family members to aid in caring for, and transmitting culture to, children. Meanwhile, some cultures fall in between.[5]

In the United States, parents normally invest extraordinary amounts of time, energy, and money in individual children. In fact, Americans' investment in children is so great that a special term has emerged for it: *neontocracy*, a child-centered culture whose primary goal is to serve children's many needs.[6] Neontocracy symbolically places children at the top of a pyramid whose lower strata hold child experts such as pediatricians, educators, and child-rearing scholars (e.g., Dr. Spock); corporations such as Disney, babyGap, and Gerber; babysitters and other caregivers; and finally, parents and grandparents. Extended family such as aunts, uncles, and cousins do not usually play much of a role in determining and meeting children's needs, nor do neighbors. Furthermore, members of older generations are very seldom considered crucial to a child's upbringing.[7]

The neontocracy heralds the nuclear family—the primary site through which investment in children is nurtured and ultimately rewarded—as central to the culture. Considerable corporate, political, legal, and moral energies are expended for the stated purpose of supporting and protecting the nuclear family as a site for transitioning the young to adulthood. Corporations claim to produce products to help raise children and promote smoother family functioning; state and federal governments enact laws that profess to better aid children's intellectual and physical development; and "family values" are always the bricks and mortar of politicians' election campaign platforms. But looking at the neontocracy from up, down, and sideways—that is, cross-culturally, historically, and holistically—leads quickly to the realization that in many cases, institutional attention to families benefits the institutions themselves more than it aids families. Turning families into consumers, demographics, and voting blocs is less about cultivating family longevity than promoting bureaucratic permanence.

Institutions in the neontocracy accomplish this by "bypassing" parents, among other means. As Ralph Nader has demonstrated, corporations spend (and make) handsome sums designing advertising and entertainment that make their self-serving messages to children appealing, even in the face of parental opposition.[8] But another factor in institutions' favor is that few adults living in the neontocracy ever question the motivations of the highly institutional practices that claim to support their efforts to ensure the health and longevity of the culture's youngest members. Americans consistently outsource parenthood to a broad range of institutional experts: social workers, nurses, child development specialists, parenting experts. As journalist Pamela Paul has put it:

> The concept of asking people for help outside the nuclear unit isn't new. Parents have always outsourced a myriad of child-rearing tasks and responsibilities, but they used to do so within their circle of extended family members and older siblings, not to hired strangers. . . . Outsourcing [today] . . . highlights how, in certain ways, children have become little businesses in which parents are supposed to invest.[9]

Whether institutional influence over families occurs through the bypassing of parents or the outsourcing of parenting itself, both routes exemplify how institutions narratively craft the experiences of family, domesticity, parenting, and childhood in the United States. What are the consequences of relying on these institutional narratives to shape and enact family? One excellent site for exploring this question may be the field of international adoption, where parents wishing to build families regularly seek out institutions and are required to comply with them. Since the early 1990s, refined reproductive technologies and increasing global communications and circulations have provided more options than ever to Americans who need help in constructing families. However, the increasing interaction between adoptive parents and institutions such as global and federal regulatory agencies, adoption agencies, and medical professionals also means that individuals often have less control over how they *enact* family. And it's not just that there's too much help; the quality of the help can be quite suspect.

This chapter examines ethnographic examples of institutional impact on families in the field of international adoption. It is a new analysis of some old concerns about neontocracy, which asks particularly whether institutional narratives and practice should replace parental intuition and intelligence in family building. Examining the controlling processes associated with the making—and breaking—of adoptive families is intended to serve as a limit case (see Eppinger, this volume), illuminating certain practices within a field where families must interact with institutions more often than is typical to show how institutions usurp the autonomy of the American family more broadly. This type of inquiry yields many ideas for rethinking the family as a creative site for present and future forms of freedom and citizenship for its members.

Adoptive Families and Faith in Institutions

I became interested in the ways that institutions influence adoptive families in 1996, when, as a graduate student, I noticed a trend in writings on adoption in popular American women's magazines. Prior to 1993, women wrote primarily about the joys and promise of domestic and international adoption, but by 1996, more women were writing about the difficulties of parenting formerly institutionalized adoptees. The solutions, adoptive mothers wrote, were few and far between, but a common thread in the articles was the desire for more biomedical theory and practice tailored to them and their families.

Three years later, in 1999, the domestic adoption rate in the United States had risen from approximately 28,000 to 36,000 per year.[10] And international adoption rates had almost quadrupled, jumping from just over 5,000 to almost 20,000 per year.[11] Meanwhile in this remarkably short period of time, thousands of children were diagnosed with Reactive Attachment Disorder (RAD) in the United States. The vast majority of these children—popularly known as "RAD kids"—were formerly institutionalized adoptees deemed unable or unwilling to attach to parental figures after placement. In addition, a range of attachment therapies—some evidence-based and some not[12]—had emerged to transform and correct the bodies and brains of RAD kids, and in turn, to attempt to transform and mend adoptive families.

In 1997, I began ethnographic research with adoptive parents whose families were at risk of dissolution and discovered that the vast majority of them believed in the RAD diagnosis and treatment enough to rely on the new field of attachment therapy to solve their post-placement problems. In 1999, I started ethnographic research at an attachment clinic in Evergreen, Colorado, the U.S. nexus of several controversial, non–evidence-based forms of attachment therapy, aiming to understand how these attachment therapists were socially constructing RAD. In the process, I conducted fieldwork with 129 families facing the possibility of dissolution (some thirty of whom had adopted from Russia). Subsequently following the trail of "informal" or unrecognized hierarchies that affected adopted children's lives,[13] I wound up conducting fieldwork with scores of international and domestic adoption facilitators and workers in five Russian orphanages as well.

During this project, I was forced to think often, intensely, and up, down, and sideways about the connections between adoptive families and institutions and the ways these links affect their lives. Elsewhere, I have analyzed biomedical discourse's role in preserving the cultural logic of adoptive family in the United States in extensive writings about the culture, practices, and philosophies of some Evergreen attachment therapists that were popular in the 1990s.[14] But a vertically integrated ethnographic approach can illuminate other sites along the adoption pipeline that are influential in the lives of adoptees. International adoption agencies, for example, are the loci of family building in global child circulation routes. As the gatekeepers of family for prospective parents, they are also an unexplored pivot point from which to obtain a vertical understanding of how global child circulation systems work—and why they sometimes fail. The principles of vertically integrated research can contextualize some of the institutional practices and strategies that adoption agencies use to increase interest in transnational adoptees to the West, to maintain global child circulation routes, and thus to maintain bureaucratic permanence for themselves. In particular, agencies' use of founding stories, testimonials, and iconography of adoptable children is an entry point for vertical analysis.

Cementing the Need for Experts: International Adoption Agencies as Gatekeepers

According to most families I interviewed at the time of my research in the late 1990s, when individuals or couples decided to adopt formerly institutionalized children, they often chose their agency based on word of mouth from friends and acquaintances or from the Internet. They also discovered that the adoption process involved many more decisions and steps than they had initially thought. Parents faced numerous choices: whether to adopt domestically or internationally, and if domestically, then whether from statewide private adoption agencies or public county agencies; whether to work through the initial stages of adoption with privately funded referral groups; whether to adopt an infant or an older child, a single child or a sibling group; whether to choose a child to match their own race or to adopt transracially; and whether they could handle adopting children with disabilities, medical problems, or histories of severe neglect or abuse. Parents also had to choose the proper agency based on the diversity of children available, the duration of the adoption process, and the origin of the adopted children. Cost was also a significant factor, particularly in international adoptions. At the time of my research in early 2000, it cost approximately $1,000 to adopt a child from domestic cultures of care, whereas adopting a child from abroad could cost up to $30,000.

In addition to this dizzying array of decisions, parents adopting through international and domestic agencies found it a highly bureaucratic process involving several state interventions. Once parents decided what kind of child they would like to parent and what agency to work with, they had to fill out general information forms, pay nonrefundable application fees, and attend information seminars to learn about their chosen agency's particular adoption process. If they still wished to adopt after this session, they were informed of several more fees. The agency assigned a licensed adoption caseworker who then conducted a home study to determine the parents' fitness to adopt. Once an agency declared the parents "fit" to adopt, agency staff members worked with them to find an available child or children.

Historically, in international adoptions, the pool of available children is limited. Parents usually do not choose the actual children they will adopt; instead, they wait for adoption agency staff to contact them about available children. Once contacted, they usually receive a file and an incomplete medical history on the child and are shown a brief video of the child. Then they have several days to decide whether to adopt the child. Parents who do not choose the child must wait, perhaps for months, until another suitable candidate for adoption passes through the agency's files. Those who do choose the child await instructions for the "pick-up date," when they fly to the child's country of origin, meet the child for the first time, and bring him or her to the United States. Adoption agency staff may schedule the "pick-up date" as soon as a week after the parents agree to adopt or as much as a year or two later. Upon arriving in the child's country of origin, the parents undergo a series of legal procedures to transfer parental rights from the state to the parents. In Russia, after about ten days, parents may file paperwork with the U.S. embassy declaring their intention to acquire the child's passport and transfer the child's citizenship. Once home, parents must finalize transfer of the child's citizenship with the Immigration and Naturalization Service.

Parents often recounted the dismay, frustration, and resigned determination they came to feel when faced with the checklist of requirements for adopting formerly institutionalized children through adoption agencies. At the same time, many expressed gratitude to the agencies. Megan Wicke, an adoptive mother of a little girl from Moscow, stated, "We actually loved the agency we worked with. We felt they supported us the whole time. They were the ones who took our phone calls, answered our questions, helped bring Katrina [to us]. It wouldn't have happened without them." Yet in the same breath, Megan articulated what she regarded as the double role of adoption agencies: "They're your 'way in' to adopting, it's like a gateway, but they're also the gatekeepers."

Inspiring Trust: International Adoption Agencies as Crafters of Family Experience

Aware of the many decisions and great risk involved in choosing an agency, adoption agencies worked out ways to attract prospective parents and maintain professional relationships with them, primarily through trust-building techniques. One such technique at the time of my research was to appeal to parents' frustrations about adopting through impersonal, institutional means by using advertising that personalized and humanized children. These ads and websites often related the agencies' founding stories to introduce potential clients to the personal stories associated with the organization's start.

For example, the Denver-area Christian nonprofit agency Hope's Promise described itself in its brochure in the late 1990s as follows:

> Paula founded Hope's Promise in 1990, after she and her husband adopted their son . . . from India. We have been serving both birth and adoptive families for over ten years. We accept applications from adoptive families who live throughout the United States and abroad, and provide counseling and support services to birth families who reside throughout Colorado. The Staff of [the agency] has both personal and professional adoption experience. We understand your needs to maintain control over the decisions that intimately affect your lives; to have accurate, timely information; and to receive support and ongoing communication.[15]

Hope's Promise administrators highlighted their position as "just plain folks" who had successfully navigated the rules, regulations, and practices associated with adoption. According to a staff member at a different agency near Denver: "They have to know that if our founder could do it, especially at a time when adopting kids from outside the United States wasn't so easy, then they can do it. And we'll help them however we can." By positioning themselves as plain folks, administrators hoped to seem less like intimidating professionals and more like friendly facilitators—parents helping other parents achieve their dreams of family. The founders' primary motivation for creating the agency was empathy: staff members understood the pure joy and importance of building families and wanted to help others do the same.

Another way international adoption agencies built trust among parents was to provide testimonials on websites and in brochures. Testimonials operated to allay parents' fears about the bureaucracy involved in adopting through a particular agency. As a hotline coordinator for an agency in Aurora, Colorado, commented: "We don't write [testimonials], let me make that clear, but we choose which testimonials we include on our sites very carefully. It's important that people have confidence in the agency ... that they understand we know what we are doing."

Testimonials included narratives addressing state interventions in the adoption process but did not dwell on the hassles. Successful testimonials demonstrated that agencies were able to conduct business with a personal touch, making adopting an enjoyable experience complete with sightseeing experiences and friends made along the way. Perhaps more importantly, families testified to the agency's ability to shield adopting parents from state interventions. According to parents I interviewed at the clinic, testimonials were particularly appealing because in their view, less state intervention during the process meant their own greater control over the process and over their family's creation.

A third agency technique for building trust was what one parent referred to as "the family catalogues": iconography of children that attested to the agency's ability to choose children who were, as one staffer put it, "good family material." This iconography usually took the form of photo listings and personality profiles of children available for adoption. Sometimes regularly published in bulletins or booklets, photo listings of adoptable children were also available on agency websites, where links such as "Waiting Children" and "Children Seeking Loving Families" connected to the photos portraying the children as happy, smiling, and aesthetically pleasing in dress and personality. According to most caseworkers I interviewed, photo listings were key to attracting parents to an agency. As one agency director stated:

> Especially today when people don't have a lot of time to investigate agencies, it's often how the kids look or seem that will help them determine which one they go with. We encourage the orphanages to try to capture the true personality of the child when they take their pictures . . . [the children] should look clean though. We want them [orphanage staff] to help them put some effort into their presentation.

Indeed, the parents I interviewed at the clinic indicated that checking out photo listings was the most "exciting" or "fun" part of looking for agencies to work with because it allowed them to fantasize about what their families would eventually look like. The photos opened the way to parents' "paradoxical grounding"[16] in the reality of adoption and magnification of their hopes for their future with children. Many of them stated that the way children looked in photographs sometimes swayed them to work with a particular agency—sometimes even before they had officially contracted with that agency, as evidenced in an interview I had with one family at an Evergreen clinic:

> RS: And what did you think when you saw the pictures of the kids?
> BM: Oh, we thought they were so cute.
> HM: Yeah, I actually had the picture from the site, and I downloaded it, and I was showing it to all the guys I played basketball with, saying, "These are gonna be my kids!"
> BM: Just really cute. We couldn't wait.

Besides providing images that allow adopting parents to project their family into the future, photo listings and personality profiles also constructed narratives that claimed to accurately depict the child's personality. The large majority of these photo listings and personality profiles included information assuring parents that despite a child's experience in institutions, she or he had the kind of personality that would smooth the transition from institutional living to the nuclear family. Personality-profile text accompanying photo listings for adoptable children from Russia commonly also assured parents that children adhered to typical gender roles—girls love to play dress-up, cook, and take care of younger siblings; boys like to fix things around the house, play sports, and take leadership roles:

Sibling Group of Three! Forever Family Found! Meet this darling sibling group! The eldest of this group has been like momma to the other two. She is a very compassionate child and loves her siblings very much. She dreams of dressing up like a princess with high heels and fancy dress and of course to have long hair! Although only 6 years old, she knows how to cook, clean, iron and sew. She is a very responsible child. She also dreams of being able to start school. Brother is lively and active. He is a leader among his peers. He is fond of sports and games. He loves to assist the adults in sweeping the leaves and cleaning off the snow from the paths. He loves to be read to. He can recite his favorite stories. The baby of the group is described as having a good personality and smile. She is lively, amusing and chubby. She loves to play with her dolls and pretend she is a nurse. The whole group loves to sing and dance. They are all friendly children and take care of each other, which is evidenced on their video. They play together and miss one another when apart. We have medicals and video on these children.[17]

He seems to be very mature for his age. At eight years, he already seems to have a grown-up, not boyish, air to him, with a courageous heart, and a harsh realization that he lives in a world where he'll have to take care of himself. When he smiles though, his childish spirit is revealed and he becomes a kid again. When asked if he has any dreams, the boy looses [sic] his smile, looks down shyly, and utters a heartbreaking "No." But if he had one wish that could come true . . . he says he would wish for a mom. His biological mother died. By the Adoption Law, both parents must travel overseas to pick up the child.[18]

Here, children are described as "compassionate," "having a good smile," "having a good personality," "responsible," and "friendly." Their productive potential is also emphasized—most often, personality profiles include information about what the child would like to be when he or she grows up. Such iconography appealed to parents' desire and sense of altruism by highlighting and confirming the child's unequivocal wish to find an adoptive family. This approach accentuated both the children's emotional availability and their acute awareness of their orphaned or abandoned status. Listings also implied that children raised in institutions understood the terms of private family life. These scenarios present potential adopting parents as the solution to a child's problems. A family and parental love can only be curative for the child.

Through such narratives, institutions assigned globally circulated children a central role in building adoptive families and allow adoptive parents to engage in "as if" biological relations.[19] Photo listings and personality profiles were instrumental, standardized narratives that encouraged, shaped, and supported prospective parents' use of biogenetic relations as a template for imagining, enacting, and maintaining adoptive family. In this scenario, children performed primarily as "emotional assets."[20] The narratives unproblematically invested children with sentimental value, unequivocally deeming children capable of particular forms of emotional returns and promising to secure for adoptive parents the intimate realm of family.

Behind the Gates: Informal Hierarchies and Distant Linkages in International Adoption

Adoption agencies' trust-building techniques aimed to ease the emotional vulnerability and anxiety many parents feel by the time they decide to adopt. However, the institutional narratives often hid informal hierarchies that negatively affect internationally adopted children's lives prior to their arrival in the United States. They also precluded parents' vertically integrated knowledge of their own potential children. In the grand narrative set up by "founding stories" and testimonials, for example, parents rarely seemed to have trouble adopting, and what they should do if they did have trouble remained unaddressed. One continuing problem with using founding stories, testimonials, and photo listings to demonstrate the "reality" of adopting institutionalized children from abroad is that they establish a framework that limits what adopting parents can ask and think about constructing families. Such narratives also do not address the range of feelings that adopted children surely have about being adopted or provide much information about children's understanding of family life, beyond the claim that the children "want one." Nor do these narratives typically address children's medical conditions, or make visible the cultural or socioeconomic preconditions of their own circulation and availability.

Another problem is that these narratives often obscure the interlocking institutions that are involved with, and benefit from, global child circulation. Though this approach to helping parents transform children raised in institutions into family members may seem normal or altruistic (as adoption agency staffers assume), several problems are associated with bureaucratic negation of adopted children's histories, including those of children adopted from institutions abroad. Reliance on adoptive children as emotional assets often goes hand in hand with the assumption that all children—especially children raised in institutions abroad—dream about, desire, and long for a family so that they may realize an attachment with a parent. For many children, however—and especially those who are raised in institutions—this is not necessarily the case. In fact, the transition from abandoned child to adoptee can create considerable conflict for children. For example, children raised in Russian state-run institutions who are expected to become emotional assets upon being abruptly integrated into American families are often disturbed by the changes. In addition to being expected to make obvious transitions, such as learning to speak a new language and acclimatizing to new sensory sensations, schedules, and places, Russian adoptees also are expected to move quickly from collective to individual behavior, from public to private living, and from deprivation to indulgence. They are also often expected to immediately understand the terms of attachment in American families, which typically call for deference to, trust in, and reliance on adults, concepts that may be foreign to them.

Numerous scholars have documented the particular relationship between the state and abandoned children in pre-Soviet and Soviet Russia that shed light on why this may be the case.[21] Prior to the revolution, Russia's attempts to modernize included the construction and maintenance of massive foundling homes to house, raise, and train Russia's future caretakers and protectors. Russia's attention to these new wards of the state, however, was short-lived and somewhat superficial, since resistance to Western bureaucracy and to the actual implementation of Enlightenment ideals was stronger than the vision for this new generation of Russian citizens. Mortality rates increased, and foundling homes decreased in popularity. Later, under the Soviet regime, the state expressed a new commitment to abandoned children, expanding an orphanage system that was charged with proving the superiority of Russian psychiatry. Children were monitored in strictly run educative environments and trained to be self-sufficient, independent, and economically useful, all in the service of the state that raised them through the age of eighteen. Since perestroika, however, attitudes about abandoned children in Russia have shifted. No longer symbolic of the state's ability to create strong, loyal, capable generations of future Soviets, abandoned children are now often grave reminders of a failing government that needs to attend to its citizens. By the late 1990s, abandoned children, stigmatized as "throw-away" children, were considered excess baggage for an already overtaxed government.[22] The status of orphans, or "children without parental care," has become an official social category, one that stigmatizes a child for life. Children carry documents that signify their orphan status and list an institution as their permanent address. They are often denied educational and professional opportunities. More and more, once they become of age, abandoned children comprise a large segment of Russia's first modern burgeoning lower class.

The stigmatization an abandoned child experiences outside an institution begins within the institution. According to one orphanage staff member interviewed by a human rights worker in 1998, "Orphans are called children with no prospects—thus they are not trainable, not treatable."[23] Many adults these children see every day, regardless of which government ministry oversees their care or whether they actually suffer from mental or physical defects, have labeled them *oligophrenic* or *debil* (heavily or lightly retarded, respectively), and thus unworthy of more than the required attention. From a very early age, then, these children must rely on themselves or their peers for amusement, education, and comfort on a day-to-day basis.

Decades of abandoned children raised in Russian institutions have thus been encouraged to remain loyal to, trust, and help one another instead of adults. In five orphanages where I conducted ethnographic fieldwork in 1996 and 2000, I observed peer-based networks in which staff expected older children to "look out" for younger children. These peer networks included initiation rites and rites of passage, often in the form of endurance tests. Peers also disciplined the younger children and taught them how to play games and perform such tasks as setting tables, washing dishes, and making beds. According to one twelve-year-old Russian adoptee adopted by a Denver couple when he was seven: "It didn't ever cross my mind to ask an adult to help me with things [in the St. Petersburg orphanage]: If you needed help it meant that you were dumb. . . . Because I didn't want to get put in a worse place, I asked [friends] Sergei and Erik to help. We helped each other get what we wanted." This is a behavior that is socially induced, and those Russian adoptees old enough to articulate their thoughts claimed that it proved more fruitful than any other behavior, for both the children and the staff. It is a means of survival. However, the type of peer-centered attachments they are encouraged to make in Russia are not considered valuable in the United States, particularly if the child is to prove an emotional asset to a family.

International adoption agencies' rituals of competence obscure a second important fact about adopting internationally from Russian state-run institutions: most Russian children placed for adoption are those who suffer from *social* orphanhood.[24] The term "social orphan" extends to orphans who have lost their parents as well as children whose parents are alive but do not provide support or care, underage children (minors) and teenagers from dysfunctional families, children in special institutions for young (or underage) delinquents, and children confined to educational homes for quasi-delinquent youth. The new term's wider scope of reference encompasses many types of children separated from parents and defines various forms of lack of social adjustment in minors. In all, the term reflects dire social conditions in post-socialist Russia.

Three important aspects of an emerging social orphanhood framework help explain the Russian state's interventions in child care in the late 1990s. First, after the fall of communism, Russia's federal authorities delegated responsibility for defending children's rights and legal interests to local authorities in the regions of Russia. That is, local authorities were given the right to formulate their own policies and regulations for improving the condition of children who needed state assistance. Policies were no longer standardized across the country.

Second, this yielded a new environment across Russia as local authorities' practices created unequal conditions among minors from different regions. For example, not all administrative subjects of the Russian Federation recognized or observed federal regulations providing jobs for socially disadvantaged minors. Also, when orphans and children without parental care graduated from their educational homes or care institutions, upon emancipation they could not expect equal treatment (as provided by federal law) regarding their housing situations. Local authorities did not follow up on the federal legislation concerning foster families, adoption, guardianship, or creation of commissions to handle minors' issues. And local laws did not provide for the rights of minors who spent court-ordered time in correctional facilities or were released from such institutions.

Third, in the 1990s local governments seldom allowed minors to stay with parents the state had labeled "dysfunctional." In 1998, Russia's Ministry of the Interior claimed that 125,000 parents across the country had "avoided their duty to educate and care for their children" or were "providing minors a negative example of family life."[25] Such parenting had serious direct negative consequences. Annually, some two million children in Russia were abused in their families. And in 1998, approximately 50,000 children left their families, preferring to live on the streets.[26] The prior decade had seen rising rates of children lacking parental care; a decline in their numbers after 1996 was mostly attributable to government agencies' inability to document all the different types of "social orphans" Russia was producing.

In this environment, Russia's state-run orphanages provided shelter, education, and opportunities for an even larger variety of social orphans than they had during the late Soviet period.[27] As mentioned, Russian children are rarely "orphaned" in the traditional sense of both biological parents having died. Most Russian children admitted to state-run orphanages are there because medical professionals in children's hospitals have referred them to an orphanage for care, because a court has appointed the institution their caretaker, and/or because parents are too poor or sick to keep them. In practice, this means that birth parents' ties to Russian children in state orphanages have not been completely severed in the ways Americans often assume or envision. For example, when I conducted fieldwork in orphanages in Vladimir and Ulyanovsk, it was common to see children speaking with their parents, who still lived in the same city, on the orphanage grounds. When I asked staff members about this, they stated that both local ministries and Russian parents sometimes saw the orphanages as places to put the children until parents got back on their feet financially, or completed state-run rehabilitation or welfare programs.

Still, even parents who had legally abdicated their parental rights visited their children in the orphanage, despite having no hope of living with them again. Many Russian children adopted from orphanages thus maintained emotional connections to their birth parents. In three cases, I witnessed Americans adopting children who had spoken or met with their biological parents only weeks or days before. Agency staff discouraged these children from speaking with their birth parents but would not go so far as to keep them from one another. Then, when children had the opportunity to go to Western nations, these same staffers told the children to be happy about their good fortune at being adopted by Westerners. The consequent abrupt shifts in family loyalties, and in the empirical experience of family, proved stressful, if not devastating, to these children.

Parenting Up, Down, and Sideways: Thinking Creatively about Family

Vertical analysis of international adoption agency narratives about family reveals their actual connections to "hidden" or "distant" institutional linkages and hierarchies affecting the lives of adoptive families in the United States. Such institutional narratives entrench certain dogmas about children, childhood, family, and domesticity in adoption circulation systems, even when the associated practices can compromise adoptees' post-placement quality of life and adoption outcomes. Further, this analysis of overt bureaucratic practices and distant, informal hierarchies in international adoption shows how the power to define and enact adoptive families begins "up"—in U.S. and foreign legislatures and welfare institutions, as well as in institutions such as adoption agencies and attachment therapy clinics—whereas control flows "down" over families, using parents primarily as channels. This situation was glaringly obvious in late 2012, when Russian President Vladimir Putin, after many years of threats and moratoriums, signed a bill banning all adoptions of Russian children by U.S. citizens. (Here it is important to note that this sweeping legislation likely was not—as is most often claimed and/or assumed—a response to maltreatment of Russian children by U.S. adoptive families or evidence of an emerging Russian commitment to the welfare of orphaned or abandoned children there, but rather diplomatic retaliation for the passage of the Magnitsky Act, signed by Barack Obama earlier in 2012, which bars Russian citizens accused of violating human rights from traveling to the United States and from owning real estate or other assets there.[28]) But just as parents can be channels for outflows of power from the family, so are they instrumental to the flow of power into families. I will conclude with some thoughts about family as a site for creatively harnessing that power, both within and outside the realm of international adoption.

In 1962, Margaret Mead wrote a sixty-page essay for the U.S. Department of Health, Education, and Welfare called *A Creative Life for Your Children*.[29] Mead used an ethnographic perspective to show Americans what they were doing—and not doing—to promote their families as active sites for freedom and democracy. Linking the concepts of creativity and citizenship, she first noted that most American parents, taking their cues from child development experts and social welfare professionals, tend to "overteach" children by preparing them to use some special talent later, in their adult lives—making great art or scientific discoveries, building new organizations, healing the sick, or pioneering world peace. Then she asked what it would be like if parents instead related to children by providing them with a creative life that values them, their capabilities, and their perspectives *as children*. In other words, rather than understanding children as future citizens, subjects, or adults, what would it mean to approach them as real people for whom each day should be lived to the fullest? And how might this approach lay a foundation for creativity and independent thought leading into the possibility of many types of adulthood?

The ethnographic data on institutions involved in international adoption clearly show that that families and children can get lost in the picture. The practices of adoption agencies and other, less visible institutions are rarely linked to the phenomenon of adoption dissolution; for example, medical professionals (and parents) tend to assign responsibility for adoption dissolution largely to the adoptees themselves, linking an adoption annulment to the child's poor behavior rather than to institutional irresponsibilitiy inherent in global child circulation systems. Meanwhile, adoption agencies continue to promote narratives that obscure the knowledge that parents need, both to understand their children's early histories (and culture) and to think more systemically about post-placement problems. Grounding Mead's ideas about creativity within this research on adoptive families allows a rethinking of these tendencies.

Take the case of Melissa Barney, a mother whom I interviewed in 2000 in Littleton, Colorado, whose four-year-old adopted daughter Carrie began to display RAD-like behaviors such as hoarding food, refusing to speak, and expressing hostility toward Melissa soon after the family brought her to the United States from Russia in 1997. Although her international adoption agency insistently pressured Melissa to obtain psychological confirmation of a diagnosis of RAD, she and her husband did not think Carrie would benefit from "being marched around from doctor to doctor." Instead they held a meeting with family and friends to reveal their family's situation and solicit ideas on how to help Carrie. "It seemed that she had been passed from person to person already," Melissa explained. "We thought what she needed was lots and lots of us." The family thought creatively about Carrie's behaviors, agreeing that she needed stability, routine, evidence that she could trust them all, and regular contact with her Russian orphanage. They also agreed that Melissa and her husband required support as well. Together they devised a plan to help Carrie bond with Melissa and to help the family with a rotating schedule of respite care and uniform child-rearing practice. Following their own paradigms about Carrie's needs and the needs of their family, rather than the needs of institutions, the Barneys and their extended family and friends ultimately were able to help Carrie. Over the course of three years, she began to show affection for Melissa and her husband. She began to speak, demonstrating that she knew much English from listening despite not having used it before, and to eat regularly at the table with other family members.

In another case, Lenore Headley, a kindergarten teacher from Minneapolis, adopted two boys from Russia in 2002. An unmarried woman in her early 40s, Lenore had long wanted children but had never met a partner to whom she wanted to make a life-long commitment. In vitro fertilization did not appeal to her, but the idea of providing an orphaned or abandoned child with her home and love had "a certain synchronicity to it." However, she placed little faith in any adoption agency to—as she put it—"broker a family for me." As a kindergarten teacher, she had taught adoptees from various countries and had seen the effects of institutionalization and the toll that the difficult transition from institutions to adoptive families could take on their learning and day-to-day lives. If she was to adopt, she thought, she wanted to do it her way.

In 2001, after saving some money and consulting with friends who ran a Russian-based NGO and had adopted a child from an orphanage in Ulyanovsk, Lenore decided to "swim upstream" to make her family. She sublet her home, moved to Ulyanovsk, found a place to live near one of the local orphanages, and became a volunteer there, working up to five days a week in both the infant house and the older children's home. For Lenore, the decision to uproot in hope of a more successful adoption outcome was logical: "I'm with children every day. I know that to make connections with children you enter their worlds, not the other way around."

Once at the orphanage, Lenore did not tell anyone that she was planning to adopt (although orphanage staff often told her she should). She also told herself that she had no expectations about what child she would adopt, and that she would not punish herself if she decided not to adopt at all. Instead she simply spent time with the children—holding the infants, preparing meals and setting tables with the older children, helping them potty train, teaching them English and learning Russian, and playing soccer with them or teaching them how to ride bikes. Over time, she connected with two boys named Alexei and Leo. They were unrelated, but best friends. Both boys, aged 10 and 12 respectively, had been abandoned to the orphanage before age three, and they had long since given up hope of being adopted. They planned to move to Moscow together to try to pursue education upon emancipation from the orphanage at age eighteen, and also thought they might try to be DJs at clubs in the city. As the months passed, however, Lenore and the boys connected over their love of soccer, and she felt herself attaching to them.

After determining that they were each adoptable and that there were no impediments to adopting them both, she asked them if they would like to return with her to the United States. Both boys were surprised and excited at the prospect, but Leo had reservations—he was nervous about learning a new language and adjusting to a new home. However, since Alexei would also come, he felt confident enough to go. Although the adoption hit bumps when Lenore brought them home—Alexei had learning disabilities that delayed his schooling for several years, and Leo suffered extreme homesickness, requiring some trips back to Ulyanovsk to visit the orphanage—Lenore's experience with the boys was ultimately what she had hoped for, and one that the boys, eventually young men in college, acknowledge has benefited them.

In both of these stories, parents decided to follow their own paradigms instead of taking all their cues about how to build their families from adoption professionals. Put another way, they were thinking *systemically* about family to create family. One might even say that they were parenting up, down, and sideways. Their stories illustrate creative thinking for building and enacting family to improve adoption outcomes and thwart adoption dissolution. When it became evident that Carrie needed help, Melissa considered her options in expansive ways, rethinking (and removing) the boundaries between adoption experts and consumers of adoption expertise. By pooling ideas from friends and family as well as from "experts" and weighing them equally, she heeded her own intuition about what a formerly institutionalized child might need in a transition period. Lenore approached adoption as a creative process from the outset. Significantly, she prioritized using the resources available to her and treated the orphanage as a preexisting family unit, and sought to include herself in a long-term reciprocal relationship with that unit instead of incorporating a child into her own preconceived notion of family. As Lenore related: "I think it was the asking them if they wanted to be a family, and not the telling them that we would be a family that made it [a success]."

The need to follow one's own paradigms to build and enact family does not apply only to adoptive families. All families in neontocracies transfer some authority to institutions to define and administer family life.[30] This transfer is a crucial part of industrialization.[31] To make the point, one need only consider the profits the Nestle Corporation has reaped from infant formula sales thanks to its role in the worldwide demonization of breastfeeding, which discourages sanitary caloric intake for already-malnourished children (and violates World Health Organization guidelines) in underdeveloped countries,[32] or the tobacco industry's marketing to children as young as thirteen despite parent opposition and mounting, undeniable evidence of smoking's negative impact on health.[33] The trick is to move beyond thinking of parents as "passive intermediaries"[34] between institutions and children in the neontocracy.

While perhaps a daunting prospect, it is possible. For example, parents' systematic boycotts of Nestle since the late 1970s have led to reduced formula sales in Third World countries (and more recently, the United States). And in 2006, after nationwide pressure from parents' groups, the American Academy of Pediatrics resolved to treat corporate advertising for tobacco that targets children and adolescents (as well as alcohol and certain forms of food and drugs) as a known health risk. The academy has even gone so far as to call for limits on advertising targeting children and adolescents.[35]

As Rose and Nathra Nader have noted, confident, creative parenting need not make headlines. Simply preparing and serving healthful, nonprocessed food to families can be a powerful act, one that is all the more powerful when vertically integrated knowledge informs consumers about the food's origins.[36] The dinner table is a deceptively subversive place from which to challenge institutional narratives and an easy, creative place to empower families and rear children with self-confidence, independent judgment, and empathy. It is a good start to the transformation toward mindsets that bypass institutions instead of parents, and acknowledge parents' resourcefulness instead of outsourcing parenting.

Notes

Some material is taken from *The Road to Evergreen: Adoption, Attachment Therapy, and the Promise of Family*, by Rachael Stryker, copyright 2010 Cornell University. Used with permission.

1. "What's Happening to the American Family? Interview with Dr. Margaret Mead, Noted Anthropologist," *US News & World Report*, 5 May 1963, http://politics.usnews.com/news/national/articles/2008/05/16/whats-happening-to-the-american-family—interview.html.
2. Laura Nader, "The Vertical Slice: Hierarchies and Children", in *Hierarchy and Society: Anthropological Perspectives on Society*, ed. Gerald M. Britan and Ronald Cohen, (Philadelphia: Institute for the Study of Human Issues, 1980), 32.
3. Abraham Rosman and Paula G. Rubel, *The Tapestry of Culture: An Introduction to Cultural Anthropology*, 6th ed. (Boston: McGraw-Hill, 1998), 128.
4. David Lancy, *Playing on the Mother-Ground: Cultural Routines for Children's Development* (New York: The Guilford Press, 1996), 12.
5. Ibid. I do not wish to overstate the case—e.g., from an ecological perspective, the family is also a site for maintaining and preserving social pathways such as religious and ethnic beliefs and traditions. See Richard H. Robbins, *Cultural Anthropology: A Problem-based Approach*, 2nd ed. (Itasca: ILF.E. Peacock Publishers, 1997).
6. Robert Levine, cited in Lancy, *Playing on the Mother-Ground*, 12–13.
7. Ibid. The neontocracy is typically contrasted with the "gerontocracy" of "child-supported" agrarian societies, in which both blood-related and local non–blood-related ancestors, elders, adults, and adolescents (in that order of importance) work together to invest in children, whom they expect to later contribute meaningfully to the household and local economies.
8. Linda Coco and Research Associates, *Children First! A Parent's Guide to Fighting Corporate Predators* (Washington, D.C.: Corporate Accountability Research Group, 1996), vi–vii.
9. Pamela Paul, *Parenting Inc.* (New York: Times Books, 2008), 225–226.
10. Adoption and Foster Care Analysis and Reporting System, "Statistics and Research" (Washington, D.C.: United States Department of Health and Human Services, Administration for Children and Families, 1999), http://www.acf.dhhs.gov/programs/cb.
11. Alison Tarmann, "International Adoption Rate Doubled in the 1990s" (Washington, D.C.: Population Reference Bureau, 2003), http://www.prb.org/Articles/2003/InternationalAdoptionRateinUSDoubledinthe1990s.aspx.
12. Evidence-based attachment interventions vary, but they tend either to attempt to enhance caregiver sensitivity to infants and children, or to change caregivers to others who can be more sensitive to the child's needs. Interventions that had no evidence base at the time of my research included some therapies associated with those practiced in Evergreen, Colorado. See Mark Chaffin et al., "Report of the APSAC Task Force on Attachment Therapy, Reactive Attachment Disorder, and Attachment Problems," *Child Maltreatment* 11, no. 1 (2006): 76–89.
13. Nader, "The Vertical Slice," 32.
14. See Rachael Stryker, *The Road to Evergreen: Adoption, Attachment Therapy, and the Promise of Family* (Ithaca, NY: Cornell University Press, 2010).
15. Hope's Promise, "About Us," 13 May 2000, http://www.hopespromise.com/about/.
16. Sara Dorow, *Transnational Adoption: A Cultural Economy of Race, Gender, and Kinship* (New York: New York University Press, 2006), 108.

17. Little Miracles, 18 May 2002, http://www.littlemiracles.org/photolisting/photolisting.
18. Denver Department of Human Services, 15 May 2003, "Denver Children Available." http//:www.denvergov.org/DenverChildren/Images
19. See Judith Modell, *Kinship with Strangers: Adoption and Interpretations of Kinship in American Culture* (Berkeley: University of California Press, 1994).
20. Viviana Zelizer, *Pricing the Priceless Child: The Changing Social Value of Children* (Princeton: Princeton University Press, 1985), 11.
21. See David Ransel, *Mothers of Misery: Child Abandonment in* Russia, (Princeton: Princeton University Press, 1988) and Alan Ball, *And Now my Soul is Hardened: Abandoned Children in Russia, 1918–1930* (Berkeley: University of California Press, 1994).
22. Clementine Creuzinger, *Childhood in Russia: Representations and Reality* (Lanham, MD: University Press of America, 1996).
23. Kathleen Hunt, *Abandoned to the State: Cruelty and Neglect in Russian Orphanages*. (New York: Human Rights Watch, 1999), 10 December 1999, http://www.hrw.or/reports98/russia.
24. See I. F. Dementieva, *Social Orphanhood: Origins and Preventions* (Moscow: Institute of Family and Youth, 2000).
25. Russian Committee on Women and Youth, *Family Report* (Moscow: The Russian Ministry of the Interior, 1998), 2.
26. Ibid., 31.
27. Ibid., 95. Local Russian governments also count on social service programs equivalent to Western foster care systems. These systems account for a low share of state interventions in child welfare, however.
28. See David M. Herszenhorn and Erik Eckholm, "Putin Signs Bill that Bars U.S. Adoptions, Upending Families," *New York Times*, 27 December 2012, http://www.nytimes.com/2012/12/28/world/europe/putin-to-sign-ban-on-us-adoptions-of-russian-children.html?pagewanted=all&_r=0#comments; and Sergei L. Loiko and Kim Murphy, "Orphans, Families in Agonizing Limbo," *Los Angeles Times*, 21 May 2013, http://www.latimes.com/news/columnone/la-fg-russian-adoptions-20130521-dto,0,135831.htmlstory.
29. Margaret Mead. *A Creative Life for Your Children* (Washington, D.C.: United States Department of Health, Education and Welfare, Social and Rehabilitation Service, Children's Bureau, 1962). The department commissioned Mead's essay to give its employees new insights into American childrearing culture.
30. Roberto Vargas, *Family Activism: Empowering your Community Beginning with Family and Friends* (San Francisco: Berrett-Koehler, 2008), 4.
31. See Steven Ruggles, "The Transformation of American Family Structure," *American Historical Review* 99 (1994): 103–128.
32. See Penny Van Esterik, *Beyond the Breast-Bottle Controversy* (New Brunswick, NJ: Rutgers University Press, 1989).
33. H. Weinstein, "Papers: RJR Went for Teens," *Los Angeles Times*, 15 January 1998, A1.
34. Nader, "The Vertical Slice," 32.
35. Donald L. Shifrin et al., "Policy Statement: Children, Adolescents, and Advertising," *Pediatrics* 118, no. 6 (2006): 2563–2569.
36. Nader and Nader, *It Happened in the Kitchen: Recipes for Food and Thought* (Washington, D.C.: Center for the Study of Responsive Law, 1991).

Chapter 8

ON TRUTH
The Repressed Memory Wars from Top to Bottom

Robyn Kliger

In 1997, a *New York Times* article headlined "Memory Therapy Leads to a Lawsuit and Big Settlement" focused national attention on the controversy of repressed memory in the United States for the first time.[1] The article recounted the case of Patricia Burgus, who had sued her therapist, his associate, and their hospital after they used hypnosis and pharmaceuticals to help her remember a horribly abusive childhood. She was then institutionalized for more than two years. Over time, however, she began to question her "recovered" memories and, after filing the malpractice suit, eventually accepted a $10.6 million settlement. In January 2004, Elizabeth Gale settled a similar lawsuit against three therapists and the Rush-Presbyterian-St. Luke's Medical Center in Chicago for $7.5 million.[2]

In 2005, repressed memory drew even more attention when Paul Shanley, a former priest assigned to a Catholic church in suburban Boston, was convicted of raping and assaulting a six-year-old boy in a case that hinged on memories of abuse the accuser said he had repressed and recovered decades later. Shanley eventually challenged his conviction, the accuser's recollections, and the science of repressed memory: "You have prominent scientists, psychologists, and psychiatrists saying this is not generally accepted. So why allow it in a court of law in a criminal proceeding?"[3]

Shanley's appeal highlighted a sharp division between two groups of experts: one that viewed "recovered memories" as a valid psychiatric condition and another that saw it as "junk science." In a unanimous ruling,

---

Notes for this chapter begin on page 189.

the Massachusetts Supreme Judicial Court upheld Shanley's conviction and said the judge made the right decision when he allowed repressed memory evidence to be used against Shanley during his 2005 trial, noting that "the lack of scientific testing did not make unreliable the theory that an individual may experience dissociative amnesia was supported in the record, not only by expert testimony but by a wide collection of clinical observations and a survey of academic literature." Thus the court officially validated the dubious evidence considered by many to be junk science.

In North America over the past twenty years, the proliferation of sexual abuse complaints based on delayed discovery of traumatic memories has had profound legal, academic, social, economic, and psychological implications. It has led to numerous expensive, high-profile lawsuits involving forensic memory experts, victims, and advocacy groups. It has also generated significant controversy within the academic community. In this chapter, I sketch the main features of the debates surrounding repressed memory in the United States. I begin by considering the sociocultural factors that have led to the emergence of communities organized around the problem of delayed discovery of traumatic memories. I then explore the complex ways in which contemporary legal and scientific notions of truth are created, often in the crucible of the courtroom. This is followed by an analysis of what is at stake for various groups affected by the debate, who are both shaping and being shaped by the repressed memory phenomenon: victims, parents, advocacy groups on both sides, academic researchers, clinicians and therapists, and legal professionals. I conclude by reflecting on anthropology as a powerful tool for making sense of this field.

Investigating a Controversy: Fieldwork in Emergent Communities

When I began my investigation into the recovered memory controversy, my inclination was to consider the etiology of one of the most significant ideological battles of the late twentieth century: the dispute over Freud's theory of repression. In my fieldwork I had witnessed the anger and confusion surrounding this controversy among accused parents, alleged victims, scientists, clinicians, and lawyers, and I felt a duty as an anthropologist to consider the cultural factors involved in the social production of such a controversial phenomenon. Initially, my aim was to understand why the phenomenon was conspicuous at this particular historical moment. Was it part of the backlash against pioneering feminist efforts to make sexual abuse a public problem?[4] Was it the result of a fin-de-siècle angst inextricably bound to fears about how we remember who we are and who is responsible for the telling? Had some cultural event, or series of events, stimulated a delayed cultural obsession with Freud's theory, and if so, why were we culturally predisposed to concern ourselves with the "memory wars" at this particular juncture?[5]

After many years of research, it became apparent to me that finding the connections between divergent communities of scholars, therapists, advocates, and their social networks is critical to understanding how and why this controversy has been kept alive and continually gains momentum in terms of academic research and of gender and individual identity formation. One of my most pressing concerns has been to assess what is at stake for whom in this debate.

For this reason, my research relies heavily upon anthropologist Laura Nader's admonition to examine all the dimensions in which power and powerlessness are manifested through the ethnographic process of "studying up, down, and sideways."[6] Only then can we truly gather connections that are fully, organically rooted in a synthesis of data that tracks the development of a sociocultural phenomenon presenting itself across time and space. Rather than likening the study of a phenomenon to a static photo, it is most revealing to participant-observe data as it changes over time.

My field site, then, is a newly emergent and newly imagined community comprised of victims and professionals who have come to define and reiterate one another's identities through agonistic practices. The concept of repression, with its now very public link to sex abuse, has powerfully forged a discussion between lawyers, victims, advocacy groups, academic research scientists, psychological practitioners, and legislators because the economic, psychological, scientific, political, and even familial stakes are so high. In many cases, a family's right to stay together relies on the contingent resolution of a complex set of scientific and legal issues that converge in the courtroom. In this institutional setting, polarized citizens assemble in the name of a social ideal: justice under the law.

Why does it matter how the *legal* world sees these cases? Why should an anthropologist consider lawyers' and judges' perceptions of repressed memory? The reason is this: the legal story and the anthropological story are interwoven, since courtroom technologies and knowledges are, in a sense, anthropological. For example, the decision to use positron emission tomography (PET) scans rather than lie detectors is culturally significant. Some scientists have suggested that it is now possible to rely on PET scan results to determine whether an individual's memories are true or false. But according to psychiatrist Roger Pitman, PET scans tell another tale.

When eight PTSD victims volunteered for an experiment at Massachusetts General Hospital, PET scans revealed that an area of their brains—the right amygdala, a small, almond-shaped structure—was abnormally active while they were reliving traumatic memories. Pitman notes, "the amygdala is the key to the conditioned-fear response in animal studies.... This study shows us that traumatic memories are activating this 'hot learning center.'"[7]

Scientists who work on the neurobiology of trauma believe that traumatic memories are processed differently from normal memories and that PET technology proves this to be the case. Their studies imply that at the time of recollection, traumatic memories are stored in specific regions of the brain and can be scientifically proven to exist through PET scan images. Psychologist Daniel Schacter has tested brains to determine what occurs when subjects have "erroneous memories." He and his colleagues recently took the first pictures of brain activity during true and false memories, whereupon he remarked: "Memory isn't a videotape; rather, it's a reconstruction using bits of sound, sights, words, and even tastes stored in different parts of the brain. Gaps in such reproductions, filled by imagination, cause error and distortions in eyewitness recollections and other aspects of everyday memory." Memory recollection appears to dominate a particular region of the brain, the hippocampus, which shows increased blood flow and oxygen use when a memory sounds truthful, as does the area where auditory memories are processed, which also "light up" on brain scans: "Our theory is that the hippocampal region tells the frontal lobes that there's something familiar out there," Schacter explains. "The latter may then search around until it finds something that fits the recollection, whether or not it's correct." Evidence for such a scenario comes from Schacter's experiments with amnesiacs who suffered damage to the hippocampal region. "These patients show reduced levels of both false and true memories," he explains. "They do not retain in their consciousness information recently given to them, say a list of words. Their frontal lobes do not get tricked into making associations that don't exist and so into building false memories." The first publication of images of false memories led to speculation that they might be used to detect false memories of rape, abuse, and murder. George Franklin, for example, spent six years in prison after his daughter recovered a memory, apparently false, that he had murdered her playmate in 1969. However, "the idea of using this technique as a lie detector is preposterous," Schacter protests.[8]

Scientists and clinicians are divided by serious controversy because, although it can be demonstrated that certain areas of the brain become flooded with blood when one thinks of certain types of memories (e.g., pleasant or painful ones), it is impossible to state definitively what this biological fact actually *means*. In other words, it is unclear whether more or less blood flow to a given area of the brain can be proven to corroborate a given memory. Many of those following the debate are avidly watching to see whether or not this technology will be allowed into courtrooms to substantiate repressed memory claims.

In the course of investigating this topic, I attended trials and interviewed plaintiffs, defendants, and attorneys for both sides. I collected legal documents and other materials relating to over 100 repressed memory cases, including the first such case in U.S. legal history, presided over by Judge Darrah of Seattle. Furthermore, in interviews and at professional conferences I documented the views of scientific professionals who study memory and often provide forensic testimony. (I call this category of informants "knowledge-producers" because they produce the current paradigms through which society at large makes sense of repressed memory claims.) In addition, I collected data from victims' organizations and support groups, such as the False Memory Syndrome Foundation and the Retractors support group (created by those who have "taken back" their claims of abuse), and I interviewed approximately 350 people involved in rendering legal opinions, including judges, plaintiffs, victims, and their representative lawyers. Finally, I interviewed many individual providers of psychological support (namely, clinicians), as well as thirty of the nation's most respected "memory scientists," many of whom have served as expert witnesses.

The Power to Determine What Is, or Is Not, Possible or True

> A change in language can transform our appreciation of the cosmos.
>
> —Benjamin Whorf, *Language, Thought and Reality* (1956)

Continuously transmuting cultural practices might be seen as connected to "epistemic shifts."[9] It seems that the types of legal concepts and technologies that are called into question at a given historical moment reflect broader sociocultural transformations. The formation of an epistemological object (in this case, memory) is inseparable from other historical processes, such as the formation of social identities—for example, the expert memory-scientist and the psychiatrist. These processes and developments are in turn inseparable from developments taking place in society in general and hence reveal much about contemporary times. The anthropologist's responsibility is to capture the motion in this ever-changing narrative about human memory: to document the changing science of memory and therefore the construction of scientific facts.

Because the memory expert interacts with both academic and legal institutions, he or she has the ability to shape contemporary legal and scientific conceptions of truth. Like ripples in a pond, each significant case ruling affects how individuals regard the psychological and scientific discourse on repression and how the law ascertains "scientific truth." This forensic assessment of the science of memory has brought about changes in memory scientists' laboratory practices and in discourses about how human memory functions. By literally embodying the link between the legal and psychological realms, the expert witness of memory plays a major role in the codification of legal and scientific epistemologies and technologies. In recent years, an extraordinary array of challenges to our notions of the stability of memory has emerged. The popular media delight in reporting cases of recovered memories, false memories, and implanted memories. Memory has become a cultural obsession for Americans (much as it was for Europeans a century ago) because in a period of modernity, memory is the key to the personal and collective identity. Personal memory has come to be seen as defining who we are. We are what we remember. We must examine memory historically and try to understand why claims to remember how one has been oppressed have extraordinary power at particular times for particular groups.[10]

In the contemporary U.S. context, the expert witness dramatically influences the court's decisions, which then influence the production of science knowledge and laboratory research. In some key repressed memory cases, the handing down of the court's decision has sent scientists back into their laboratories to rethink paradigms that did not hold up under cross-examination or appeared deficient in addressing specific issues raised by the court. Sometimes, the scientists have forged new paradigms that might better deal with anomalies that arose in the courts. Thus, throughout the course of this controversy, legal decisions and sensibility have directly influenced the types of research design either abandoned or embraced by top scientists working in the memory field today. The academic production of knowledge, in conjunction with "the law" as both a discourse and a cultural site (again, the courtroom), has dramatically shaped the trajectory of this controversy. The study of repression illustrates how scientific and legal knowledge is produced and epistemic agreements negotiated.

Cultural affairs outside the lab—a process otherwise known as politics—profoundly influence scientific "facts" and "truths," even as external factors affect how these facts and truths are deployed. Consider the "expert" authority who is one of a mere handful of international experts with the power to define a domain of cultural reality—for instance, the domain of psychology. Awesome power resides in naming "that which is possible" through language, "authoring" and inventing new psychopathological categories; in sitting on committees that advocate for the truth or falsehood of clinical diagnoses (based upon alleged scientific veracity, or perhaps one's own clinical phenomenological experiences); and indeed, in possessing the authority to state what is experientially possible (subjectively and objectively) and to answer the question: What is true? It is worth mentioning that these same experts also wield power by influencing the political economic realm as well: the pharmaceutical industry, insurance companies, health care conglomerates, and research foundations are all affected by the "expert."[11]

From a different perspective, the actors who "name" a given phenomenon through language alter our very perception of reality. Perhaps unwittingly, they are potentially preventing the creation of alternative spaces within which we can see and feel a cultural imperative to realize "the ability to think otherwise."[12] Antonio Gramsci's ideas about power and his concept of hegemony—"to make an historical study of the means for procuring consensus and defining reality"[13]—is analytically useful in this moment, as the salience of the dispute over scientific "fact production" lies particularly in its rigorous documentation of how scientific practices develop in relation to social and cultural concerns.[14] This well-defined corpus of scholarly writings has established what I often encountered in my research: that scientific phenomena are not discovered but socially determined, and in significant ways.

A cautionary note: I am not focusing on "science" in some abstract sense, for one might plausibly argue that there is no unitary entity called "'science" but instead various sciences with procedures and styles of reasoning that do not coincide. Rather, I am focusing on the particular sciences implicated in this controversy—experimental psychology, cognitive psychology, and neuropsychology. The distinctive characteristics of fact-making (or consensus-making) in these sciences have three prominent features: the process typically takes place very gradually, over long periods of time (the given controversy has affected changes in the field of human memory for at least twenty years, though interaction with the legal community has expedited the process of scientific fact-making); contested views exist alongside one another and there is no institutional authority analogous to juridical authority that can resolve this process or contestation; and different views often coincide with different audiences within the scientific community.

Key to better understanding the contradictions and conflict surrounding sexual abuse and incest in our society today is cognizance of the various social institutions or networks that have breathed life into this cultural configuration focused on the science of traumatic memory and the war between clinical and legal truths.

Does this mean that the repressed memory controversy is not about sexual abuse and the exploitation of women by men who dominate—both in a very real physical sense and in a sociological sense related to patriarchal institutional controls? In many ways, this is too facile a question. Clearly, domineering men's sexual abuse and exploitation of girls and women is a grave social problem in the United States (as in many societies worldwide). The Department of Health and Human Services reported that an estimated 68,000 children (of a total 74,924,121) were victims of sexual abuse in forty-nine U.S. states in 2008.[15] The debate over traumatic memory and sexual abuse has inspired polarized dialogue and action in North America for several possible reasons, and scholars have offered a wide variety of explanations, including the ascension of the so-called memory sciences (memoro-politics) in the twentieth century;[16] psychoanalytic and clinical efforts to organize women's distress around the diagnostic constellation of PTSD and sexual abuse;[17] and the rise of what some scholars have called "somatized" cultural hysteria.[18]

These explanations, though useful, do not take into account a crucial dimension of the problem, namely, that clinical truth-claims and realities have sought legitimacy in courts of law. This dynamic has propelled the debate forward and continues to push us as a society to rethink the relationship between clinical trauma and the science of memory. The effort toward legitimacy has been arduous. As one justice wrote: "Perhaps no area of the law has been more productive of controversy, than the academic and judicial controversy surrounding the admissibility and reliability of repressed recollections, as well as the admissibility of supportive expert testimony.[19]

The inability to translate "truth in the clinic" into "truth under the law" has resulted in a series of complicated epistemological negotiations involving top knowledge-producers, who translate truth claims from one cultural context into another. The scientific memory-expert appears in the courtroom to make legal sense of a clinical truth, or conversely to destroy the legitimacy of clinical truth claims through juridical commonsense. This social fact has elicited a relationship of intense intellectual exchange: for these two separate domains (the clinic and the courtroom) to understand one another, a translator is required, in part because the scientific and legal domains have different end goals.

These types of statements are challenged in legal settings because the primary concern in the courtroom is whether or not the alleged abuse occurred. It is worth recalling that legal discourse assumes that (1) truth can be known in some objective and ascertainable way; and (2) objective measures can uncover this truth while functioning independently of the patient's internal reality. Yet this same standard cannot be said to exist in the clinical encounter. Thus a fundamental problem arises in the repressed memory debate: truth claims cannot be assessed by the same standards because this social phenomenon is constructed uniquely in at least two different cultural realms.

By moving their battlefield to the courtroom, recovered memory advocates and their opponents are transforming conventional discourse on both human memory and forensic standards of truth. The law, as both discourse and site, has been drawn into the process of scientific fact-making about human memory. Its involvement has, as noted above, encouraged scientists to make conceptual shifts in the way they understand human memory, which in turn prompt them to alter their research foci. As more and more participants in the controversy began to seek resolution through legal channels, the customary scientific processes of fact negotiation were altered.[20] Ultimately, the outcomes of this process are a revision of standards within both the legal and scientific domains, an accelerated rate of production of particular types of scientific knowledge, and a concomitant greater dependence upon notions of "good science" within the legal world. This process eventually alters forensic standards of truth and influences how modern memories are both made and unmade in the courtroom.

On Being a Victim

A pervasive sense of victimization infuses memory politics, as most if not all of my informants—clinicians, lawyers, scientists, alleged abusers, and alleged victims of incest—perceived themselves to be in a situation of intense domination and victimization as a result of the controversy. Domination by whom? The domination is apparently everywhere. As historian Mark Poster has noted: "Critical theory faces the formidable task of unveiling structures of domination when it appears that no one is dominating, no thing is being dominated and no ground exists for a principle of domination."[21] In a paradoxical sense, the same can be said of the repressed memory debate, which sets the task of unveiling structures of domination even though all players involved are simultaneously dominating and dominated, and multiple grounds exist for a principle of domination.

Scientific and legal knowledge networks play vital (though often elusive) roles in ubiquitous perceptions of victimization and domination. Because the sense of victimization exists everywhere, the recovered memory debate has become an extremely polarized field, with families and professionals on all sides feeling exploited, misunderstood, misrepresented, betrayed, and angry. Once immersed in the recovered memory debate, I realized I was in a war zone. Informants saw themselves as under siege, and I sometimes found myself implicated in these struggles. To illustrate this point, I offer a few fieldwork anecdotes.

Anecdote 1

When I began my fieldwork well over a decade ago, my plan was to study the changes in legal case law regarding repressed memories and scientific memory research regarding repressed memories over the twenty-year span from 1990 to 2010. The first "cold call" I made, in 1997, was to a highly successful self-identified feminist attorney in Seattle named Barbara Jo, who had been a plaintiff's attorney for several women in recovered memory cases. She had almost single-handedly managed to initiate and lobby for the passage of the first state legislation allowing the delayed discovery rule to be applied to repressed memories of sex abuse. This legislation enables sex abuse cases to be tried long after the normal statute of limitations. Washington was the first such state to pass this legislation. Today, approximately thirty other states have adopted similar laws.

Steve Moen, an experienced defense attorney in the Seattle area, told me, "Barbara Jo has been laboring in the accusers' vineyards for years; we got blindsided by her. We didn't know what hit us. She managed to get this legislation passed without presenting the other side of the story. Back then, people didn't realize that there was another side to the story."

Barbara Jo answered the phone, and once I had introduced myself as a researcher studying the recovered memory controversy, she immediately asked: "That's all fine, but what side are you on?"

"What side am I on?" I asked slowly, as I distinctly sensed she was asking me for an answer I was not prepared to give.

"Yes," she said, in a tone that led me to believe she was immune to insecurity. "What side are you on? You see, I don't want to speak with you unless you are on my side. Our side has been burned too many times by reporters and journalists and researchers, and frankly, I don't want to talk with you. If you're not going to offer a report favorable to my side, I don't want to waste my time."

My first-year graduate student readings on rapport-building flashed across my mind, but nothing truly applicable appeared. I decided to tell her exactly how I felt. I heaved a sigh of relief when she continued to speak with me.

Anecdote 2

In 2006, I phoned the office of a famous forensic psychiatrist in San Francisco who has testified in court numerous times and was an expert witness in the Franklin case, the first criminal case in American history to rest on "recovered memory" testimony.[22] Eileen Franklin had recalled memories of her father raping and killing her best friend approximately twenty years after the fact. At first, the psychiatrist—I will call her "Dr. X"—declined to speak with me. I told her receptionist that I had been able to interview other experts from Stanford and Harvard, and that I had received a grant from the Social Science Research Council to study and document this debate. The receptionist asked me to call back the next day, when the doctor would be in. The following day, our conversation went something like this:

"Hello, Dr. X, thank you for speaking with me."

"Yes, I'm glad to do it. I understand that you have received a very prestigious grant to do your work."

"Yes, I'm quite happy and privileged to have received it."

"Well, it's really too bad you didn't get this grant last year. You see, the whole thing has blown over now, and nobody is interested anymore."

Recoiling from the blow, I pressed Dr. X to tell me how she had arrived at this conclusion. She answered: "A lot of professionals have used this subject, exploiting the fact that it is sensational to make money and become famous. . . . But actually the whole controversy has been created by the media and these professionals because they have had nothing better to focus their attention upon. Once the Gulf War came upon us, they stopped being interested in the subject of repressed memories of sex abuse."

When I asked Dr. X if she would meet with me, she said, "Well, I just don't want to be positioned in this debate . . . I've been unfairly positioned so far . . . if I made an appointment with you, I'd probably just cancel it at the last minute. . . . How do I know that you are not just another one of those professionals trying to use this controversy? After all, you're obviously very ambitious or you wouldn't have been able to get that grant."

When I mentioned the level of animosity this debate had evoked, she replied, "Sure, there's been a lot of name calling in this debate, but I haven't done any of it." And when I asked if she could recommend any other researchers in the field, she said emphatically, "Sure, but I doubt that they'll speak with you."

Later, I asked another expert on the subject, an academic sociologist, why Dr. X might feel that the whole thing had blown over. He answered, "Of course it stands to reason that she thinks the whole thing has blown over; that's because it has, *for her*."

These ethnographic accounts illustrate how polarized the repressed memory debate has become. Yet at the same time, an almost symbiotic relationship prevails between at least two groups: academic researchers and legal professionals. To understand the mutual influence between the legal and scientific epistemological spheres, it is useful to examine the construction of this controversy in the three different social realms of academic researchers, clinicians (or therapists), and legal professionals.

Is Repressed Memory Real? Debates among Academic Researchers

Academic researchers of the repressed memory debates include memory scientists and psychological researchers. In 1995, the American Psychological Association formed an emergency task force to decide once and for all whether or not repression was a legitimate construct. The committee was comprised of three academic memory scientists and three therapeutic practitioners of psychology. After much debate, the committee opinion was split. All three memory scientists viewed repression as dubious, there being little or no scientific evidence to support its existence. By contrast, every therapeutic practitioner concluded that repression was entirely possible and that empirical data supported this assertion.

Since then, the polarization between academic scientists and therapeutic practitioners has been increasingly acute. What is relevant here are the different (and frequently opposed) ways in which each group views the controversy, and how each group produces knowledge about it. For memory scientists, the debate is not about sexual abuse but about how human memory works. They are chiefly concerned with research paradigms that might scientifically prove that memory works in a specific manner. In other words, memory scientists ask whether research proves empirically that there exists a genuine mechanism that enables human beings to dissociate from, and later recall, traumatic events. They also ask: Does the science show that such a memory mechanism exists? Respected scientists have argued both sides of this question, but generally speaking, most academic research scientists do not find that the scientific evidence exists.

It is worth reiterating that for memory scientists, this debate is not about the prevalence or existence of a history of sex abuse, but rather about scientific conceptions of human memory. Ever since the "memory wars" played out in the courtroom, memory experts have been asked to elaborate on the scientific data regarding how the human brain processes traumatic experience. From one perspective, the main effort is to either prove or disprove (depending upon the position held by the memory scientist) the human ability to forget traumatic events, and the social practices involved in doing so are anchored to the notion that the "other side" is conducting pseudoscience, according to legal standards. In the courtroom, each side accuses the other of inventing and appropriating "junk" science. (As one attorney recently told me: "The scientific experts on *our* side do real science.") Whether in academic labs or clinicians' offices, the war is ideological, based upon legal notions of "good" versus "junk" science.

The cognitive and behavioral sciences currently offer at least two traceable research trajectories—for and against the idea of repression. The research paradigms "against" repression are designed to prove that memory is continually subject to revision, and therefore that repression is implausible. Research "for" repression focuses scientific efforts on proving that memory exists in a more stable condition, and that an external event leaves a neurobiological "trace" within the subject, making repression possible. The former regards the subject as an active constructor of memory, whereas for the latter the subject is a passive recipient who records an exact copy of the event.

The first trajectory deals with research paradigms that attempt to account for—and empirically prove—the reality of memory malleability. To this end, cognitive psychologists like Beth Loftus at the University of Washington have conducted studies that indicate, through replicable laboratory experiments, that a person can be led to revise his or her memory of events and to remember events that did not truly happen. In Loftus's experiments, researchers implant false memories into unsuspecting participants to demonstrate that social influence has a powerful effect upon human recollection, and therefore that human memory works in a more process-oriented, reconstructive fashion. Loftus notes: "One of the things that I have found over and over in these couple of decades of research is that when people are exposed to misleading information [after an event has occurred] . . . they adopt the misinformation and they claim it as their own memory."[23] Loftus, who has worked in both the field and the laboratory studying human memory for over two decades, has testified in the courtroom that recovered memories of sexual abuse are scientifically unreliable and should not be viewed as legitimate in a court of law, given the high stakes in a criminal trial.[24]

The second research trajectory attracts scientists sympathetic to the idea of memory repression. These researchers tend to view memory, or "memory traces," as capable of existing unchanged over time in a preserved biological state, analogous to the way an insect is preserved in amber.[25] These scientists seek to prove the reality of a unique kind of forgetting that involves both the human capacity to dissociate from painful events as they occur, and the ability to suddenly recall these same memories accurately years later. As forensic psychiatrist Lenore Terr explained to me: "Repression is not the same as forgetting. It is a kind of motivated forgetting on the part of the person. For example, if I just forget where I place an object, that is not repression. Yet, if I lose a pen someone important to me gives me, and I am angry with that person, this probably involves some form of repression."[26]

Both groups of scientists are conducting new research to address questions raised in the courts. At a recent conference the American Psychological Association sponsored for its legal subdivision, some research suggested that individuals with histories of childhood sexual abuse who had trouble with their "general adult memory" revealed "less overall memory."[27] If this were indeed proven true, then a psychological test could be administered to assess an individual's general level of recollection, and its findings could then be used in a court of law in an attempt to corroborate allegations of sexual abuse. Recently, pro-repression researchers have sought to design research protocols that conceptually split memory continuity from memory accuracy. Emblematic of this research in memory accuracy is the work of Jennifer Freyd, a cognitive psychologist at the University of Oregon. Freyd has proposed the following explanation for amnesia related to childhood trauma: the greater an individual's closeness to and dependence on the perpetrator of abuse, the less likely he or she is to consciously and cognitively acknowledge the betrayal. Freyd has been a prominent figure in both the academic and survivor communities because she has accused her father of childhood sexual abuse, based upon therapeutically recovered memories.[28]

The effort to scientifically prove amnesia for a traumatic event is fraught with methodological complexity. Basically, academics who support or refute the scientific validity of repression are contesting only two things: (1) contrasting ideas about how purposively forgotten memories are stored in the brain and later retrieved, and (2) the accuracy with which the recovered memory content reflects the relationship between the recovered memory content and the event or experience in which the memory was born. However, because this debate has moved into the courts, often in the form of criminal cases, the stakes are extraordinarily high. Consequently, both groups of scientists are rapidly developing scientific protocols that address legal considerations. Each seeks to develop research designs that will hold up under legal scrutiny and meet the requirements of forensic standards of truth.

Debates among Clinicians and Therapists over Memory

The second group involved in the repressed memory debate consists of clinicians and therapists, for whom the debate primarily concerns the relationship between the recovered memory content and the event in which the memory was born. For many clinicians, the crucial issues in this debate are the healing of abuse victims and concern about the conditions under which academic scientists produce "truth." Clinicians often regard academic scientists as failing to understand the complex way that traumatic events become neurologically encoded and thereby make repression a key to individual survival.[29]

Many academic researchers assert that memories are frequently reinvented and reconstituted as they are pulled into our consciousness. In this view, memories resemble videotaped events more than static snapshots. Many clinicians who work with trauma victims vehemently disagree, stating emphatically that the human mind clearly has the capacity to dissociate in the midst of a traumatic event, thereby repressing the event from consciousness. The animosity between these "two poles"—academic researchers versus practitioners—has grown increasingly virulent. Jennifer Freyd recently made a similar point: "Laboratory scientists with their enormous cognitive authority to define reality for the rest of the population, must be especially conservative when arguing that lab results on memory generalize to contested memories of abuse . . . scientists must attend to their power to define reality for others."[30]

Initiating Lawsuits and Defending the Accused: Legal Perspectives

Lawyers representing accused parents shape the aforementioned scientific knowledge to best serve the interests of their clients. Their goal is to liberate the defendant, usually an accused parent, from criminal or civil charges related to sexual abuse or rape. Lawyers for accused parents may also initiate suits against doctors or therapists who have allegedly damaged wrongly accused parents and their families, an act made possible by a fairly recent ruling that a third party—such as a parent involved in a therapeutic process with an adult child that results in an accusation of sexual abuse—has the legal right to sue the professional mental health care provider. The New Hampshire Supreme Court, in this case of "first impression" (with no existing precedent), ruled:

> We hold that a therapist owes an accused parent a duty of care in the diagnosis and treatment of an adult patient for sexual abuse where the therapist or the patient, acting on the encouragement, recommendation, or instruction of the therapist, takes public action concerning the accusation. In such instances, the social utility of detecting and punishing sexual abusers and maintaining the breadth of treatment choices for patients is outweighed by the substantial risk of severe harm to falsely accused parents, the family unit, and society.[31]

In this context, lawyers often submit to the court a motion for summary judgment asking that the case be dismissed on the basis of insufficient scientific evidence for the theory of repression. This argument for dismissal is based on an interpretation of the United States Supreme Court's *Frye* (1923) and *Daubert* (1993) rulings, which have greatly influenced the development of legal case law because they established guidelines as to what is "junk" versus "legitimate" science (a concern shared by the scientific community at large).[32] In other words, they seek to answer the questions: What is "good" science? Who makes that determination? And how do concerns over "good" science play out within the legal community?

Because all these cases involve a witness wanting to testify about his or her recovered memories, expert testimony supporting the accuser is brought in to establish the scientific validity of memory repression and recovery. Given the highly controversial nature of the repression principle, and its purportedly uncertain accuracy, the defense's counterargument is that the witness's testimony and his or her supporting cast of experts should not be allowed to testify. For example, one of the key legal rules of evidence (Federal Rules of Evidence #157k555.2) states that for scientific testimony to be admissible, the trial court must conclude that scientific testimony is not only relevant but also "reliable" scientific knowledge:

> One factor [among others] to be considered when deciding whether proffered testimony is valid "scientific knowledge" [sic] and therefore reliable is whether the theory has attained general acceptance within the relevant

scientific community. . . . We must determine nothing less than whether the experts' testimony reflects "scientific knowledge," whether their findings are derived by the scientific method and whether their work product amounts to "good science."[33]

If an expert meets this standard, he or she may testify before the court in support of—or against—repression. But if the expert fails to prove to the court's satisfaction that the general scientific community upholds his or her opinion, then the case may be dismissed. In the words of a Superior Court judge sitting on a panel of federal and state judges at a professional conference:

We judges are the gatekeepers. If we allow a repressed memory case into our courtroom, knowing that even the leading experts of this nation cannot agree upon whether or not the theory of repression meets the minimal standards of scientific reliability and is considered to be generally reliable and valid within the relevant scientific communities, we are putting an undue burden upon our jury, which is comprised of individuals who are most certainly not experts in this field. So, if the nations' leading academics and scholars here today cannot even come close to agreeing, is it moral to ask a jury to decide? We all know that expert witnesses are hired guns; and most court cases will never have the caliber of scholars representing *both sides* as we have here today. This is terribly confusing to me; so I say, let's just keep these cases out of our courts, and let you famous experts all fight it out with one another. My thought is that until such time as you *can* reach an agreement, repressed memory cases should be thrown out of the courts.[34]

In sum, the legal literature indicates that expert witness knowledge has increasingly been shaped by legal standards and rules of evidence, and that to distinguish "true memories" from "false memories" within the courtroom, an ever-increasing reliance upon "good science" has prevailed within the legal domain. Further illustrating this point are two rulings from early repressed-memory cases. In *Loomis v. Mecklenburg*, which occurred in 1991, the judge's opinion centered on whether the statute of limitations had expired.[35] By contrast, the judge in *Mateu v. Hagen*, a repressed-memory case in King County, Washington, was mainly concerned not with the statute of limitations or the moral question of "fair play," but with the question of whether the complaint was legally admissible based upon the science of memory. In *Mateu vs. Hagen*, which occurred in 1993, the procedural issue of import was whether or not the expert witness testimony was admissible—in other words, was it "good science"?[36] Only secondarily did the legal concern over the statute of limitations enter into the analysis. In *Loomis vs. Mecklenburg*, the science of memory was not invoked at all in the courtroom negotiation. An attorney involved in these cases told me: "This shows you just how much more information was available in only two years, as both judges are thoughtful, fair persons."[37]

Regardless of whether the information was available, unavailable, or simply overlooked, comparing these two early cases illustrates how the science of memory was introduced into legal deliberations and became increasingly central to the outcome of repressed memory litigation. This development set public and professional discourses moving in an entirely different direction.

Shifts in legal knowledge tell the story of the developing science of repressed memories, and vice versa. The court's admissibility rulings largely hinge on the court's assessment of "good" versus "junk" science, based on the testimony of expert witnesses who are academic scientists working in the field. After court decisions are handed down, these scientists return to their labs to reformulate research design in accordance with forensic standards of evidence. This reciprocal relationship enables the scientists—who are also expert witnesses—to improve their chances of surviving the next round of juridical inquisition, should they choose to testify again. Most expert witnesses of memory do testify in subsequent cases for reasons having to do with money, status, and advocacy. This is just one of many examples that demonstrate the evolution of scientific research in response to court decisions.

Conclusion: Drawing Connections

Laura Nader's notion of "studying up, down, and sideways"—that is, making connections and studying a "problem across class, or at least on a vertical slice"—offers a fruitful approach to making sense of the repressed memory debates.[38] I will conclude by considering each of these dimensions more fully.

Studying *up* reveals specific actions taken by those who have the power to effect change: judges and lawyers representing accusers and the accused, cognitive psychologists and other academic researchers who specialize in how human memory works, clinicians involved in providing therapy for their patients, and the editors and contributors of the current edition of the *Diagnostic and Statistical Manual of Psychological Disorders*. These knowledge producers have been extraordinarily influential in shaping the contours of a national debate with significant impacts for thousands of people.

The reality of studying *down* translates into taking seriously the suffering of those who feel victimized, whether it is the alleged victim of sexual abuse or the adult accused of such heinous acts, who often sincerely feels innocent. In many such cases, the victim's life is devastated, as is that of the accused adult facing a criminal case and potentially a long prison sentence. The personal and emotional stakes are extremely high.

Finally, "studying sideways" may make room for new perceptions along the margins of the hegemonic interpretations produced by "experts." Social and ideological hegemony is never complete; there is always the possibility that liminal interpretations will arise. A feeling of being compelled by a sense of "wrongness" regarding current understandings of this debate leads to feeling compelled "to work [in order] to think differently."[39] Some individuals, while uninvolved personally, are affected through their own social and kinship networks. I am invoking the term "sideways" to connote a lateral, or non-hierarchical, relationship with someone injured or deeply affected by this polemic. Those who witness the suffering inflicted by the "war" over what is the truth of repression, but who necessarily are outside the immediacy of the front lines, experience this phenomenon from a lateral or horizontal subject-position.

For the anthropologist, memory is not an object waiting to be discovered (as it is in legal discourse), but rather an object that is constructed in the course of scientific research and legal proceedings. This is consistent with both the long-standing anthropological concern with the relationship between culture, knowledge, and power, and a more specific interest in documenting contemporary North American views on what it means to be human, as reflected in the contemporary sciences of human memory.

Studying up, down, and sideways is a means to draw connections between communities and social networks, thereby animating this debate. Seeing these connections is key to an anthropological understanding of the phenomenon of repressed memory. Such an understanding has potential to more lucidly analyze the various orders of engagement, victimization, and complicity that exist alongside the most salient tragic figure in this controversy: the alleged sex abuse victim.

Acknowledgments

I would like to express my gratitude to Laura Nader, Margaret Singer, Beth Loftus, Alan Young, Michael Spolan, and my extraordinarily wise and loving sons, Maurice and Jacob.

Notes

1. Pam Belluck, "Memory Therapy Leads to a Lawsuit and Big Settlement," *New York Times*, 6 November 1997, http://www.nytimes.com/1997/11/06/us/memory-therapy-leads-to-a-lawsuit-and-big-settlement.htm.
2. Hal Dardick, "Psychiatric Patient Tells of Ordeal in Treatment," *Chicago Tribune*, 13 February 2004, http://articles.chicagotribune.com/2004-02-13/news/0402130313_1_psychiatric-treatment-psychiatric-illnesses-childhood-trauma.
3. Katie Zezima and Benedict Carey, "Ex-Priest Challenges Abuse Conviction on Repressed Memories," *New York Times*, 10 September 2009, http://www.nytimes.com/2009/09/11/us/11priest.html?_r=0.
4. See, e.g., Florence Rush, *The Best Kept Secret: Sexual Abuse of Children* (New York: Sulzburger and Graham, 1980).
5. Even more puzzling: In 1896 Freud published three papers stating that he had uncovered, in all of his patients, deeply repressed memories of early childhood sexual abuse. Freud recorded that his patients were not consciously aware of these memories, which must therefore be present as unconscious memories if they were to result in hysterical symptoms or obsession neurosis. Patients were subjected to considerable pressure to "reproduce" infantile sexual abuse "scenes" that Freud was convinced had been repressed into the unconscious. Patients were generally unconvinced that their experiences of Freud's clinical procedure indicated actual sexual abuse. He reported that even after a supposed "reproduction" of sexual scenes, the patients assured him emphatically of their disbelief. This flies directly in the face of all of my own research findings, data outcomes, and ethnographic interviewing. Why is it now culturally believable by women rather than refuted, as it was directly by Freud's clients and often directly to him in his own clinical milieu? See Sigmund Freud, *The Aetiology of Hysteria*, trans. J. Strachey and A. Freud (London: Hogarth Press 1952 [1896]).
6. Laura Nader, "Up the Anthropologist: Perspectives Gained from Studying Up," in *Reinventing Anthropology*, ed. Dell H. Hymes (New York: Pantheon Books, 1972), 292.
7. Judith Hooper, Hannah Bloch, and Lisa Towle, "Targeting the Brain," *Time*, 18 September 1996, http://jackiewhiting.net/Psychology/AbPsych/AnxietyTreatment.htm.
8. Daniel Schacter, quoted in William Cromie, "False Memories," *Harvard Gazette*, 19 September 1996, http://www.news.harvard.edu/gazette/1996/09.19/FalseMemories.html. See also Daniel Schacter, *Searching for Memory: The Brain, the Mind, and the Past* (New York: Basic Books, 1996).
9. Michel Foucault, *Discipline and Punish: The Birth of the Prison* (New York: Vintage Books, 1979).
10. Michael Roth, *The Ironist's Cage: Memory, Trauma, and the Construction of History* (New York: Routledge, 1995).
11. For an overview, see Troyen A. Brennan et al., "Health Industry Practices That Create Conflicts of Interest," *JAMA* 295, no. 4 (25 January 2006): 429–433.
12. Michel Foucault, *The History of Sexuality: An Introduction* (New York: Vintage Books, 1984).
13. Antonio Gramsci, *Selections from the Prison Notebooks* (New York: International Publishers, 1973), 4.
14. Andrew Pickering, ed., *Science as Practice and Culture* (Chicago: University of Chicago Press, 1992); Bruno Latour, *Science in Action: How to Follow Scientists and Engineers*

through Society (Cambridge: Harvard University Press, 1987); H. M. Collins, *Changing Order: Replication and Induction in Scientific Practice*, 2nd ed. (Chicago: University of Chicago Press, 1992).

15. See U.S. Department of Health and Human Services, *Child Maltreatment 2008*, http://www.acf.hhs.gov/programs/cb/pubs/cm08/table3_12.htm.
16. Ian Hacking, *Rewriting the Soul: Multiple Personality and the Sciences of Memory* (Princeton: Princeton University Press, 1995).
17. J. Haaken, "The Debate over Recovered Memory of Sexual Abuse: A Feminist-Psychoanalytic Perspective." *Psychiatry* 58, no. 2 (May 1995): 189–198.
18. Elaine Showalter, *The Female Malady* (New York: Pantheon, 1986).
19. Supreme Court of Rhode Island, *State of Rhode Island v. Quattrocchi* (1995), case number 95–343, http://www.fmsfonline.org/quattrocchi.html.
20. See Latour, *Science in Action*; see also Thomas Kuhn, *The Structure of Scientific Revoutions* (Chicago: University of Chicago Press, 1962).
21. Mark Poster, *Critical Theory and Poststructuralism: In Search of a Context* (Ithaca, NY: Cornell University Press, 1989).
22. For a description of the Franklin case see "Repressed Memory Versus False Memory: Going to Court" (n.d.), http://www.libraryindex.com/pages/1437/Repressed-Memory-Versus-False-Memory-GOING-COURT.html (accessed 22 October 2010).
23. Elizabeth Loftus, personal communication, 2008. See also Alan W. Sheflin and D. Brown, "Repressed Memory of Dissociative Amnesia: What the Science Says," *Journal of Psychiatry and Law* 24 (1996): 143–188.
24. See Supreme Court of New Hampshire, *State of New Hampshire v. Joel Hungerford* (1997), case number 95–429, and *Joel Hungerford v. Susan L. Jones* (1998), case number 97–657.
25. Robyn Kliger, "Somatization: Social Control and Illness Production in a Religious Cult," *Culture, Medicine, and Psychiatry* 18 (1994): 215–245; Robyn Kliger, "Anthropology of Memory Technologies" (unpublished Ph.D. manuscript, University of California, Berkeley, 2000).
26. Lenore Terr, personal communication, March 2003.

Robyn Fivush and V. J. Edwards, "Remembering and Forgetting Childhood Sexual Abuse," *Journal of Child Sexual Abuse* 13 (2004): 1–19.

27. Freyd's parents responded by founding the most important parent advocacy group in existence, the False Memory Syndrome Foundation, which has garnered the support of many influential scientific researchers, some of whom sit on the organization's advisory board. See "Repressed Memory Versus False Memory." See also Jennifer Freyd, *Betrayal Trauma: The Logic of Forgetting Childhood Abuse* (Cambridge: Harvard University Press, 1997).
29. Allan Young, *The Harmony of Illusions: Inventing Post-Traumatic Stress Disorder* (Princeton: Princeton University Press, 1997). The argument is that the diagnostic category of PTSD was invented, in part to lend veracity to the psychological trauma that Vietnam veterans had suffered so that they might receive insurance coverage for treatment once it was established as a "legitimate" diagnosis.
30. Jennifer Freyd, "Science in the Memory Debate," *Ethics and Behavior* 8, no. 2 (1998): 109.
31. Supreme Court of New Hampshire, *Hungerford v. Jones*.
32. See U.S. Supreme Court, *Daubert v. Merrell Dow Pharmaceuticals* (1993) and U.S. Supreme Court, *Frye v. United States* (1923).
33. See *US Federal Rules of Evidence*, 297.

34. Quotation from comments at "Repressed Memories And The Courts: A Mock Trial," presented at the biennial meeting of the American Psychology/Law Society, Jacksonville, FL, 5–7 March 2008.
35. Steven Moen, personal communication, May 1998.
36. King County Superior Court, Mateu v. Hagen (1993), case number 91-2-08053-1.
37. Steven Moen, personal communication, May 1998.
38. Nader, "Up the Anthropologist," 292.
39. Michel Foucault, *The Foucault Reader*, ed. Paul Rabinow (New York: Pantheon, 1984).

Chapter 9

ON COMMON SENSE
Lessons on Starting Over from Post-Soviet Ukraine

―≪≫―

Monica Eppinger

What happens when life stops making sense? When plans, projects, life trajectories, and power hierarchies suddenly lose their salience, not just for an individual but for a nation? Imagine, for example, waking up to find your country erased from the map of the world. This was the situation for the people of the Soviet Union in 1991. Within the span of a few months, the USSR, a country 6,000 miles wide, disappeared from the map. Remainders of the Soviet Union—such as Ukraine, where I conducted anthropological fieldwork—became politically independent states. Socialism as an ideology was discredited; the Communist Party in Ukraine was even outlawed for a short period. Ukrainians faced the completely unforeseen problem of coming up with a new basis on which to organize society, imagining new forms of self and collective governance, finding new ways to make a living and new reasons why, all while hurtling toward an unforeseen future. The disappearance of the Soviet Union shipwrecked Ukrainians on an unknown shore; "home" was a past to which they could not return. Even fifteen years on, when I arrived to conduct fieldwork, Ukrainians were only just beginning to find their footing, and even then, the grounding for experience was more quicksand than bedrock.

What transpired in post-Soviet Ukraine is not the familiar twentieth-century problem of dizzyingly rapid social change. Rather, the frame within which change happens itself disappeared. What was once "common" became fragmented or extinguished; what used to "make sense"

Notes for this chapter begin on page 208.

lost justification. Received wisdom that had guided thoughtful choices and unconscious patterns became glaringly out of place. The nature of this in situ dislocation unsettled "common sense," the term I use to indicate a subgenre of shared intuitions concerning practical evaluations of possible courses of action. It is a mode of thought attentive to the future. "Common sense" is also intimately related to frame. It involves reflecting on a frame, and a frame may present boundary conditions for common sense appraisals. Contesting boundaries of commonality and exclusion—part of the work of constituting group and self—is a familiar target of anthropological attention. But what happens when a frame like Soviet socialism dissolves, when the rug is pulled out from under a whole group of people? What lessons can we learn? Figuring out how people make sense, and how they continue in its sudden absence, may be useful to others who find themselves in conditions of upheaval or rupture.

Metaphor plays a particular role in common sense. Humans use metaphors to understand the world and our place in it. Metaphors using space—particularly up and down—have long been a tool for understanding human relations, affect, and thought in Western social science. Canonical images—for example, Marx's "base" and "superstructure," Freud's subconscious and superego, or "revolution" literatures from Rousseau to Lenin on order turned upside down—are underwritten by spatial metaphors that depend on intuition of up and down. The anthropological metaphor of "social structure" depicts social relations as patterned and layered, with a clear top and bottom, like a building or a wire diagram. More recent social science has used up-down metaphors to think about dominant and subordinate culture, the powerful and the powerless, and relationships between power and resistance.[1]

Laura Nader's provocative critique in her article "Up the Anthropologist" falls squarely within this tradition of spatial metaphor. Nader takes on anthropologists' affinity for studying the less powerful, the poor, and the colonized. She calls on anthropologists to address a blind spot in the discipline and encourages them to turn the ethnographic gaze upon those who have relatively more power or wealth.[2] Her call to study "up, down, and sideways" presages a new wave in anthropology of studying lawyers, scientists, and other higher-echelon subjects. Her admonition to make connections between down and up, and to understand them in relation to each other, bears close attention as much today as when she wrote it.

I had Nader's work in mind when I designed a research project in legal anthropology focusing on the former USSR in 2006. I went to study what happened when institutions and people use law to create private property to replace a system based on state and collective property ownership.

I ran into problems when I actually executed this project, though, that I suspect are of interest to anyone trying to understand life up, down, and sideways. In short, I found that the approach itself presumes preexisting frames whose existence is, instead, a matter for empirical inquiry. The problems I encountered alert us to both obvious and obscure framing devices that structure thought and action. In this chapter, I look at some ways that spatial metaphors like up, down, and sideways operate as framing devices as well as ways that framing devices sometimes deceive us. My hope is to identify when to use such framings, when to use caution with them, and how we might think and act differently altogether. Particularly, I raise two problems related to directionality and fragmentation that I encountered in my own attempts to "study up, down, and sideways." I also propose ways to respond to these challenges that may help others trying to reorient themselves in the throes or wake of rupture of the ordinary work of cultural or social reproduction.

The first problem is figuring out which way is "up." In many contexts, this is a matter of "common sense," the kind of given that anthropologists are trained to discern and analyze. What happens, though, in the case of people living in the USSR? One participant-observer described life at the breakup of the USSR as "waking up one morning to find that the laws of gravity no longer are working." Deciding which way is up, or creating a new up and a new down, becomes a fundamental project in this context. The second problem that arose in my fieldwork context is that of many emergent possible "ups." By this, I do not mean the familiar problem of conflict between social orders underwritten by mutually contradictory normative orders, each competing to be on top: it is not a contentious version of pluralism.[3] Rather, in a context where "ups" are new or still forming, sometimes they compete with each other—but only sometimes. More often, they actually stand in no systematic relation to each other, and it is the problem of the participant or observer to decide on a focus or path in a realm of unconnected dead-ends, floating signifiers, and domains that vanish while the eternal lingers and the extinct reappears. Examining this problem also means examining how pasts are reproduced and why we sometimes take continuity for granted until it is disrupted.

Ethnographic Context: Misrecognition as a Symptom and Diagnostic Tool

> I take a hat
> It turns out to be a frog.

> I hug my wife
> But it is a pillow.
> I pat a cat;
> It turns out to be an iron.
> I open a window and suddenly feel
> The dampness of a closet streaming
> Into my face.
> —"Metamorfozi" (Metamorphoses) by Stranniye Igri (Strange Games), after the poem by Jean Gardier

The 1987 song "Metamorfozi" by the Soviet band Stranniye Igri ("Strange Games") conveys the persistent sense of misrecognition at the beginnings of post-Socialism. Misrecognition, or mistaking something alien for something familiar, may be symptomatic of a particular social condition that affects how one might "study up." How misrecognition may be a complicating factor will become clearer from a description of how my research was supposed to proceed.

As mentioned, I originally formulated a research question that struck me as particularly amenable to "studying up." I focused on what appeared to me to be intentional social change via dramatic legal projects in post-Soviet Ukraine—a new Constitution, fundamental legislative codes—aimed at creating what would come next. When Ukraine became an independent country in 1991, it inherited a set of basic laws that referred to a country (the USSR) and state institutions (e.g., the central planning agency Gosplan, the Supreme Court of the USSR, the KGB) that no longer existed. The basic legal framework—Constitution, Civil Code, Criminal Code, Land Code—referred to legal elements and the social system of a regime that had vanished. The disappearance of the old country, as well as the creation of the newly independent Ukraine, demanded new basic laws.

This seemed a promising area for researching intentional social change for two reasons. First, law-making is a practice in which Ukrainians articulate, dispute, and reiterate emergent alternatives through routines that are easy to identify and observe. In particular, the process of drafting and passing basic framework legislation offers a striking opportunity to analyze law-making as a matter of both verbal performance[4] and performative speech.[5] This leads to the second reason law-making seemed such a fertile area: post-Socialists themselves treat legal change as central to remaking their economies, infrastructure, and citizenry. After the Soviet Union dissolved in 1991 and political and social reconstitution began, one activity that bewildered ex-Soviet citizens have used to make sense of their world is law-making. Debates over constitutional reforms, civil and criminal codes, and private property ownership consumed private conversations and public airwaves for a decade and a half; and implementation of fundamental changes after laws passed has changed the daily life of literally every citizen of the country. Taking on this topic required me to study up and down, and back again.

I first lived in Ukraine as a U.S. diplomat, serving in Embassy Kiev from 1995 to 1997 including as the U.S. government's liaison to the parliament from 1996 to 1997. I returned in 2006 for fourteen months as an anthropologist specializing in the study of normative orders and political structure. Concentrating on the creation of private property, I first studied the parliamentarians who made the privatization laws, as well as the former collective farmers receiving land and urban residents receiving apartments under the laws. Up, down, and sideways. So far, so good. As a general matter, I already knew who was up here, having been assured by the political scientists of several continents that across Central and Eastern Europe the majority of the post-Socialist economic elite are holdovers from the socialist political elite.[6] Down and sideways largely correlated with spatial distribution: rural meant down, urban meant sideways.

It was the "up" that gave me the first inkling of trouble. Background research on elite subjects, it seemed, would be the equivalent of flipping open the *Komsomol* yearbook, the Ukrainian Communist Party leadership rolls, and the Ukrainian SSR parliamentary list from the late 1980s and taking notes.

Consider the following fairly typical life history, though, of Volodymyr Lytvyn, one of the many persistent figures in the Ukrainian political elite, and we begin to get a sense of how the seemingly straight-forward orientation of up, down, and sideways becomes suspended. Lytvyn climbed the governmental hierarchy of a ministry through the 1980s and was a member of the top Communist Party body of the Ukrainian SSR in 1991; Lytvyn was speaker of the Ukrainian parliament in 2002. So far, predictions regarding the nomenklatura's survival into the post-Socialist order seem borne out. But now add some background information provided by one of Lytvyn's peers in parliament: "Lytvyn headed the Party training school and was an insider with the Central Committee of the Communist Party of Ukraine at the end of the USSR. After the Soviet Union fell apart, Lytvyn finally found a job as a security guard."

This changes the view of Lytvyn's trajectory. From Lytvyn's point of view, he was pursuing a specific life path, with both personal ambitions and collective hopes for the future well defined, when suddenly, the Communist-only parliament of the Ukrainian SSR voted Ukraine independent and outlawed the Communist Party. In 1991, Lytvyn is out of a job, out of a future, without paycheck or "marketable skills." — And so is most of the rest of Ukraine: the period from 1991 to 1993 was a period of de facto collective unemployment and galloping inflation. All workplaces were "state-owned," but the new state had inherited no financial resources, nor had it yet developed the capacity to finance itself. "Wage arrears," the rather anonymous term for a post-Soviet period in which people worked without receiving pay, ran for months on end. "Galloping inflation" exceeded 1,000 percent annually; Soviet-era savings, carefully collected over years, were wiped out overnight. Which way was up, then? "We were all spinning in circles, scrambling," one of my interlocutors recalls. "There was no up and no down, just spinning."

Lytvyn, like others, worked his contacts and scrambled his way back into a suit and tie, and eventually into political leadership. But unlike the Lytvyn of 1989, the Lytvyn of 1999, like most of his compatriots, knew what it was like to face complete uncertainty regarding his material well-being in the present, his beliefs and investments of the past, and his future, and to be lucky to find work as a security guard.

Now we can revisit the finding that many of the post-Socialist economic elite are "the same as" the Socialist political elite. When we look "up" to see who was on top at the end of the Soviet period and compare it to now, do we really see "the same people?" Regardless of faces, names, and other superficial markers of continuity, if we think they are "the same," perhaps we are engaging in wide-scale misrecognition. Did intervening experiences have no effect on the social order in which they were "up" or "down," or even the way they defined "up" or "down?" The same kind of disruption and misrecognition could also figure, I found, when I "studied down." Lytvyn and his contemporaries' paths remind us to heed Laura Nader's demand for contextualization: studying up, down, and sideways requires also that we insert ethnography into history. The spatial analytic demands a temporal element; making connections between up, down, and sideways requires learning what has happened over time to constitute, reconstitute, or unmoor "up" and "down."

The problem of misrecognition led me to reconsider the research question. Instead of merely inquiring into how the "old" Lytvyn learned new slogans and electoral tricks of parliamentary democracy in passing privatization legislation and the like, I had to first ask whether the current Lytvyn is the "same person" as the old. Does the disappearance of the prior frame of reference (and basis for the prior hierarchy)—as well as debating, legislating, and implementing new ways of life—work recursively in the production of post-Socialist subjects? The question "Is the old dog learning new tricks?" leads to a prior question: "Is this really the same old dog?" Admitting the possibility of misrecognizing the new dog as "the same" as the old dog opens the way to investigating how and why the dog has changed or not. In other words, the problem of misrecognition made me attentive to a new set of issues: in addition to *what* was going on inside the new borders of a new country, I needed to be aware of *who* was emerging within those borders. A different relationship between practice and subjectivity needed to be accounted for, to understand this new place, and assumptions about "up" and "down" were not of use to that end. Instead of a narrow focus on the role of legal change in the construction of post-Soviet social and economic hierarchies, I began also to look at the role of legal change in the creation of the post-Soviet self.

This leads to a diagnostic insight that is key to the analytical work of studying up, down, and sideways. Misrecognition of the seemingly familiar—cat for iron, window for closet, Lytvyn for Lytvyn—may be symptomatic of a particular form of social change. Unlike other periods of rapid social change within a given frame, the type of social change at issue in the post-Soviet context involves the dissolution of a frame and a resulting disorientation. The change is marked not just by amount or rapidity, but by its peculiar nature. Recognizing this and dealing with it conceptually and methodologically became my first research challenge.

Problem 1: Suspension of Gravity

Discursive Rupture and the Limit Case

We normally distinguish social change by pace: rapid social change during modernization or glacial cumulative change through reiterations of the traditional. In my research, it became worthwhile to distinguish between qualitatively different types of social change as well, in order to isolate and understand better one that poses interesting challenges to studying up.

Change, after all, is a defining feature of the post-Socialist context. I found that at least initially, the change at issue was itself defined by discontinuity. "Post-Socialism" is named not by what it is, but by what it succeeds. This points to a peculiar core feature: post-Socialism is identified to some extent by what has been lost, or is missed, or recognized as never coming. For a post-Socialist subject, this particular understanding of one's self—naming presence by an absence—may be descriptive or constitutive. Loss has at times seemed profound and formative. Subjectivity is in flux; confusion and redefinition, common. In the new states emerging from the dissolution of the USSR, the problem of what to call oneself, how to form an identity, what to do next, became basic questions. Contemporary Ukraine may not be a typical context in which to test "up and down" as settled propositions, but it may serve well as a limit case[7] because of the peculiar experience of post-Socialism. It may also illuminate some of the landscape for any person facing a context of profound rupture.

What is peculiar in the case of post-Soviet Ukraine is the break in business as usual and the unraveling of what was once taken for granted. This created the opening for emergent forms across the board. The complex of profound changes that took place in the Soviet Union in the span of just a few years in the late 1980s has been called "discursive rupture."[8] In this section, I describe the discursive production that preceded post-Socialism to better explain what is meant by discursive rupture, and then discuss some implications for contemporary fieldwork. I understand discursive rupture in reference to an "always already" quality of discourse.[9] Suddenly, what was for "always" was no more, and the presumed "already" was removed. More than "transition," post-Socialism is falling into and climbing out of a gap.

Before the Break

To understand the gap, we may explore its last solid edge, Socialism. From the present vantage, "late Socialism" in the USSR is understood as a period of stagnation (*zastoi*), which usually means flattening trajectories of material production over the post–World War II period. However, there is an alternative characterization and explanation. After the 1917 Socialist Revolution, authoritative discourse remained fluid through a lively, Party-led interactive process of forming and reforming a Party line through the 1930s and 1940s. This fluidity froze in 1950 when a Stalin article in *Pravda* declared that language stood outside of revolutionary time and did not change with every transformation of base and superstructure. With this and subsequent statements, Stalin was saying there was no position for anyone, including himself, to originate meta-discourse, or commentary on public (and private) conversations; Stalin destroyed the Party leadership's position of authorship of a fluid authoritative discourse. From that point, a hegemony of forms prevailed in the production of authoritative discourse in the USSR.[10]

We might do well to discuss two literary genres, the novel and the epic, to understand two discursive modes at play in this paradigm shift to late Socialism.[11] The novel is an emergent form, free and flexible. It "reflects the tendencies of a new world still in the making."[12] It renews its language by incorporating many forms of spontaneous speech like street language, conversation, banter, or spats. These forms of spontaneous speech that originate outside of formal grammars and codes of literature come from many strands and may be dissonant with each other. The novel is "permeated with laughter," irony, humor, elements of self-parody, and indeterminacy. The epic, by contrast, is fixed. Its defining feature is that the "authorial position" (the position of the one who utters the epic word) is "the environment of a man."[13]

These characterizations of the novel and the epic may help us grasp the change in authoritative discourse that is the hallmark of late Socialism. After Stalin's paradigm shift in 1950 and death in 1953, interactive production of an authoritative discourse was replaced by reproduction. Rather than continually posing contemporary questions and answers, nuanced changes in Party line, or new suggestions for ethics or comportment, late Socialism was marked by the reproduction of authoritative discourse through repetition and citation.[14] The work of local Komsomol secretaries resembles that of the tellers of the epic: "it is memory, and not knowledge, that serves as the source and power for the creative impulse. That is how it was, it is impossible to change it: the tradition of the past is sacred."[15] In late Socialism, this opened a growing gap between emergent discourses and authoritative discourse, between contemporary discussion of emerging conditions and reproduction of the authoritative word.

This continued until the next dramatic shift in production of authoritative discourse, when in 1986 Gorbachev called for experts outside the Party structures to advise on policy and management. The capacity for meta-discourse was reopened, but under new management. Gorbachev ceded the Party's monopoly on public self-reflection and correction, seemingly inadvertently removing the center from a centralized authority.[16] How was authoritative discourse to be produced or reproduced, if authority declared itself inadequate to the task? In terms of discursive production, "post-Socialism" in the former Soviet space, then, may be seen as the gap left when the authorities called into question their own authority, and authoritative discourse collapsed in on itself like quicksand, a kind of discontinuity characterized as discursive rupture.

To summarize, by the 1980s, "up" had a very clear referent: it referred to those entrusted with reproducing authoritative discourse. Gorbachev changed the rules of the game though, when he called for extra-Party experts to produce rather than reproduce, and in doing so unwittingly brought an end to the game itself. This gives a clear picture of the situation in 1991, the point at which Ukrainian Communist Party members of parliament voted Ukraine independent and, shortly thereafter, their party against the law. The game disappeared, leaving only a field of former players.

The Catalogue of Lack, Perhaps Including an Upside

Absence, shortage, and lack become commanding features of this Socialist landscape, at least as figured in the academic literature. Many emphasize Socialism as a time and space of shortages. Some go so far as to call state Socialism an "economy of shortage."[17] Socialism has also been depicted as rich in lacks of various kinds: practices (some of those practices, for example, associated with liberalism like basic civil liberties and public accountability) and sensational or material lacks associated with physical amenities (like spacious housing, bright color, variety of tastes, or consumer choice).[18] A typical reference to Socialism and post-Socialism runs, "'Socialism had trained them to desire. Capitalism stepped in to let them buy,'"[19] as if the end of Socialism meant an end to lack or scarcity.

The evidence on post-Socialism disappoints these expectations. Observers catalogue a different set of lacks in the post-Socialist space. Familiar goods of bygone days are in short supply.[20] Demand for Socialist-era goods surged, possibly reflecting nostalgia for the work that produced them and for the identity that work had entailed, during a time of widespread lack of employment.[21] Scarcity of Socialist material amenities decimates the post-Socialist standard of living, and the sense of loss is widespread—not just for the extraordinary, like the forty-eight orchestras that played free concerts on summer evenings in Gorky Park under high Stalinism, but also for the simple Ferris wheel of a small-town park.[22] Understandings of value are disordered, and the experience of devaluation is profound and widespread in the former Socialist space.[23]

This shift in terms of trade in both material and symbolic capital lay behind one of the most pronounced scarcities in post-Socialism: the unforeseen disappearance of life-long companions, familiar faces, and stable sociability. In Ukraine, under Socialism, residential mobility was infrequent and largely confined to limited social groups at expected periods of life, such as college students going to university or military families assuming a new rotation. This life structure has changed radically. The post-Soviet Ukrainian population has fallen from 52 million in 1991 to an estimated 47 million today, largely because of emigration.[24] Internal migration, or so-called labor migration, accounts for even more displacement and sometimes for a persistent sense of the absence of those who have left.[25] On a collective level, eradicating the Iron Curtain has engendered not cosmopolitanism, but massive flight and a growing localism for those who have stayed behind.

For some of those who remain behind, post-Socialism's defining characteristic is its "culture of symbolic shortages" in which people lack the tools to express the new or explain the changes befalling them.[26] Speechlessness, particularly the widespread inability to describe one's own identity, may be one more symptom of discursive rupture.[27] Speechlessness can be distinguished from silence. Unlike the previously studied transitional silence, which comes from distancing oneself from the past, speechlessness comes from a lack of speech for the present. It is an inability to put into words new ideals and goals, or an inability to express or interpret changes that have already happened. This collective speechlessness may be related to a fundamental scarcity of post-Socialism, the absence of a collective utopia. This loss of an internally persuasive discourse—namely, that the performance of everyday life is also performative of a better future for all—is staggering. There is no epic for the present; discourse is dominated by the novel, if we take the "emergent" to mean both the new and the new expressions of nostalgia for the past.

Thus the end of the USSR was marked by the end of a certain mode of reproduction of authoritative discourse. Over the first fifteen years of Ukrainian independence, close to 10 percent of the population of the Ukrainian SSR has been lost to emigration, rising mortality, and falling birth rates. Those who remain are engaged in fashioning authority and authoritative discourse while also attending to other pressing material and psychological demands. Social networks, understandings of the world, and means of providing for material needs quickly become untethered quickly, and, for most, have yet to be firmly nailed down again. Open-ended discursive modes dominate the present in place of an authoritative discourse. What that means for Ukrainians' everyday life today is that rather than drawing on an established frame of reference to evaluate personal success or failure, experience happiness or sadness, formulate life goals and daily expectations, or retell the history of their country or themselves, they feel they are making it up as they go along.

Social Change, Culture Change, and Discursive Rupture

Setting and implementing the rules for post-Socialism is a process contested at every step. These disputes have very concrete and measurable outcomes, but they still do not always clearly indicate which way is up. Consider the following example, related by a member of a disbanded collective farm:

> The land regulations specified that farmland would be distributed to those who had worked the farm through the last years of Socialism, but did not specify exactly how the land would be divvied up. The farm director took

charge of deciding who got which plots of land, awarding the richer fields to himself and his special cronies. That continued until disgruntled farmers held a town meeting, which ended in the farm director receiving a sound thrashing. The director died from his injuries. After that, no one wanted to be in charge of the land apportionment. The farmers ended up numbering the land plots on a giant map and drawing numbers out of a transparent fishbowl at a meeting with all present.

The un-mooredness of post-Socialism is thus by definition difficult to model. The first years after the dissolution of the USSR in Ukraine were a time of deeply sensed rupture, sometimes experienced as shock, uncertainty, fear, or tingling possibility. By the late 1990s, some uncertainty had abated: some possibilities were perceived as precluded, and new probabilities regarding class formation, gender positions, distribution of wealth, assets, and property rights, identity, consumption, and production patterns had emerged.

Even so, describing the situation in using the relatively stable, albeit rearranged, elements of something like a "configuration" would terminologically fail to capture the fluidity and flux. Post-Socialism, as discussed, does include familiar-looking forms from the prior era but they are prone to misrecognition. These forms, together with the completely unexpected, yield new aspects of life and conditions of possibility. The past, rather than foisting inherited fixities, yields an assemblage marked by fracture, movement, and lines of flight.[28]

This state has also been described as a sensation of "disorientation in place."[29] The post-Soviet setting offers a peculiar vantage to anthropologists who would study up, down, and sideways. The methodological imperative to "study up" seemingly presumes a shared sense of direction. However, if a defining element of post-Socialism is that a certain form of authority and authoritative discourse has been left behind, and the post-Soviet context is more like a world in which gravity has been suspended, then the methodology could be adapted in interesting ways. A study of post-Socialist subjectivity, or other contexts marked by discursive rupture, would benefit from taking emergent forms—practice, iteration, and performance—as central objects.

A look back at law is warranted at this juncture. Law can be described as one subgenre of "performative speech," the kind of speech whose utterance changes reality.[30] Certain minimal conditions permit performative speech to be felicitous, that is, to succeed. One necessary condition is that the person producing the utterance has to be the correct authority. For an accused defendant to be sentenced as guilty, for example, it has to be a judge, not an actor playing a judge, who bangs a gavel and pronounces him or her "Guilty." That raises the key question, though, about where authority comes from. A post-Socialist world of zero gravity might provide an opportunity to ascertain just how one figures out how authoritative discourse (and authority) is produced and reproduced—and then, how people create, subvert, seize, evade, and ignore authority itself. In other words, conditions of discursive rupture might offer an opportunity to examine closely how people discern or create which way is up.

Problem 2: Polyphony

In the former Soviet space, the past seems to inflect the present in rich and novel ways. The indeterminacy of a post-Soviet "transition" with no clear linear progression presents the possibility of multiply rupturing lines or curves without a discernible endpoint. It contrasts with a process in, say, eastern Germany, with a presumed (albeit occasionally resisted) endpoint of the extension of West German modes of subjectivity, governance, and economic practices across the space of unified Germany.[31] This difference between Central Europe and the former Soviet space reveals an opening for inquiry: how do relationships to the past change the experience of the present and orientation to the future, in a period following discursive rupture? Ukraine, for example, has not emulated an East German repudiation of past abuses nor a South African vetting of truth and attempt at reconciliation. There has been no standardized, collective subject formation. Ukrainians are forming, learning, and internalizing new norms outside of a formal process of recasting the past and articulating a consensus vision of the present and future, largely on their own. In a present created by the collapse of a certain process of reproduction of an authoritative discourse, the conflicting ways of understanding the world inherent to post-Soviet Ukraine are forming without an initial center of gravity.

In conversations with my interlocutors, I have tested this multiplicity using research inquiries along a couple of lines: what it means to lead a "good life," and who or what is up and who or what is down in Ukraine. The first led to discussions about protecting one's family from material discomfort and attaining a certain level of material comfort, yet not making pursuit of material gain the central focus of one's life. Confusing? Yes. This patently unclear combination is a small taste of what life is like in conditions of discursive rupture. The second line of inquiry takes Nader's call literally and starts by asking directions. The answers, particularly regarding who is up, grow increasingly less confident.

To inquire from a different angle with some interlocutors, I re-raised a question initiated in the 1960s by a persistently disdainful and caustic commentator on Soviet life—writer Vladimir Nabokov, "What is *poshlost'*?"[32] (*Poshlost'* may be translated as vulgarity, tackiness, or garishness, although none of those terms fully captures its sense.) When queried, Nabokov himself answered, "*poshlost'* has many nuances, and evidently I have not described them clearly enough if you think anyone can be tempted by *poshlost'*. Corny trash, vulgar clichés, Philistinism in all its phases, imitations of imitations, bogus profundities, crude, moronic, and dishonest pseudo-literature—these are obvious examples."[33] I thought it was worth re-posing Nabokov's question as a methodology for exploring or delineating limits in what had become a limitless world. If it is difficult, in conditions of discursive rupture, to identify who or what is "up," then perhaps one could at least make out the contours of what is aspired to, by exploring what is repulsive. Given the importance in Soviet culture of being *kulturniy* (cultured), maybe inquiring into post-Soviet *poshlost'* might give an idea of its opposite—namely, virtues manifest in leading a "good life."

Regarding *poshlost'*, informants in separate interviews have all agreed on two points: that *poshlost'* includes sexual vulgarity as a subset but not as a synonym, and that a quality of *poshlost'* marks an activity, performance, behavior, or speech as inferior in class. All, however, distinguish *poshlost'* from post-Soviet material success. A focus group of Kyiv forty-something office workers gathers in a Kyiv restaurant chosen by one of "the girls" for its tasteful setting and affordable menu. Several of the group are Kyiv natives, meaning they had enjoyed a certain level of family privilege in Soviet times; others rode star-student status to Kyiv, where they met the Kyivans in graduate school at a prestigious technical university. All would now be considered "middle class," if one adopts a defining criterion of the American middle class: being physically comfortable but unable to miss four paychecks in a row without risk of falling into poverty. "*Poshlost'* is above all a spiritual matter," one of my informants tells me. "It has nothing to do with rich or poor. A *nouveau riche* person could be the most *poshliy*, and a poor person these days could be the most cultured." However, in the same conversation this same informant told me, "Which way is up? Well, the easy way to decide is on a material level. Those who have money are up and those who don't are down."

Really? During a walk along a park-lined street with another Kyiv interlocutor, I am told, "Thinking something is *poshliy* marks it as inferior in a class sense. As a matter of fact, even contemplating this distinction implies you are trying to figure out who is inferior to you, and that in itself makes your question *poshliy*." A classically trained musician in his mid-forties, who now makes his living teaching music in middle school and playing music for hire, has some specific descriptions.

> What is *poshlost'*? Oh man, these days . . . I play piano in the evenings, and there are some places I won't play. People come to cafés with different aims. Some come to hang out with friends, read, think quietly to themselves, talk. That is one kind of public, and it forms around a certain kind of place. Others come to party, throw money around, be wild, forget. That is another kind of public. Those places don't attract intellectuals. The people there treat the musicians like servants. I don't need it.

These answers indicate that these interlocutors clearly consider some conduct *poshliy*. But which way is up for them? And which way is up for the person who does party, throw money around, or attract or impress friends by showing off materially?

Parliamentarians I have interviewed likewise show simultaneous, multiple, and sometimes mutually contradictory senses of "up" and "down." Among them, their voters, and ascendant property-holders that would seek to influence them, both ideas and social formations rise and fall before a single vote is held or law is passed. Political parties proliferate, and the majority do not even last a term in office. Coalitions both do in their opponents and fall apart themselves in the opening weeks of a parliamentary session. Party platforms are superseded by the disappearance of both the keynote speaker from the dais and the raison d'etre of the party as the party congress is held. A clamorous discourse around "corruption" takes on what is proper or desirable for public officials: Does honest policy failure or voter disappointment amount to "corruption"? What are ethics? Duty?

This period of multiple, competing senses of which way is up call to mind a Bakhtinian heteroglossia. However, marked as it is by dissonance and clamor, I suggest that a better descriptor of discourse in this context is polyphony. In a period of such active production of new forms of thought and evaluation, American anthropology's tradition of considering material culture, ideational culture, and social structure as distinct domains of inquiry clouds the picture. Rather than breaking analysis down between culture and society, I use the concept of discourse and discursive production to allow for a more holistic consideration of emergent forms than breaking analysis down between culture and society. This approach also allows for a more interactive understanding of the relationship between past and present, and recasts the bounded nature of the time at issue. Both the present and the past emerge as an echoing call-and-response pattern rather than analytically separate realms. A reengineered conceptualization taking the material, the ideational, and the social holistically, as well as a more interwoven temporality, may be contributions to theory that come from the study of an unsettled period involving many perceived possible "ups." Discourse analysis might also offer some very practical methodological benefits to those "studying up, down, and sideways" in a period dominated by contradictory understandings of the world.

Extending Studying Up: When the Bottom Drops Out

"Studying up" continues the rich heritage of spatial metaphor in social science, not least because the imperative to study "up, down, and sideways" can lead in unexpected directions. I have considered a particular kind of fieldwork setting, a scene of discursive rupture where the bottom drops out and gravity is suspended. In this context, appearances can be deceiving. A person, institution, ritual, or process may not be "the same" as it "always" was. The problem of misrecognition itself may serve to alert us to a context in which the frame is unstable, dissolving, or dissolved. Trying to "study up, down, and sideways" leads us to consider which way is up, and how our interlocutors discern and create an up and a down. It may aid investigation into the formation and performance of authority, the process of establishing a position from which one may issue performative speech acts.

In a context of fragments and fluidity, we also run into the problem of multiple, emergent, and disappearing "ups." Older studies of pluralism and pluralistic societies provide some insights, but pluralism assumes a stability within the discourses at issue, and in the relationships between them, that is absent in a setting where trial runs at establishing which way is up have the half-life of a Cheshire cat multiplied into several litters of chimerae. In a context of many ways of seeing, "studying up" allows inquiry into how multiple senses of "up" might be tolerated, and how demand, aspiration, hope, and ambition are created or abandoned.

This ethnographic context stands as a warning against over-internalizing, or becoming blind to, our own spatial metaphors. Staying alert to instances of misrecognition can aid in diagnosing periods of dissolution and emergence. Recurrent misrecognition might sound an alarm that the past is confusing our understanding of the present rather than illuminating it, and noticing misrecognition might help to identify a certain milieu marked not by change within a frame but by dissolution of the frame. In such a milieu, it may be appropriate to suspend the assumption that there is a well-recognized or relatively stable up, or down, to study.

Even though these problems come from the specific context of the former Soviet Union, they may provide food for thought and action for anyone for whom life has become fundamentally unpredictable, disrupted, or disorienting. The problems that disrupted my research show that even in a context in which it is no longer clear which way is up, or in which multiple divergent "ups" are at play, "studying up" initiates a line of inquiry and action without which some of the more unforeseen, interesting, and even disorienting results might not come to light. Thinking about orientation in times of upheaval may allow us to more lucidly recognize and respond to certain forms of social change. The dissolution of the USSR is but one of many instances of rupture that have disturbed common sense in recent years. We are surrounded by examples closer to home: How are we to make sense of the rewriting of civil liberties and norms of executive power in the United States after 9/11? Or government administration's framing of violence as a way of life in the name of peace? Or the meltdown of a financial-legal apparatus that enabled an American dreamscape in which one's home is one's castle and the object of desire is a domain of sovereign individuality? Or the dissolution of public education in all but name? Can we recognize, in time to think and act afresh, those instances in which a common frame for thought, action, and power disappears and common sense becomes nonsensical?

Post-Soviet Ukraine wakes us up with the clarity of comparative consciousness.[34] This ethnographic context reminds us that the most unexpected events can occur, that dissolution of an entire lifeway can happen, and that in even the most solid-seeming systems, the most improbable turn is possible. It poses to us the bracing challenge of dealing with an open future.

Notes

1. See, e.g., James Scott, *Weapons of the Weak* (New Haven: Yale University Press, 1985); Dick Hebdige, *Subculture: The Meaning of Style* (London and New York: Routledge, 1979); T. J. Jackson-Lear, "The Concept of Cultural Hegemony: Problems and Possibilities," *American Historical* Review 90, no. 3 (1985): 567–593.
2. Laura Nader, "Up the Anthropologist: Perspectives Gained from Studying Up," in *Reinventing Anthropology*, ed. Dell H. Hymes (New York: Pantheon Press, 1972).
3. See, e.g., Max Gluckman, *Politics, Law, and Ritual in Tribal Society* (Oxford: Blackwell, 1965). Legal scholars have also puzzled over how to administer justice in a polity that includes differing legal or normative orders. See, e.g., Eugen Ehrlich, *Fundamental Principles of the Sociology of Law*, trans. W. Moll (New York: Russell and Russell, 1962 [1913]).

For some answers proposed in the doctrine known in the Anglo-American legal tradition as "Conflicts of Laws," see Walter Wheeler Cook, "The Logical and Legal Basis of the Conflict of Law," *Yale Law Journal* 33 (1933): 457; David P. Currie, Herma Hill Kay, and Larry Kramer, *Conflict of Laws: Cases, Comments, Questions* (St. Paul, MN: West, 2001); R. A. Leflar, "Conflicts Law: More on Choice-Influencing Considerations," *California Law Review* 54 (1966): 1584–88; and Ernst Rabel, *The Conflict of Laws: A Comparative Study* (Ann Arbor: University of Michigan Press, 1945).

4. Richard Bauman, "Verbal Art as Performance," *American Anthropologist* 77, no. 2 (1975): 290–311.
5. John Austin. *How to Do Things with Words* (Cambridge: Harvard University Press, 1962).
6. See, e.g., Gil Eyal, Ivan Szeleny, and Eleanor Townsley, *Making Capitalism Without Capitalists: Class Formation and Elite Struggles in Post-Communist Central Europe* (London: Verso, 1998); Jozsef Borocz and Akos Rona-Tas, "Small Leap Forward: Emergence of New Economic Elites," *Theory and Society* 24 (1995): 751–781; Eric Hanley, Natasha Yershova, and Richard Anderson, "Russia—Old Wine in New Bottle? The Circulation and Reproduction of Russian Elites, 1983–1993," *Theory and Society* 24 (1995): 689; Akos Rona-Tas, "The First Shall be the Last? Entrepreneurship and Communist Cadres in the Transition from Socialism," *American Journal of Sociology* 100 (1994): 40–69; and Jacek Wasilewski, "The Forming of the New Elite: How Much Nomenklatura Is Left?" *Polish Sociology Review* 2 (1995): 133.
7. A "limit case," a concept adopted from calculus, refers to a bounding condition that can be approached but not attained. To understand what this means, consider the temperature of water. Water can be heated to 50° Fahrenheit, 100° F, 150° F, but at 212° F it boils, undergoes a phase transition, and is no longer water but steam. Thus 212 + n° F (where n is any positive number) is the limit case for heating water. Water can be cooled to 50° F, 40° F, but at 32° F it undergoes a phase transition and is no longer water but ice. Likewise, 32 − n° F is the limit case for cooling water. The post-Socialist context is like a stable substance, say, ice, that has undergone a phase transition, say, to water. It may not be the typical case for studying what happens under conditions of normal discursive reproduction. The typical "studying up" case study is analogous to studying a property of a stable substance, like ice, and the research question, "Why does ice float?" gets at an essential and important scholarly problem. Studying post-Socialist Ukraine is like studying ice at 32° F. It may be illuminating in the special way that a limit case can be illuminating.
8. Alexei Yurchak, *Everything Was Forever until It Was No More: The Last Soviet Generation* (Princeton, NJ: Princeton University Press, 2005).
9. Louis Althusser, "Ideology and Ideological State Apparatuses: Notes towards an Investigation," in *Lenin and Philosophy, and Other Essays*, ed. Louis Althusser (London: New Left Books, 1971).
10. Yurchak, *Everything Was Forever until It Was No More*.
11. Mikhail M. Bakhtin, "Epic and Novel," in *The Dialogic Imagination: Four Essays*, ed. Michael Holquist and Caryl Emerson, trans. Michael Holquist (Austin: University of Texas Press, 2002 [1975]).
12. Ibid., 7.
13. Ibid..
14. Yurchak, *Everything was Forever until It was No More*.
15. Bakhtin, "Epic and Novel," 15.
16. Yurchak, *Everything Was Forever until It Was No More*.
17. Janosz Kornai, quoted in Katherine Verdery, "Theorizing Socialism: a Prologue to the 'Transition,'" *American Ethnologist* 18 (1991): 423.

18. Václav Havel, "The Power of the Powerless," in *Living in Truth*, ed. Václav Havel (London: Faber and Faber, 1986).
19. Borneman, quoted in Jonathan Bach, "The Taste Remains: Consumption, (N)ostalgia, and the Production of East Germany," *Public Culture* 14, no. 3 (2002): 551.
20. Bach, "The Taste Remains"; Daphne Berdahl, "(N)ostalgia for the Present: Memory, Longing, and East German Things," *Ethnos* 64, no. 2 (1999): 192–211.
21. Berdahl, "(N)ostalgia for the Present."
22. Diana Blank, "Fairytale Cynicism in the Kingdom of Plastic Bags: Powerlessness of Place in a Ukrainian Border Town," *Ethnography* 5, no. 3 (2004): 349–378.
23. Katherine Verdery, *The Vanishing Hectare: Property and Value in Postsocialist Transylvania* (Ithaca, NY: Cornell University Press, 2004).
24. Konovalchuk, however, attributes a small proportion of the population decline to women's decisions not to bear children after the Chernobyl nuclear disaster—in other words, as another response to an event central to the advent of discursive rupture in Ukraine. Vladimir Konovalchuk, *A Computable General Equilibrium Analysis of the Economic Effects of the Chernobyl Nuclear Disaster*, unpublished Ph.D. dissertation archived at: http://etda.libraries.psu.edu/theses/approved/WorldWideIndex/ETD-1337/index.html (accessed March 2006).
25. Blank, "Fairytale Cynicism in the Kingdom of Plastic Bags."
26. Oushakine, "In the State of Post-Soviet Aphasia," 1010.
27. Ibid., 997.
28. Gilles Deleuze and Felix Guattari, "Introduction: Rhizome," in *A Thousand Plateaus: Capitalism and Schizophrenia*, ed. Gilles Deleuze and Felix Guattari, trans. Brian Massumi, (Minneapolis: University of Minnesota Press, 1987), 3–4.
29. Yuri Andrukhovich, Дезорієнтація на Місцевості [*Disorientation in Place*], (Ivano-Frankivsk: Liliya, 2006). The title is a play on words using word-for-word translation of the Russian idiom for the competition of racing with use of compasses and topographical maps known as orienteering—literally, "orientation in place."
30. Austin, *How to Do Things with Words*.
31. Berdahl, "(N)ostalgia for the Present."
32. Vladimir Nabokov, *Nikolai Gogol* (New York: New Directions, 1961); Vladimir Nabokov, interviewed by Harold Gould, "Vladimir Nabokov," *The Paris Review* 41 (1967).
33. See Harold Gould's interview of Nabokov, "Vladimir Nabokov," *The Paris Review* 41 (1967): 12.
34. Laura Nader, "Comparative Consciousness," in *Assessing Cultural Anthropology*, ed. Robert Borofsky (New York: McGraw-Hill, 1994).

Chapter 10

ON CARING

Solidarity Anthropology (or, How to Keep
Health Care from Becoming Science Fiction)

————∞∞∞————

Adrienne Pine

As a lead educator for the California Nurses Association (CNA) from 2004 to 2007, I taught continuing education courses defined broadly by the California Board of Registered Nursing as including social science lessons germane to nursing issues. I taught hundreds of daylong seminars on technology, disaster prevention, electoral process, corporate politics, health care reform, and U.S. labor history to thousands of nurses throughout and outside California. In the process, I brought anthropological tools to workers in the "caring" profession of nursing.

These classes contextualized registered nurses' (RNs) day-to-day struggles as they fought to protect their patients and themselves in the face of larger corporate agendas. Nurses shared many stories both in and out of class about the different ways that hospitals and clinics monitored and controlled the workplace. Through these examples I came to better understand nurses' experiences as workers and caregivers within a broader structural context.

Staff RNs hold a strong view of themselves as the moral locus of hospitals and clinics. RNs spend more time than perhaps anyone else in the hospital with patients; they are charged with the bulk of "caring"; doctors' contact with patients is more limited. And nurses' commitments to their patients run deep. Unlike doctors, who "diagnose" patients, nurses more personally assess patients and create their "care plans." As a largely

---

Notes for this chapter begin on page 231.

female and historically feminized profession, nursing is intertwined with understandings of women as natural caregivers. Nursing overlaps with other "feminine" professions (e.g., elementary school teaching, factory sewing, and housekeeping); nursing is often understood as an extension of women's care work in the home, and this belittling view is reflected in pay inequity and degrading treatment.

Management discourses that contrast professionals with unskilled workers tie in with registered nurses' attempts to gain respect. In conjunction with their focus on professionalism, professional nurse organizations traditionally eschew the union label, opting instead to encourage members to further professionalize and outsource more tedious or unpleasant tasks to less skilled workers. Legal overlap with discourses of professionalism is another factor in defining nurses relative to other hospital-based employees. This classifies them as ineligible to form unions or to collectively oppose management decisions harmful to them and their patients. Classifying nurses as professionals with supervisory duties is the key to the 2006 "Kentucky River" National Labor Relations Board decisions,[1] where a majority Bush-appointed board stacked with professional union-busting attorneys ruled that virtually any skilled U.S. worker can be considered management and therefore ineligible for protection under the National Labor Relations Act. The original case centered around RNs.

As the keyword in the healthcare industry, "care" is a tool that different actors use in often-contradictory ways. In this chapter, I explore some of the ways "care" has been used in the controlling processes of labor restructuring in its clinical, corporate, ideological, and technological manifestations in U.S. hospitals. Politicians, hospital management, and technology corporations (along with other health care profiteers) manipulate concepts of care in ways that can harm patients and their human caregivers. When used by RNs, however, the concept of care has revolutionary potential.

A History of Clinical Restructuring

In the 1990s, the CNA demanded that hospitals implement safe nurse-to-patient ratios. Patient loads had risen to unmanageable levels, they argued, and RNs could not adequately care for their patients.[2] Hospital executives retorted that avoiding ratios was, in fact, the *only* way to care for patients. They would like to hire more nurses, they claimed, but there was a nursing shortage; complying with ratios would mean turning away patients. The industry spent hundreds of millions of dollars over a decade to advance this argument, the California Hospital Association (CHA) paying for lobbying fees, public advertising campaigns, and consultant fees.

In fact, the executives' just-so story of the 1990s nursing shortage masked the active role that hospital management played in creating a supply-demand imbalance and the strong likelihood that ratios would—as they ultimately did—ameliorate the problem. A previous nursing shortage in the mid 1980s had been reversed by replacing fragmented labor models with "primary care nursing," which made one nurse responsible for a patient throughout the patient's stay, allowing her to focus time and energy on her patient. This had a salutary effect on health-based outcomes and on nurses' job satisfaction, making the profession more attractive to newcomers as well. Many nurses today look back on primary care nursing as a golden period preceding the horrors to come.[3]

In 1993 and 1994, the Clinton administration's *Statements of Antitrust Enforcement Policy in Health Care* encouraged hospitals to merge in the name of competition, giving hospital corporations the ideological go-ahead to restructure their businesses based on the deeply flawed libertarian claim that market competition would lead to better care.[4] Hospitals shifted their assets from for-profit to nonprofit entities to avoid paying taxes, moved patients to facilities with less oversight, and most importantly, squeezed their labor force to attain the added capital necessary for their corporate expansion.[5]

In the clinic/ward—the RNs' shop floor—employees experienced this labor restructuring as a massive influx of management consultants from a broad range of industries, all giving orders. Nurses whom I asked in class about consultants mentioned dozens of names of companies who had sent them, from Andersen to Marriott. Consultants are near-universally despised among nurses. Paid exorbitant sums—sometimes in the hundreds of millions—for their services, they bring manufacturing-sector models to the hospital workplace. For example, using the "just-in-time" production approach, consultants reframed empty beds as a profit loss rather than as a necessary element in preparing for inevitable, unpredictable patient surges. Consultants used statistical models of "average" day-to-day hospital needs to rationalize cuts in staffing as a means to maximize profits. Thousands of registered nurses were fired. The language management used to rationalize changes imposed on nurses and patients diverged from the discourse of profit they aimed at stockholders and business partners, which spoke of care, efficiency, and patient satisfaction.

"Patient-focused care!" nurses would exclaim sarcastically in class, referring to one of the most bitterly remembered (and in some cases ongoing) models that came to replace primary-care nursing. It was easy to talk about restructuring in nurses' own terms, for regardless of party politics or their position vis-à-vis the union, nearly every nurse I met agreed that "patient-focused care" was anything but. Under patient-focused care, hospitals transformed a nurse's job from holistic primary care to a task-based model in which she or he was made to supervise unlicensed assistive personnel. When cheaper workers (e.g., Licensed Vocational/Practical Nurses, Medical Assistants, and even housecleaning staff) were brought in to take over RN duties (from changing bedpans and taking vital signs to monitoring intensive-care patients), hospitals saved money by both lowering salaries and firing the workers who were actually properly trained to do all these jobs. Between 1994 and 1997, tens of thousands of nurses lost their jobs in California alone; many RNs left nursing altogether due to downsizing. Nurses who remained were left in an untenable position: separated from bedside tasks that labor consultants deemed unimportant, they were unable to spend adequate time with their patients but still medically necessary for proper patient assessment and care. As "team leaders," nurses were held responsible when something went wrong due to an unlicensed worker's error. The RN's license, her profession, and her patients' lives were on the line.

Simultaneously, universities and colleges were receiving less state funding and downsizing nursing school programs. As potential students saw fewer job openings, applications dwindled. "Side effects" of this corporate-induced nursing shortage, to borrow the medical euphemism for iatrogenesis (harm caused by medical treatment), have included an aging workforce, increased hiring of more easily exploitable, cheaper migrants from the Philippines, China, South Korea, India, and elsewhere (which precipitates nursing shortages in sending countries); and the outsourcing of RN labor, facilitated by a host of new "medical" technologies.[6] The "shortage" also caused the deaths of untold numbers of unattended patients.[7]

Because the staffing issue was morally clear to most RNs, nurse-patient ratios became a galvanizing issue, the nexus of the struggle between nurses and a market-based healthcare industry armed with its consultants' definitions of patient care. Even nurses who had previously avoided engaging in collective struggle in the name of professionalism organized collectively in the mid 1990s in the name of professionalism—that is, in the name of care. A long series of legislative and ballot wars against the CHA pitted the CHA's spending power against nurses' organizing power. Ultimately, the nurses won. In October 1999, then governor Gray Davis signed AB 394, the first bill in the nation to mandate safe staffing standards.

In 2004, one day after a clear ballot victory for his team, a jubilant Governor Arnold Schwarzenegger issued an emergency declaration delaying the implementation of ratios (with the clear aim of rescinding them altogether) at the behest of the CHA. As with many states of emergency, the exception in question was little more than a pretext for rescinding civil protections.[8] Schwarzenegger quoted the CHA's argument that compliance would lead to an increase in hospital closures, a phenomenon in reality traceable to the same market-based actions that caused the nursing shortage in the first place.[9] But Schwarzenegger underestimated the importance of the nurses' "patient care" victory over their employers, a mistake for which he paid dearly the following year, when nurses led a citizen revolt against his special election ballot measures attacking the public sector. Two days after an expensive and embarrassing November 2005 defeat at the ballot box, Schwarzenegger quietly dropped his yearlong fight against RN ratios. However, the nurse-patient ratio struggle continued daily in wards across the state as nurses strove to ensure compliance with the law despite a governor-appointed Department of Health Services that was unenthusiastic about enforcement. Ratio compliance continues to be the primary justification for strikes, and nurse militancy in the form of job stoppages has become a lucrative source of employment for scab laborers and the firms that facilitate their hiring, like Scab.org ("a site for Travel and Replacement Nurses"), which operated from 2000 to 2008 before being replaced by MobileRN.com.

The ratio fight has been the backdrop for all political mobilization of nurses in the past fifteen years, not just in California but nationwide. It exemplifies how nurses can successfully wrest the rhetoric of "patient care" from their employers. They did not do this by "speaking truth to power." As most workers who have tried that approach know, power is not particularly interested in truth. The nurses won the battle over the language of care by collectively and forcefully *shouting* the truth to the public, politicians, and hospitals. Since nurses have been the "undisputed leader" in Gallup's annual Honesty and Ethics of Professions poll every year but 2001 (when firefighters won), they have also *embodied* that truth.[10] Ironically, the same gendering that has kept them underpaid and undervalued has, when used as a political mobilizing tool, given them moral authority in an anti-union climate to win high wages as well as larger political battles.

Technology as Controlling Process

Although nurses have enjoyed notable success in the fight for safe staffing, they now face another challenge that could easily dismantle these gains: the move of restructuring into the realm of science fiction. In 1999, the Institute of Medicine (IOM), a branch of the National Academy of Science that advises the U.S. government, released a study containing the now-famous claim that every year in U.S. hospitals, between 44,000 and 98,000 deaths result from medical error. Responses to the IOM study noted flaws in its definition and measurement of "errors," including the omission of the systemic understaffing in hospitals and clinics as a type of "medical error."[11] However, although numerous medical researchers studying the same issues have called the study's methodology and conclusions into question, the upper figure has now become a ubiquitous, unquestioned, bipartisan political truth.

One of the biggest critiques of the IOM study was that "[u]nless the epidemiologic science of error detection improve[d] greatly, the effort to prevent errors [would] deteriorate into a marketing ploy."[12] Indeed, one beneficiary of the blanket acceptance of the 98,000 deaths statistic is clear: the medical technology industry. As implied by the IOM study's title, "To Err is Human," errors occur only through human judgment. Also implied is that computers do not make mistakes. This tautology justifies the IOM's prescription: the computerization of hospital decision-making and monitoring functions from the bedside to the national level. Hospitals are enthusiastically on board, spending billions of dollars to implement "healthcare information technology" (HIT). Having pushed for greater HIT implementation, Congress established the Agency for Healthcare Research and Quality, a government entity dedicated to technology-driven health care restructuring. President Bush made HIT a central priority, establishing a cabinet-level HIT position and appointing a wealthy HIT executive. President Obama's Affordable Care Act emphasizes the importance of HIT. Not even single-payer health care advocates like Senator Sheila Kuehl and filmmaker Michael Moore have questioned the assumption that such technology leads to improvements in care.[13]

Using computers to eliminate medical errors has little to do with health care but everything to do with the boundaries of science. Rhetoric that redefines medical science is a highly profitable tool for the medical technology industry—not because it is reduces error (it does not), but because it is hegemonic. As Laura Nader points out, boundaries of science are boundaries of power.[14] The way these boundaries are redrawn deeply affects those who carry out the day-to-day work of science. Our society's blind faith in computers and its much-theorized effect on the patient-as-cyborg is only part of the picture. Changing boundaries of science intersect with and justify both increasingly oppressive forms of labor organization and their effects on not just the practices of care, but our health.

Hospitals have participated in every major industrial management trend of the past century, from Taylorism to Fordism to the Toyota model of continuous improvement, to the current incarnations of so-called Total Quality Management and Enterprise Resource Planning, involving information technology. These models use scientific rhetoric to justify evolving forms of decentralized worker control. The language of industrial restructuring bleeds into everyday discourse of workers in contradictory ways. For example, rather than talk about hard work and doing a good job, managers speak of reducing errors, of quality, of (continuous) improvement, evidence, efficiency, value-added activities, and "best practices." Productivity can be improved, they claim, through harmonious labor relations achieved through joint governance or labor-management partnerships. "Benchmarks" are deployed to measure success and achievement.

Indeed, what could someone have against best practices? How could one possibly argue that reducing errors is not a laudable goal? Can I honestly claim to oppose the use of evidence? But decoding business doublespeak is central to the job of all workers who recognize the fundamental conflict between themselves and the owners of the means of production. Any good bargaining team member—anyone at all, in fact—needs to understand the corporate hijacking of language. Like former President Bush's "Healthy Forest" and "Clear Skies" initiatives, which increased industrial logging and reduced air pollution controls, pleasant-sounding management phrases must be deconstructed and their beneficiaries identified as part and parcel of studying up.

For example, take the concept of the "error." Six Sigma is a lucrative management consulting offshoot of Motorola. It sells a business restructuring model that uniformly dictates businesses should achieve fewer than 3.4 errors per million opportunities (the "6th Sigma" of errors). Originally developed to prevent defects in assembly-line products, Six Sigma places central emphasis on one Best Practice: the elimination of variation. Manufacturing and business processes, its proponents argue, can be measured, analyzed, improved, and controlled. To eliminate variation in the product, it is necessary to eliminate variation in the production process. The innovation of Six Sigma and other models like it is the standardization, through centralized Enterprise Resource Planning IT systems, of the monitoring of every aspect of the workplace: production measures, time management, worker movement, product movement, and inventory control. The unwanted variation is not just in the fetishized commodity (which in the case of the hospital is not a widget, but a human being): variation in the *workers* is also identified and eliminated, scientifically, through a panopticon of information technology.

So how do Six Sigma and similar industrial organization models define an error? In the hospital context, some errors are obvious to all: the wrong limb is amputated, patients are given the wrong medication or dosage, poor hygiene leads to hospital-acquired infections and other forms of iatrogenesis. Other errors are not so clear. Medical professionals can disagree about the best protocols for treating different diseases. Is it best to "shoot first and ask questions later" by giving all Emergency Department patients with diagnosis X the same expensive medication before determining whether it will actually help in the individual case? Should all patients with diagnosis Y be kept in the hospital after they are ambulatory, or should they be monitored? Medical experts' opinions intertwine with their financial interests, including profit sharing in hospitals and owning shares in drug or medical technology companies. And none of this discussion takes into account the embodied experience and full range of hospital workers' or patients' desires, either.

Six Sigma's definition of error, also used by the IOM and other workplace technology corporations, erases ambiguity and subjectivity, and with them the role judgment plays for health care providers—for in human judgment lies the capacity for error. Individualized treatment plans are reduced to universal protocols and given important-sounding names like "clinical pathways." Doctors' and nurses' compliance is increasingly monitored through a series of integrated technologies using supermarket technologies like bar codes and Radio Frequency Identification chips (now FDA-certified as subcutaneous "medical" devices), along with so-called "electronic medical records" and a host of heroic- and magical-sounding programs, from Pyxis the drug-dispensing robot to Stargate call-center software. These technologies have explicitly redefined a medical error as a deviation from the prescribed algorithm embedded in the "medical" software.

Powerful scientistic rhetoric maintains the authority of the independent-judgment-as-error concept. Scientism refers to the *ideology* of science, rather than science as a category or practice (i.e., it is the belief that science is more critical, more legitimate, and somehow better than other forms of knowledge production, even when it is not borne out as such). The Best Practices embedded in nurses' computerized protocols, for example, are "evidence-based." Use of the term "evidence" here is, by any thoughtful definition, anti-scientific. In reality, the only admissible evidence for the purposes of computerization, by definition, is that which can be quantified. Quantification reifies the results of statistical studies done on raced, classed, gendered, sometimes colonized human subjects by human researchers who themselves are culturally situated subjects with corporate and governmental funders. Such results represent an incomplete truth at best. At worst, they medicalize and rhetorically neutralize vast power inequalities. Furthermore, the "evidence-based" algorithms used in designing workplace information technologies ignore another fundamental of honest scientific inquiry: being proprietary, they are inaccessible to the user. Transparency is lost.

Best practices that nurses recognize as "common sense"—basic hygiene, for instance—can work to obscure flaws in Best Practices that exist because they are "evidence-based," i.e., because "science" says so. Computers may be programmed based on medical science, but nurses point out that computer orders are suspiciously in line with management goals of shortening lengths of stay, prescribing more expensive treatments, and lowering patient acuity, which enables their bosses to save money through understaffing. The concept of best practices also serves non-IT purposes through the simple codification of management's desires: nurses recounted how protocols serving no other purpose than worker monitoring were described by management as best practices, too.

On being introduced to nurses, management terms that are common across industries, like "best practices" and "evidence-based," are depicted as part of improved scientific medical practice and the true essence of care. In the classes I taught, nurses argued about whether evidence-based medicine was necessary to the nursing process and whether their work would be unscientific without this "evidence." An exasperated nurse once exclaimed in class, "I don't understand why they think evidence is new ... what do they think we were basing our decisions on before: voodoo?"

Reducing Variation

In addition to the emergence of technology as a controlling process in the field of healthcare, specific practices and technologies have been quietly reshaping the definition of care in the hospital context through Enterprise Resource Planning (ERP). This form of workplace restructuring, along with the technologies that enable it, inevitably results in speeding up, deskilling, disempowering, dehumanizing, and ultimately eliminating bedside RNs. It also further exacerbates patients' problems of access and treatment. ERP is characterized by several technologies and best practices that reduce worker variation, including scripting, call-center nursing, standardized decision-making technology, and outsourcing and remote care.

Scripting

At U.S. movie theaters, you often hear, "Would you like to get the jumbo size popcorn combo? It's only a dollar more," followed by, "Thank you and enjoy the show." Then you walk away slightly confused and with more popcorn than you could possibly eat. Anyone who regularly stays in hotels knows their signature lines: "Good morning, Ms. Pine, this is Jenny at your service," or a bored, "It's always a great day here at the Auburn Holiday Inn. How can I help you?" Scripting manipulates customer psychology in order to increase profits. As a patient, you might feel comforted by phrases like, "I'm closing the curtain now to give you privacy," or "Is there anything else I can do for you? I have the time." When the nurse asks, "Is there anything else I can do to give you very good service today?" you might marvel at her concern, even if her parting "Thank you for letting me serve you" strikes you as a little odd.

As the nursing shortage of the 1990s gained visibility, particularly through nurses' very public protests during the ratio battle, the tactic of scripting nurses became part of hospitals' strategy for winning the "care" war. Rather than invest money in things nurses identified as care, such as providing patients with adequate skilled personnel to best move toward the goal of improving patient health, hospitals invested in ways to make patients *feel* like they were being cared for, within a service sector model. They shifted the blame for declining patient satisfaction from their policy of understaffing to the nurses themselves, who, management alleged, made patients unhappy by not "caring" enough. Hospitality sector consultants brought with them obligatory slogans like "Journey to Excellence" and "Key Words for Key Times." Nurses in San Bernardino County recounted how their bosses described their consultant-led training as "charm school."

Scripting is ubiquitous: it is on posters in the break room, in management newsletters, on personal badges reminding nurses of their "key phrases." A nurse's superiors monitor her compliance with scripts, in some cases shadowing her and in others, entering rooms after she has left to ask patients what she said. They also use audio or video technology to listen in on and/or observe nurses at patients' bedsides. Some hospitals employ "secret shoppers," or "mystery patients"—people posing as patients to check up on nurses' compliance.[15]

Scripts infuriate most nurses, especially when they force nurses to tell lies. Having to use the phrase, "I have the time" draws the most ire. Statements like "I am here to provide you very good service" are qualitatively different from, for example, "This may hurt a little," or "Breathe normally, and don't worry if the gas makes you feel a little light-headed." But although many nurses refused to comply with scripting, others admitted that although it was humiliating, they went along because they felt intimidated. Some argued that certain scripted phrases were good reminders, to which others would inevitably retort: "Do they think we don't have any social skills?" adding that sometimes responding to a "code" in one room was more important than "playing the maid" to a patient in the next.

Under extreme time pressure, scripting not only takes the emphasis off skill but also encourages the active deskilling of the work. The principle this practice follows—that of separating thinking from doing—is central to Taylorism, a restructuring scheme that promotes worker alienation as a conscious management goal. Scripted nurses are standardized: their necessarily human conversations with their patients and each other are limited and controlled in the name of quality and efficiency. Scripting also involves speedup, as it forces nurses to spend more time on hospitality tasks and decreases the time available to assess patients and provide skilled care. Scripting is often linked to increases in other required, monitored, and non–medically necessary tasks, like thirty-minute checks. Under such standardization, nurses can neither prioritize aspects of their job based on patient acuity nor employ the judgment they are ethically and legally required to use. And the less time they have to practice skills, the more distant those skills become. As one nurse complained, "it gets harder to think for yourself when they're trying to turn you into a robot."

A week or two after returning home, patients receive a survey from the hospital. Hospitals refer to these surveys as "customer," "client," or "guest" surveys, which points to their role in reframing hospital care as a consumer choice rather than a human need. Nursing scripts are designed based on these surveys. For example, if the survey lists "excellent" as the top choice in questions about care, nurses are likely to be made to repeat the word "excellent" in numerous phrases, such as "Is there anything else I can do to give you excellent care?" Survey questions about privacy and hygiene lie behind nurses' tediously repeated declarations that they are carrying out bedside tasks "for your privacy" or "for your hygiene." And of course, surveys always ask patients if the nurse had time for them. Patients also receive reminders to give their providers a high score. RNs are often required to follow up with patients in phone calls timed to take place just before the survey arrives. The callers reiterate key phrases and encourage the patient to fill out and return the survey. Pre-survey reminders are also mailed, like a refrigerator magnet from an Oakland, California, Kaiser clinic picturing a box marked X next to the word Excellent.

When this sort of administrative persuasion results in improved customer satisfaction scores, hospitals are rewarded. Hospitals advertise their higher scores and post them on "consumer" websites to attract more "customers." More importantly, satisfaction scores weigh heavily in the Joint Commission on Accreditation of Healthcare Organizations'

(JCAHO) overall scores for hospitals. Only JCAHO-accredited organizations meet the Centers for Medicare and Medicaid Services' certification requirements allowing for reimbursement from Medicare—which in California accounts for almost 40 percent of a hospital's income, on average.[16] Thus, although nurses argue that this practice is inversely correlated with care, it has been reified as a central part of profit-oriented "outcomes assessment," which is then used as a powerful tool to contradict nurses who argue that models like "patient-focused care" do not actually work: if success is defined as Best Practices, then Best Practices lead to success!

Nurses in my classes frequently commented on the patient surveys' inadequacy for measuring what they do measure. In fact, nurses do a lot that patients are not aware of. Much of the nurse's job is nonverbal: nurses look for changes in patients' behavior, in their perspiration, in their skin tone, and in their vital signs to assess their conditions. Patients themselves are sometimes confused, delirious, or even unconscious while they are receiving their most important care. And sometimes, nurses find it medically necessary to do things that patients don't like. Patients, themselves schooled as consumers, only know how to answer questions geared around hospitality, which they are trained to perceive as valid indicators of care. Because of the nature of nursing, however, the patient survey is a deficient tool for measuring how well a nurse actually does her or his job. But then again, that is not what the survey is *meant* to do. It is meant to change the job. As customer survey results factor into hospital accreditation, individual nurses' qualifications for merit pay, and other divisive economic incentives, nursing care itself becomes redefined as a branch of the hospitality industry. Unless nurses actively and collectively resist these changes, they find themselves forced to "care to the survey"—the nursing equivalent of "teaching to the test."

Call Centers

As nurses become more mechanized and alienated from their work, their human product is transformed into a commodity fetish.[17] The Best Practice of saying the same non–care-related things to every patient/consumer obscures differences of class, culture, and gender. This is facilitated by the "population-based care" approach necessary for (yet predating) computerization, which portrays patients as conglomerations of demographic and epidemiologic averages with certain quantifiable traits or "risk factors." And from a management perspective, the use of scripting—astutely seen as "roboticizing" nurses by the nurse quoted above—is in fact much more effective when controlled directly through computers.

Today, call centers are the place where computers most clearly control nurses' speech. Over the course of my work at the CNA, I met dozens of "advice nurses" from Kaiser call centers in California and developed friendships with several of them. One of the first call center nurses I had the opportunity to speak with told me I should research her work setting because "we have been protocoled into oblivion." I soon came to see what she meant. Call center nurses have much more in common with robots than with floor nurses. Expert-systems software, programmed using "evidence-based" research to create algorithms for assessment and protocol, guide the entire nurse-patient interaction. Every patient is asked the same questions, which the call center nurse reads from a screen. The nurse then must pigeonhole the patient's narrative into one of several clickable options on her screen, which then leads her to a new screen with a new question, and so on.

Call center–dependent HMOs refer to expert systems software compliance as a best practice for patients, but the workplace practices of call centers belie this claim. Teleservice representatives (TSRs) first answer patient calls. Most have no training in the healthcare field—one call-center nurse referred disparagingly to TSRs as "Arby's graduates." These workers work for far less pay than nurses, and their wages and work discipline are oriented toward three primary management goals: (1) finishing the call as quickly as possible, (2) preventing costly hospital visits, and (3) preventing calls from actually transferring to RNs. Kaiser gives bonuses of up to 10 percent to TSRs who comply with these goals.[18] Nurses refer to this practice as a "morbidity" or "mortality" bonus—apt descriptions of the effect of merit pay in the hospital as well.

Call-center nurses' jobs are structured much like TSRs': the nurses too are paid and monitored to work fast and divert patients from hospital care. Supervisors can listen in on calls, which are recorded and timed through the computer system. Nurses I spoke with had to maintain an average of 7.5 minutes or less per call to avoid being disciplined, and like TSRs, they are encouraged to keep patients away from costly care. Needless to say, such a system neither benefits patients nor takes advantage of nurses' many years of bedside training. And nurses tend to be bad at it. Because their training emphasizes independent judgment and creative thinking, they often find it impossible to comply. They can recognize when the computer is wrong.

It was challenging to talk about these issues in class. Although most call-center nurses agreed with analysis suggesting that the imposition of expert-systems assessment software is harmful to their practice, there was always a risk that they would feel personally attacked. One nurse protested: "[B]ut I do use my judgment—it's programmed into the computer. I have to click a box at the bottom of every screen that asks if I used my judgment!" But was she being asked to use *her* judgment? This digitized guarantee of independent thinking put her in a double bind, for if she were to click a box affirming that her judgment accorded with the computer-generated advice to advance the call, and then the patient's condition subsequently worsened, she—not her employer—would be held liable. Her boss can also hide behind the magical aura of evidence-based Best Practice algorithms that explicitly deny the role of nurse judgment. One Kaiser regional operations director for Northern California denied that patients were put at risk, stating to the *Contra Costa Times*: "Computer scripts—not operators—assess patient needs."[19]

This particular nurse also did not realize that this programming afterthought was likely a nod to organized CNA call-center nurse resistance that ultimately led to laws (AB 285, SB 969) providing that telephone medical advice may be given only by a registered nurse or physician licensed in California. Call centers are a key strategy in labor outsourcing across all industries; U.S. prisoners and English speakers in developing countries around the world provide the labor for such centers. Not just in California but around the country in the late 1990s, TSRs and outsourced labor from states with lower wages and laxer consumer protections entirely replaced call-center nurse jobs.[20] Bad computer advice does not hinder TSRs, who have neither health care experience nor a professional moral imperative. Patients seldom know when they are not talking to a nurse. And like less skilled workers and technology call center nurses, the nurses themselves are being actively deskilled. Like children who learn math on calculators and college students who write their papers in the postliterate age of spell-check, nurses who carry out day-to-day patient care through computers run the risk of becoming unable to do their job without their computer aids.

Through legal and collective actions, the experienced Kaiser call-center nurses were able to assert the right to maintain the use of "judgment" in California health care. And many stubbornly defend their right to circumvent computer scripts when they recognize bad advice. But like any form of workplace resistance, asserting professional authority over computer authority succeeds only when done collectively. Those who protest alone are easily singled out for punishment or firing. Call-center nurses are particularly vulnerable from a legal standpoint. Not only are they held responsible for bad patient outcomes resulting from advice they read off the computer screen, but if something should go wrong after they give advice contradicting the Best Practice on the screen, they are also vulnerable to the accusation of intentional harm. Moreover, they risk greater liability than they would in the absence of the scientific Best Practices. The fact that juries in malpractice cases understand best practices in the common sense of the term, rather than as a tool in a pan-industrial worker-crushing strategy, is additional incentive for nurses to simply do as the computer tells them. As I would point out to my students, "If it's not Best Practice, it's malpractice!"

Decision-Support Technology

Until a decade ago, expert-systems diagnostic health care technologies were mostly confined to call centers. But their scope is broadening as hospitals are spurred on by the IOM report and the aggressively pro-HIT stance at all levels of government. Hospital and HMO systems like Kaiser, Catholic Healthcare West, and Sutter invest hundreds of millions, and sometimes billions, of dollars in restructuring programs under names like HealthConnect and CareConnect, which aim to increase revenues by disempowering workers and patients. Meanwhile, these hospital systems impede patients' access to care along race and class lines through overcharging and clinical and corporate restructuring (resulting in fewer qualified personnel per patient and fewer facilities per population, respectively).[21]

When health care workers demand job security, pensions, and measures intended to improve patient health, hospitals cite a lack of resources and their "care-centered" and (where applicable) nonprofit missions. But nonprofit hospitals, regardless of their lofty claims of community involvement, are no better than most for-profits in terms of prioritizing money over patients and rationalizing this through technology. Nurses around the state confirmed that even public health care facilities—which are rapidly disappearing, having been stranded in a market-based health care system by politicians who refuse to tax the rich more or reallocate war funding to health care—adopt labor-replacing technologies to compete in the race to the bottom.

Although ERP systems incorporate billing, drug dispensing, and automatic input from a wide variety of nurse- and patient-monitoring technologies, the most dangerous element of healthcare ERP is Computerized Provider Order Entry Software (CPOE). CPOE is commonly referred to as "decision-support technology," a phrase that stresses the doctor's supposed final authority. In today's information age and with so much scientific progress, the argument goes, there is no way doctors can know everything; these programs are designed to help them know everything. But the deskilling and disempowering effects of expert-systems technologies are not limited to nurses, so decision support technologies become decision-replacement technologies for all health care providers. Doctors are no more immune to the pressure to be scientific, the lure of money, or the threat of punishment than are their lower-paid yet often more experienced feminized coworkers.

CPOE brings call center technology to the bedside, presenting patients and care providers with a whole new set of problems. Like their deskilling predecessor computerized charting, CPOE computers have a physical presence. The computer mediates the nurse's interactions with the patient, radically altering the nurse-patient relationship. Nurses look at the computer screen, not the patient, to devise a "care" plan. Sometimes the RN is even forced to sit with her back to her patient throughout an assessment. Many complained to me that they felt like the computer had *become* the patient. Also, since few hospitals equip every bed with networked machines, nurses must wheel large, heavy, awkward computer carts (sometimes called "COWs," short for Computers on Wheels) from patient to patient.

Patients, in turn, express feeling dehumanized by these methods. A dramatic example from one of my classes involved a home health nurse from Northern California who was using a new expert-systems software program to interview an elderly patient in his home. During her visit he expressed increasing frustration with her stilted computer-generated questions and her attention to the machine, which he felt interfered with his care, she said. She explained to him that it was a new technology required for her job, and that they would both have to get used to it. At a later point, she got up to use the bathroom. On returning, she found her computer had been smashed to pieces with a walker. The home health workers in her district had used paper charting ever since, she told the class, which then broke into applause.

Provider inexperience and incompetence are cited as justifications for the implementation of "decision-support technology." One Medicare consultant (himself an MD) told me: "I see your point about deskilling for the good doctors, but the problem as I see it is that there are so many bad doctors out there. Frankly, most of the doctors I know, I wouldn't feel safe having them treat me. I think having some sort of computer backup is the only way we can ensure any standard of quality."

Nurses, with their scientific training, are particularly vulnerable to the hegemonic ideology of computers as "scientific," authoritative containers of medical truth. Through collective action based on confidence in their own skills as caregivers, usually associated with years of bedside nursing, some nurses have been able to resist this. For others, however—particularly inexperienced and/or younger nurses, who tend to be more accepting of computers than their colleagues—the threats of monitoring, pay cuts, and litigation are compounded by their lack of confidence in their own judgment with respect to the technologies into which their employers have invested so much money and which they themselves view as authoritative.

Management uses this generational gap in its labor-dividing strategy. Younger, more technologically proficient nurses are promoted to leadership positions, while more experienced nurses are passed by. This tactic is apt to destroy the solidarity among nurses that is required to humanly care for their patients, that is, the solidarity of purpose that challenges the capitalist contradiction inherent in making caring into an act of wage labor. On several occasions in class, I had to diffuse angry confrontations between more and less experienced nurses. Experienced nurses accused their younger colleagues of lacking interest in true nursing care, failing to learn basic skills of nursing, and blindly relying on technologies. Younger nurses argued that they too wanted to provide the best care for patients. One successful strategy for countering generational divisions has been mentorship programs for new nurses, who may not know the extent to which they are *not* learning because of their reliance on job-replacing technologies, or the devastating history of restructuring and nurses' resistance to it. By identifying intergenerational discord as a conscious management strategy and encouraging cooperation as a response, I attempted to calm tensions without coercing classroom harmony.[22]

Nurses and doctors alike are told that each new hospital technology frees them up for patient care. In my classes, even avid devotees of evidence-based medicine scoffed at this claim, primarily because most find themselves working longer hours to comply with the extensive yet constrictive documentation demands of programs like computer charting. Nurses empirically reject the "more technology = more time" argument: whenever a new practice or technology gives them more time, rather than being able to devote it to "care"—here discursively separated from the masculinized concept of skill to be replaced by the technology in question—nurses wind up being saddled with more tasks, more patients, and fewer colleagues. The argument that job-restructuring technology will alleviate their overwork again masks the fact that restructuring is the primary cause of that overwork. In much the same way that drug companies might market patented drugs to alleviate the "side effects" of their other patented drugs, fighting the clinical restructuring fire with technological gasoline is a Best Practice.

Outsourcing and Remote Care

Decision-support technology is decision-replacement technology, and decision-replacement technology is job-replacement technology. The same is true of technologies like automatic blood pressure machines and automatic IV drips, which are marketed to simplify marginalized but crucially important "tasks." This is not new. For centuries, replacing workers and their skills with technology has been perhaps the most important controlling process associated with labor restructuring. Job-replacing technologies are a specific and ongoing target of worker actions. But nurses, like those in many salaried professions, tend to think of themselves as irreplaceable.[23] They are wrong.

Radiologists once considered themselves irreplaceable too. Now, thanks to the electronic technology of teleradiology, American radiologists' jobs are outsourced to countries like Australia, India, Switzerland, Israel, and Lebanon, where workers in some cases earn one-tenth of what U.S. doctors are paid. A quick scan of news media articles on this burgeoning field supplies the most common arguments in favor of teleradiology: First, it will fix the restructuring-caused "shortage" of U.S. radiologists. Second, it will meet "exploding demand for more sophisticated scans to diagnose scores of ailments."[24] The source of this demand, these articles imply, is not technology corporations or doctors who charge high fees for services, but patients. Third, there is the management-friendly argument that "the outsourcing of radiology could make health care affordable again."[25] This is an attractive proposition, but its underlying assumption is that increased hospital earnings are necessarily passed on to patients in the form of lower charges. This is simply untrue.

Only because hospitals now technologically render patients as data is it possible to imagine remote "care" as a possibility. Beyond being dehumanized, patients are disincorporated, disembodied, fragmented, and reinscribed as electronic text, as computers themselves—the present-day version of man-as-machine. As sociologist Sarah Nettleton writes, "[t]he medical body has not only escaped; it is also e-scaped in the sense that it is 'viewable' through the electronic infoscape that is the internet."[26] As long as the subject is acted upon, even at the bedside, as the sum—nay, as an aggregation—of its quantifiable parts, why not use technological advances to allow doctors to provide care from the comfort of their homes in . . . Australia?

Many nurses did not question the outsourcing of doctors when it began in the early 2000s, because, as they complain, doctors all too often are disengaged and physically absent from the bedsides of the patients for whom they are responsible anyway. But remote care outsourcing is now hitting them more directly. The availability of remote charting allows some nurses now to take part of their work home—a classic form of labor intensification masked as increased choice. And hospitals around the country have been setting up eICUs—electronic intensive care units—that enable one internist to "care" for up to fifty patients at a time, helping to alleviate the "shortage" of internists. From a distance, through an array of monitoring technologies including highly sensitive cameras that capture for perpetuity, along with the patient's data, every *action* of the presiding nurse, a doctor *virtually* cares.

Finally, alongside scripting and technologies designed to turn human nurses and doctors into robots, actual robots compete with and replace humans. "Nurse Penelope," for example, is a voice-activated "scrub nurse" that, according to its inventor "[eliminates] the need for a human being and [frees] a nurse for patient care."[27] U.S. taxpayers fund these robots through the National Science Foundation and the Department of Defense, the latter by way of the U.S. Army Telemedicine and Advanced Technology Research Command (TATRC). Like its projects for remote killing, the department's vision of remote healing is generously financed. The Defense Advanced Research Projects Agency has already poured well over twelve million dollars into the development of "trauma pods" through TATRC. Computer models of these "trauma pods," which look suspiciously like one of the military's violent recruiting video games,[28] show a desert-camouflaged soldier being automatically and remotely "evacuated" by a trauma pod, lifted into a "mobile unit" that looks like a tank, and then scanned—his electronic likeness graphically displayed on the unmanned computer screen—and robotically operated upon by a relative of Penelope.[29]

CNA nurses have developed several responses to technological incursions on their scope of practice, from on-the-job resistance to bargaining for contract language barring the introduction of deskilling technologies and preserving a nurse's right to circumvent computerized protocols whenever, in her judgment, they are wrong. But HIT is a juggernaut, and most people do not notice the disappearance of their skills and/or scope until it is too late. As with all incremental power concessions, whether ceded in the name of convenience, security, or simply being too busy to notice, nurses and patients run the risk of waking up one day soon and realizing it is just too late to care.

Conclusion

Technologies can do wonderful things. But doctors in the United States do CAT scans to avoid lawsuits, do C-sections to better fit their schedules, and receive higher reimbursements from insurance companies and greater rewards from JCAHO for using expensive technologies that are sometimes invasive and risky.[30] New diagnostic and risk-assessing technologies broaden the scope of the preexisting condition, an invention of the insurance industry intended to exclude wide segments of society (not just the poor) from receiving care. Noting this technological euphoria's coexistence with vast numbers of people who lack access to the most basic health care, skeptics may ask to what extent procedures are performed "*because* of the existence of the technology." I would also ask to what extent technologies are being used to increase profits by overcharging patients and controlling the health care workforce. If the money spent on technologies were spent differently, e.g., on hiring enough nurses and doctors to provide basic hands-on healthcare to underserved communities, would actual health outcomes for the whole society—as opposed to customer satisfaction scores—improve? For that matter, would tax breaks and other governmental incentives that health care institutions receive for implementing HIT be better allocated back to the working people who create those surpluses, in the form of a single-payer health care system that would serve all?

In her classic essay "Sex and Death in the Rational World of Defense Intellectuals," Carol Cohn described how learning to speak the language of nuclear scientists deprived her of the ability to think critically about nuclear weapons.[31] Likewise, our capitulation to the hegemonic language of corporate restructuring can blind us to its crushing effect on a democracy that encourages everyday acts of civic engagement, such as prioritizing consumer protections over "evidence-based" protocols, waging direct action campaigns against corporate-owned politicians, and smashing computers.

Indeed, Laura Nader's claim that "never before have so few, by their actions and inactions, had the power of life and death over so many members of the species" is particularly true in the deadly realm of corporate health care today.[32] Nurses repeatedly demonstrate that it is still possible to wrest the shared language of "care" from those who profit through its technological replacement, and anthropologists (who themselves are past, present, and future patients) can and must play a central role in confronting that power by helping to expose its workings. Caring does not just take place in hospitals. Caring, and how we care, is reflected in the ways we challenge the dehumanizing practices and technologies of institutional hierarchies—and of corporate capitalism itself—on a daily basis. As such, an integrated practice of studying up, down, and sideways with "indignation as motive" is a form of caring in itself. Studying up is necessary for our health: our democracy, our world, and our lives are at stake.

Notes

Some material is taken from the article From Healing to Witchcraft: On Ritual Speech and Roboticization in the Hospital, by Adrienne Pine, published in *Culture, Medicine, and Psychiatry* May 2011, 35(2): 262–284.

1. National Labor Relations Board, "NLRB Issues Lead Case Addressing Supervisory Status in Response to Supreme Court's Decision in Kentucky River," 3 October 2006, http://www.nlrb.gov/shared_files/Press percent20Releases/2006/r2603.htm.
2. DeMoro, Don, "Engineering a Crisis: How Hospitals Created a Shortage of Nurses," *Revolution* 1, no. 2 (2000): 16–23.
3. Donald L. Barlett and James B. Steele, *Critical Condition: How Health Care in America Became Big Business—and Bad Medicine* (New York: Doubleday, 2004); Suzanne Gordon, "Nursing against the Odds : How Health Care Cost Cutting, Media Stereotypes, and Medical Hubris Undermine Nurses and Patient Care" In *The Culture and Politics of Health Care Work*, (Ithaca, NY: ILR Press, 2005); Dana Beth Weinberg, *Code Green: Money-Driven Hospitals and the Dismantling of Nursing* (Ithaca, NY: ILR Press, 2003).
4. U.S. Department of Justice, and Federal Trade Commission (Washington, DC: U.S. Department of Justice, 1996) *Statements of Antitrust Enforcement Policy in Health Care*.
5. Donald L. Barlett and James B. Steele, *Critical Condition*.
6. P. Buerhaus, D. O Staiger, and D. I Auerbach, *The Future of the Nursing Workforce in the United States: Data, Trends and Implications* (Salisbury: Jones and Bartlett, 2008).
7. L. H. Aiken et al., "Implications of the California Nurse Staffing Mandate for Other States," *Health Services Research*, 20 April 2010, 18.
8. Giorgio Agamben, *State of Exception* (Chicago: The University of Chicago Press, 2005).
9. Mergers and acquisitions facilitated by the 1994 antitrust laws sped up privatization. The public sector has been drastically underfunded (due largely to politicians' reluctance to tax their corporate donors) and thus set up to fail, creating a service-sector vacuum that benefits the same corporations that profit from under-taxation.
10. Lydia Saad, "Honesty and Ethics Poll Finds Congress' Image Tarnished," *Gallup*, 9 December 2009, http://www.gallup.com/poll/124625/Honesty-Ethics-Poll-Finds-Congress-Image-Tarnished.aspx.
11. Troyen A. Brennan, "The Institute of Medicine Report on Medical Errors—Could It Do Harm?" *New England Journal of Medicine* 342, no. 15 (13 April 2000): 1123–1125.
12. Ibid.
13. An exception to this was the single-payer Conyers-Kucinich bill, HR 676, which explicitly called for careful review of new technologies and for clear prioritization of providers' judgment in all cases.
14. Laura Nader, *Naked Science: Anthropological Inquiry into Boundaries, Power, and Knowledge* (New York: Routledge, 1996), 4.
15. Shirley S. Wang, "Health Care Taps 'Mystery Shoppers,'" Wall Street Journal, 8 August 2006, http://online.wsj.com/news/articles/SB115499684792929340.
16. Medicare reimbursements represent 36.11 percent of net patient revenue in short-term hospitals in California (excluding Kaiser), "Institute for Health & Socio-Economic Policy Calculation of California Office of Statewide Health Planning and Development (OSHPD) Data for 2006." Thanks to Jane Morrison for this information.
17. A commodity fetish is a commodity-object in-and-of-itself that mystifies the relations of production involved in its creation. Karl Marx, *Capital: A Critique of Political Economy* (Harmondsworth and New York: Penguin Books, 1976).

18. Charles Ornstein, "Kaiser Clerks Paid More for Helping Less: Bonuses were Given for Limiting Members' Calls and Doctor's Appointments. HMO Defends Program but Has Dropped It," *Los Angeles Times*, 17 May 2002.
19. Judy Silber, "Critics Hung Up Over Kaiser's Call Center," *Contra Costa Times*, 9 August 2003.
20. Barlett and Steele, *Critical Condition*.
21. Institute for Health and Socioeconomic Policy, *The Third Annual IHSP Hospital 200: The Nation's Most—and Least—Expensive Hospitals Fiscal Year 2003/2004* (Orinda, CA: Institute for Health and Socioeconomic Policy, 2005).
22. Laura Nader, "Coercive Harmony: The Political Economy of Legal Models," *Kroeber Anthropological Society Papers* 80 (1996): 1–13.
23. Jeff Schmidt, *Disciplined Minds: A Critical Look at Salaried Professionals and the Soul-Battering System that Shapes Their Lives* (Lanham, MD: Rowman and Littlefield, 2000).
24. Associated Press, "Some US Hospitals Outsourcing Work: Shortage of Radiologists Spurs 'Growing Telemedicine Trend," 6 December 2004, http://www.msnbc.msn.com/id/6621014.
25. David Leonhardt, "Political Clout Matters in the Age of Outsourcing," *International Herald Tribune*, 19 April 2006, http://www.iht.com/articles/2006/04/19/business/outsource.php.
26. Sarah Nettleton, "The Emergence of E-Scaped Medicine?" *Sociology* 38, no. 4 (2004): 661–679.
27. Bill Meltzer, "Coming Soon to an OR Near You: Meet Penelope, the $100,000 Robotic Scrub Nurse," *Outpatient Surgery Magazine* (February 2004), http://www.outpatientsurgery.net/2004/os02/news.php.
28. U.S. Army, "America's Army: Special Forces," *The Official Army Game: America's Army*, 2008, http://www.americasarmy.com/.
29. SRI International, "Image Bank: Trauma Pod," *SRI International—News*, 16 March 2006, http://web.archive.org/web/20120113031928/http://www.sri.com/news/imagebank/trauma-pod.html; "Robot Medic Will Deploy by 2009: Live from DARPATech," *Popular Mechanics Blogs, Technology News*, 7 August 2007, http://www.popularmechanics.com/blogs/technology_news/4220163.html.
30. Neil Postman, *Technopoly: The Surrender of Culture to Technology* (New York: Vintage Books, 1993), 101–105.
31. Carol Cohn, "Sex and Death in the Rational World of Defense Intellectuals," *Signs* 12, no. 4 (1987): 687–718.
32. Laura Nader, "Up the Anthropologist: Perspectives Gained from Studying Up," in *Reinventing Anthropology*, ed. Dell H. Hymes (New York: Pantheon Books, 1972), vi, 470.

Conclusion

ON POWER

Barbara Rose Johnston, Roberto J. González, and Rachael Stryker

This collection of essays adds to the wealth of materials that demonstrate how thinking, teaching, mentoring, research, and writing can move anthropology from a largely static engagement with and depiction of reality, to a deeper critical questioning of the means by which realities are shaped, as well as recognition of the means by which realities might be transformed. Inspired by Laura Nader's insights on the controlling processes and constructs of hegemonic culture, the contributors to this book demonstrate an anthropology that consciously considers what it means to jump in, swim in, be affected by, and attempt to change the loci and meaning of power. These efforts to identify and understand the currents and consequences of power in the varied facets of human life necessarily involve excursions into systems of power, a process of immersion that both engages and disturbs the current and flow of power. In these concluding comments, we revisit specific inquiries to ask: What are the implications of these ripples in the pond? What does this work say about the identification and critical scrutiny of architectures of power; the destruction of autonomy and corresponding dependence; the material basis and social relationships that generate power and sustain it; the ways power is consolidated and amplified, influenced, or challenged; and the ramifications of such engagement? We conclude this book with a review of these main themes, which cut across the various chapters.

Critically Analyzing Architectures of Power

Several of the contributions to this volume support and extend Laura Nader's original ideas by mapping the bureaucratic power structures that create, implement, or reinforce controlling processes. These chapters might be seen as critical analyses of architectures of power that shape, transform, and sometimes constrain behavior.

For example, in her essay "On Bureaucracy," Ellen Hertz delves into issues of power and responsibility, recounting her efforts to apply insights and help shape a decision-making process at a United Nations International Labour Organisation meeting on working conditions in the information and technology industries, specifically, the labor implications of the globalized production of computer hardware. Her ethnographic snapshot of a particular United Nations meeting, the political negotiations process, the eventual outcome, and the relative social impact of her work offers an inside look at the workings of a controlling bureaucratic process that was created to insure justice yet too often serves as a mechanism for maintaining the distance between injustice and accountability. An outline of the chain of events that brought her to the meeting, her role as an adviser and representative of the Swiss government, and her insights on three days of negotiations, conflict, and consensus provides the descriptive context for her primary points: By trying to "study up" and confront "might" with "right," she demonstrates that "up" is relative. Power relationships and the controlling processes that produce and reproduce them are dynamic, fluid, and relative to contexts and situations. Hertz demonstrates that the structural mechanisms that shape and facilitate the movement of power—both the bureaucratized hierarchies of governance and the socialized experience of being an elite actor with the power to shape government policy—operate as controlling processes that restrain, temper, and co-opt the transformative potential that exists in any gathering of diverse actors and agendas.

Monica Eppinger's essay "On Common Sense" presents a focused consideration of praxis, especially in her thoughtful discussion of the difficulties of applying the up/down/sideways spatial metaphor as a research framework when the focus of study is located in a rapidly changing realm where the shape and meaning of power morphs constantly. Eppinger's research in post-Soviet Ukraine occurred at a time when the social, economic, and political norms that had once shaped the fabric of reality no longer held currency. Her original plan, to map out new architectures of power by examining the role of legal change in the construction of post-Soviet social and economic hierarchies, implied a methodological focus on social relationships, agendas, and the means by which power is generated, concentrated and controlled—an impossible task, given the individual and societal ramifications of the dissolution of the Soviet state, where status and standing changed overnight. Eppinger concludes that studying up, down, and sideways in such times requires a broader analytical focus on process (how people regain a sense of perspective and identity so as to build the legal structure and means to operate a post-Soviet state), rather than a more focused study of the mechanisms used to concentrate and exercise power. This work demonstrates both the importance of orientation in times of upheaval and the value of open-ended inquiry into evolving forms of power. Eppinger's chapter illustrates both how and why an anthropological focus is needed on those times and contexts where the kaleidoscope lens is shifting, and where one understanding of "the world" ends and another begins.

Similarly, Adrienne Pine's point of entry to ethnographic research with nurses coincided with a pivotal point of change as privatization and other forces pushed a techno-intensive approach to managed health care, profoundly impacting the meaning and experience of nursing. Her essay "On Caring" uses the studying up/down/sideways methodology to identify driving forces and controlling processes that fueled transformative change in an evolving and contested healthcare context. Mapping out the process and ramifications of change from an individual patient–centered model of health care to a techno-intensive managed care delivery system, Pine examines dehumanizing practices and the technologies of institutional medical hierarchies to identify how these changes have transformed the meaning and nature of nursing. A core finding in this work is that a fundamental transformation has taken place in the conceptual meaning and human experience of "care," and that manipulation of concepts of care—by politicians, hospital management, and the medical supply food chain (technology, information, pharmaceutical, and other industries)—harms both patients and their human caregivers. Studying up, down, and sideways also allows Pine to observe how these changes reactively and dynamically impact nursing. Thus, she documents how nurses confront this co-optation of the conceptual meaning of care and use individual and collective strategies to reclaim their power and voice in patient-centered care. Documenting the controlling processes and driving forces that shape health care delivery and studying the relative meaning of change up, down, and sideways reveals the power of Laura Nader's constructs: they help us to grasp what it means to be an actor in this evolving facet of American life and then, armed with this knowledge, to capably question whether "those with might have it right."

Destroying Autonomy, Fostering Dependence

Adrienne Pine's work, like other contributions to the volume, also illustrates another theme that Laura Nader has discussed at length in her work on controlling processes: institutional practices that lead to the erosion of autonomy and corresponding dependence on large-scale organizations. Pine's research illuminates the ways in which health itself has become subject to large HMOs and impersonal protocols that render patients and nurse practitioners dependent upon bureaucracies.

In a similar vein, Liza Grandia's essay "On Dispossession" considers how international organizations employ controlling processes to shape, facilitate, and legitimize land dispossession in Q'eqchi' Maya communities in Guatemala's Petén Department. To understand how and why dysfunctional Guatemalan governance (i.e., state-sponsored plunder) systematically destroys its citizens' means of sustaining life, she examines the agendas and assumptions of the World Bank, which designed and financed the state. In this case, a land titling project structured by neoliberal assumptions promised to improve the lives of small landholders in Guatemala by breaking up communal title, retitling land in individual hands, and facilitating national land reform legislation to establish a market value for land and thence secure credit to develop, buy, and sell land. But whereas land transactions increased, for various reasons land insecurity and poverty increased. Despite this outcome, the World Bank and the Guatemalan government define the initiative as a success, and additional loans are now financing the initiative in other regions. How is failure interpreted as success, and why? Grandia points to the belief systems that shape World Bank–financed initiatives; the financier's power to shape agendas, priorities, and plans and determine the key indicators of success; the vast distance that exists between those who formulate plans (their goals, notions of development and success, experience in the world, understanding of place and people) and the intended beneficiaries; and the insulated distance between those who profit and those who live with the day-to-day results of inept, flawed, corrupt governance. She also observes that ulcerating social, economic, or environmental consequences of dysfunctional governance often implode, creating contexts in which denial is no longer an option. In times of explosive crisis, the belief systems propping up the legitimacy of governments, institutions, and corporate entities fail. At such times, Grandia argues, resistance and social transformation might be achieved.

Besides critique, viable social change must also present an alternative vision worth struggling for. The essay "On Food," by Roberto González, offers both the critique and the vision, drawing on detail and insights from studying up, down, and across the food chain in Oaxaca, Mexico, and beyond. Initially focusing on the traditional values, knowledge, behavior, and material conditions that sustain a Rincón Zapotec way of life, González identifies the linkages between food and power as they have evolved over time, demonstrating the complex and synergistic relationship between cultural diversity and biodiversity and food's key role in nourishing this life. As the historical trajectory passes through the "modern tragedies" of the twenty-first century and into the present day, González identifies the controlling processes that have undermined and eroded a functional food/power system, and then lays out the ramifications of this degenerative change. Although the varied human and environmental consequences of this erosion are particular to place and case, the controlling processes are part of a broader global economy that increasingly intersects, dismantles, and controls the food/power relationships in regions, communities, and cultures around the world. Understanding how food and farming has changed among the Rincón Zapotec, and what has been lost in the process, both informs and inspires. Ultimately, González argues, reclaiming control over our food production systems and repairing our deeply dysfunctional relationship with food requires an understanding and appreciation of how functional food/power relationships are structured.

Rachael Stryker's essay "On Family," another example of vertically integrated research, allows insight into the controlling processes involved in the construction and deconstruction of family through a particular focus on institutional incursions into adoptive families. Concentrating on the bureaucratic maze of international placement agencies, orphanages, and state institutions—that is, the loci of family building in global child circulation routes—Stryker examines the experiences of American parents who attempted to locate, receive, and care for Russian adoptees and, in the event the placement did not work out, return a child to his or her Russian institution of origin. This essay depicts many pitfalls of adoptive family construction, zeroing in on cultural disconnects influenced by varied forces that sell the promise or generate the expectation of an instant family. These disconnects include the many reasons for Russian children's institutionalization, adoption agencies' disinclination to communicate children's personal histories to prospective parents, the emotional needs and expectations of adoptive parents who seek a substitute for a biological child, and the difficulties of achieving an intimate and happy family-bond for a Russian-born child whose notion of family life is shaped by, among other things, the work expectations and peer group structure of an orphanage. When problems emerge, adoptive families turn to the U.S.

biomedical support system, which typically diagnoses a behavioral or emotional disorder. This may eventually disrupt the legalization process and, in extreme cases, prompt the child's return to Russia. In this analysis of the construction of adoptive families, power resides largely in the institutional bureaucracies and agencies that place children and counsel adoptive parents. Agencies often frame adoptive parents as passive recipients in the family-building business, and other controlling processes that dictate the norms and behavior of American family life reinforce this passiveness. Stryker's chapter illustrates how the ability to create autonomous families has come under pressure from bureaucratic organizations fostering a kind of dependence, and helps us think more broadly about the extent to which institutional surrogacy impacts modern families.

Stigmatization as a Controlling Process

Yet another theme that emerges from this collection building on Nader's work on controlling processes is social stigmatization's function as a form of control—in other words, the ways that powerful institutions scapegoat, manipulate, or otherwise stigmatize individuals or small groups. Rachael Stryker's ethnographic description of adoptive family construction (discussed above) vividly illustrates this theme by exposing the processes by which adoptive children, families, birth families, and sending countries can become stigmatized.

Likewise, Robyn Kliger's essay "On Truth" examines the controlling processes that shape and determine what is credible truth in the social quagmire of child abuse allegations, especially in cases involving repressed memory of child abuse. For Kliger, studying up, down, and sideways means delving into the multidimensional nature of the debates surrounding repressed memory to identify and explore how controlling processes shape the perception and experience of victims, parents, advocacy groups on both sides, academic researchers, clinicians and therapists, and legal professionals. By exploring the sociocultural factors that support or disabuse a determination of truth in different clinical and courtroom settings, and critically deconstructing the means by which legal and scientific notions of truth are contested, determined credible, or dismissed, Kliger is able to recognize the contradictions that emerge from a clash between two controlling processes shaped by very different assumptions of truth. Examining the relative power of actors and the consequences of acting within these two controlling domains, Kliger demonstrates the power of one institutional force to influence and change the other. By illuminating the linkages between court cases, admissibility rulings, and public and scientific discourse over the science of memory, Kliger demonstrates how scientific research evolves in response to court decisions, with legal standards and rules of evidence both controlling and driving scientific knowledge production.

The social relevance of these points is further illustrated in Linda Coco's essay "On Debt," which explores the legal, social, and cultural norms that shape the social meaning of debt in the United States. Coco's analysis sheds light on the hugely contradictory experience of debt, in which the stigmatized individual consumer can only obtain the court's forgiveness through public demonstration of an honest failure, even though "the consumer debtor is considered as simply part of the natural ebb and flow of the capitalist market" and "the morality of the actor is irrelevant." This characterization of the deeply inequitable social consequences of the contradictions of capitalism offers insight into the question of why corporate wrongdoing is so rarely penalized. Coco observes that just as individual debtors' standing is shaped by the history, laws, and sentiments of a "deeply encultured notion of individual responsibility," so too is corporate actors' standing shaped by deeply encultured notions: the free marketplace is the essential feature in our economic landscape; corporate entities are the engines that drive and sustain our capitalist society; corporate debt is a natural and inevitable facet of a healthy economy; the corporate debtor unquestionably deserves privileged standing. Coco's conclusions are profoundly relevant to understanding the various contradictions in catastrophic economic collapse. Between 1997 and 2011, some 6.2 million families were forced to declare bankruptcy and some 4 million U.S. families saw their homes foreclosed upon, and by January 2012 another 4 million loans had been reported as delinquent. Meanwhile, Wall Street has transformed its collapse into a juggernaut, powering on to new heights as wealth accumulates in the hands of failed corporations, banks, and investment firms that have risen again under new names but with the same powers and might. Coco's analysis lays bare how and why the individual citizen bears "the moral burden of the marketplace under capitalism in the U.S."

The Consequences of Corporate Capitalism

This volume also clearly extends Laura Nader's work through its ethnographic commitment to highlighting the deleterious consequences of corporate capitalism—also called neoliberalism—implemented on a global scale. The chapters by Adrienne Pine and Liza Grandia (see above) clearly illustrate how these forces have impacted health care delivery in the United States and land tenure in Guatemala, respectively.

Alongside these contributions, Jay Ou's analysis of the social and cultural effects of corporate capitalism and economic crisis in Asia in the late twentieth and early twenty-first centuries says much about the how the architecture of power is structured and sustained, generating deeply inequitable conditions with profound social ramifications. Using a vertically integrated approach to research the social meaning of labor in a stratified workplace, Ou explores the experiences and the linkages between workers and managers in a globalized military-industrial system that straddles three nations: Korea, Indonesia, and the United States. Having conducted ethnographic research before, during, and after a severe regional economic crisis, Ou is able to identify and explore the social architecture of labor, the machinations of power in contemporary commerce, and the consequential impact of these controlling processes on the lives of workers. By mapping out the antecedents, controlling processes, intersects, and consequences of a regional transnational economic crisis in human terms, Ou demonstrates the usefulness of the vertical slice concept to construct a multidimensional exploration of how those with power obtain, exercise, and maintain their might, and at what cost. In a world characterized by escalating crisis, economic convulsions, and social upheaval (bank failures and home foreclosures, job loss and systemic unemployment, human and environmental rights abuse in globalized extractive and manufacturing industries, mass public protests over the consequences of corrupt governance in service to a corporate elite), effectively confronting and challenging such realities requires a critical understanding of the structure, function, *and* dysfunction of power in our global economy.

Similarly, in her essay "On Environment," Patricia Urteaga-Crovetto explores the evolution and anatomy of dysfunctional human environmental relationships, utilizing the vertical slice concept to study the structure and consequences of petroleum development in Peru. In this case, a multi-sited ethnography of power examines the belief systems that shape and legitimize neoliberal models of development, the political and economic mechanisms that legitimize extractive industry as the primary and inevitable vehicle for societal progress, and the social relationships that produce and reproduce a culture of governance largely dependent on foreign corporations, nations, and multilateral financiers. This approach allows Urteaga-Crovetto to situate specific actors within the currents of power and trace their trajectory through time. The end result is the recognition of social, political, and economic incest among the power elite and the complex means by which the state's priorities, responsibilities, and actions are corrupted. In mapping out the dynamics in the structural architecture of plunder, Urteaga-Crovetto demonstrates how the privatization of governance occurs, and how this erosion of sovereignty has generated abusive relationships and ulcerating conditions that make victims out of the supposed beneficiaries of progress—indigenous peoples living on customary lands—whose livelihood and future now sustains the wealth of a power elite.

Ripples in the Pond: Envisioning Alternatives

Collectively, the contributors to this volume identify and explore the architecture of power and the ramifications of exercising power. They do so by examining the material, social, and cultural means by which power is generated, consolidated, amplified, and deployed. From the family living room (Stryker) to the picket lines of nursing unions in the United States (Pine); from indigenous collective movements to address and curtail food insecurity (González), land dispossession (Grandia), and corporate resource appropriation (Urteaga-Crovetto), to the efforts to re-theorize and deconstruct power and control in the cultures of Wall Street (Ou and Coco), neoliberal development bureaucracies (Hertz), and established and emerging forms of Western law (Coco, Eppinger, and Kliger), this volume provides mental tools and frameworks to help citizens envision alternatives to current power structures and engage in vertically integrated social reform. Many of its chapters not only provide a model for envisioning alternate futures, but also describe in detail the actual ways in which the vertical slice impacts public policy, social reform, or citizen action.

The contributions to the volume clearly demonstrate that mapping out the multidimensional universe of power allows us to recognize varied loci of power and the conditions that change these loci, and discern linkages between micro and macro conditions and actual experience. The resulting picture of reality is a dynamic, multifaceted construct that both demonstrates and questions the ramifications of exercising power, explaining and predicting, for example, how and why corrupt and dysfunctional governance occurs, or how notions of credible science and ideology are constructed and why they are employed.

By allowing a focus on the linkages between condition and outcome, studying up, down and sideways illuminates the relationships between ulcerating crisis, contestation and conflict, transformative change, and dynamic backlash. The issues examined here are central to twenty-first century life: corporate capitalism as it affects labor, debt as it affects the poor, land dispossession of indigenous peoples, food and hunger, energy, bureaucracies, health and mind-control. There is considerable power in analyses such as these. Such work helps us recognize and deal with immediate issues of the present and future—not just as academics, but as a citizenry armed with sound information and hope for the future.

Contributors

Linda Coco is Assistant Professor of Law at Barry University's Dwayne O. Andreas School of Law. She has also served as Research Professor at St. John's University School of Law in Queens, NY. Her research topics include professional responsibility, law and anthropology, and corporate bankruptcy reorganizations. She is a Ph.D. candidate in Anthropology at the University of California, Berkeley. The author of several articles and essays, she also conducted research for Ralph Nader's book *Children First: A Parent's Guide to Fighting Corporate Predators* (1996). She has also clerked in bankruptcy courts in Maryland and California.

Monica Eppinger is Assistant Professor of Law and Assistant Professor of Anthropology at Saint Louis University. She earned a Ph.D. in Anthropology from University of California, Berkeley, and a J.D. from Yale Law School. She served nine years as a diplomat in the U.S. Foreign Service with tours of duty in West Africa, Eurasia, and Washington, D.C., where her responsibilities included transition policies in the former Soviet Union, Caspian energy development, poverty alleviation, and West African security. She has also spent two years as a volunteer in northeastern China. Her research is guided by an interest in ideas and practices that produce settings for the individual and collective self and attendant modes of power. This led to lines of inquiry in property, national security, and sovereignty.

Roberto J. González is Professor of Anthropology at San Jose State University. He is author of *Zapotec Science: Farming and Food in the Northern Sierra of Oaxaca* (2001), *American Counterinsurgency: Human Science and the Human Terrain* (2009), and *Militarizing Culture: Essays on the Warfare State* (2011). He and Laura Nader recently co-produced the documentary film *Losing Knowledge: 50 Years of Change* (2012). He is a founding member of the Network of Concerned Anthropologists.

Liza Grandia is Associate Professor of Anthropology in the Department of Native American Studies at University of California, Davis. Her research explores the impacts of trade and corporate globalization on northern Guatemala and southern Belize. She is a permanent emeritus board member of ProPeten (a former affiliate of Conservation International). She speaks both Spanish and Guatemala's second largest indigenous language, Q'eqchi' Maya. From 2006 to 2007, she was a fellow in the Program in Agrarian Studies at Yale University. Her most recent book is *Enclosed: Conservation, Cattle, and Commerce among the Q'eqchi' Maya Lowlanders* (2012).

Ellen Hertz is Professor of Anthropology at the Institut d'ethnologie of the University of Neuchâtel, Switzerland, where she has served as department head and dean. Before coming to work in Switzerland, she studied Chinese, law, and anthropology in the United States. Her research focuses on the interplay of economic, legal, and cultural regimes of thought and action, and she has done fieldwork on the creation of the Shanghai stock market, on indigenous people's rights in the U.N. system, and on local courts and the social welfare regime in Switzerland. She is the author of *The Trading Crowd: An Ethnography of the Shanghai Stock Market* (1998). Her research interests include complex supply chains, state law, and corporate social responsibility in the electronics industry in China and Taiwan. Her chapter in this volume reflects a field experience that served as the starting point for this research.

Robyn Kliger received her Ph.D. in anthropology from University of California, Berkeley. She is an independent scholar and the author of the article "Somatization: Social Control and Illness Production in a Religious Cult" (*Culture, Medicine, and Psychiatry*, 1995). Her research interests include ideological control, cults, and the cultural construction of memory and experience.

Jay Ou received his Ph.D. in anthropology at University of California, Berkeley. His interest in the connections between culture, food, and environment led to his entry into the world of organic food. Drawing on his training in environmental science and socio-cultural anthropology, he has launched several successful organic and fair trade businesses and NGOs, including Cacao Green Global, Red Mango Global, and Ecologic, all focused on sustainability and wellness.

Adrienne Pine is Assistant Professor of Anthropology at American University in Washington, D.C. A former educator with the California Nurses Association (CNA), she is a militant medical anthropologist who has worked in Honduras, Mexico, Korea, the United States, and Egypt. She is the author of *Working Hard, Drinking Hard: On Violence and Survival in Honduras* (2008). Prior to and following the June 2009 military coup in Honduras, she collaborated with numerous organizations and individuals to bring international attention to the Honduran struggle to halt state violence in its multiple forms. She has also conducted extensive research on the impact of corporate health care and health care technologies on labor practices in the United States.

Rachael Stryker is Assistant Professor of Anthropology in the Department of Human Development and Women's Studies at California State University, East Bay. She is the author of *The Road to Evergreen: Adoption, Attachment Therapy, and the Promise of Family* (2010). Her research interests include the anthropology of childhood; adoption, migration, and globalization; and public interest ethnography. Her public interest research with female prisoners in California is included in the anthropology textbook *Conformity and Conflict: Readings in Cultural Anthropology* (14th ed., 2011; 15th ed., 2015). Her latest book, *Public Interest Ethnography: A Primer*, is under contract with Left Coast Press.

Patricia Urteaga-Crovetto is a lawyer and anthropologist who teaches at the Pontificia Universidad Católica del Perú. Her research focuses on legal and political themes related to the predicament of indigenous peoples of the Peruvian Amazon basin. She is the author of *La Problemática Minera y los Pueblos Indígenas en Madre de Dios, Perú* (2003) and co-author (with Rutgerd Boelens) of *Derechos Colectivos Políticas Hídricas en la Región Andina* (2006). She was a member of the Water Law and Indigenous Rights Programme (WALIR), led by the University of Wageningen (Netherlands), and CEPAL. She was also the Peruvian coordinator of the Concertación Programme. As part of an interdisciplinary research team at the Pontificia Universidad Católica del Perú, she is currently working on water scarcity and agribusiness on the Peruvian coast. She will soon publish a book on extractive industries and water.

References

Adoption and Foster Care Analysis and Reporting System. "Statistics and Research." Washington, D.C.: United States Department of Health and Human Services, Administration for Children and Families. 1999. http//:www.acf.hhs.gov/programs/cb.

Agamben, Giorgio. *State of Exception*. Chicago: The University of Chicago Press, 2005.

Aiken, L. H., et al. "Implications of the California Nurse Staffing Mandate for Other States." *Health Services Research* (April 2010): 18.

Althusser, Louis. "Ideology and Ideological State Apparatuses: Notes towards an Investigation." In *Lenin and Philosophy, and Other Essays*, ed. Louis Althusser, 85–126. London: New Left Books, 1971.

Anders, Gerhard. "The 'Trickle-Down' Effects of Civil Service Reform in Malawi: Studying Up." In *The Commission on Folk Law and Legal Pluralism, Proceedings of the XIII International Congress*, comp. Pradhan Rajendra, 131–150. Chiang Mai, Thailand: The Commission on Folk Law and Legal Pluralism, 2002.

Anderson, Eugene. *Ecologies of the Heart: Emotion, Belief, and the Environment*. Oxford: Oxford University Press, 1996.

Andrukhovich, Yuri. *Дезорієнтація на Місцевості* [*Disorientation in Place*], Ivano-Frankivsk: Liliya, 2006.

Aronson, Naomi. "Working Up an Appetite." In *A Woman's Conflict: The Special Relationship between Women and Food*, ed. J.R. Kaplan, 203–229. New York: Prentice-Hall, 1980.

Associated Press. "Some US Hospitals Outsourcing Work: Shortage of Radiologists Spurs 'Growing Telemedicine Trend." 6 December 2004. http://www.msnbc.msn.com/id/6621014.

Austin, John. *How to Do Things with Words*. Cambridge, MA: Harvard University Press, 1962.

Baba, Marietta L. "Organizational Culture: Revisiting the Small-Society Metaphor." *Anthropology of Work Review* 10, no. 3 (September 1989): 7–10.

———. "Beyond Dilbert: The Cultural Construction of Work Organizations in America." In *Ethnographic Essays in Cultural Anthropology: A Problem-Based Approach*, ed. R. Bruce Morrison and C. Roderick Wilson, 183–210. Itasca, IL: F. E. Peacock, 2001.

Bach, Jonathan. "The Taste Remains: Consumption, (N)ostalgia, and the Production of East Germany." *Public Culture* 14, no. 3 (2002): 545–556.

Bagdikian, Ben. *The New Media Monopoly*. Boston: Beacon Press, 2004.

Bakhtin, Mikhail M. "Epic and Novel." In *The Dialogic Imagination: Four Essays*, ed. Michael Holquist and Caryl Emerson and trans. Michael Holquist, 3–40. Austin: University of Texas Press, 1975.

Ball, Alan. *And Now My Soul Is Hardened: Abandoned Children in Russia, 1918–1930*. Berkeley: University of California Press, 1994.

Bankruptcy Abuse Prevention and Consumer Protection Act of 2005. 11 U.S.C. § 707.
Barlett, Donald L., and James B. Steele, eds. *Critical Condition: How Health Care in America became Big Business—and Bad Medicine*. New York: Doubleday, 2004.
Bauman, Richard. "Verbal Art as Performance." *American Anthropologist* 77, no. 2 (1975): 290–311.
Bellier, Irène. "Dernières Nouvelles du Groupe de Travail sur le Projet de Déclaration des Droits des Peuples Autochtones à l'ONU." *Recherches Amérindiennes au Québec* 33, no. 3 (2003): 93–99.
Belluck, Pam. "Memory Therapy Leads to a Lawsuit and Big Settlement." *New York Times*. 6 November 1997. http://www.nytimes.com/1997/11/06/us/memory-therapy-leads-to-a-lawsuit-and-big-settlement.htm.
Beltran, Gonzalo Aguirre. *Regions of Refuge*. Washington, D.C.: Society for Applied Anthropology, 1979.
Berdahl, Daphne. "(N)ostalgia for the Present: Memory, Longing, and East German Things," *Ethnos* 64, no. 2 (1999): 192–211.
Bernard, Tara Siegel, and Jenny Anderson. "Downturn Drags More Consumers into Bankruptcy," *New York Times*. 16 November 2008.
Berreman, Gerald. "Anemic and Emetic Analyses in Social Anthropology." *American Anthropologist* 68, no. 2 (1966): 346–354.
Blank, Diana. "Fairytale Cynicism in the Kingdom of Plastic Bags: Powerlessness of Place in a Ukrainian Border Town." *Ethnography* 5, no. 3 (2004): 349–378.
Bodley, James. *Anthropology and Contemporary Human Problems*. Menlo Park, CA: Cummings, 1976.
———. "Alternatives to Ethnocide: Human Zoos, Living Museums, and Real People." In *Western Expansion and Indigenous Peoples*, ed. Elias Sevilla-Casas, 31–50. The Hague and Paris: Mouton, 1977.
Bodley, John. *Victims of Progress*. Menlo Park, NJ: Cummings, 1975.
———. "The World Bank Tribal Policy: Criticisms and Recommendations." Testimony presented before US House Committee on Banking, Finance, and Urban Affairs and U.S. House Subcommittee on International Development, Institutions, and Finance. 29 June 1983.
Bonfil Batalla, Guillermo. *Diagnóstico Sobre el Hambre en Sudzal, Yucatán*. Mexico City: INAH, 1962.
———. "Conservative Thought in Applied Anthropology: A Critique." *Human Organization* 25, no. 2 (1966): 89–92.
Borocz, Jozsef, and Akos Rona-Tas, "Small Leap Forward: Emergence of New Economic Elites." *Theory and Society* 24 (1995): 751–781.
Bossevain, Jeremy. *Friends of Friends: Networks, Manipulators, and Coalitions*. Oxford: Basil Blackwell, 1974.
Bourdieu, Pierre. *Invitation to Reflexive Sociology*. Chicago: University of Chicago Press, 1992.
———. *Practical Reason: On the Theory of Action*. Palo Alton: Stanford University Press, 1998.
Bourgois, Phillipe I. *In Search of Respect: Selling Crack in El Barrio*. New York: Cambridge University Press, 1995.
Brennan, Troyen A. "The Institute of Medicine Report on Medical Errors—Could It Do Harm?" *New England Journal of Medicine* 342, no. 15 (April 2000): 1123–1125.
———et al., "Health Industry Practices That Create Conflicts of Interest." *JAMA* 295, no. 4 (25 January 2006): 429–33.
Buerhaus, P., D. O. Staiger, and D. I. Auerbach, *The Future of the Nursing Workforce in the United States: Data, Trends and Implications*. Salisbury: Jones and Bartlett, 2008.

Burke, Peter. *The French Historical Revolution: The Annales School, 1929–1989*. Cambridge: Polity Press, 1990.
Campodónico, Humberto. *La Política Petrolera 1970–1985: El Estado, las Contratistas y Petroperú*. Lima: Desco, 1986.
Canby, Peter. "Retreat to Subsistence." *The Nation*. 16 June 2010.
Carpenter, Novella. *Farm City: The Education of an Urban Farmer*. New York: Penguin, 2010.
Casper, Monica J. "Feminist Politics and Fetal Surgery: Adventures of a Research Cowgirl on the Reproductive Frontier." *Feminist Studies* 23, no. 2 (1997): 232–262.
Castellanos, Javier. *El Maiz en Yojovi, Villa Alta, Oaxaca*. Mexico City: Primer Lugar, 1988.
Center for Environmental Cooperation. *Maize and Biodiversity: The Effects of Transgenic Maize in Mexico* (Montreal: CEC, 2004). http://www.cec.org/Storage/56/4837_Maize-and-Biodiversity_en.pdf (accessed 22 August 2010).
Center for Food Safety. "Genetically Modified Food." http://centerforfoodsafety.org/geneticall7.cfm (accessed 29 October 2010).
Center for Media and Democracy. "Paul Dundes Wolfowitz." http://www.sourcewatch.org/index.php?title=Paul_Dundes_Wolfowitz (accessed 21 August 2013).
Chaffin, Mark, et al., "Report of the APSAC Task Force on Attachment Therapy, Reactive Attachment Disorder, and Attachment Problems." *Child Maltreatment* 11, no. 1 (2006): 76–89.
Chang, Ha-Joon, Gabriel Palma, and D. Hugh Whittaker, eds. *Financial Liberalization and the Asian Crisis*. New York: Palgrave Macmillan, 2001.
Chang, S. S., et al. "Was the Economic Crisis 1997–1998 Responsible for Rising Suicide Rates in East/Southeast Asia? A Time-Trend Analysis for Japan, Hong Kong, South Korea, Taiwan, Singapore, and Thailand." *Social Science and Medicine* 68, no. 7 (April 2009): 1322–1331.
Clements, Jeffery D. *Corporations Are Not People: Why They Have More Rights Than You Do and What You Can Do About It*. San Francisco: Barrett-Koehler, 2012.
Coco, Linda, and Research Associates. *Children First! A Parent's Guide to Fighting Corporate Predators*. Washington, D.C.: Corporate Accountability Research Group, 1996.
Cohen, Felix. "Transcendental Nonsense and the Functional Approach." *Columbia Law Review* 35, no. 6 (June 1935): 809–849.
Cohn, Carol. "Sex and Death in the Rational World of Defense Intellectuals," *Signs* 12, no. 4 (1987): 687–718.
Colby, Gerard, and Charlotte Dennett. *Thy Will Be Done: The Conquest of the Amazon, Nelson Rockefeller, and Evangelism in the Age of Oil*. New York: Harper Collins, 1995.
Coleman, Simon, and Peter Collins, eds. *Locating the Field: Space, Place and Context in Anthropology* (ASA Monographs 42). Oxford and New York: Berg, 2006.
Collins, H. M. *Changing Order: Replication and Induction in Scientific Practice*, 2nd ed. Chicago: University of Chicago Press, 1992.
The Compact Edition of the Oxford English Dictionary. Oxford University Press, 1971.
Cook, Walter Wheeler. "The Logical and Legal Basis of the Conflict of Law." *Yale Law Journal* 33 (1933): 457.
Creuzinger, Clementine. *Childhood in Russia: Representations and Reality*. Lanham, MD: University Press of America, 1996.
Critser, Greg. *Fat Land: How Americans Became the Fattest People in the World*. Boston: Houghton-Mifflin, 2003.
Cromie, William. "False Memories." *Harvard Gazette*. 19 September 1996. http://www.news.harvard.edu/gazette/1996/09.19/FalseMemories.html.
Cumings, Bruce. *The Korean War: A History*. New York: Modern Library, 2011.
Cummings, Claire Hope. "Risking Corn, Risking Culture." *WorldWatch* (15 October 2002). http://www.worldwatch.org/node/525 (accessed 2 November 2010).

Currie, David P., Herma Hill Kay, and Larry Kramer. *Conflict of Laws: Cases, Comments, Questions*. Saint Paul: West, 2001.

Czarniawska, Barbara, Guje Sevon, Stewart R. Clegg, and Ralph E. Stablein, eds. *Global Ideas: How Ideas, Objects and Practices Travel in the Global Economy*. Malmö: Liber, 2005.

Dardick, Hal. "Psychiatric Patient Tells of Ordeal in Treatment." *Chicago Tribune*. 13 February 2004. http://articles.chicagotribune.com/2004-02-13/news/0402130313_1_psychiatric-treatment-psychiatric-illnesses-childhood-trauma.

de Aguirre, David Martínez. "Situación, Oportunidades y Riesgos del Proyecto Camisea." *Estudios Amazónicos* 2, no. 2 (2005): 71–89.

Deininger, Klaus. *Land Rights for Poor People Key to Poverty Reduction, Growth: Summary of a World Bank Policy Research Report*. Washington, D.C.: Center for International Private Enterprise, 2003.

Delaporte, Francois, ed. *A Vital Rationalist: Selected Writings from Georges Canguilhem*. New York: Zone Books, 2000.

Deleuze, Gilles, and Felix Guattari. "Introduction: Rhizome." In *A Thousand Plateaus: Capitalism and Schizophrenia*, ed. Gilles Deleuze and Felix Guattari and trans. Brian Massumi, 3–25. Minneapolis: University of Minnesota Press, 1987.

Dementieva, I. F. *Social Orphanhood: Origins and Preventions*. Moscow: Institute of Family and Youth, 2000.

DeMoro, Don. "Engineering a Crisis: How Hospitals Created a Shortage of Nurses." *Revolution* 1, no. 2 (2000): 16–23.

Denver Department of Human Services. "Denver Children Available." 15 May 2003. http//:www.denvergov.org/DenverChildren/Images.

de Onis, Juan. *The Green Cathedral: Sustainable Development of Amazonia*. New York: Oxford University Press, 1992.

Descalzi, Carlos Herrera. "Assessment on the Camisea Pipeline Project in Peru." Testimony presented before the U.S. Senate Committee on Foreign Relations hearing on "Multilateral Development Banks: Development Effectiveness of Infrastructure Projects." 12 July 2006. http://www.etechinternational.org/07-13-06_Carlos%20Herrera%20Descalzi_testimony_US_senate.pdf.

de Soto, Hernando. *The Mystery of Capital: Why Capitalism Triumphs in the West and Fails Everywhere Else*. New York: Basic Books, 2000.

de Sousa Santos, Boaventura. *Toward a Common Sense: Law, Science and Politics in the Paradigmatic Transition*. New York: Routledge, 1995.

Dirección General de Salud Ambiental. *Informe de Ensayo Hidrobiológico No. 0463, Laboratorio de Hidrobiología, Microbiología de Aguas*. 18 July 2006.

Donald, Leland. "Review: Reinventing Anthropology by Dell Hymes." *American Anthropologist* 76, no. 4 (1974): 861.

Dorow, Sara. *Transnational Adoption: A Cultural Economy of Race, Gender, and Kinship*. New York: New York University Press, 2006.

Doukas, Dmitra. *Worked Over: The Corporate Sabotage of an American Community*. Ithaca, NY: Cornell University Press, 2003.

Ego, Manual Dammert. *La República Lobbysta: Amenaza contra la Democracia Peruana en el Siglo XXI*. Lima: Medios y Enlaces SRL, 2009.

Ehrlich, Eugen. *Fundamental Principles of the Sociology of Law*, trans. W. Moll. New York: Russell and Russell, 1962 [1913].

El Comercio. 5 May 2009.

"El MEM Autoriza Instalar Hidroeléctrica en Cobán." *El Periódico*. 10 July 2010.

Elias, Norbert. *The Civilizing Process: Sociogenetic and Psychogenetic Investigations*, trans. E. Jephcott. Oxford: Blackwell, 1994.

Espinoza, Roberto, and Beatriz Huertas. *Evaluación Social del Proyecto Camisea y Defensa de los Pueblos Indígenas Auto Aislados*. Report commissioned by Aprodeh. Unpublished manuscript, 2003.

Ewen, Stanley, and Arpad Pusztai. "Effect of Diets Containing Genetically Modified Potatoes Expressing *Galanthus nivalis lectin* on Rat Small Intestine." *Lancet* 354 (1999): 1353.

Ewen, Stuart. *Captains of Consciousness*. New York: McGraw-Hill, 1976.

Eyal, Gil, Ivan Szeleny, and Eleanor Townsley. *Making Capitalism Without Capitalists: Class Formation and Elite Struggles in Post-Communist Central Europe*. London: Verso, 1998.

Farmer, Paul. *Pathologies of Power: Health, Human Rights, and the New War on the Poor*. Berkeley: University of California Press, 2004.

Ferguson, James, and Akhil Gupta. "Spatializing States: Toward an Ethnography of Neoliberal Governmentality." *American Ethnologist* 29, no. 4 (2002): 981–1002.

Fernandez-Kelly, Maria Patricia. *For We Are Sold, I and My People: Women and Industry in Mexico's Frontier*. Albany: SUNY Press, 1983.

Fischer, J. L. "*Reinventing Anthropology* (Review)," *Journal of American Folklore* 87, no. 346 (1974): 376–377.

Fivush, Robyn, and V. J. Edwards. "Remembering and Forgetting Childhood Sexual Abuse." *Journal of Child Sexual Abuse* 13 (2004): 1–19.

Forbes.com. "US Foreclosures Rise in December, Reach 2.2 Mln in 2007." 29 January 2008. http://www.forbes.com/feeds/afx/2008/01/29/afx4584956.html.

Foucault, Michel. *Discipline and Punish: The Birth of the Prison*. New York: Vintage Books, 1979.

———. *The Foucault Reader*, ed. Paul Rabinow. New York: Pantheon, 1984.

———. *The History of Sexuality: An Introduction*. New York: Vintage Books, 1984.

Fresia, Marion. "Une élite transnationale: la fabrique d'une identité professionnelle chez les fonctionnaires du Haut Commissariat aux réfugiés", *Revue Européenne des Migrations internationals*, 25 n° 3, 2010

Freud, Sigmund. *The Aetiology of Hysteria*, trans. J. Strachey and A. Freud. London: Hogarth Press 1952 [1896].

Freyd, Jennifer. *Betrayal Trauma: The Logic of Forgetting Childhood Abuse*. Cambridge, MA: Harvard University Press, 1997.

———. "Science in the Memory Debate," *Ethics and Behavior* 8, no. 2 (1998): 101–113.

Fromm, Erich. *Escape from Freedom*. New York: Farrar & Rinehart, 1941.

———. *The Heart of Man: Its Genius for Good or Evil* (Religious perspectives; v. 12). New York: Harper and Row, 1964.

Frontline (PBS). "Timeline of the Panic" (1999). http://www.pbs.org/wgbh/pages/frontline/shows/crash/etc/cron.html.

Gabel, Medard, and Henry Bruner. *Global Inc.: An Atlas of the Multinational Corporation*. New York: The New Press, 2003.

Galeano, Eduardo. *Upside Down: A Primer for the Looking-Glass World*. New York: Metropolitan Books, 2001.

Galinat, Walter C. "El Origen del Maiz: El Grano de la Humanidad." *Economic Botany* 49, no. 1 (1995): 3–12.

Galliher, John F. "Social Scientists' Ethical Responsibilities to Superordinates: Looking Upward Meekly." *Social Problems* 27, no. 3 (1980): 298–308.

Garsten, Christina. "The United Nations—Soft and Hard: Regulating Social Accountability for Global Business." In *Organizing Transnational Accountability*, ed. Magnus Boström and Christina Garsten, 27–45. London: Edward Elgar Publishing, 2008.

George, Susan, and Fabrizio Sabelli. *Faith and Credit: The World's Bank Secular Empire*. London: Penguin Books, 1994.

Gerth, H. H., and C. W. Mills, eds. *From Max Weber: Essays in Sociology*. New York: Oxford University Press, 1946.

Geslin, Philippe, and Ellen Hertz. "Public International Indigenes." In *Making Things Public: Atmospheres of Democracy*, ed. Bruno Latour and Peter Weibel, 578–585. Karlsruhe: ZKM Editions and Cambridge MA: MIT Press, 2005.

Giddens, Anthony. *Central Problems in Social Theory: Action, Structure and Contradiction in Social Analysis*. Los Angeles: University of California Press, 1990.

Gluckman, Max. *Politics, Law, and Ritual in Tribal Society*. Oxford: Blackwell, 1965.

Erving Goffman. *Frame Analysis: An Essay in the Organization of Experience*. Cambridge, MA: Harvard University Press, 1974.

Goldman, Michael. *Imperial Nature: The World Bank and Struggles for Social Justice in the Age of Globalization*. New Haven: Yale University Press, 2006.

Goldschmidt, Walter. "*Reinventing Anthropology* (Review)," *Science* 180, no. 4086 (11 May 1973): 612–613.

González, Roberto J. "Brave New Workplace." In *Essays on Controlling Processes*, special issue, *Kroeber Anthropological Society Papers* 80 (1996): 14–31.

———. *Zapotec Science: Farming and Food in the Northern Sierra of Oaxaca*. Austin: University of Texas Press, 2001.

Goodenough, Ward. "Componential Analysis and the Study of Meaning," *Language* 32 (1958): 195–216.

Gordon, Suzanne. "Nursing against the Odds: How Health Care Cost Cutting, Media Stereotypes, and Medical Hubris Undermine Nurses and Patient Care." Ithaca, NY: ILR Press (an imprint of Cornell University Press), 2005.

Goritti, Gustavo. "Camisea ¿Cómo sea?" *Ilustración Peruana Caretas*. 14 June 2007.

Gould, Harold. "Vladimir Nabokov." *The Paris Review* 41 (1967): 12.

Graeber, David. *Debt: The First 5,000 Years*. London: Melville House, 2011.

Gramsci, Antonio. *Selections from the Prison Notebooks*. New York: International, 1973.

Grandia, Liza. *Unsettling: Land Dispossession and Enduring Inequity for the Q'eqchi' Maya in the Guatemalan and Belizean Frontier Colonization Process*. Ph.D. diss., University of California, Berkeley, 2006.

———. *Tz'aptzooqeb'*. Guatemala City: AVANCSO, 2009.

———. *Enclosed: Conservation, Cattle, and Commerce among the Q'eqchi' Maya Lowlanders*. Seattle: University of Washington Press, 2012.

Grignon, Claude, and Jean-Claude Passeron. *Le Savant et le Populaire : Misérabilisme et Populisme en Sociologie et en Littérature*. Paris: Gallimard, 1989.

Groth, Stefan. *Negotiating Tradition: The Pragmatics of International Deliberations on Cultural Property* (Göttingen: Universitätsverlag Göttingen (Göttingen Studies in Cultural Property), vol. 4 (2012).

Guggenheim, Scott. "Crises and Contradictions: Understanding the Origins of a Community Development Project in Indonesia." In *The Search for Empowerment: Social Capital as Idea and Practice at the World Bank*, ed. Arthur Bebbington, Michael Woolcock, Scott Guggenheim, and Elizabeth Olson, 111–144. Sterling, VA: Kumarian Press, 2006.

Gupta, Akhil, and James Ferguson. "Beyond 'Culture': Space, Identity, and the Politics of Difference." *Cultural Anthropology* 7, no. 1 (1992): 6–23.

Gusterson, Hugh. "Studying Up Revisited," PoLAR 20, no. 1 (May 1997): 119.

———. *Nuclear Rites: A Weapons Laboratory at the End of the Cold War*. Berkeley: University of California Press, 1998.

Haaken, J. "The Debate over Recovered Memory of Sexual Abuse: A Feminist-Psychoanalytic Perspective." *Psychiatry* 58, no. 2 (May 1995): 189–198.

Hacking, Ian. *Rewriting the Soul: Multiple Personality and the Sciences of Memory*. Princeton, NJ: Princeton University Press, 1995.

Hanley, Eric, Natasha Yershova, and Richard Anderson. "Russia—Old Wine in New Bottle? The Circulation and Reproduction of Russian Elites, 1983–1993." *Theory and Society* 24 (1995): 689.

Hardt, Michael, and Antonio Negri. *Empire*. Cambridge, MA: Harvard University Press, 2000.

Hart, Gillian. "Denaturalizing Dispossession: Critical Ethnography in the Age of Resurgent Imperialism." *Antipode* 38 (2006): 977–1004.

Hart-Landsberg, Martin. *The Rush to Development: Economic Change and Political Struggle in South Korea*. New York: Monthly Review Press, 1993.

Hartley, Matt. "Grain Farmer Claims Moral Victory in Seed Battle against Monsanto." *Globe and Mail* (Canada). 20 March 2008.

Harvey, David. *The New Imperialism*. Oxford: Oxford University Press, 2003.

———. *A Brief History of Neoliberalism*. Oxford: Oxford University Press, 2005.

Havel, Václav. "The Power of the Powerless." In *Living in Truth*, ed. Václav Havel. London: Faber and Faber, 1986.

Hebdige, Dick. *Subculture: The Meaning of Style*. London and New York: Routledge, 1979.

Herszenhorn, David M., and Erik Eckholm. "Putin Signs Bill that Bars U.S. Adoptions, Upending Families." *New York Times*. 27 December 2012. http://www.nytimes.com/2012/12/28/world/europe/putin-to-sign-ban-on-us-adoptions-of-russian-children.html?pagewanted=all&_r=0#comments.

Ho, Karen. *Liquidated: An Ethnography of Wall Street*. Durham, NC: Duke University Press, 2009.

Hooper, Judith, Hannah Bloch, and Lisa Towle. "Targeting the Brain." *Time*. 18 September 1996. http://jackiewhiting.net/Psychology/AbPsych/AnxietyTreatment.htm.

Hope's Promise. "About Us." 13 May 2000. http://www.hopespromise.com/about/.

House of Representative Hearings in the Committee on Oversight and Government Reform. The Federal Bailout of AIG. 27 January 2010.

Howard, Manny. *My Empire of Dirt*. New York: Scribner, 2010.

Huertas, Beatriz. "El Proyecto Camisea y los Derechos de los Pueblos Indígenas." In *Asuntos Indígenas 3/03: Terrorismo, Conflictos y Derechos*, 20–31. Copenhagen: International Work Group for Indigenous Affairs, 2002.

Hunn, Eugene S. *A Zapotec Natural History*. Tucson: University of Arizona Press, 2008.

Hunt, Kathleen. *Abandoned to the State: Cruelty and Neglect in Russian Orphanages*. New York: Human Rights Watch, 1999. http//:www.hrw.or/reports98/russia.

Hunt, Katie. "Time to Reform the IMF?" *BBC News*. 9 October 2008. http://news.bbc.co.uk/2/hi/business/7647015.stm.

Ingrassia, Paul. *Crash Course: The American Automobile Industry's Road to Bankruptcy and Bailout*. New York: Random House, 2010.

Institute for Health and Socioeconomic Policy. *The Third Annual IHSP Hospital 200: The Nation's Most—and Least—Expensive Hospitals Fiscal Year 2003/2004*. Orinda, CA: Institute for Health and Socioeconomic Policy, 2005.

Instituto Nacional de Estadística e Informática. *Perú: Compendio Estadístico 1996–1997*. Lima: Instituto Nacional de Estadística e Informática, 1997.

International Labour Organisation. "Note on the Proceedings: Tripartite Meeting on the Production of Electronic Components for the IT Industries: Changing Labour Force Requirements in a Global Economy." TMITI/2007/10. Geneva: International Labour Office, 2007. http://www.ilo.org/public/english/dialogue/sector/.

---. "The Production of Electronic Components for the IT industries: Changing Labour Force Requirements in a Global Economy." TMITI/2007. Geneva: International Labour Office, 2007. http://www.ilo.org/public/english/dialogue/sector/techmeet/tmiti07/report.pdf.

---. "Report on the Committee on Sectoral and Technical Meetings and Related Issues." GB.200/16. 2007. http://www.ilo.org/wcmsp5/groups/public/—ed_norm/—relconf/documents/meetingdocument/wcms_087418.pdf.

"iOvulate." http://www.iovulate.com (accessed 31 August 2010).

Jackson-Lear, T. J. "The Concept of Cultural Hegemony: Problems and Possibilities." *American Historical Review* 90, no. 3 (1985): 567–593.

Jefferson, Thomas. *Notes on the State of Virginia.* New York: Penguin Books, 1999 [1785].

Johnson, Chalmers. *Blowback: The Costs and Consequences of American Empire.* New York: Metropolitan/Owl Book, 2004.

Kaplan, David. "The Anthropology of Authenticity: Everyman His Own Anthropologist," *American Anthropologist* 76, no. 4 (1974): 824–839.

King County Superior Court. *Mateu v. Hagen* (1993), case number 91–2-08053–1.

Klein, Naomi. *The Shock Doctrine: The Rise of Disaster Capitalism.* New York: Picador, 2008.

Kliger, Robyn. "Somatization: Social Control and Illness Production in a Religious Cult." *Culture, Medicine, and Psychiatry* 18 (1994): 215–245.

---. "Anthropology of Memory Technologies." Unpublished Ph.D. manuscript, University of California, Berkeley, 2000.

Kluckhohn, Clyde. *Mirror for Man: The Relationship of Anthropology to Everyday Life.* New York: Whittlesey House, 1949.

Konovalchuk, Vladimir. *A Computable General Equilibrium Analysis of the Economic Effects of the Chernobyl Nuclear Disaster.* Unpublished Ph.D. diss., The Pennsylvania State University, 2006. http://etda.libraries.psu.edu/theses/approved/WorldWideIndex/ETD-1337/index.html.

Kuhn, Thomas. *The Structure of Scientific Revolutions.* Chicago: University of Chicago Press, 1962.

Lancy, David. *Playing on the Mother-Ground: Cultural Routines for Children's Development.* New York: The Guilford Press, 1996.

Lappé, Frances Moore. *Diet for a Small Planet.* New York: Ballantine Books, 1971.

Latour, Bruno. *Science in Action: How to Follow Scientists and Engineers through Society.* Cambridge, MA: Harvard University Press, 1987.

Layne, Linda L. "Introduction." *Science, Technology, and Human Values* 23, no. 1 (1998): 4–23.

Layton, Lyndsey. "FDA Says Basic Food Flavors Knew Plant Was Contaminated with Salmonella," *Washington Post.* 10 March 2010.

Lee, Richard. "The Impact of Development on Foraging Peoples: A World Survey." In *Tribal Peoples and Development Issues: A Global Overview*, ed. John Bodley. Mountain View, California: Mayfield, 1982.

Leflar, R. A. "Conflicts Law: More on Choice-Influencing Considerations." *California Law Review* 54 (1966): 1584–1588.

Leonhardt, David. "Political Clout Matters in the Age of Outsourcing." *International Herald Tribune.* 19 April 2006. http://www.iht.com/articles/2006/04/19/business/outsource.php.

Leopold, Jason. "Shady Background of Dick Cheney's Halliburton." *Centre for Research on Globalisation.* 16 April 2003. http://globalresearch.ca/articles/LEO304B.html.

Little Miracles. 18 May 2002. http://www.littlemiracles.org/photolisting/photolisting.

Liu, Henry C. K. "U.S. Dollar Hegemony Has Got to Go." *Asia Times Online.* 11 April 2002. http://www.atimes.com/global-econ/DD11Dj01.html (accessed 11 July 2013).

Local Loan Co. v. Hunt. 292 US 234, 243 (1934). (citing Williams v. US Fidelity & Guaranty 236 US 549, 554 [1915]).

Loiko, Sergei L., and Kim Murphy. "Orphans, Families in Agonizing Limbo." *Los Angeles Times*. 21 May 2013. http://www.latimes.com/news/columnone/la-fg-russian-adoptions-20130521-dto,0,135831.htmlstory.

Losey, John, Linda Rayor, and Maureen Carter. "Transgenic Pollen Harms Monarch Larvae." *Nature* (20 May 1999): 214.

Lutz, Catherine. *Homefront: A Military City and the American Twentieth Century*. Boston: Beacon Press, 2011.

Lynd, Robert S. *Knowledge for What? The Place of Social Science in American Culture*. Princeton, NJ: Princeton University Press, 1939.

Madigan, Carleen. *The Backyard Homestead*. North Adams, MA: Storey, 2009.

Malkki, Liisa H. "Citizens of Humanity: Internationalism and the Imagined Community of Nations." *Diaspora* 3, no. 1 (1994): 41–68.

Malpica, Carlos. *La Verdad Sobre el Gas de Camisea*. Lima: Ediciones La Escena Contemporánea, 1989.

Manco, Jorge Eusebio. *Privatización e Hidrocarburos: Mito y Realidad, Perú 1991–2002*. Lima: Fondo Editorial, Universidad Nacional Mayor de San Marcos, 2002.

Manning, Robert. *The Consequences of America's Addiction to Credit*. New York: Basic Books, 2000.

Marcus, George. *Ethnography through Thick and Thin*. Princeton, NJ: Princeton University Press, 1998.

Marcus, George, and Michael M. J. Fischer, eds. *Anthropology as Cultural Critique*. Los Angeles and Berkeley: University of California Press, 1986.

Marx, Karl. *The Eighteenth Brumaire of Louis Bonaparte*. New York: International, 1963.

———. *Capital: A Critique of Political Economy*. Harmondsworth and New York: Penguin Books, 1976.

Mattei, Ugo, and Laura Nader. *Plunder: When the Rule of Law is Illegal*. Malden, MA: Blackwell, 2008.

Mauss, Marcel. *The Gift: The Form and Reason for Exchange in Archaic Societies*, trans. H. W. Halls. New York: W. W. Norton, 1950.

Mayorga, Eleodoro. The *Social and Economic Effects of Petroleum Development in Peru*. Geneva: ILO, 1987.

McMillan, Tracie. "Urban Farmers' Crops Go from Vacant Lot to Market." *New York Times*. 7 May 2008.

Mead, Margaret. *A Creative Life for Your Children*. Washington, D.C.: United States Department of Health, Education, and Welfare, Social and Rehabilitation Service, Children's Bureau, 1962.

Meltzer, Bill. "Coming Soon to an OR Near You: Meet Penelope, the $100,000 Robotic Scrub Nurse." *Outpatient Surgery Magazine (Online)* (February 2004). http://www.outpatientsurgery.net/2004/os02/news.php.

"Mexico Issues First Permits to Grow GM Corn." *Reuters*. 15 October 2009. http://www.reuters.com/article/idUSN1527085220091016 (accessed 30 October 2010).

Mills, C. Wright. *White Collar: The American Middle Classes*. New York: Oxford University Press, 1951.

———. 1972 [1956]. *The Power Elite*. London, Oxford, and New York: Oxford University Press.

———. *The Sociological Imagination*. New York: Oxford University Press, 1959.

Mills, Clare. "Could Genetically Modified Foods Be a New Source of Allergens?" *SciDevNet*. 1 March 2005. http://www.scidev.net/en/policy-briefs/could-genetically-modified-foods-be-a-new-source-o.html (accessed 2 November 2010).

Mintz, Sidney. *Sweetness and Power: The Place of Sugar in Modern History*. New York: Viking, 1985.

Modell, Judith. *Kinship with Strangers: Adoption and Interpretations of Kinship in American Culture*. Berkeley: University of California Press, 1994.

Mondragón, Héctor. "Colombia: Agrarian Reform, Fake and Genuine." *Land Research Action Network*. 2005. https://www.foodfirst.org/files/bookstore/pdf/promisedland/8.pdf (accessed 5 February 2014).

Monsanto. "Now What?" http://www.monsanto.com/pdf/sustainability/advertisement_now_what.pdf (accessed 12 November 2008).

Moss, Pamela, and Margo L. Matwychuk. "Beyond Speaking as an 'As A' and Stating the 'Etc.': Engaging in a Praxis of Difference." *Frontiers: A Journal of Women's Studies* 21, no. 3 (2000): 82–104.

Mosse, David. "Anthropologists at Work at the World Bank: An Institutional Ethnography." In *Terms of Reference: The Anthropology of Expert Knowledge and Professionals in International Development*, ed. David Mosse. Oxford: Berghahn Books, 2008.

Muehlebach, Andrea. "'Making Place' at the United Nations: Indigenous Cultural Politics at the U.N. Working Group on Indigenous Populations." *Cultural Anthropology* 16, no. 3 (2001): 415–448.

Müller, Birgit (ed.), *The Gloss of Harmony. The Politics of Policy-Making in Multilateral Organisations*. London: Pluto Press, 2013.

Muhlke, Christine. "Growing Together." *New York Times*. 8 October 2010.

Nabokov, Vladimir. *Nikolai Gogol*. New York: New Directions, 1961.

Nader, Laura. "Up the Anthropologist: Perspectives Gained from Studying Up." In *Reinventing Anthropology*, ed. Dell H. Hymes, 285–311. New York: Pantheon Books, 1972.

———. "The Vertical Slice: Hierarchies and Children." In *Hierarchy and Society: Anthropological Perspectives on Society*, ed. Gerald M. Britan and Ronald Cohen, 31–43. Philadelphia: Institute for the Study of Human Issues, 1980.

———. "Barriers to Thinking New about Energy." *Physics Today* 34 (1981): 99–102.

———. "1984 and Brave New World: The Insidious Threat of Covert Control," Radcliffe Quarterly (December 1983), 2–3.

———. *Harmony Ideology: Justice and Control in a Zapotec Mountain Village*. Stanford: Stanford University Press, 1990.

———. "Comparative Consciousness." In *Assessing Cultural Anthropology*, ed. Robert Borofsky, 84–96. New York: McGraw-Hill, 1994.

———. "Coercive Harmony: The Political Economy of Legal Models." *Kroeber Anthropological Society Papers* 80 (1996): 1–13.

———. "Controlling Processes: Tracing the Dynamic Components of Power." *Current Anthropology* 38, no. 5 (1997): 711–739.

———. "Homo Sapiens and The Longue Durée." *Journal of Developing Societies* 24, no. 1 (2008): 83–94.

———, ed. *Naked Science: Anthropological Inquiry into Boundaries, Power and Knowledge*. New York: Routledge, 1996.

Nader, Rose, and Nathra Nader. *It Happened in the Kitchen: Recipes for Food and Thought*. Washington, D.C.: Center for the Study of Responsive Law, 1991.

Nash, June. "Anthropology of the Multinational Corporations." In *New Directions in Political Economy: An Approach from Anthropology*, ed. Madeleine Barbara Leons and Frances Rothstein, 421–446. Westport, CT: Greenwood Press, 1979.

———. *We Eat the Mines and the Mines Eat Us*. New York: Columbia University Press, 1979.

Nasiripour, Shahein. "Don't Look Back: Major Players Continue to 'Walk Away' From Poor Mortgages." *Huffington Post*. 26 January 2010.

National Labor Relations Board. "NLRB Issues Lead Case Addressing Supervisory Status in Response to Supreme Court's Decision in Kentucky River." 3 October 2006. http://www.nlrb.gov/shared_files/Press%20Releases/2006/r2603.htm.

Nettleton, Sarah. "The Emergence of E-Scaped Medicine?" *Sociology* 38, no. 4 (2004): 661–679.

Neuman, William. "Keeping Their Eggs in Their Backyard Nests." *New York Times*. 3 August 2009.

Newman, Katherine S. *Falling From Grace: Downward Mobility in the Age of Affluence*. Berkeley: University of California Press, 1999.

Norconsult. *Social and Economic Effects of Petroleum Development Programmes: Consultant's Report*. Geneva: ILO, 1984.

Nordstrom, Carolyn. *Shadows of War: Violence, Power, and International Profiteering in the Twenty-First Century*. Berkeley: University of California Press, 2004.

Ong, Aihwa. *Spirits of Resistance and Capitalist Discipline: Factory Women in Malaysia* Albany: SUNY Press, 1987.

Ordonez, Jennifer. "Hamburger Joints Call Them 'Heavy Users'—But Not to Their Faces." *Wall Street Journal*. 12 January 2000.

Ornstein, Charles. "Kaiser Clerks Paid More for Helping Less: Bonuses were Given for Limiting Members' Calls and Doctor's Appointments. HMO Defends Program but has Dropped it." *Los Angeles Times*. 17 May 2002.

OSINERG. Official letter no. 7514. 24 September 2004.

Ou, Jay. "Native Americans and the Monitored Retrievable Storage Plan for Nuclear Wastes." *Kroeber Anthropological Society Papers* 80 (1996): 32–89.

Oushakine, Sergei. "In the State of Post-Soviet Aphasia: Symbolic Development in Contemporary Russia." *Europe-Asia Studies* 52, no. 6 (2000): 991–1016.

Oxfam International. "Offside! Labour Rights and Sportswear Production in Asia." Oxford: Oxfam International, 2006. http://www.oxfam.org/sites/www.oxfam.org/files/OffsideExecSummary.pdf.

Páez, Ángel, and Milagros Salazar. "Kuczinski y la Red Financiera de las Empresas de Camisea." *La República*. 10 March 2006.

Parry, Richard L. "Suharto Snubs IMF's Plan to Save Indonesia." *The Independent* (UK). 9 March 1998. http://www.independent.co.uk/news/suharto-snubs-imfs-plan-to-save-indonesia-1149253.html.

Pasour, E. C., and Randal Rucker. *Plowshares and Pork Barrels: The Political Economy of Agriculture*. Oakland, CA: Independent Institute, 2005.

Paul, Pamela. *Parenting Inc*. New York: Times Books, 2008.

Pearse, Damien. "Afghan Civilian Death Toll Reaches Record High." *The Guardian*. 4 February 2012.

Peru Congreso de la República. *Informe Final de la Comisión Investigadora Encargada de la Investigación del Transporte del Gas (Gasoducto) del Proyecto Camisea, las Causas y Consecuencias de los Reiterados Accidentes Producidos en el Mismo y la Determinación de las Responsabilidades Políticas, Administrativas y Penales a que Hubiere Lugar, así como el Estudio y Evaluación de los Compromisos Asumidos en los Contratos Suscritos*. 20 June 2006. http://www.amazonwatch.org/newsroom/view_news.php?id=1173 (accessed 18 October 2010).

Peru Defensoría del Pueblo. "El Proyecto Camisea y sus efectos en los derechos de las persona." Report No. 103 (2006). http://www.eclac.cl/dmaah/noticias/paginas/7/27987/DEFENSORIA_PUEBLO_CAMISEA.pdf.

———. "Superposición de Lotes de Hidrocarburos con áreas Naturales Protegidas y Reservas Territoriales en la Amazonía Peruana." Report No. 009–2007-DP/ASPMA.CN. 2007. http://www.petronoticias.com/noticias.php?op=NoticiaCompleta&id=152.

Petroleumworld. "Out of Order." 09/26/08. http://www.petroleumworld.com/issues08092601.htm

Picciotto, Sol. "Fragmented States and International Rules of Law." *Social and Legal Studies: An International Journal* 6, no. 2 (1997): 259–279.

Pickering, Andrew, ed. *Science as Practice and Culture*. Chicago: University of Chicago Press, 1992.

Pineyro-Nelson, A., et al. "Transgenes in Mexican Maize: Molecular Evidence and Considerations for GMO Detection in Landrace Populations." *Molecular Ecology* 18 (18 December 2008): 750–761.

Poleman, Thomas. *The Papaloapan Project: Agricultural Development in the Mexican Tropics*. Stanford: Stanford University Press, 1964.

Pollan, Michael. "Farmer in Chief." *New York Times*. 9 October 2008.

———. *In Defense of Food*. New York: Penguin, 2008.

Poster, Mark. *Critical Theory and Poststructuralism: In Search of a Context*. Ithaca, NY: Cornell University Press, 1989.

Postman, Neil. *Technopoly: The Surrender of Culture to Technology*. New York: Vintage Books, 1993.

Quist, David, and Ignacio Chapela. "Transgenic DNA Introgressed into Traditional Maize Landraces in Oaxaca, Mexico." *Nature* (29 November 2001): 541–542.

Rabel, Ernst. *The Conflict of Laws: A Comparative Study*. Ann Arbor: University of Michigan Press, 1945.

Rachel Maddow Show. "That Was Then. This is Then." 26 May 2010.

Rachel Maddow Show. "When These Things Happen, We are Not Well-Equipped to Deal with Them." 15 June 2010.

Randeria, Shalini. "Protecting the Rights of Indigenous Communities in the New Architecture of Global Governance: The Interplay of International Institutions and Post-Colonial States." In *The Commission on Folk Law and Legal Pluralism, Proceedings of the XIII International Congress*, comp. Pradhan Rajendra, 175–189. Chiang Mai, Thailand: The Commission on Folk Law and Legal Pluralism, 2002.

Randerson, James. "World's Richest 1 percent Own 40 percent of All Wealth, UN Report Discovers." *The Guardian* (UK). 6 December 2006. http://www.guardian.co.uk/money/2006/dec/06/business.internationalnews.

Ransel, David. *Mothers of Misery: Child Abandonment in Russia*. Princeton, NJ: Princeton University Press, 1988.

RealtyTrac. "Record 2.9 Million U.S. Properties Receive Foreclosure Filings in 2010 Despite 30-Month Low in December." 12 January 2011. http://www.realtytrac.com/content/foreclosure-market-report/record-29-million-us-properties-receive-foreclosure-filings-in-2010-despite-30-month-low-in-december-6309.

———. "2011 Year-End Foreclosure Report: Foreclosures on the Retreat." 9 January 2012. http://www.realtytrac.com/content/foreclosure-market-report/2011-year-end-foreclosure-market-report-6984.

———. "1.8 Million U.S. Properties With Foreclosure Filings in 2012." 14 January 2013. http://www.realtytrac.com/content/foreclosure-market-report/2012-year-end-foreclosure-market-report-7547.

"Repressed Memory Versus False Memory: Going to Court." N.d. http://www.libraryindex.com/pages/1437/Repressed-Memory-Versus-False-Memory-GOING-COURT.html.

Riesman, David (in collaboration with Reuel Denney and Nathan Glazer). *The Lonely Crowd: A Study of the Changing American Character*. New Haven and London: Yale University Press, 1950.

Robbins, Richard H. *Cultural Anthropology: A Problem-based Approach*, 2nd ed. Itasca, IL: F.E. Peacock, 1997.

Robertson, Campbell, and Henry Fountain. "BP Caps its Leaking Well, Stopping the Oil after 86 Days." *New York Times*. 16 July 2010, A16.

"Robot Medic Will Deploy by 2009: Live from DARPATech." *Popular Mechanics Blogs, Technology News*. 7 August 2007. http://www.popularmechanics.com/blogs/technology_news/4220163.html.

Roe, Mike J. and David Skeel. "Assessing the Chrysler Bankruptcy." 108 *Michigan Law Review* (2010): 727

Roitman, Janet. "Unsanctioned Wealth, or, The Productivity of Debt in Northern Cameroon." *Public Culture* 15, no. 2 (2003): 211–237.

Rona-Tas, Akos. "The First Shall Be the Last? Entrepreneurship and Communist Cadres in the Transition from Socialism." *American Journal of Sociology* 100, no. 1 (1994): 40–69.

Rose, Nikolas. *Powers of Freedom*. New York: Cambridge University Press, 1999.

Rosman, Abraham, and Paula G. Rubel. *The Tapestry of Culture: An Introduction to Cultural Anthropology*, 6th ed. Boston: McGraw-Hill, 1998.

Roth, Michael. *The Ironist's Cage: Memory, Trauma, and the Construction of History*. New York: Routledge, 1995.

Roy, Arundhati. *The Algebra of Infinite Justice*. London: Harper Collins, Flamingo Imprint, 2001.

Royte, Elizabeth. "Street Farmer." *New York Times*. 1 July 2009.

Ruggles, Steven. "The Transformation of American Family Structure." *American Historical Review* 99 (1994): 103–128.

Rush, Florence. *The Best Kept Secret: Sexual Abuse of Children*. New York: Sulzburger and Graham, 1980.

Russian Committee on Women and Youth. "Family Report." Moscow: The Russian Ministry of the Interior, 1998.

Saad, Lydia. "Honesty and Ethics Poll Finds Congress' Image Tarnished." *Gallup*. 9 December 2009. http://www.gallup.com/poll/124625/Honesty-Ethics-Poll-Finds-Congress-Image-Tarnished.aspx.

Sahlins, Marshall. *Stone Age Economics*. Chicago: Aldine-Atherton, 1972.

Sawyer, Suzana. *Crude Chronicles: Indigenous Politics, Multinational Oil, and Neoliberalism in Ecuador*. Durham, NC: Duke University Press, 2004.

Schacter, Daniel. *Searching for Memory: The Brain, the Mind, and the Past*. New York: Basic Books, 1996.

Schlosser, Eric. *Fast Food Nation*. Boston: Houghton-Mifflin, 2001.

Schmidt, Jeff. *Disciplined Minds: A Critical Look at Salaried Professionals and the Soul-Battering System that Shapes Their Lives*. Lanham, MD: Rowman and Littlefield, 2000.

Schwartz, John. "Claims to BP Fund Attract Scrutiny." *New York Times*. 2 October 2010, A21.

Scott, James. *Weapons of the Weak*. New Haven: Yale University Press, 1985.

Sheflin, Alan W., and D. Brown. "Repressed Memory of Dissociative Amnesia: What the Science Says." *Journal of Psychiatry and Law* 24 (1996): 143–188.

Sheng, Andrew. *From Asian to Global Financial Crisis: An Asian Regulator's View of Unfettered Finance in the 1990s and 2000s*. Cambridge: Cambridge University Press, 2009.

Shifrin, Donald L., et al. "Policy Statement: Children, Adolescents, and Advertising." *Pediatrics* 118, no. 6 (2006): 2563–2569.

Shorett, Peter. "Dogmas of Inevitability: Tracking Symbolic Power in the Global Marketplace." *Kroeber Anthropological Society Papers* 87 (2005): 219–241.

Showalter, Elaine. *The Female Malady*. New York: Pantheon Books, 1986.

Sieber, Joan E. "On Studying the Powerful (Or Fearing to Do So): A Vital Role for IRBs," *IRB: Ethics and Human Research* 11, no. 5 (1989): 1–6.

Silber, Judy. "Critics Hung Up Over Kaiser's Call Center." *Contra Costa Times*. 9 August 2003.

Sklar, Holly. "CEO Pay Still Outrageous." *Dissident Voice*. 1 May 2003. http://dissidentvoice.org/Articles4/Sklar_CEO-Pay.htm.

"Sleep Analyzer." http://itunes.apple.com/us/app/sleep-analyzer/id296266786?mt=8 (accessed 31 August 2010).

Smith, Anthony Oliver. *Defying Displacement: Grassroots Resistance and the Critique of Development*. Austin: University of Texas Press, 2010.

Solomon, Deborah. "Big Man on Campus." *New York Times Magazine*. 24 September 2009.

Soria, Carlos. "Camisea: ¿Por qué Cuesta Tanto el Gas Barato?" *ICONOS: Revista de Ciencias Sociales* 21 (January, 2005): 47–55.

SRI International. "Image Bank: Trauma Pod." *SRI International—News*, 16 March 2006, http://web.archive.org/web/20120113031928/http://www.sri.com/news/imagebank/trauma-pod.html.

Stavenhagen, Rodolfo. "Decolonizing Applied Social Science." *Human Organization* 30, no. 4 (1971): 333–344.

Stiglitz, Joseph E. *Globalization and Its Discontents*. New York: W. W. Norton, 2002.

Stocking, George. *The Ethnographer's Magic and Other Essays in the History of Anthropology*. Madison: University of Wisconsin Press, 1992.

Striffler, Steve. *Chicken: The Dangerous Transformation of America's Favorite Food*. New Haven: Yale University Press, 2007.

Stryker, Rachael. *The Road to Evergreen: Adoption, Attachment Therapy, and the Promise of Family*. Ithaca, NY: Cornell University Press, 2010.

Supreme Court of New Hampshire. State of New Hampshire v. Joel Hungerford (1997), case number 95–429.

———. Joel Hungerford v. Susan L. Jones (1998), case number 97–657.

Supreme Court of Rhode Island. State of Rhode Island v. Quattrocchi (1995), case number 95–343. http://www.fmsfonline.org/quattrocchi.html.

Tarmann, Alison. "International Adoption Rate Doubled in the 1990s." *Population Reference Bureau Population Bulletin*. Washington, D.C.: Population Reference Bureau, 2003. http://www.prb.org/Articles/2003/InternationalAdoptionRateinUSDoubledinthe1990s.aspx.

Tello, Hernán. "Actividad Petrolera." In *Amazonia Hoy, Politicas Publicas, Actores Sociales y Desarrollo Sostenible*, ed. Martha Rodríguez Achung, 51–64. Lima: IIAP, PUCP, 1994.

Tett, Gillian. *Fool's Gold: The Inside Story of J.P. Morgan and How Wall St. Greed Corrupted Its Bold Dream and Created a Financial Catastrophe*. New York: Free Press, 2009.

Thomson, Koy, and Nigel Dudley. "Transnationals and Oil in Amazonia." *The Ecologist* 19, no. 6 (November/December 1989): 219–224.

Thoreau, Henry David. *Civil Disobedience*. New York: Empire Books, 2011 [1849].

———. *Walden*. New York: Empire Books, 2013 [1854].

Toppo, Greg, and Janet Kornblum. "Ads on Tests Add Up for Teacher." *USA Today* (December 2, 2008). http://www.usatoday.com/news/education/2008–12–01-test-ads_N.htm.

Traweek, Sharon. *Beamtimes and Lifetimes: The World of High Energy Physicists*. Cambridge, MA: Harvard University Press, 1988.

Ugarteche, Óscar. *Adiós Estado Bienvenido Mercado*. Lima: Friedrich Ebert Stiftung, UNMSM, 2004.

United Nations News Centre. "Afghan Civilian Deaths Drop but Attacks on Women, Children, and Political Targets Rise." 19 February 2013. http://www.un.org/apps/news/story.asp?NewsID=44170#.UdITdpyfb2Z.

Urteaga-Crovetto, Patricia. *Negotiating Identities and Hydrocarbons: Territorial Claims in the Southeastern Peruvian Amazon.* Unpublished Ph.D. diss., University of California, Berkeley, 2005.

U.S. Army. "America's Army: Special Forces." *The Official Army Game: America's Army.* 2008. http://www.americasarmy.com/.

U.S. Department of Health and Human Services. *Child Maltreatment 2008.* 2008. http://www.acf.hhs.gov/programs/cb/pubs/cm08/table3_12.htm.

U.S. Department of Justice and Federal Trade Commission. *Statements of Antitrust Enforcement Policy in Health Care.* Washington, D.C.: U.S. Department of Justice, 1996.

U.S. Supreme Court. Frye v. United States. 1923.

———. Daubert v. Merrell Dow Pharmaceuticals. 1993.

Van Esterik, Penny. *Beyond the Breast-Bottle Controversy.* New Brunswick, NJ: Rutgers University Press, 1989.

Vargas, Roberto. *Family Activism: Empowering your Community Beginning with Family and Friends.* San Francisco: Barrett-Koehler, 2008.

Verdery, Katherine. "Theorizing Socialism: A Prologue to the 'Transition,'" *American Ethnologist* 18 (1991): 423.

———. *The Vanishing Hectare: Property and Value in Postsocialist Transylvania.* Ithaca, NY: Cornell University Press, 2004.

Vine, David. *Island of Shame: The Secret History of the US Military Base on Diego Garcia.* Princeton, NJ: Princeton University Press, 2009.

Von Biel, Victoria. "The iPhone Health Plan." *Bon Appetit* (January 2010): 32.

Wang, Shirley S. "Health Care Taps 'Mystery Shoppers.'" *Wall Street Journal.* 8 August 2006. http://online.wsj.com/article/SB115499684792929340-search.html.

Warman, Arturo, et al., eds. *De Eso Que Llaman Antropología Mexicana.* Mexico City: Nuestro Tiempo, 1970.

Wasilewski, Jacek. "The Forming of the New Elite: How Much Nomenklatura is Left?" *Polish Sociology Review* 2 (1995): 133.

Waterston, Alisse. *Street Addicts in the Political Economy.* Philadelphia: Temple University Press, 1997.

Wax, Murray L. "Paradoxes of 'Consent' to the Practice of Fieldwork." *Social Problems* 27, no. 3 (1980): 272–283.

Weatherford, Jack. *Indian Givers: How Native Americans Transformed the World.* New York: Three Rivers Press, 1988.

Weaver, Thomas. *To See Ourselves: Anthropology and Modern Social Issues.* New York: Random House, 1973.

Weber, Max. *The Protestant Ethic and the Spirit of Capitalism.* New York: Routledge, 1930.

Wedel, Janine. *Shadow Elite: How the World's New Power Brokers Undermine Democracy, Government, and the Free Market.* New York: Basic Books, 2009.

Weinberg, Dana Beth. *Code Green: Money-driven Hospitals and the Dismantling of Nursing.* Ithaca, NY: ILR Press, 2003.

Weinberg, Neil. "What Devaluation Hath Wrought." *Forbes.* 5 October 1998. http://www.forbes.com/forbes/1998/1005/6207053a.html.

Weinstein, H. "Papers: RJR Went for Teens." *Los Angeles Times.* 15 January 1998, A1.

Wells, Ken, et al. "From the Gulf, a Portrait of Business Owners on the Brink." *Bloomberg Businessweek.* 10 June 2010. http://images.businessweek.com/ss/10/07/0708_lost_summer/2.htm.

Wells, Pete. "Not in My Backyard." *New York Times*. 20 October 2010.
"What's Happening to the American Family? Interview with Dr. Margaret Mead, Noted Anthropologist." *US News & World Report*. 5 May 1963. http://politics.usnews.com/news/national/articles/2008/05/16/whats-happening-to-the-american-family—interview.html.
Whelan, Robbie. "Foreclosure Machines Still Running on 'Low.'" 31 July 2012. http://blogs.wsj.com/developments/2012/07/31/foreclosure-machines-still-running-on-low/.
Whittell, Giles. "Flooding from Hurricane Katrina Was Man-Made Disaster, Judge Rules." *The Sunday Times* (UK). 20 November 2009. http://www.timesonline.co.uk/tol/news/world/us_and_americas/article6924125.ece.
Wilkinson, Rupert. "'The Lonely Crowd,' at 60, Is Still Timely." *Chronicle of Higher Education*, 12 September 2010. http://chronicle.com/article/The-Lonely-Crowd-at-60-Is/124334/.
Wolf, Eric. *Sons of the Shaking Earth*. Chicago: University of Chicago Press, 1959.
———. *Peasants*. Englewood Cliffs, NJ: Prentice-Hall, 1966.
———. *Europe and the People without History*. Berkeley: University of California Press, 1982.
Worthy, Ken. "Biotechnology, Enclosures, and the Privatization of Life." *Biotechnology and Society* (2001): 12. http://www.rpp.com.pe/portada/economia/49340_1.php.
Young, Allan. *The Harmony of Illusions: Inventing Post-Traumatic Stress Disorder*. Princeton, NJ: Princeton University Press, 1997.
Yurchak, Alexei. *Everything Was Forever until It Was No More: The Last Soviet Generation*. Princeton, NJ: Princeton University Press, 2005.
Zelizer, Viviana. *Pricing the Priceless Child: The Changing Social Value of Children*. Princeton, NJ: Princeton University Press, 1985.
Zezima, Katie, and Benedict Carey. "Ex-Priest Challenges Abuse Conviction on Repressed Memories." *New York Times*. 10 September 2009. http://www.nytimes.com/2009/09/11/us/11priest.html?_r=0.

Index

adoption
  and hierarchies, 149–50, 153, 159, 163
  and institutional influence, 151–65, 167
  processes, 153–54
  and Reactive Attachment Disorder, 152–53, 165
  and Russia, 153, 155, 157, 160–66, 169n27, 237–38
Affordable Care Act, 216
Afghanistan, 2
Africa, 86, 111, 129
Amazon (region), 86, 127, 129–31, 133, 139–40
American Federation of Labor (AFL), 66
American International Group (AIG), 27, 41, 43n33
American Psychological Association (APA), 181–83
"anthropological imagination," 59–60
apolitical anthropology, 9
Arendt, Hannah, 101
Argentina, 127
Atlantic Richfield Company (ARCO), 129, 131
Australia, 228
authoritative discourse, 199–200, 202–4
autonomy, 5, 18, 115, 121, 123, 133, 152, 233, 236, 238
Avatar (film), 85–87, 104

Bankruptcy
  Bankruptcy Code, 31–32, 36–37, 40, 43n26
  chapters, 29, 32, 35
  and corporations, 28–29, 32–33, 40
  and courts, 28, 31–35
  individual filings, 27
  and individualism, 39–41
  in Korean corporations, 45
  meeting of creditors, 32, 34–36, 38
  and United States Trustee Office, 34–35, 37
Belgium, 66
Belize, 17, 86, 89
Berger, Oscar, 100
bin Laden, Osama, 101
Blackwater, 86
"blowback," 101
Boas, Franz, 9
Bodley, James, 128, 133
Bolivia, 86, 131
Bourgois, Phillipe, 39
Brazil, 94, 131
Bretton Woods Agreements, 54
British Petroleum, 2, 17, 88, 102–3, 105n26, 106n28
Bush, George W., 55, 120, 212, 216–17

cadastre, 91, 95–97
California Hospital Association (CHA), 213–15
California Nurses Association (CNA), 19, 211–12, 223–24, 229

call centers (nursing), 223–26
Calvinism, 31
Cameron, James, 85–86
Camisea Gas Project, 17–18
   Article 4 of the Gas Law, 135
   Consortium, 127, 131–33, 135, 137–38, 140–41
   definition of, 127
   depiction of, 128
   and García Alan,137
   hydrocarbons, 128, 130–132, 134, 137–38, 141–42
   and indigenous peoples, 127–34, 138–42
   and inevitability, 18, 128, 133–34, 141–42
   management, 132
   Ombudsman, 138–40, 146n52
   Program for Institutional Strengthening and Support for the Environmental and Social Spills, 134, 136, 138–40, 142
Canada, 115–16
Canadian First Nations, 86
capitalism, 6, 30, 41, 86, 99, 201, 239
Carter, Jimmy, 55
Cayman Islands, 100
Cheney, Dick, 56, 62n13
Chevron Corporation, 102, 131
China, 44, 70, 79, 87, 214
Chrysler Corporation, 27, 41
Chun Doo Hawn, 55–57
"clinical pathways," 218
Clinton, Bill, 55, 213
Cohn, Carol, 230
Cold War, 7, 67
Columbia, 94–95
Commission for Environmental Cooperation (CEC), 119–21
"committed contingency," 60
communism, 54, 67, 162
Communist party, 192, 196, 200
comparative consciousness, 208
"constructive engagement," 55
consumption, 60

controlling processes, 10–12, 14, 18, 23n42, 41, 64, 65, 123, 127–28, 133, 141, 152, 163, 212, 215–19, 228, 233–40
corn, 91, 93, 102, 108–14, 116–21
corporate capitalism, 16, 29, 44, 46, 54, 59–60, 67, 102, 230, 239–41
corporatization. *See* privatization
creditors (of debtors), 36
Cuba, 66
cultural relativism, 9
Czechoslovakia, 66

debt, 42n4, 42n16
   and corporate debtors, 27–30, 32–33, 40
   definition of, 29
   and identity, 27, 29, 31–38, 40
   individual, 16, 28–34, 36, 38–40
   morality, 31–33, 41
   and stigma, 28–31, 35, 38
   Supreme Court interpretations of, 32
Deininger, Klaus, 94, 105n10
democracy, 1, 3–5, 9, 14, 18–19
"disorientation in place," 203
dispossession, 17, 86, 96–102, 104
   and "blowback," 101
   and capitalist exploitation, 99
   and corporate capitalism, 102
   definition of, 85
   and Empire, 99
   facilitators, 101
   and government, 99
   and imperialism, 99
   and privatization, 101
   Q'eqchi' Maya, 17, 88, 91–94, 97–98, 100–101, 104, 104n3, 236
   rationale, 101–2
Dow Chemical Company, 118
doxa, 30, 42n14
DuPont Chemical Company, 118–19
Durkheim, Emile, 46

economic crisis, 60, 240
economic integration, 54

"economic virtue," 31
Ecuador, 104, 129
egalitarian society, 4
Egypt, 71
EICC Initiative, 74, 82n28
Energy Regulator Institution, 138–140
Enlightenment, the, 31
"epistemic shifts," 174
"erroneous memories," 173
E-Tech International, 139, 145n43
Ewen, Stuart, 123
expert witnesses, 174–75, 180, 186–87
Exxon Corporation, 102

fact-making, 176, 178
False Memory Syndrome Foundation, 174, 190n27
family, 149, 151–53, 155–65, 167
"fancied needs," 123
Farmer, Paul, 15
fast food, 121, 123
Ferguson, James, 65, 68, 78
"First World countries," 104, 127
Fischer, Michael, 129
food security, 107
Ford, Gerald, 55
Fordism, 216
Foster, George, 10
France, 66, 98
freedom, 4–6, 18–19, 31, 39, 67, 152, 164
Freud, Sigmund, 171, 189n5, 193
Freyd, Jennifer, 183–84, 190n27
Fromm, Erich, 5–6, 19, 21n15
"frontier mentality," 40
Fukushima Daiichi nuclear disaster, 2–3

Galeano, Eduardo, 19
García, Alan, 130, 134, 137
Gas Law (Camisea Gas Project), 134–35
Geithner, Timothy, 41, 43n33
General Motors, 27, 41
genetically modified organisms (GMOs), 117–21

Geneva, Switzerland, 16, 65, 68–71, 73, 77
Germany, 70, 204
gerontocracy, 168n7
global economic crisis, 57
globalization, 17, 67–68, 79, 98, 129, 133
Gompers, Samuel, 66
Gorbachev, Mikhail, 200
Gramsci, Antonio, 98, 176
Group of Eight, the (G8), 98
Guatemala, 17, 85–86, 88–92, 94–100, 104, 236, 240
Gulf Coast, 17, 102–4, 105n26
Gulf of Mexico, 2, 102
Gupta, Akhil, 65, 68, 78
Gusterson, Hugh, 13, 15

habitus, 30
"haciendas," 88
Haiti, 98
Hardt, Michael, 17, 88, 98–101
Hart, Gillian, 103
Harvey, David, 17, 88, 99, 101
Health Maintenance Organizations (HMOs), 223, 225, 236
hegemony, 5, 12, 20, 41, 58, 98, 134, 176, 188, 199, 216, 226, 230, 233
hierarchy, 65, 68, 78, 149–150, 153, 159, 163, 192, 196–98, 230, 234, 235
Ho, Karen, 14
Hoemardani, Soedjono, 56–57
housing market collapse, 27
Hunt, Ray,(Hunt Oil Company), 136–37
Hunt Oil Company, 132–33, 136–37, 144n35
Hurricane Katrina, 2
Hydrocarbons Commission, 131, 143n11

indigenismo, 132
indignation, 7–8
individualism, 39–40

Indonesia
  and Asian financial crisis of
    1997–1998, 45–46, 54, 61
  foreign debt, 57
  and the International Labour
    Organisation, 70
  and the International Monetary
    Fund, 45, 57–59
  Japanese manufacturing in, 55
  and Korea, 240
  Korean-owned factories in, 16,
    44–49, 58–59
  and migrant workers in Korea,
    58–60
  neoliberal revolution in, 55
  and the United States, 44, 55, 240
"inevitability argument," 128,
  133–34, 141–42
information technology
  "decision-support technology,"
    225, 226, 228
  electronic Intensive Care Units,
    229
  "electronic medical records," 218
  "evidence-based" practices,
    218–19, 223–24, 227, 230
  "Healthcare Information
    Technology," 216, 225, 227,
    230
  and the International Labour
    Organisation meeting, 65, 69,
    73
  "Nurse Penelope," 229
  Pyxis, 218
  Radio Frequency Identification
    Chips, 218
  Six Sigma, 217–18
  Stargate call-center software, 218
  "trauma pods," 229
Institute of Medicine (IOM), 215–16,
  218, 225
"integrating agenda," 128, 132–33,
  136–37, 139–40, 142, 143n10,
  145n40
International Fund, 94

International Labour Organisation
  (ILO)
  and "best practices," 69, 75
  function, 66
  Governing Body, 69, 71–72, 76
  and indigenous peoples, 70, 140
  International Labour Conference,
    66–67, 69, 71
  and the Nobel Peace Prize, 67
  and power, 67, 77, 79
  report, 69–70
  Sectoral Activities Programme,
    69, 75
  and Social Dialogue Sector, 69,
    73–74
  and technology, 63, 65, 69–70, 77
International Monetary Fund (IMF),
  98, 127, 136, 145n39
  austerity measures, 45, 51–53
  bailouts, 56–57
  and Empire, 98
  and Indonesia, 45, 56–57
  and Korea, 45, 51–54, 57–59
  and power, 98, 136
  structural adjustment policies, 127
  and Suharto, 56
International Organizations (IOs),
  17, 65, 71, 79, 81n14–15, 236
International Petroleum Company,
  144n34
Iraq, 86
Iron Curtain, 201
Israel, 228
Italy, 66
Ixtoc oil spill (1979), 102

Japan, 2–3, 40, 50, 54, 55, 62n17, 66, 70
Jefferson, Thomas, 4, 6
Joint Commission on Accreditation
  of Healthcare Organizations
  (JCAHO), 221–22, 229–30

Kaiser Permanente, 221, 223, 225
Kantianism, 31, 40
"Kentucky River" decisions, 212

Keynesian economics, 100
King, Martin Luther, 74
Kluckhohn, Clyde, 108
"knowledge producers," 174
Korea
   38th parallel, 54
   and Asian financial crisis of 1997–1998, 45–46, 54, 61
   and corporate capitalism, 44, 54
   debt, 45, 57
   economic development, 54–55
   exports, 55
   factory management in Indonesia, 50–54
   Indonesian industrial trainees in, 47–54
   Indonesian migrant workers in, 48–50, 53, 58, 60
   industrial investments in Indonesia, 44–45, 240
   and the International Labour Organisation, 70
   and the International Monetary Fund, 45, 52, 53, 57–58
   and Japan, 50, 54–55, 62n17
   Korean War, 54
   and labor, 51, 53, 54
   manufacturing in Indonesia, 16, 44–45, 56–59
   and NGOs, 52–53
   and the United States, 50, 54–55, 240, 62n8
Kuczynski, Pedro Pablo, 132, 136–37, 144n34, 145n37–38
Kuhn, Thomas, 8

Lappé, Frances Moore, 118
Latin America, 8, 120, 142n1
League of Nations, 66
Lebanon, 228
Lee, Richard, 129
legal drift, 102
Lenin, Vladimir, 193
Liberalism, 100
Loftus, Beth, 182–83

L'ouverture, Toussaint, 98
Lutz, Catherine, 14–15
Lynd, Robert, 6, 19, 21n16
Lytvyn, Volodymyr, 196–98

Machiguenga (people), 130–31, 133, 138
maize. *See* corn
Marcus, George, 13, 129
Marx, Karl, 46, 104, 193
Mateu v. Hagen (1993), 186–87
Mattei, Ugo, 17, 88, 100–101
Mauritius, 15
Maya Biosphere Reserve, 90, 92, 104n4
McCarthy, Joseph, 9
McDonald's (restaurant), 122, 149
Mead, Margaret, 149, 164, 169n27
Medicare, 222, 226, 231n16
Melville, Herman, 5–6
"memory scientists," 174
Mesoamerica, 110–12, 119
Mexico, 92, 107–8, 111, 114–20, 120, 155–57
Middle East, 111
Mills, C. Wright, 4, 20n7, 21n25, 59–60, 64, 72
Ministry of Energy and Mines, 132, 137, 139–42, 145n45
Mintz, Sidney, 10, 110–111
misrecognition, 194–95, 197–98, 203, 207
Mitchell, Clyde, 13
Monsanto, 117–19
Moore, Michael, 216
Morales, President Evo, 86
Morgan Stanley, 28
Motorola, 217–18
Multinational Corporations (MCs), 9, 15, 17, 47, 116, 123, 128

Nabokov, Vladimir, 205
Nader, Laura, 3, 7–14, 16–17, 19, 23n42, 46, 63–65, 68, 77, 79, 88, 94, 100–103, 123, 129, 133, 141, 149,

172, 187, 193, 197, 204, 216, 230, 233–36, 238–39
Nader, Nathra, 167
Nader, Ralph, 151
Nader, Rose, 167
Nanti community, 131, 138
Nash, June, 10
National Academy of Science, 215–16
Native Americans, 4, 129
Navajo Nation, 86
Negri, Antonio, 17, 88, 98–101
neoliberalism, 14, 67, 121
   and economics, 45, 54–55, 57, 61, 127
   and privatization, 86, 88, 94, 99, 128, 133–36, 141–42, 236
   and public health, 15
   repercussions, 17, 239–41
neontocracy, 18, 150–52, 167, 168n7
network analysis, 11, 15, 23n35, 30, 46, 79, 151, 172, 177, 179
"New Imperialism," 17, 88, 99, 101
Newman, Katherine, 40
Nigeria, 104
Nike Corporation, 44, 53–55, 60
9/11, 208
Nongovernmental Organizations (NGOs), 47, 52–54, 68, 70–72, 74, 120–21, 90, 165
Nordstrom, Carolyn, 15
North American Free Trade Agreement (NAFTA), 115–17, 120
North Atlantic Treaty Organization (NATO), 98
nuclear
   energy, 12
   reactors, 2–3
   waste, 129
   weapons, 7, 15, 230
nursing
   and AB 394, 214
   "advice nurses," 223
   "best practices," 217, 219, 222, 225
   call centers, 223–25
   "care," 211–16, 220–22, 224–30, 235
   and downsizing for profit, 213–14
   and "Enterprise Resource Planning" (ERP) systems, 219, 225
   and information technology, 216–18, 225, 227–29
   and judgment, 216, 218, 221, 223–24, 227, 229
   and labor restructuring, 213, 228
   and nurse-patient ratios, 212–15, 220
   and "patient-focused care," 213–14, 222
   patient surveys, 221–22
   primary care nursing, 213
   and "population-based care," 222
   Registered Nurses' (RNs) responsibilities, 211
   scripting, 219–21
   shortage, 212–13
   solidarity, 227

Oaxaca, Mexico, 8, 17, 107, 112, 114–15, 118–20
Obama, Barack, 105n26, 164, 216
"objectivity," 7–8
Odría, Manuel, 133
Organismo Supervisor de la Inversión en Energía y Minería (OSINERGMIN), 138–40
Organization of Economic Co-operation and Development (OECD), 50, 53
"organized irresponsibility," 3, 20n7
Orwell, George, 107

Pacific Islands, 111
Pakpahan, Muchtar, 53
Paniagua, Valentín, 132
Paul, Pamela, 151
Paulson, Hank, 28
"performative speech," 203, 207

Peru, 142
    and the Amazon, 127, 129–31, 133, 139–40, 142
    and the Camisea Gas Project, 17, 127–34
    and congress, 132, 137–40
    and Fujimori, Alberto, 127, 131–32
    Lima, 132
    Ministry of Energy and Mines, 132, 137, 139–42
    neoliberalism in, 136
    and the Organismo Supervisor de la Inversion en Energia, 138–40
    and petroleum, 127–31, 134, 240–41
    and Shell-Mobil Corporation, 131
Perupetro, 131–32, 135, 146n52
Peten, 89–91, 93, 95–97, 100, 236
Philippines, 5, 70, 214
plunder, 17, 88–94, 98–101, 128, 236, 241
pluralism, 207
Pluspetrol Perú Corporation, 132–33, 136, 140, 144n35
Poland, 66
polyphony, 206
poshlost, 205–6
Positron Emission Tomography (PET) scans, 172–73
Post-Socialism, 198–203, 209n7
Post-Traumatic Stress Disorder (PTSD), 173, 177, 190n29
"power elite," 9, 11, 68, 72, 240–41, 80n8
privatization, 2, 127, 142n1, 231n9, 236, 241
Puerto Rico, 39
Putin, Vladimir, 163

Q'eqchi' Maya, 17, 86–98, 100–101, 103–4, 236

Reactive Attachment Disorder (RAD), 152–53, 165
Reagan, Ronald, 56–57, 100
"reasonable man" standard, 31

recovered memory. *See* repressed memory
Redfield, Robert, 10
Reinventing Anthropology, 7, 12, 64
repressed memory
    and academic research, 181–84
    and clinicians and therapists, 184, 189n5
    in court, 172, 174–75, 177–78, 180, 182–87, 238, 239
    debates, 178, 181, 184
    and experts, 170–71, 174–77, 180–82, 185–88
    lawsuits, 170
    and reliability, 177, 185–86
    science, 170–79, 181–88
    and victimization, 178–79
Repsol Exploración Peru, 133, 144n35
"revolving door" policies, 136–37, 141
Riesman, David, 5–6, 19
Rose, Nikolas, 31
Rousseau, Jean-Jacques, 193
Roy, Arundhati, 101
Russia, 160–63, 165–67

Saba, Daniel, 146n52
Sahlins, Marshall, 7, 10
Saudi Arabia, 87
Schwarzenegger, Arnold, 214–15
science and technology studies (STS), 63
scientific adequacy, 9
"scientific truth," 175
sexual abuse, 18, 171, 177–80, 181–83, 185
Seychelles, 15
Shell, (Royal Dutch), 102, 130–31, 143n11
Shinai Serjali, 138, 145n41
Sinclair, Upton, 5–6
"social dialogue," 67, 74
social orphanhood, 161–62
Socialism, 192, 195–204, 199–200, 209n7

Sonatrach Peru, 144n35
South Africa, 94, 204
South America, 86
South Korea. *See* Korea
sovereignty, 98, 135, 138, 241
Soviet Union, 54, 192–205, 208
Spain, 71, 86, 88–89, 127
Stalin, Joseph, 199–200
Stranniye Igri, 194–95
"structural adjustment," 15, 127
studying up, down, and sideways, 7, 9, 13–14, 17–18, 22n27, 22n29, 23n35, 23n42, 41, 63–64, 129, 141, 194, 234
   in Asia, 54
   and the Camisea Gas Project, 141
   and children, 149–50
   and "common sense," 193–94, 208, 219
   and corporate capitalism, 54, 60, 239
   and corporations, 128
   and debtors, 29
   and the elite, 13
   and food, 17, 124, 236
   as framing device, 193–94, 197–98, 234
   and the global economy, 46–47, 54, 56
   and healthcare, 19, 230, 235
   at the International Labor Organization, 77–79
   and management phrasing, 217
   on neontocracy, 151
   and political upheaval, 18–19, 196–200, 203–8, 209n7, 234–35
   and power, 63, 172, 240
   and the Q'eqchi' Maya, 85–104
   and repressed memory, 187–88, 238
   and research, 11, 13
   vertical slice, 11, 14, 16, 18, 46, 53, 64, 149–50, 240
Suharto, 45, 54–59

Supreme Court
   on bankruptcy, 32
   and *Local Loan v. Hunt*, 32
   and *Marrama v. Citizens Bank of Massachusetts*, 32
Switzerland, 70–71, 76, 228

Taylorism, 216, 221
Tec, Rigoberto, 96, 100–101
Techint, 132, 136
Technical Group for Interinstitutional Coordination, the (GTCI), 132, 140
Tecpetrol del Perú, 132–33, 144n35
Tett, Gillian, 14
Thailand, 57
Thatcher, Margaret, 100
"Third World countries," 67, 95, 100, 167
Thoreau, Henry David, 4–6
Toledo, Alejandro, 132, 135–37
Toyota Corporation, 216–17
transnational corporations, 129
Transportadora de Gas del Perú (TGP), 132–33, 136–40
traumatic memory, 177
Traweek, Sharon, 40
"tripartism," 67
"trustanoia," 103
Twain, Mark, 5–6

Ukraine
   and the Central Committee of the Communist Party of Ukraine, 196
   Communist party, 192, 196, 200
   and "galloping inflation," 197
   law, 193, 195–96, 203
   political independence, 192, 195, 200
   population decline, 202
   Post-Soviet era, 18, 192, 195, 197–99, 201–5, 208, 209n7, 234
   and "wage arrears," 197

United Nations
  Biosafety Protocol, 119
  Conference on Trade and
    Development, 71
  Food and Agriculture
    Organization, 120–21
  Working Group on Indigenous
    Peoples, 81n15
underwater mortgages, 29
Union of Soviet Socialist Republics
  (USSR), 192–96, 198–99, 202–3,
  208
United Kingdom, 66
United Nations (UN), 2, 66, 71,
  119–21, 234

United States, 2, 6, 34–35, 40, 45–46,
  86, 107, 110, 208
  and adoption, 151–155, 237–38
  and Asia, 44, 47, 50, 54–58, 60, 240
  and the Camisea Gas Project, 127
  and dispossession, 100, 102
  and family, 143–155, 159, 161,
    163–67
  financial crisis of 2008, 27–28
  and food, 3, 107, 110, 117–18,
    121–24
  and healthcare, 229, 240
  and the International Labour
    Organisation, 66, 70, 75–76
  and the North American Free
    Trade Agreement, 115–17
  and repressed memory, 170–71, 185
  and sexual abuse, 177
United States Army Corps of
  Engineers, 2, 20
United States Bankruptcy Courts, 29,
  31, 33, 36, 41
University of California, Berkeley,
  7, 118
Upstream Consortium, 144n35
Usabiaga, Javier, 119
Ussury, Jeff, 103

Veblen, Thorstein, 5–6

"vertical slice," 11, 14, 16, 18–19,
  46, 14, 18, 53, 64, 78, 149–50, 187,
  240–41
  and children, 149–50
  and corporate capitalism, 46, 54,
    60, 239
  and debtors, 28
  and the global economy, 46–47
  and Korea, 16, 46, 53, 60–61
  and vertical analysis, 60–61, 153
  and vertical integration, 11, 14, 18,
    237, 240–41
Vine, David, 15

Walmart, 124
Waterston, Alisse, 15
Wall Street, 27, 239–41
war, 59
  Afghanistan, 2
  Cold War, 7, 67
  criticism of, 9
  economic, 50
  Guatemalan Civil War, 90, 92, 96,
    101
  Gulf War, 180
  Korean War, 54
  Vietnam War, 7
  World War I, 66
  World War II, 54
war economy, 8
Weber, Max, 30, 46
Wedel, Janine, 15
"white man's burden," 62n17, 67
"white messiah," 86
Whorf, Benjamin, 174
Wise, Timothy, 116
Wolf, Eric, 10
Wolfowitz, Paul, 56, 62n13
World Bank, 17, 54, 136–37,
  145n39
  land governance, 94–97
  land titling projects, 86–87, 91,
    94–97, 236
  and neoliberalism, 54, 94
  and plunder, 98–101

and the Q'eqchi' Maya, 86, 90, 94 236
structural adjustment policies, 127–28
World Trade Organization (WTO), 117

Yaxcal, Sebastian, 93–94

Zapotec
farming, 107–17, 119–24
food, 17, 108–110, 111–12, 121, 237
lifestyle, 109
and Mesoamerican influences, 110–12
and modernization, 115
people, 108